STECK-VAUGHN
GED

W9-AWN-361

Writing Skills

PROGRAM CONSULTANTS

Myra K. Baum
New York, New York

Sheron Lee Chic
Community School South
East Palo Alto, California

June E. Dean
Parent and Adult Education
Detroit Public Schools
Detroit, Michigan

Ruth E. Derfler, M.Ed.
State GED Chief Examiner
Massachusetts Department of
    Education
Malden, Massachusetts

Joan S. Flanery
Adult Education and Literacy
    Program
Ashland Independent Board
    of Education
Ashland, Kentucky

Michael E. Snyder, Ed.S.
Tennessee Department of
    Corrections
Pikeville, Tennessee

STECK-VAUGHN
C O M P A N Y
ELEMENTARY · SECONDARY · ADULT · LIBRARY

Staff Credits

Executive Editor:	Ellen Northcutt
Senior Editor:	Tim Collins
Design Manager:	John J. Harrison
Cover Design:	Rhonda Childress
Photo Editor:	Margie Foster

Editorial Development: McClanahan & Company, Inc.

Photography: Cover: (computer) © Dominique Sarraute/The Image Bank; (letters) © Elle Shuster/The Image Bank. p.32 © Judy Gelles/Stock Boston; p.100 © Frank Siteman/Stock Boston; p.160 © Jean-Claude Lejeune/Stock Boston.

ISBN 0-8114-7361-9

Copyright © 1996 Steck-Vaughn Company.

Printed in the United States of America.

2 3 4 5 6 7 8 9 BP 00 99 98 97 96

Contents

To the Learner

What Is the GED Test?

You are taking a very big step toward changing your life with your decision to take the GED test. By opening this book, you are taking your second important step: preparing for the test. You may feel nervous about what is ahead, which is only natural. Relax and read the following pages to find out the answers to your questions.

The GED test, the Test of General Educational Development, is given by the GED Testing Service of the American Council on Education for adults who did not graduate from high school. When you pass the GED test, you will receive a certificate that is regarded as being equivalent to a high school diploma. Employers in private industry and government, as well as admissions officers in colleges and universities, accept the GED certificate as they would a high school diploma.

The GED test covers the same subjects people study in high school. The five subject areas are: Writing Skills, Interpreting Literature and the Arts, Social Studies, Science, and Mathematics. You will not be required to know all the information that is usually taught in high school. You will, however, be tested on your ability to read and process information. Certain U.S. states also require a test on the U.S. Constitution or on state government. Check with your local adult education center to see if your state requires such a test.

Each year hundreds of thousands of adults pass the GED test. The *Steck-Vaughn GED Series* will help you develop and refine the reading and thinking skills you need to pass the GED test.

GED Scores

After you complete the GED test, you will get a score for each section and a total score. The total score is an average of all the other scores. The highest score possible on a single test is 80. The scores needed to pass the GED test vary depending on where you live. The chart on page 2 shows the minimum state requirements. A score of *40 or 45* means that the score for each test must be 40 or more, but if one or more scores is below 40, an average of at least 45 is required. A minimum score of *35 and 45* means that the score for each test must be 35 or more and an average of at least 45 is required.

Area	Minimum Score on Each Test		Minimum Average on All Five Tests
UNITED STATES			
Alabama, Alaska, Arizona, Connecticut, Georgia, Hawaii, Illinois, Indiana, Iowa, Kansas, Kentucky, Maine, Massachusetts, Michigan, Minnesota, Montana, Nevada, New Hampshire, North Carolina, Ohio, Pennsylvania, Rhode Island, South Carolina, Tennessee, Vermont, Virginia, Wyoming	35	and	45
Arkansas, California, Colorado, Delaware, District of Columbia, Florida, Idaho, Maryland, Missouri, New York, Oklahoma, Oregon, South Dakota, Utah, Washington, West Virginia	40	and	45
Louisiana, Mississippi, Nebraska, New Mexico, North Dakota, Texas	40	or	45
New Jersey (42 is required on Test 1; 40 is required on Tests 2, 3, and 4; 45 is required on Test 5; and 45 average on all 4 tests.)			
Wisconsin	40	and	50
CANADA			
Alberta, British Columbia, Manitoba, New Brunswick (English and French), Northwest Territories, Nova Scotia, Prince Edward Island, Saskatchewan, Yukon Territory	45		—
Newfoundland	40	and	45
U.S. TERRITORIES & OTHERS			
Guam, Kwajalein, Puerto Rico, Virgin Islands	35	and	45
Panama Canal Area, Palau	40	and	45
Mariana Islands, Marshall Islands, Micronesia	40	or	45
American Samoa	40		—

Note: GED score requirements change from time to time. For the most up-to-date information, check with your state or local GED director or GED testing center.

This chart gives you information on the content, number of items, and time limit for each test. In some places you do not have to take all sections of the test on the same day. If you want to take all the test sections in one day, the GED test will last an entire day. Check with your local adult education center for the requirements in your area.

Test	Content Areas	Number of Items	Time Limit (minutes)
Writing Skills Part I	Sentence Structure Usage Mechanics	55	75
Writing Skills Part II	Essay	1	45
Social Studies	Geography U.S. History Economics Political Science Behavioral Science	64	85
Science	Biology Earth Science Physics Chemistry	66	95
Interpreting Literature and the Arts	Popular Literature Classical Literature Commentary	45	65
Mathematics	Arithmetic Algebra Geometry	56	90

≡Where Do You Go to Take the GED Test?

The GED test is offered year-round throughout the United States, its possessions, U.S. military bases worldwide, and in Canada. To find out when and where tests are held near you, contact the GED Hot Line at 1-800-62-MY-GED (1-800-626-9433) or one of these institutions in your area:

♦ An adult education center

♦ A continuing education center

♦ A local community college

♦ A public library

♦ A private business school or technical school

♦ The public board of education

In addition, the Hot Line and the institutions can give you information regarding necessary identification, testing fees, and writing implements. Schedules vary: some testing centers are open several days a week; others are open only on weekends.

Why Should You Take the GED Test?

A GED certificate can help you in the following ways:

Employment

People without high school diplomas or GED certificates have much more difficulty changing jobs or moving up in their present companies. In many cases employers will not hire someone who does not have a high school diploma or the equivalent.

Education

If you want to enroll in a technical school, a vocational school, or an apprenticeship program, you often must have a high school diploma or the equivalent. If you want to enter a college or university, you must have a high school diploma or the equivalent.

Personal

The most important thing is how you feel about yourself. You have the unique opportunity to turn back the clock by making something happen that did not happen in the past. You can attain a GED certificate that will help you in the future and make you feel better about yourself now.

How to Prepare for the GED Test

Classes for GED preparation are available to anyone who wants to take the GED. The choice of whether to take classes is up to you; they are not required. If you prefer to study by yourself, the *Steck-Vaughn GED Series* has been prepared to guide your study. *Steck-Vaughn GED Exercise Books* are also available to give you additional practice for each test.

Most GED preparation programs offer individualized instruction and tutors who can help you identify areas in which you may need help. Many adult education centers offer free day or night classes. The classes are usually informal and allow you to work at your own pace and with other adults who also are studying for the GED. In addition to working on specific skills, you will be able to take practice GED tests (like those in this book) in order to check your progress. For information about classes available near you, contact one of the institutions in the list on page 3.

What You Need to Know to Pass Test One: **Writing Skills**

The GED Writing Skills Test is divided into two parts. Part I focuses on grammar, and Part II asks you to write an essay. The *Steck-Vaughn GED Writing Skills* book teaches you the skills you need to pass Writing Skills Part I. These writing skills are also necessary when you write the essay for Part II. For more information on Part II, see *Steck-Vaughn GED: The Essay*.

Part I of the GED Writing Skills test takes 75 minutes and has 55 items. The items will test your knowledge of three areas of grammar: mechanics, usage, and sentence structure.

Mechanics

Thirty percent of the test items examine correct punctuation, spelling, and capitalization. Punctuation includes using commas correctly in sentences. For example, in the sentence Sara, left her house., a comma should not be placed after the subject Sara. Spelling errors include use of possessives, contractions, and homonyms—words that sound the same but are spelled differently (such as *their, they're,* and *there*).

Usage

Thirty-five percent of the test items ask you to correct errors in usage. Usage includes using the right verb or pronoun to agree with the subject of the sentence. For example, the sentence A man need food., incorrectly uses a plural verb for a singular subject. Correct usage also includes determining the right verb tense for the situation. In the sentence Tomorrow I went home., the verb went is past tense, but the sentence needs will go, the future tense. As mentioned above, usage also involves the correct use of pronouns. In the sentence Everyone wanted their seat close to the window., Everyone is a singular pronoun and their is a plural pronoun. Therefore, their must be changed to his or her.

Sentence Structure

Thirty-five percent of the test items examine the way sentences are put together. You have to identify and fix sentences that are missing important parts, that are worded in a way that changes the original meaning, or that are punctuated incorrectly. You may be asked to rewrite a sentence in a different way, or to combine two sentences. The goal of the sentence structure items is to make sure you know how to write a clear and logical sentence that has a subject, a complete verb, and the right punctuation.

The Writing Skills Test, Part I consists of paragraphs that are from ten to thirteen sentences long. Each item is based on one or two sentences from that paragraph. Always read the paragraph first. You will need to know what the paragraph is about to decide what subject, verb, or pronoun a sentence from the paragraph may need.

The items on the Writing Skills Test, Part I fall into three basic types. About half of the items ask you to correct something in a sentence, a third ask you to change a sentence or sentences, and the rest ask you either to combine two sentences or to rewrite a single sentence.

Correct a Sentence

These items use a sentence from the paragraph and ask you to choose a correction for an error in the sentence. You have to say if you want to change, replace, or remove words or punctuation. You might be asked if you want to change the spelling of a word, to move a word or phrase to a different location in the sentence, or to capitalize a word. No more than one error will appear in these sentences, and some sentences will be correct as written.

Change a Sentence or Sentences

These items give you either one or two sentences from the paragraph. The parts you need to focus on will be underlined. You will then have to select a change in the wording or punctuation or choose to leave the sentence as it stands.

Rewrite a Sentence or Combine Two Sentences

These items test your skill at writing new sentences. You may be asked to rewrite a sentence from the paragraph beginning with a different set of words. You have to decide which choice will result in a sentence that is free of errors and keeps the meaning of the original sentence. The item may take two sentences and ask you how they would best be combined. Only one of the choices will result in a clear, logical sentence.

Sample Passage and Items

The following paragraph and items shows how the writing skills test works. Although the paragraph is much shorter than those on an actual GED test, the items that follow are similar to those on the actual GED. Following each item is an explanation of the skill area the item tests as well as an explanation of the correct answer.

<u>Items 1 to 4</u> refer to the following paragraph.

(1) Some parents look forward to there children leaving home at last. (2) This group of parents want peace and quiet. (3) A number of adult children, however, move back home. (4) Parents continue to support them. (5) Sometimes the children are charged rent by those parents.

1. Sentence 1: **Some parents look forward to there children leaving home at last.**

What correction should be made to this sentence?

(1) change <u>parents</u> to <u>parent's</u>
(2) change <u>look</u> to <u>looks</u>
(3) replace <u>to</u> with <u>too</u>
(4) replace <u>there</u> with <u>their</u>
(5) no correction is necessary

Answer: **(4) replace <u>there</u> with <u>their</u>**

Explanation: This is an example of correcting a sentence. The item covers mechanics; you must know the correct spelling of the word in the answer. Option (4) is correct because it replaces there with their, which is the needed possessive form. It shows whose children these are. Option (1) is incorrect because the possessive form for parents is not needed. Option (2) is incorrect because it gives the plural subject a singular verb. Option (3) replaces to with its homonym too, which means "also."

2. Sentence 2: **This group of parents want peace and quiet.**

Which of the following is the best way to write the underlined portion of this sentence? If you think the original is the best way, choose option (1).

(1) group of parents want
(2) group of parents, want
(3) group of parents wanting
(4) group of parents wants
(5) group of parents to want

Answer: **(4) group of parents wants**

Explanation: This is an example of changing a sentence in order to correct it. This item covers usage; you must use the form of the verb that agrees with the subject. Option (4) is correct because it gives the singular subject <u>group</u> a singular verb, <u>wants</u>. Option (1) leaves the subject and verb in disagreement. In option (2), the comma separates the subject from the verb. Option (3) changes the verb to a form that is not complete; without a complete verb, the sentence is a fragment. Option (5) also changes the verb to a form that does not act as a verb.

3. Sentences 3 and 4: **A number of adult children, however, move back home. Parents continue to support them.**

The most effective combination of sentences 3 and 4 would include which of the following groups of words?

(1) home where parents
(2) home even if parents
(3) home, but parents
(4) home; instead, parents
(5) home, parents

Answer: **(1) home where parents**

   Explanation: This is an example of an item that asks you to combine two sentences. The area covered is sentence structure; you must choose the words that best connect the two sentences while keeping the meaning the same. Option (1) is correct because it uses the word where to put the two sentences together. In option (2), even if implies that the children would have moved home regardless, an idea not present in the two sentences. Options (3) and (4) show a contrast between the two ideas that is not meant. Option (5) incorrectly connects the sentences using only a comma.

4. Sentence 5: **Sometimes the children are charged rent by those parents.**

If you rewrote sentence 5 beginning with

Sometimes parents

the next words should be

(1) are charged rent
(2) charging the children
(3) charged the children
(4) charges the children
(5) charge the children

Answer: **(5) charge the children**

   Explanation: This is an example of an item that asks you to rewrite a sentence. The area covered is usage; you must figure out the verb that agrees with the new subject. Option (5) is correct because it makes the verb agree with the plural subject and keeps the present tense of the sentence. Option (1) results in a sentence that does not have the same meaning as the original sentence. Option (2) changes the verb to a form that is not a complete verb, resulting in a fragment. Option (3) uses the past tense, but the original is in the present tense. Option (4) uses a singular verb, charges, that does not agree with the plural subject, children.

The *Steck-Vaughn GED Writing Skills* book helps you develop the necessary grammar skills by giving detailed explanations for each answer. The answer key for each item has an explanation of why the correct answer is right and the incorrect answers are wrong. By studying these explanations, you will learn strategies for understanding and thinking about grammar. To prepare for the essay portion of the Writing Skills test, consider *Steck-Vaughn GED: The Essay.*

Test-Taking Skills

The GED Writing Skills Test is not the kind of test you can cram for. There are, however, some ways that you can improve your performance on the test.

Answering the Test Items

♦ Never skim the directions. Read them carefully so that you know exactly what to do. If you are unsure, ask the test-giver if the directions can be explained.

♦ First read the passage to get a general idea about what it is about. Notice the overall verb tense and the way the sentences relate to each other. Then read the items once. Read each sentence carefully before answering the question about it.

♦ Read all of the answer options carefully, even if you think you know the right answer. Some of the answers may not seem wrong at first glance, but one answer will always be better than the others.

♦ Answer all the items. Wrong answers will not be subtracted from your score. If you cannot find the correct answer, reduce the number of possible answers by eliminating all the answers you know are wrong. Then go back to the passage to figure out the correct answer. If you still cannot decide, make your best guess.

♦ Fill in your answer sheet carefully. To record your answers, mark one numbered space on the answer sheet beside the number that corresponds to the item. Mark only one answer space for each item; multiple answers will be scored as incorrect.

♦ Remember that the GED is a timed test. When the test begins, write down the time you have to finish. Then keep an eye on the time. Do not take a long time on any one item. Answer each item as best you can and go on. If you are spending a lot of time on one item, skip it. If you finish before time is up, go back to the items you skipped or were unsure of, and give them more thought.

♦ Don't change an answer unless you are certain your answer was wrong. Usually the first answer you choose is the correct one.

♦ If you feel you are getting nervous, stop working for a moment. Take a few deep breaths and relax. Then begin working again.

Study Skills

Study Regularly

- If you can, set aside an hour to study every day. If you do not have time every day, set up a schedule of the days you can study. Be sure to pick times when you will be the most relaxed and least likely to be bothered by outside distractions.

- Let others know your study time. Ask them to leave you alone for that period. It helps if you explain to others why this is important.

- You should be relaxed when you study, so find an area that is comfortable for you. If you cannot study at home, go to the library. Most public libraries have areas for reading and studying. If there is a college or university near you, find out if you can use its library. All libraries have dictionaries, encyclopedias, and other resources you can use if you need more information while you're studying.

Organize Your Study Materials

- Be sure to have pens, sharp pencils, and paper for any notes you might want to take.

- Keep all of your books together. If you are taking an adult education class, you probably will be able to borrow some books or other study material.

- Make a notebook or folder for each subject you are studying. Folders with pockets are useful for storing loose papers.

- Keep all of your material in one place so you do not waste time looking for it each time you study.

Read Regularly

- Read the newspaper, read magazines, read books. Read whatever appeals to you—but read! Regular, daily reading is the best way to improve your reading skills.

- Use the library to find material you like to read. Check the magazine section for publications of interest to you. Most libraries subscribe to hundreds of magazines ranging in interest from news to cars to music to sewing to sports. If you are not familiar with the library, ask a librarian for help. Get a library card so that you can check out material to use at home.

≣Take Notes

- ◆ Take notes on things that interest you or things that you think might be useful.

- ◆ When you take notes, do not copy the words directly from the book. Restate the information in your own words.

- ◆ Take notes any way you want. You do not have to write in full sentences as long as you can understand your notes later.

- ◆ Use outlines, charts, or diagrams to help you organize information and make it easier to learn.

- ◆ You may want to take notes in a question-and-answer form, such as: *What is the main idea? The main idea is . . .*

≣Improve Your Vocabulary

- ◆ As you read, do not skip a word you do not know. Instead, try to figure out what the word means. First, omit it from the sentence. Read the sentence without the word and try to put another word in its place. Is the meaning of the sentence the same?

- ◆ Make a list of unfamiliar words, look them up in the dictionary, and write down the meanings.

- ◆ Since a word may have several meanings, it is best to look up the word while you have the passage with you. Then you can try out the different meanings in the context.

- ◆ When you read the definition of a word, restate it in your own words. Use the word in a sentence or two.

- ◆ Use the Glossary at the end of this book to review the meanings of the key terms. All of the words you see in **boldface** type are defined in the Glossary. In addition, definitions of other important words are included. Use this list to review important vocabulary for the content areas you are studying.

≣Make a List of Subject Areas that Give You Trouble

- ◆ As you go through this book, make a note whenever you do not understand something. Then ask your teacher or another person for help. Later go back and review the topic.

Taking the Test

Before the Test

* If you have never been to the test center, go there the day before the test. If you drive, find out where to park. This way you won't get lost the day of the test.

* Prepare the things you need for the test: your admission ticket (if necessary), acceptable identification, some sharpened No. 2 pencils with erasers, a watch, glasses, a jacket or sweater (in case the room is cold), and a snack to eat during breaks.

* You will do your best work if you are rested and alert. So do not cram before the test. In fact, if you prepared for the test, cramming should be unnecessary. Instead, eat a meal and get a good night's sleep. If the test is early in the morning, set the alarm.

The Day of the Test

* Eat a good breakfast. Wear comfortable clothing. Make sure that you have all of the materials you need.

* Try to arrive at the test center about twenty minutes early. This allows time if, for example, there is a last-minute change of room.

* If you are going to be at the test center all day, you might pack a lunch. If you have to find a restaurant or if you wait a long time to be served, you may be late for the rest of the test.

Using this Book

* Start with the Pretest. It is identical to the real test in format and length. It will give you an idea of what the GED test is like. Then use the Pretest Correlation Chart to figure out your areas of strength and the areas you need to review. The chart will tell you exact units and page numbers to study.

* As you study, use a copy of the Study Record Sheet to keep track of the times and pages you study. Use the GED Cumulative Review and the Performance Analysis chart at the end of each unit to find out if you need to review any lessons before continuing.

* After you complete your review, use the Posttest to decide if you are ready for the real GED test. The Correlation Chart will tell you if you need additional review. Then use the Simulated Test and its Correlation Chart as a final check.

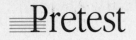Pretest

WRITING SKILLS

Directions

The Writing Skills Pretest is intended to measure your ability to use clear and effective English. It is a test of English as it should be written, not as it might be spoken.

This test consists of paragraphs with numbered sentences. Some of the sentences contain errors in sentence structure, usage, or mechanics (spelling, punctuation, and capitalization). After reading the numbered sentences, answer the multiple-choice questions that follow. Some questions refer to sentences that are correct as written. The best answer for these questions is the one that leaves the sentence as originally written. The best answer for some questions is the one that produces a sentence that is consistent with the verb tense and point of view used throughout the paragraph.

You should spend no more than 75 minutes answering the 55 questions on this test. Work carefully, but do not spend too much time on any one question. Do not skip any items. Make a reasonable guess when you are not sure of an answer. You will not be penalized for incorrect answers.

When time is up, mark the last item you finished. This will tell you whether you can finish the real GED Test in the time allowed. Then complete the test.

Record your answers to the questions on a copy of the answer sheet on page 332. Be sure that all required information is properly recorded on the answer sheet.

To record your answers, mark the numbered space on the answer sheet that corresponds to the answer you choose for each question on the test.

Example:

Sentence 1: **We were all honored to meet governor Phillips.**

What correction should be made to this sentence?

(1) insert a comma after <u>honored</u>
(2) change the spelling of <u>honored</u> to <u>honered</u>
(3) change <u>governor</u> to <u>Governor</u>
(4) replace <u>were</u> with <u>was</u>
(5) no correction is necessary   ① ② ● ④ ⑤

In this example, the word <u>governor</u> should be capitalized; therefore, answer space 3 would be marked on the answer sheet.

When you finish the test, use the Correlation Chart on page 30 to determine whether you are ready to take the real GED Test, and, if not, which skill areas need additional review.

Do not rest the point of your pencil on the answer sheet while you are considering your answer. Make no stray or unnecessary marks. If you change an answer, erase your first mark completely. Mark only one answer space for each question; multiple answers will be scored as incorrect. Do not fold or crease your answer sheet.

Adapted with permission of the American Council on Education.

Directions: Choose the best answer to each item.

Items 1 to 8 refer to the following paragraphs.

(1) Getting a speeding ticket is a stressful experience that can ruin your day. (2) You have an appointment with your Doctor and you are running a little late. (3) The traffic is light so you drive faster than the speed limit. (4) All of a sudden you hear a siren. (5) You look at your speedometer, and see that you are going over the speed limit. (6) When you look in the rearview mirror. (7) You see the flashing lights on the police car. (8) Your heart starts to beat faster you get a panicky feeling and start to look for a place to pull over.

(9) You wait for a period of time that seems like forever. (10) As people drive by your car, everyone slows down and stares at you. (11) The police officer approaches your car and says, "may I see your driver's license, please?"

(12) While the officer is writing your speeding ticket, you are thinking of the gas car repairs food, and clothes you could have purchased with the money you will have to pay for the ticket.

1. Sentence 2: **You have an appointment with your Doctor and you are running a little late.**

   Which of the following is the best way to write the underlined portion of this sentence? If you think the original is the best way, choose option (1).

   (1) Doctor and
   (2) doctor; and
   (3) Doctor; and
   (4) doctor, and
   (5) Doctor, and

2. Sentence 4: **All of a sudden you hear a siren.**

   What correction should be made to this sentence?

   (1) change you to yous
   (2) change hear to heard
   (3) change hear to here
   (4) change siren to Siren
   (5) no correction is necessary

3. Sentence 5: **You look at your speedometer, and see that you are going over the speed limit.**

   What correction should be made to this sentence?

   (1) change your to you're
   (2) remove the comma after speedometer
   (3) insert a comma after are
   (4) change are to is
   (5) no correction is necessary

4. Sentences 6 and 7: **When you look in the rearview mirror. You see the flashing lights on the police car.**

   Which of the following is the best way to write the underlined portion of these sentences? If you think the original is the best way, choose option (1).

   (1) rearview mirror. You
   (2) rearview mirror; you
   (3) rearview mirror, you
   (4) rearview Mirror, you
   (5) rearview mirror you

5. Sentence 8: **Your heart starts to beat faster you get a panicky feeling and start to look for a place to pull over.**

   What correction should be made to this sentence?

   (1) change Your to You're
   (2) change starts to started
   (3) insert a comma after faster
   (4) insert a semicolon after faster
   (5) insert a comma after feeling

6. Sentence 10: **As people drive by your car, everyone slows down and stares at you.**

   Which of the following is the best way to write the underlined portion of this sentence? If you think the original is the best way, choose option (1).

   (1) everyone slows down and stares
   (2) everybody slows down and stares
   (3) they slows down and stare
   (4) they slow down and stares
   (5) they slow down and stare

7. Sentence 11: **The police officer approaches your car and says, "may I see your driver's license, please?"**

   What correction should be made to this sentence?

   (1) change your to you're
   (2) change says, "may to Says, "may
   (3) change says, "may to says, "May
   (4) change the spelling of license to lisense
   (5) change please?" to please"?

8. Sentence 12: **While the officer is writing your speeding ticket, you are thinking of the gas car repairs food, and clothes you could have purchased with the money you will have to pay for the ticket.**

   Which of the following is the best way to write the underlined portion of this sentence? If you think the original is the best way, choose option (1).

   (1) gas car repairs food,
   (2) gas car repairs, food,
   (3) gas, car repairs, food
   (4) gas, car repairs, food,
   (5) gas, car, repairs, food,

Items 9 to 16 refer to the following paragraphs.

(1) Daydreaming is a popular pastime. (2) Songs, fiction stories, and movies often contains passages about daydreaming. (3) Daydreaming is not bad if you controlled it and do not let it control your life.

(4) Daydreaming can help you relax and improve your mood when your having a bad day. (5) You need to be sure your daydreams do not get to the point where you will begin to confuse dreams with reality.

(6) Sometimes we daydream while doing a boring, repetitive job. (7) Pushed a lawn mower around and around the yard. (8) You might find yourself daydreaming. (9) While you are driving alone along a straight road for a long time. (10) It can be very dangerous to daydream while using machinery, operating electrical controls, or when you drive a car. (11) Daydreaming, like many other things, is often okay if not done to excess.

9. Sentence 1: **Daydreaming is a popular pastime.**

   What correction should be made to this sentence?

   (1) replace Daydreaming with daydreaming
   (2) change is to was
   (3) replace is with are
   (4) change popular to Popular
   (5) no correction is necessary

10. Sentence 2: **Songs, fiction stories, and movies often contains passages about daydreaming.**

    What correction should be made to this sentence?

    (1) change fiction stories to Fiction Stories
    (2) change movies to Movies
    (3) change contains to contain
    (4) change contains to will contain
    (5) no correction is necessary

11. Sentence 3: **Daydreaming is not bad if you controlled it and do not let it control your life.**

    Which of the following is the best way to write the underlined portion of this sentence? If you think the original is the best way, choose option (1).

    (1) if you controlled it and do not
    (2) if you control it and do not
    (3) if you control it; and do not
    (4) if you control it and Do Not
    (5) if you control it, and, you do not

12. Sentence 4: **Daydreaming can help you relax and improve your mood when your having a bad day.**

    Which of the following is the best way to write the underlined portion of this sentence? If you think the original is the best way, choose option (1).

    (1) mood when your
    (2) mood, when you're
    (3) mood, when your'
    (4) mood when you're
    (5) mood, when your

13. Sentence 5: **You need to be sure your daydreams do not get to the point where you will begin to confuse dreams with reality.**

What correction should be made to this sentence?

(1) change will begin to began
(2) change will begin to begin
(3) change your to you're
(4) change will begin to has begun
(5) no correction is necessary

14. Sentences 6 and 7: **Sometimes we daydream while doing a boring, repetitive job. Pushed a lawn mower around and around the yard.**

The most effective combination of sentences 6 and 7 would include which of the following groups of words?

(1) job, push a lawn mower
(2) job such as push a lawn mower
(3) job, such as pushing a lawn mower
(4) job; such as push a lawn mower
(5) job; push a lawn mower

15. Sentences 8 and 9: **You might find yourself daydreaming. While you are driving alone along a straight road for a long time.**

Which of the following is the best way to write the underlined portion of this sentence? If you think the original is the best way, choose option (1).

(1) daydreaming. While you are
(2) daydreaming while you are
(3) daydreaming; while you're
(4) daydreaming while your
(5) daydreaming; while your

16. Sentence 10: **It can be very dangerous to daydream while using machinery, operating electrical controls, or when you drive a car.**

What correction should be made to this sentence?

(1) change operating to operation of
(2) change electrical to electricity
(3) change when you drive a car to driving a car
(4) change when you drive a car to when a car is driven
(5) change drive to drove

Items 17 to 24 refer to the following paragraphs.

(1) Yes anyone can learn to be a handy person around the house. (2) Start with simple things like changing a light bulb, oiling a lock, and the screws in the door can be tightened. (3) A reference guide, *The Handyman's Book of Tricks* is full of helpful hints.

(4) As you try more difficult jobs, you first need to analyze the job. (5) It often helps to consider what advance preparations is necessary and to make a list before you start. (6) For example, if you decide to paint the walls in your bedroom, what do you need to do? (7) Painting can be messy, and you will need to cover the floor. (8) You need to decide on the color and the type of paint to use. (9) There is oil-base and latex paints on the market. (10) Are a paintbrush to do the trim and, a roller to do the large flat areas adequate?

(11) If you want to try more technical jobs, you should first consult someone who has experience. (12) No one was born a handy person, the best way to learn is by doing.

17. Sentence 1: **Yes anyone can learn to be a handy person around the house.**

Which of the following is the best way to write the underlined portion of this sentence? If you think the original is the best way, choose option (1).

(1) Yes anyone
(2) Yes Anyone
(3) Yes, anyone
(4) Yes, Anyone
(5) Yes; anyone

18. Sentence 2: **Start with simple things like changing a light bulb, oiling a lock, and the screws in the door can be tightened.**

Which of the following is the best way to write the underlined portion of this sentence? If you think the original is the best way, choose option (1).

(1) and the screws in the door can be tightened
(2) and the door screws can be tightened
(3) and tightening the screws in the door
(4) and tighten the screws in the door
(5) and how to make the screws in the door tighter

19. Sentence 3: **A reference guide, *The Handyman's Book of Tricks* is full of helpful hints.**

    What correction should be made to this sentence?

    (1) remove the comma after <u>guide</u>
    (2) change <u>Book</u> to <u>book</u>
    (3) add a comma after <u>Tricks</u>
    (4) change <u>is</u> to <u>are</u>
    (5) no correction is necessary

20. Sentence 5: **It often helps to consider what advance preparations is necessary and to make a list before you start.**

    What correction should be made to this sentence?

    (1) insert a comma after <u>necessary</u>
    (2) change <u>is</u> to <u>are</u>
    (3) change <u>is</u> to <u>were</u>
    (4) change <u>is</u> to <u>was</u>
    (5) no correction is necessary

21. Sentence 7: **Painting can be messy, and you will need to cover the floor.**

    If you rewrote sentence 7 beginning with

    <u>Because painting can be</u>

    the next words should be

    (1) messy; you will
    (2) messy, you will
    (3) messy; and, you will
    (4) messy you will
    (5) messy, you, will

22. Sentence 9: **There is oil-base and latex paints on the market.**

    What correction should be made to this sentence?

    (1) change <u>There is</u> to <u>There are</u>
    (2) change <u>oil-base</u> to <u>Oil-Base</u>
    (3) change <u>latex paints</u> to <u>Latex paints</u>
    (4) change <u>latex paints</u> to <u>latex Paints</u>
    (5) no correction is necessary

23. Sentence 10: **Are a paintbrush to do the trim and, a roller to do the large flat areas adequate?**

    What correction should be made to this sentence?

    (1) change <u>Are</u> to <u>Is</u>
    (2) add a comma after <u>trim</u>
    (3) remove the comma after <u>and</u>
    (4) change the question mark to a period
    (5) no correction is necessary

24. Sentence 12: **No <u>one was born a handy person, the</u> best way to learn is by doing.**

    Which of the following is the best way to write the underlined portion of this sentence? If you think the original is the best way, choose option (1).

    (1) one was born a handy person, the
    (2) one is born a handy person, the
    (3) one is born a handy person; the
    (4) one was born a handy person; the
    (5) one is born a handy person the

Items 25 to 32 refer to the following paragraphs.

(1) AIDS is a deadly disease, it is also a very misunderstood disease. (2) There is a lot of hysteria, ignorance, and some people get emotional about AIDS. (3) It is important to learn all the facts.

(4) You won't get AIDS just by being around someone with the disease. (5) You won't get AIDS from sharing an office with an infected person; you can't get AIDS from being coughed or sneezed on. (6) You won't get AIDS from shaking hands with, hugging, or even kissing someone with the disease. (7) We won't get AIDS from using public toilets, telephones, drinking fountains, or swimming pools.

(8) You can get AIDS by coming into direct contact with the HIV virus. (9) The virus is carried in the blood and other bodily fluids of someone already infected. (10) You risk contact with the HIV virus if contaminated blood or other bodily fluids get into a cut on your skin, in your mouth, or in your eyes. (11) In the past, you could get AIDS from receiving contaminated blood in a transfusion, but now all blood is carefully screened so you're risk is very small.

(12) You can be exposed to the HIV virus if you have unprotected sex. (13) Always use condoms during sex if either you or your partner is unsure of having been exposed to the HIV virus. (14) You can be exposed to the virus by using a contaminated needle. (15) Never share needles; always wear a face mask, gloves, and long-sleeved top when giving medical care to a person with AIDS or someone suspected of being HIV positive.

(16) If you think you may have been exposed to the virus that causes AIDS, get tested. (17) You won't have to give the health clinic your name. (18) There is still no cure for AIDS, but there are treatments to slow the disease and lessen it's symptoms. (19) These medicines work best if the infection is diagnosed early.

25. Sentence 1: **AIDS is a deadly disease, it is also a very misunderstood disease.**

Which of the following is the best way to write the underlined portion of this sentence? If you think the original is the best way, choose option (1).

(1) disease, it
(2) disease; and
(3) disease; it
(4) disease; and,
(5) disease it

26. Sentence 2: **There is a lot of hysteria, ignorance, and some people get emotional about AIDS.**

What correction should be made to this sentence?

(1) replace is with are
(2) change the spelling of ignorance to ignorence
(3) replace some people get emotional with emotion
(4) replace ignorance with ignorant
(5) no correction is necessary

27. Sentence 5: **You won't get AIDS from sharing an office with an infected person; you can't get AIDS from being coughed or sneezed on.**

If you rewrote sentence 5 beginning with

You can't get AIDS from being coughed or sneezed on,

the next word should be

(1) and
(2) though
(3) but
(4) although
(5) however

28. Sentence 7: **We won't get AIDS from using public toilets, telephones, drinking fountains, or swimming pools.**

What correction should be made to this sentence?

(1) change We to You
(2) change We to They
(3) change We to Them
(4) change get to got
(5) no correction is necessary

29. Sentences 9 and 10: **The virus is carried in the blood and other bodily fluids of someone already infected. You risk contact with the HIV virus if contaminated blood or other bodily fluids get into a cut on your skin, in your mouth, or in your eyes.**

The most effective combination of sentences 9 and 10 would include which of the following groups of words?

(1) infected; and you
(2) infected; you
(3) infected you
(4) infected, you
(5) infected, because

30. Sentence 11: **In the past, you could get AIDS from receiving contaminated blood in a transfusion, but now all blood is carefully screened so you're risk is very small.**

Which of the following is the best way to write the underlined portion of this sentence? If you think that the original is the best way, choose option (1).

(1) you're
(2) your'
(3) their
(4) your
(5) my

31. Sentence 15: **Never share needles; always wear a face mask, gloves, and long-sleeved top when giving medical care to a person with AIDS or someone suspected of being HIV positive.**

What correction should be made to this sentence?

(1) remove the comma after mask
(2) insert a comma after top
(3) insert a semicolon after top
(4) change the spelling of needles to needels
(5) no correction is necessary

32. Sentence 18: **There is still no cure for AIDS, but there are treatments to slow the disease and lessen it's symptoms.**

What correction should be made to this sentence?

(1) change symptoms to symtoms
(2) remove the comma after AIDS
(3) change it's to its
(4) change there to their
(5) no correction is necessary

Items 33 to 38 refer to the following paragraphs.

(1) Some experts tell the public that they should legalize the use of marijuana. (2) People which want drugs legalized often make a comparison to Prohibition. (3) These people say that when the sale of liquor became legal, it solved the crime and other problems associated with Prohibition.

(4) Legalizing drugs might reduce the criminal element and the profit motive it would result in lower prices and increased accessibility to purer drugs. (5) The legalization of drugs may encourage more people to try drugs whom were reluctant before due to cost, fear of contaminated drugs, and fear of arrest. (6) Legalizing drugs is not the answer to the drug problem; education is the answer. (7) Education will help people become aware of how drugs affects the body and brain.

33. Sentence 1: **Some experts tell the public that they should legalize the use of marijuana.**

Which of the following is the best way to write the underlined portion of this sentence? If you think the original is the best way, choose option (1).

(1) public that they should legalize the use of marijuana.
(2) public, "the use of marijuana should be legalized."
(3) public, "They should legalize the use of marijuana."
(4) public that the use of marijuana should be legalized.
(5) public "The use of marijuana should be legalized."

34. Sentence 2: **People which want drugs legalized often make a comparison to Prohibition.**

What correction should be made to this sentence?

(1) change People to Peoples
(2) change which to who
(3) change which to whom
(4) change the spelling of comparison to comparason
(5) no correction is necessary

35. Sentence 4: **Legalizing drugs might reduce the criminal element and the profit <u>motive it</u> would result in lower prices and increased accessibility to purer drugs.**

Which of the following is the best way to write the underlined portion of this sentence? If you think the original is the best way, choose option (1).

(1) motive it
(2) motive but it
(3) motive, and it
(4) motive; but it
(5) motive, it

36. Sentence 5: **The legalization of drugs may encourage more people to try drugs whom were reluctant before due to cost, fear of contaminated drugs, and fear of arrest.**

What correction should be made to this sentence?

(1) change the spelling of <u>encourage</u> to <u>encurage</u>
(2) change <u>whom</u> to <u>which</u>
(3) change <u>whom</u> to <u>who</u>
(4) change <u>were</u> to <u>was</u>
(5) no correction is necessary

37. Sentence 6: **Legalizing drugs is not the answer to the drug problem; education is the answer.**

What correction should be made to this sentence?

(1) change the spelling of <u>answer</u> to <u>anser</u>
(2) remove the semicolon after <u>problem</u>
(3) change <u>education</u> to <u>Education</u>
(4) change the spelling of <u>education</u> to <u>edecation</u>
(5) no correction is necessary

38. Sentence 7: **Education will help people become aware of how drugs affects the body and brain.**

What correction should be made to this sentence?

(1) change <u>become</u> to <u>became</u>
(2) change <u>become</u> to <u>becomes</u>
(3) change <u>affects</u> to <u>affect</u>
(4) replace <u>affects</u> with <u>effects</u>
(5) no correction is necessary

Items 39 to 44 refer to the following paragraphs.

(1) We have come a long way from the 1400s when j. gutenberg invented the printing press to today's fax machines that send pages of text around the world in seconds. (2) Prior to the invention of the printing press, written material was all done by hand. (3) It took an hour or more to hand print a page. (4) Days, weeks, or months to do a whole book like the Bible.

(5) There are few books and very little written information. (6) That is not true today. (7) Some people would say we have too much written material. (8) You even hear about an organization "floating on a sea of paperwork" (printed pages of information).

(9) The printing press enabled many copies of the same printed page to be made once the page of type had been set quickly and easily. (10) Once this was possible, it spread widely and rapidly, people became more educated, and civilization advanced. (11) The invention of the printing press is probably the most important single invention ever made.

39. Sentence 1: **We have come a long way from the 1400s when j. gutenberg invented the printing press to today's fax machines that send pages of text around the world in seconds.**

What correction should be made to this sentence?

(1) change j. gutenberg to J. Gutenberg
(2) change printing press to Printing Press
(3) change that send to who send
(4) change world to World
(5) no correction is necessary

40. Sentences 3 and 4: **It took an hour or more to hand print a page. Days, weeks, or months to do a whole book like the Bible.**

Which of the following is the best way to write the underlined portion of these sentences? If you think the original is the best way, choose option (1).

(1) page. Days,
(2) page; days,
(3) page; and days
(4) page; therefore, days,
(5) page and days,

41. Sentence 5: **There are few books and very little written information.**

What correction should be made to this sentence?

(1) change There to Their
(2) replace are with is
(3) replace are with were
(4) change books to book
(5) no correction is necessary

42. Sentence 8: **You even hear about an organization "floating on a sea of paperwork" (printed pages of information).**

Which of the following is the best way to write the underlined portion of this sentence? If you think the original is the best way, choose option (1).

(1) You even hear
(2) You even here
(3) We even here
(4) We even hear
(5) They even hear

43. Sentence 9: **The printing press enabled many copies of the same printed page to be made once the page of type had been set quickly and easily.**

What correction should be made to this sentence?

(1) move quickly and easily to the beginning of the sentence
(2) move quickly and easily after many copies
(3) change printing press to Printing Press
(4) move quickly and easily after to be made
(5) no correction is necessary

44. Sentence 10: **Once this was possible, it spread widely and rapidly, people became more educated, and civilization advanced.**

Which of the following is the best way to write the underlined portion of this sentence? If you think the original is the best way, choose option (1).

(1) it spread
(2) it spreads
(3) information spread
(4) information, spread
(5) information will spread

(1) Life insurance can protect your family if you die. (2) If you buy life insurance when you are young. (3) The cost is low. (4) Life insurance can be a good investment. (5) There is in every state three basic kinds of life insurance—term, whole life, and universal life.

(6) Term insurance is the lowest cost, usually has no cash value, and is best for a temporary need (less than 10 years). (7) The most economical term insurance increase in cost each year as you get older.

(8) Whole life insurance is permanent, and is the most expensive kind. (9) Whole life has cash value, and you can often stop paying for it after a few years and let it pay for itself. (10) Whole life insurance can provide income when you retire. (11) It forces you to save an amount of money on a regular basis.

(12) Universal life insurance is a flexible plan to accomodate everyone. (13) You can change the amount of insurance and the premium each year to fit your changing needs. (14) Shop carefully for life insurance, and buy from a reputable company and agent you trust.

45. Sentences 2 and 3: **If you buy life insurance when you are young. The cost is low.**

Which of the following is the best way to write the underlined portion of these sentences? If you think the original is the best way, choose option (1).

(1) young. The
(2) young, however, the
(3) young, the
(4) young, because the
(5) young and the

46. Sentence 5: **There is in every state three basic kinds of life insurance—term, whole life, and universal life.**

What correction should be made to this sentence?

(1) change There is to Their is
(2) change There is to There are
(3) change There is to There's
(4) change state to states
(5) no correction is necessary

47. Sentence 7: **The most economical term insurance increase in cost each year as you get older.**

What correction should be made to this sentence?

(1) change term insurance to Term Insurance
(2) change increase to increases
(3) insert a comma after increase
(4) change year to years
(5) no correction is necessary

48. Sentence 8: **Whole life insurance is permanent, and is the most expensive kind.**

What correction should be made to this sentence?

(1) change the spelling of <u>permanent</u> to <u>permenant</u>
(2) change the spelling of <u>permanent</u> to <u>permanant</u>
(3) change <u>is permanent</u> to <u>are permanent</u>
(4) remove the comma after <u>permanent</u>
(5) change <u>and</u> to <u>or</u>

49. Sentence 9: **Whole life has cash value, and you can often stop paying for it after a few years and let it pay for <u>itself</u>.**

Which of the following is the best way to write the underlined portion of this sentence? If you think the original is the best way, choose option (1).

(1) itself
(2) it self
(3) theirself
(4) themself
(5) themselves

50. Sentence 10: **Whole life insurance can provide income when you retire.**

If you rewrote sentence 10 beginning with

<u>When you</u>

the next words should be

(1) retire, whole life
(2) retire; whole life
(3) retire; and whole life
(4) retire, Whole Life
(5) retire; Whole Life

51. Sentence 12: **Universal life insurance is a flexible plan to accomodate everyone.**

What correction should be made to this sentence?

(1) change <u>is</u> to <u>are</u>
(2) change the spelling of <u>accomodate</u> to <u>accommadate</u>
(3) change the spelling of <u>accomodate</u> to <u>accommodate</u>
(4) change <u>is</u> to <u>were</u>
(5) no correction is necessary

Items 52 to 55 refer to the following paragraphs.

(1) Lifestyles change greatly from generation to generation. (2) Our lifestyles are becoming more casual today then in the past.

(3) There is still many people with the "me first" instant gratification lifestyle. (4) However, on account of this we are beginning to be concerned about such things as the environment and our impact on it. (5) We, as a nation, is becoming more health conscious and aware of the importance of diet, exercise, low cholesterol, and high fiber. (6) We are more casual; our dress and activities are less formal than in the past.

(7) Where would we be without our jeans, denim jackets, leather jackets, and tennis shoes? (8) Not only fast food places but also the expensive restaurant now welcome customers without a suitcoat and necktie.

52. Sentence 2: **Our lifestyles are becoming more casual today then in the past.**

Which of the following is the best way to write the underlined portion of this sentence? If you think the original is the best way, choose option (1).

(1) today then in
(2) today, than in
(3) today or in
(4) today, then in
(5) today than in

53. Sentence 3: **There is still many people with the "me first" instant gratification lifestyle.**

What correction should be made to this sentence?

(1) change There is to There are
(2) replace There with Their
(3) change lifestyle to Lifestyle
(4) replace me with myself
(5) no correction is necessary

54. Sentence 4: **However, on account of this we are beginning to be concerned about such things as the environment and our impact on it.**

Which of the following is the best way to write the underlined portion of this sentence? If you think the original is the best way, choose option (1).

(1) However, on account of this we
(2) However on account of this we
(3) However we
(4) However, we
(5) However, We

55. Sentence 5: **We, as a nation, is becoming more health conscious and aware of the importance of diet, exercise, low cholesterol, and high fiber.**

What correction should be made to this sentence?

(1) remove the comma after nation
(2) change nation, is to nation, are
(3) replace conscious with conscience
(4) change aware to awares
(5) no correction is necessary

Answers are on page 252.

Pretest Correlation Chart: Writing Skills

Name: _____ Class: _____ Date: _____

This chart can help you determine your strengths and weaknesses on the content and skill areas of the Writing Skills GED Test. Use the Answer Key on pages 252–256 to check your answers to the test. Then circle on the chart the numbers of the test items you answered correctly. Put the total number correct for each content area and skill area in each row and column. If you answered fewer than 55 questions correctly, look at the total items correct in each column and row and decide which areas are difficult for you. Use the page references to study those areas. Use a copy of the Study Record Sheet on page 31 to guide your studying.

Content/ Item Type	Sentence Correction	Sentence Revision	Rewrite/ Combine	Total Correct	Page Ref.
Mechanics *(Pages 32–99)*					
Capitalization	7, 39	1		_____ out of 3	34–39
Commas	3, 19, 23, 48	8, 17, 31	50	_____ out of 8	44–59
Semicolons	37	25		_____ out of 2	60–65
Apostrophes and Quotation Marks	32	12, 30		_____ out of 3	66–73
Spelling	2, 51			_____ out of 2	74–99
Usage *(Pages 100–159)*					
Subject-Verb Agreement	10, 20, 22, 38 46, 47, 53, 55			_____ out of 8	108–113
Verb Tenses and Irregular Verbs	9, 13, 41	11	14	_____ out of 5	114–127
Personal Pronouns	28, 34, 36	49		_____ out of 4	128–135
Pronouns and Antecedents		33, 44		_____ out of 2	136–141
Indefinite Pronouns		6		_____ out of 1	142–147
Adjectives and Adverbs					148–153
Sentence Structure *(Pages 160–218)*					
Sentence Fragments		4, 15, 40, 45		_____ out of 4	162–167
Run-on Sentences	5	24, 35		_____ out of 3	168–173
Combining Sentences			29	_____ out of 1	174–181
Parallel Structure	16, 26	18		_____ out of 3	182–187
Subordination		21, 27, 52		_____ out of 3	188–193
Misplaced Modifiers	43			_____ out of 1	194–199
Shift of Focus		42		_____ out of 1	200–205
Revising Sentences		54		_____ out of 1	206–211

For additional help, see the Steck-Vaughn GED Writing Skills Exercise Book.

Study Record Sheet

Name: ______________________ **Class:** ______________ **Date:** ________

Use this chart to help you track your studies after you take the Pretest, Posttest, or Simulated Test. After each test, use the Writing Skills Correlation Charts on pages 30, 234, and 250 to help you figure out the areas you need to study. Then, make a copy of the Study Record Sheet for you to complete. In the column on the left, write the content and skill areas you want to study. Then, after each session, write the date and the pages you studied. Use the sheet to review your study habits from time to time. Are you studying regularly? Are you reviewing the material you need to cover? Do you need to schedule more frequent sessions?

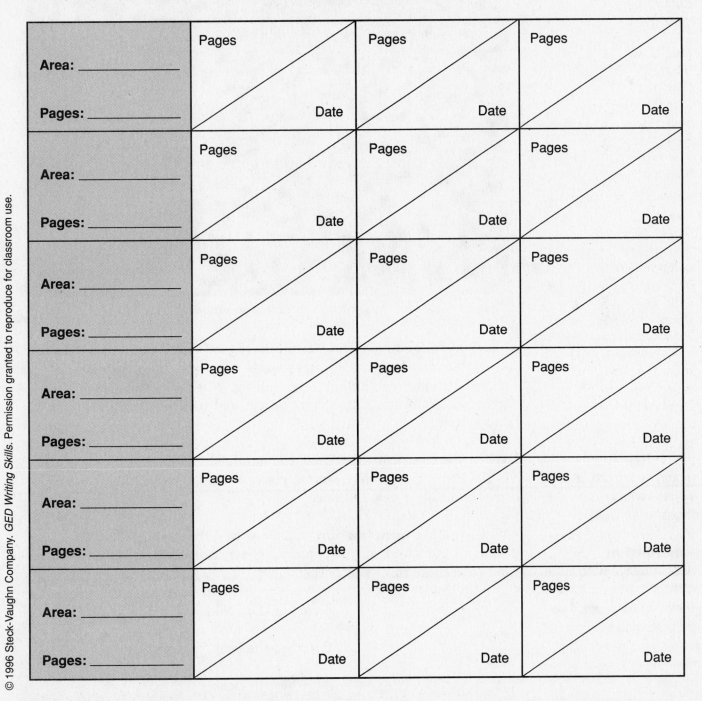

Area: ____________ **Pages:** ____________	Pages / Date	Pages / Date	Pages / Date
Area: ____________ **Pages:** ____________	Pages / Date	Pages / Date	Pages / Date
Area: ____________ **Pages:** ____________	Pages / Date	Pages / Date	Pages / Date
Area: ____________ **Pages:** ____________	Pages / Date	Pages / Date	Pages / Date
Area: ____________ **Pages:** ____________	Pages / Date	Pages / Date	Pages / Date
Area: ____________ **Pages:** ____________	Pages / Date	Pages / Date	Pages / Date

Good spelling can be useful in a variety of situations.

Your understanding of the mechanics of good writing will be helpful in everything you write. Writing is easier when you know the rules for capitalization, punctuation, and spelling. When you write, each instance of capitalization, punctuation, and spelling gives information to the reader.

capitalization
beginning a word or proper name with a capital letter

When you use **capitalization,** you emphasize. You show that a word is the name of a specific person, place, or thing; or you show that you are beginning a new sentence.

punctuation
marks that show how the parts of a sentence are related to each other so the reader can understand the exact meaning of what is written

When you use **punctuation,** you show how the sentence should "sound." For example, you can show the difference in meaning between these three sentences:

Give her the book.

Give her the book?

Give her the book!

Punctuation is used within a sentence, as well as to show where a sentence ends. Punctuation indicates a pause. It shows which words are in a list or are a **direct** or **exact quotation**. It shows how the parts of the sentence are related to each other. Punctuation marks help the reader to move along quickly and understand the exact meaning of what is written.

Correct **spelling** also makes writing clear and accurate. Some misspellings cause the reader to mistake your meaning. But even if the reader knows what you mean, he or she may notice the misspellings before noticing what you have to say.

Writing that is **mechanically correct**—that is, writing that has correct capitalization, punctuation, and spelling—always makes a better impression than writing that contains errors.

This unit gives you an opportunity to test your skill in spotting mechanical errors. You will learn how to avoid some of the most common mistakes in capitalization, punctuation, and spelling so that you can write more easily and correctly. You will learn some useful rules to help you improve your mechanical skills in all these areas. You will learn that it is sometimes good to pay attention to your instincts in spelling. If a word "looks wrong," you can check it by applying the rules you will learn or by looking it up in the dictionary.

How you use the mechanics of writing tells a lot about you as a person and as a writer. Are you careless and unobservant? Or are you careful and aware? The following lessons should help you master many areas of mechanics and ensure that your writing makes a positive statement about you.

direct quotation
words telling exactly what somebody said

spelling
putting the correct letters of a word in the correct order

mechanically correct
writing that uses correct capitalization, punctuation, and spelling

SEE ALSO: Steck-Vaughn GED Writing Skills Exercise Book, Unit 1: Mechanics

Lesson 1

Using Capitalization

 tip **Capitalize *I*, the first letter of proper nouns, and the first word of each sentence.**

This letter has four parts: address, salutation, body, and complimentary close. Read the letter and notice where capital letters are used.

ADDRESS:	3453 Ridgefield Road Oklahoma City, Oklahoma 83346 March 12
SALUTATION: **BODY:**	Dear Wilma Mae, As you know, I was going to ask for vacation time during the month of August. Last Friday when I asked my boss, Mr. Driscoll, he said only old-timers could get summer vacation. I have to take my vacation during the fall, and I probably won't even get off on Thanksgiving or Christmas. There goes our chance to take a vacation together!
COMPLIMEN-TARY CLOSE:	As ever, Mattie

Notice that all sentences begin with a capital letter and that the following words or phrases also begin with a capital.

ADDRESS:	name of street (Ridgefield Road) name of city (Oklahoma City) name of state (Oklahoma) name of month (March)
SALUTATION:	salutation (Dear) name of person (Wilma Mae)
BODY:	I name of month (August) name of day (Friday) title of person (Mr.) name of person (Driscoll) name of holiday (Thanksgiving, Christmas) Note: The names of seasons, *summer* and *fall*, are not capitalized.
COMPLIMEN-TARY CLOSE:	first word of closing (As ever) name of person (Mattie)

You capitalize the name of a *specific* person, place, or thing. This shows that someone, someplace, or something is one of a kind.

Always capitalize:

♦ the specific names of people, places, and organizations
♦ the specific names of days, months, and holidays
♦ the first word of a sentence
♦ the first word of a sentence in quotation marks
♦ the word *I*
♦ the first, last, and other important words in the titles of books, stories, movies, and so on. Articles (*a, the*), conjunctions (*and, or, but*), and prepositions (*on, in, to*) are not considered important words.

☰Titles

Titles are often part of a person's name and are capitalized when they refer to a specific person. Titles are often abbreviated.

Examples: Alice went to see Dr. Jones.
The mayor appointed a new police chief.

Titles, along with such family names as *mother, father, grandmother,* and *grandfather,* are capitalized when they are used to address a person directly.

Examples: When do you think you will be able to visit, Mother?
Do you think, Doctor, that she will recover?

☰Names

Brand names are *always* specific names, so they are capitalized.

Example: Here is a Kleenex.

☰Places

Direction words sometimes indicate a specific place. They are capitalized only when they refer to a specific area of the world, a country, a region, or a city.

Examples: Laura grew up in the South.
The Barnards live in the Middle East.
We took a tour of the East.
Note: A proper adjective that is formed from a specific place name is also capitalized *(Middle Eastern, American).*

Items 1 to 4 refer to this friendly letter. Choose the best answer to each item.

ADDRESS:	(1) 1582 percy drive indianapolis, indiana 48958 (2) April 24
SALUTATION:	(3) Dear John,
BODY:	(4) We are planning to move to a bigger house during May. (5) Last wednesday we signed a lease with the landlord, mr. larry garwood. (6) Mr. garwood was looking for someone to move in before summer. (7) we hope to be out of our present house by memorial day. (8) Since the fourth of july is on saturday, please plan to join us for a Holiday picnic.
COMPLIMENTARY CLOSE:	(9) Sincerely yours, (10) Tom

1. Address: **1582 percy drive indianapolis, indiana 48958**

   What capitalization corrections are needed in the address?

   (1) Percy, Indianapolis, Indiana
   (2) Percy Drive, Indianapolis, Indiana
   (3) Percy Drive, Indiana
   (4) Indianapolis, Indiana
   (5) no correction is necessary

2. Sentence 5: **Last wednesday we signed a lease with the landlord, mr. larry garwood.**

   What capitalization corrections are needed in this sentence?

   (1) Mr. Garwood
   (2) Mr. Larry Garwood
   (3) Larry
   (4) Wednesday, Mr. Larry Garwood
   (5) no correction is necessary

3. Sentences 6 and 7: **Mr. garwood was looking for someone to move in before summer. we hope to be out of our present house by memorial day.**

   What capitalization corrections are needed in these sentences?

   (1) Garwood, Summer, We
   (2) Garwood, We, Memorial Day
   (3) Garwood, Summer, We, Memorial
   (4) Garwood, Memorial
   (5) no correction is necessary

4. Sentence 8: **Since the fourth of july is on saturday, please plan to join us for a Holiday picnic.**

   What capitalization corrections are needed in this sentence?

   (1) Fourth, July, Saturday, holiday
   (2) The Fourth Of July
   (3) Fourth, July, Saturday
   (4) July, Saturday, holiday
   (5) no correction is necessary

Items 5 to 9 refer to the following sentences.

(1) When Secretary of State Kissinger served under President Nixon, he went all over the world, especially to the middle East.
(2) After Nixon resigned from the office of the presidency, Vice President ford became President.
(3) On Election Day in the Fall, Americans will go to the polls, hoping to elect a President to solve both old and new problems.
(4) Many Presidents, such as Bill Clinton, have been from the south.
(5) The nation's most populous State, California, has produced only two presidents, Richard Nixon and Ronald Reagan.

5. Sentence 1: **When Secretary of State Kissinger served under President Nixon, he went all over the world, especially to the middle East.**

What correction should be made to this sentence?

(1) change Secretary of State to secretary of state
(2) change Kissinger to kissinger
(3) change President to president
(4) change middle East to Middle East
(5) no correction is necessary

6. Sentence 2: **After Nixon resigned from the office of the presidency, Vice President ford became President.**

What correction should be made to this sentence?

(1) change presidency to Presidency
(2) replace Vice President ford with Vice President Ford
(3) change Vice President ford to vice President Ford
(4) change Nixon to nixon
(5) no correction is necessary

7. Sentence 3: **On Election Day in the Fall, Americans will go to the polls, hoping to elect a President to solve both old and new problems.**

What correction should be made to this sentence?

(1) change Election Day to election day
(2) change Fall to fall
(3) change Americans to americans
(4) change polls to Polls
(5) no correction is necessary

8. Sentence 4: **Many Presidents, such as Bill Clinton, have been from the south.**

What correction should be made to this sentence?

(1) change Clinton to clinton
(2) change Bill to bill
(3) change the to The
(4) change south to South
(5) no correction is necessary

9. Sentence 5: **The nation's most populous State, California, has produced only two presidents, Richard Nixon and Ronald Reagan.**

What correction should be made to this sentence?

(1) change nation's to Nation's
(2) change State to state
(3) change California to california
(4) change presidents to Presidents
(5) no correction is necessary

Items 10 to 13 refer to the following paragraph.

(1) John f. Kennedy was the first Catholic President of the United States. (2) At his inauguration on January 20, 1961, President Kennedy said, "let the torch be passed to a new generation of Americans." (3) Kennedy supported an offensive by the Attorney General and the Federal Bureau of Investigation against organized crime. (4) After his assassination, many people suggested that we establish a new national holiday, similar to Washington's Birthday, to celebrate Kennedy's birthday.

10. Sentence 1: **John f. Kennedy was the first Catholic President of the United States.**

What correction should be made to this sentence?

(1) change John f. Kennedy to John F. Kennedy
(2) change Catholic to catholic
(3) change elected to Elected
(4) change the United States to The United States
(5) no correction is necessary

11. Sentence 2: **At his inauguration on January 20, 1961, President Kennedy said, "let the torch be passed to a new generation of Americans."**

What correction should be made to this sentence?

(1) change inauguration to Inauguration
(2) change January to january
(3) change President to president
(4) change let to Let
(5) no correction is necessary

12. Sentence 3: **Kennedy supported an offensive by the Attorney General and the Federal Bureau of Investigation against organized crime.**

What correction should be made to this sentence?

(1) change Attorney General to attorney general
(2) change Federal Bureau of Investigation to federal Bureau of Investigation
(3) change Federal Bureau of Investigation to Federal Bureau of investigation
(4) change organized crime to Organized Crime
(5) no correction is necessary

13. Sentence 4: **After his assassination, many people suggested that we establish a new national holiday, similar to Washington's Birthday, to celebrate Kennedy's birthday.**

What correction should be made to this sentence?

(1) change assassination to Assassination
(2) change holiday to Holiday
(3) change Washington's Birthday to Washington's birthday
(4) change Kennedy's birthday to Kennedy's Birthday
(5) no correction is necessary

Items 1 to 5 refer to the following paragraph.

(1) Both the Rumford and Valdez families enjoy camping in the beautiful scenery of the American west. (2) The Valdezes and the Rumfords took their Winnebagos to the Grand Canyon last Spring. (3) their April trip was full of mishaps. (4) The Rumfords' daughter, Susan, got sick in Colorado and had to see a Doctor. (5) In Texas, Rosa Valdez broke the Coleman lantern, and her mother tried to buy a new one at a camping store. (6) When that store did not have one, Rosa said, "We should try Sears, Mother."

1. Sentence 1: **Both the Rumford and Valdez families enjoy camping in the beautiful scenery of the American west.**

   What correction should be made to this sentence?

   (1) change Rumford to rumford
   (2) change Valdez to valdez
   (3) change families to Families
   (4) change west to West
   (5) no correction is necessary

2. Sentence 2: **The Valdezes and the Rumfords took their Winnebagos to the Grand Canyon last Spring.**

   What correction should be made to this sentence?

   (1) change Valdezes to valdezes
   (2) change Winnebagos to winnebagos
   (3) change Grand Canyon to grand canyon
   (4) change Spring to spring
   (5) no correction is necessary

3. Sentence 3: **their April trip was full of mishaps.**

   What correction should be made to this sentence?

   (1) change their to Their
   (2) change April to april
   (3) change trip to Trip
   (4) change mishaps to Mishaps
   (5) no correction is necessary

4. Sentence 4: **The Rumfords' daughter, Susan, got sick in Colorado and had to see a Doctor.**

   What correction should be made to this sentence?

   (1) change daughter to Daughter
   (2) change Susan to susan
   (3) change Colorado to colorado
   (4) change Doctor to doctor
   (5) no correction is necessary

5. Sentence 5: **In Texas, Rosa Valdez broke the Coleman lantern, and her mother tried to buy a new one at a camping store.**

   What correction should be made to this sentence?

   (1) change Texas to texas
   (2) change Rosa Valdez to rosa valdez
   (3) change mother to Mother
   (4) change camping store to Camping Store
   (5) no correction is necessary

Answers are on page 257.

Lesson 2

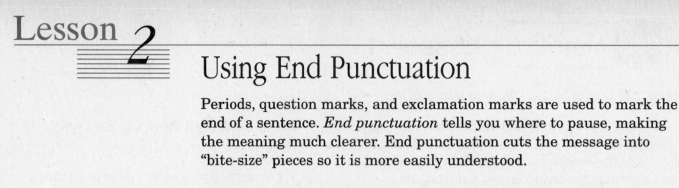

Using End Punctuation

Periods, question marks, and exclamation marks are used to mark the end of a sentence. *End punctuation* tells you where to pause, making the meaning much clearer. End punctuation cuts the message into "bite-size" pieces so it is more easily understood.

Read the paragraph about an upcoming wedding and notice the end punctuation marks.

(1) What time would be best for us to schedule the wedding? (2) I have always wanted to be married in a church at 8 P.M. with candlelight. (3) Do you think that is too late? (4) When the wedding is over, I want people to come to a dance. (5) Wow! (6) That's a wonderful idea, isn't it?

≡Question Mark

Rule: A question mark is used at the end of direct questions. A direct question requires an answer.

Examples: (Sentence 1) What time would be best for us to schedule the wedding?
(Sentence 3) Do you think that is too late?
(Sentence 6) That's a wonderful idea, isn't it?

≡Period

Rule: Use a period at the end of a group of words that makes a statement and expresses a complete thought or command.

Example: (Sentence 4) When the wedding is over, I want people to come to a dance.

Rule: Periods are used in abbreviations, such as A.M and P.M.

Example: (Sentence 2) I have always wanted to be married in a church at 8 P.M. with candlelight.

≡Exclamation Mark

Rule: Use an exclamation mark at the end of a word or a sentence that expresses strong feelings, such as surprise, shock, or enthusiasm.

Example: (Sentence 5) Wow!

> **tip** To figure out whether to use a period, question mark, or exclamation mark to indicate the end of each sentence, say the sentence to yourself and decide whether it is a statement, a question, or an exclamation.

Items 1 to 6 refer to the following note. Choose the best answer to each item.

(1) I have been looking forward to this wedding for a long time. (2) Please meet me at Brown's Department Store to help me select a wedding present? (3) On Friday I will get paid, so I can buy a wedding present then? (4) Do you think the bride and groom would like something for their kitchen! (5) I'm not going to spend $100 for towels. (6) I think I can buy a nice wedding present for about $25?

1. Sentence 1: **I have been looking forward to this wedding for a long time.**

   What correction should be made to this sentence?

   (1) change the period to a question mark
   (2) change the period to an exclamation mark
   (3) no correction is necessary

2. Sentence 2: **Please meet me at Brown's Department Store to help me select a wedding present?**

   What correction should be made to this sentence?

   (1) change the question mark to a period
   (2) change the question mark to an exclamation mark
   (3) no correction is necessary

3. Sentence 3: **On Friday I will get paid, so I can buy a wedding present then?**

   What correction should be made to this sentence?

   (1) change the question mark to a period
   (2) change the question mark to an exclamation mark
   (3) no correction is necessary

4. Sentence 4: **Do you think the bride and groom would like something for their kitchen!**

   What correction should be made to this sentence?

   (1) change the exclamation mark to a period
   (2) change the exclamation mark to a question mark
   (3) no correction is necessary

5. Sentence 5: **I'm not going to spend $100 for towels.**

   What correction should be made to this sentence?

   (1) change the period to a question mark
   (2) change the period to an exclamation mark
   (3) no correction is necessary

6. Sentence 6: **I think I can buy a nice wedding present for about $25?**

   What correction should be made to this sentence?

   (1) change the question mark to a period
   (2) change the question mark to an exclamation mark
   (3) no correction is necessary

Answers are on page 258.

Directions: Choose the <u>best answer</u> to each item.

<u>Items 1 to 5</u> refer to the following paragraph.

(1) Is it possible to lose weight without exercising or dieting! (2) Don't believe it for one second! (3) Despite what you may read in advertisements for weight-loss products, no one has developed a miracle diet pill? (4) Many nutritionists and other Health Professionals believe that a combination of dieting and exercise is the best way to lose weight. (5) Forget miracle products now. (6) If you are trying to lose weight, talk to your doctor about a sensible diet and exercise program. (7) It's easy to increase your level of physical activity. (8) For example, you can take a walk from 6 P.M. to 7 P.M. instead of watching television.

1. Sentence 1: **Is it possible to lose weight without exercising or dieting!**

   What correction should be made to this sentence?

   (1) change the exclamation mark to a period
   (2) change the exclamation mark to a question mark
   (3) no correction is necessary

2. Sentence 2: **Don't believe it for one second!**

   What correction should be made to this sentence?

   (1) change the exclamation mark to a period
   (2) change the exclamation mark to a question mark
   (3) no correction is necessary

3. Sentence 3: **Despite what you may read in advertisements for weight-loss products, no one has developed a miracle diet pill?**

   What correction should be made to this sentence?

   (1) change the question mark to a period
   (2) change <u>you</u> to <u>You</u>
   (3) no correction is necessary

4. Sentence 4: **Many nutritionists and other Health Professionals believe that a combination of dieting and exercise is the best way to lose weight.**

   What correction should be made to this sentence?

   (1) change the period to a question mark
   (2) change <u>Health Professionals</u> to <u>health professionals</u>
   (3) no correction is necessary

5. Sentence 5: **Forget miracle products now.**

   What correction should be made to this sentence?

   (1) change the period to an exclamation mark
   (2) change the period to a question mark
   (3) no correction is necessary

Items 6 to 10 refer to the following paragraph.

(1) My friend Kevin asked his wife, Sabrina, not to plan a surprise party for him. (2) He was turning thirty-five years old on the first day of March? (3) To make sure she didn't try to throw a party, he arranged to spend the weekend of his birthday out of town! (4) Friday night they arrived at the morris Hotel in Buffalo. (5) Kevin carried his bags upstairs to the room and waited for Sabrina to open the door. (6) What did he hear when Sabrina turned the key? (7) "Surprise?"(8) Of all the people who were there, I think Kevin enjoyed the party the most.

6. Sentence 1: **My friend Kevin asked his wife, Sabrina, not to plan a surprise party for him.**

   What correction should be made to this sentence?

   (1) change the period to an exclamation mark
   (2) change the period to a question mark
   (3) change wife to Wife
   (4) change Sabrina to sabrina
   (5) no correction is necessary

7. Sentence 2: **He was turning thirty-five years old on the first day of March?**

   What correction should be made to this sentence?

   (1) change the question mark to a period
   (2) change the question mark to an exclamation mark
   (3) change first to First
   (4) change March to march
   (5) no correction is necessary

8. Sentence 3: **To make sure she didn't try to throw a party, he arranged to spend the weekend of his birthday out of town!**

   What correction should be made to this sentence?

   (1) change the exclamation mark to a period
   (2) change the exclamation mark to a question mark
   (3) change weekend to Weekend
   (4) change birthday to Birthday
   (5) no correction is necessary

9. Sentence 4: **Friday night they arrived at the morris Hotel in Buffalo.**

   What correction should be made to this sentence?

   (1) change the period to an exclamation mark
   (2) change morris to Morris
   (3) change Hotel to hotel
   (4) change Buffalo to buffalo
   (5) no correction is necessary

10. Sentence 7: **"Surprise?"**

    What correction should be made to this sentence?

    (1) change the question mark to an exclamation mark
    (2) change the question mark to a period
    (3) change Surprise to surprise
    (4) change "Surprise?" to "Surprise?
    (5) no correction is necessary

Answers are on page 258.

Lesson 3

Using Commas

 Use a comma to indicate a pause or to show how the parts of a sentence are related to each other.

Read the memorandum and notice the commas.

MEMORANDUM

DATE: April 23
TO: Members of Fellowship Hall
SUBJECT: Bake sale

(1) The members of the Fellowship Hall will hold a bake sale on Monday or Tuesday or Wednesday. (2) Cakes, pies, and cookies will be sold. (3) The president of the hall believes that this year's will be the best, biggest sale yet. (4) The secretary is concerned that not enough posters and fliers have been made. (5) Please attend a meeting on Thursday.

Here are some rules to help you use commas correctly.

Items in Series

When items in a list appear one after the other, the items are referred to as items in series. Items in series can be words or phrases.

Rule: Use commas to separate more than two items in a list. Place a comma before the conjunction. Do not use a comma after the last item in a list unless another punctuation rule requires one.

Example: (Sentence 2) Cakes, pies, and cookies will be sold.

Rule: If all of the items in a list are joined by conjunctions, do not use commas between the items.

Example: (Sentence 1) The members of the Fellowship Hall will hold a bake sale on Monday or Tuesday or Wednesday.

Rule: Do not use commas to separate only two items in series.

Example: (Sentence 4) The secretary is concerned that not enough posters and fliers have been made.

Rule: Two adjectives that describe the same noun are separated by a comma if *and* could be used between them without changing the meaning.

Example: (Sentence 3) The president of the hall believes that this year's will be the best, biggest sale yet.

 **Practice** Using Commas

Items 1 to 5 refer to the following memorandum. Choose the best answer to each item.

MEMORANDUM

DATE: September 12
TO: Staff
SUBJECT: Half-price sale

   (1) The Short Stop Cafe will have a half-price sale on Friday Saturday, and Sunday. (2) Sandwiches drinks, desserts, and salads will be included in the sale. (3) The sandwiches will be ham and cheese roast beef and tuna salad. (4) The manager expects a 100 percent increase in the sale of drinks, and desserts. (5) Invite your friends and relatives!

---

1. Sentence 1: **The Short Stop Cafe will have a half-price sale on Friday Saturday, and Sunday.**

    What correction should be made to this sentence?

    (1) insert a comma after sale
    (2) insert a comma after on
    (3) insert a comma after Friday
    (4) remove the comma after Saturday
    (5) no correction is necessary

2. Sentence 2: **Sandwiches drinks, desserts, and salads will be included in the sale.**

    What correction should be made to this sentence?

    (1) insert a comma after Sandwiches
    (2) remove the comma after drinks
    (3) remove the commas after drinks and desserts
    (4) insert a comma after salads
    (5) no correction is necessary

3. Sentence 3: **The sandwiches will be ham and cheese roast beef and tuna salad.**

    What correction should be made to this sentence?

    (1) insert a comma after ham
    (2) insert a comma after cheese
    (3) insert a comma after roast
    (4) insert commas after both cheese and beef
    (5) no correction is necessary

4. Sentence 4: **The manager expects a 100 percent increase in the sale of drinks, and desserts.**

    What correction should be made to this sentence?

    (1) insert a comma after expects
    (2) insert a comma after manager
    (3) insert a comma after increase
    (4) remove the comma after drinks
    (5) no correction is necessary

5. Sentence 5: **Invite your friends and relatives!**

    What correction should be made to this sentence?

    (1) insert a comma after friends
    (2) insert a comma after and
    (3) change the exclamation mark to a period
    (4) change the exclamation mark to a question mark
    (5) no correction is necessary

Answers are on page 259.

Interrupting Words or Phrases

Words or phrases that interrupt the main thought are sometimes used in sentences. A common type of interrupter that further explains a noun or pronoun is called an **appositive.** If an appositive or a nonessential phrase is left out of the sentence, the sentence still expresses a complete idea.

Rule: Use a comma to separate a descriptive word or group of words (an appositive) from the noun being described. A comma is used before and after the appositive.

Example: Chuck Garr, his neighbor, pays more rent than he.

Rule: If the information in the phrase is necessary or essential to make the meaning of the sentence clear, do not set off the phrase with a comma.

Example: A driver who uses a radar detector is more likely to avoid a speeding ticket. (The phrase who uses a radar detector limits the meaning of driver and so is essential to the sentence.)

Example: Paul Tyler, his friend, uses a radar detector to avoid speeding tickets. (The phrase his friend is nonessential to the meaning of the sentence.)

Words or phrases that are essential to the meaning of a sentence are also called *restrictive*. Phrases that are nonessential are also known as *nonrestrictive* phrases.

Example: Her sister Eva will also be at the party. (The word *Eva* is essential to the meaning of the sentence. It is a *restrictive appositive.)*

Another common interrupter is the **parenthetical expression.** A parenthetical expression adds nothing to the meaning of the sentence, so it is set off with commas. Some common expressions are:

for example	I am sure	incidentally	of course
however	I know	nevertheless	on the one hand

Rule: Set off expressions that are not essential to the meaning of the sentence.

Example: The grandfather clocks, for example, will be on sale.

Introductory Elements

An introductory element is a word or a group of words located at the beginning of a sentence that is not part of the main idea of the sentence. Introductory elements may be such common expressions as *yes, well, however,* and *oh.*

Rule:	Use a comma to separate introductory words from the rest of the sentence.
Example:	Yes, we will be open on Memorial Day.
Rule:	When a person's name or title is used in direct address, use commas to set it off from the rest of the sentence.
Examples:	Marcy, did you lock the door when you came home? The choice is now yours, delegates.
Rule:	Use a comma after a long introductory phrase.
Example:	As a result of overspending, Ron's funds are low.
Note:	If the introductory phrase is short and has no verb, the comma is frequently omitted.
Example:	In 1990 the Census forms were mailed.
Note:	If the sentence might be misread without the comma, insert a comma.
Example:	According to the report, that is not likely to happen.
Direct Quotations	When the exact words someone uses are given in a sentence, you have a **direct quotation.** Such phrases as *he replied, she stated,* and *I said* are clues that the sentence contains a direct quotation.
Rule:	Use a comma to separate a quotation from the rest of a sentence. Place a comma before the quote.
Example:	Ben Franklin said, "A penny saved is a penny earned."
Rule:	When the phrase that identifies the speaker interrupts the quotation, the first comma is placed inside the quotation marks. A comma also follows the interrupting phrase.
Example:	"A penny saved," said Ben Franklin, "is a penny earned."

Commas with Dates and Place Names

Dates and names of places may have several parts. Separate the parts of a date, or place name with commas.

Rule:	Use a comma to separate the name of a town from a country or state. *Washington* and *D.C.* are also separated by a comma.
Rule:	Use a comma to separate the day of the week from the name of the month in a date and to set off the year from the rest of the sentence.
Example:	The reunion will be Sunday, August 3, 1997, at Miller Park in Columbus, Ohio.

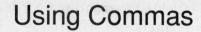 Using Commas

Items 1 to 5 refer to the following paragraph. Choose the best answer to each item.

(1) People are afraid, angry, and, confused over the news that radon gas may be in their homes. (2) Radon, a gas from uranium in the soil, can enter homes through cracks in basements, walls, and floors. (3) According to Floyd Whellan a government official, "There is a definite connection between breathing radon gas and dying from lung cancer." (4) Radon, a radioactive gas is invisible and has no color or odor. (5) We should do more research on the connection between radon gas and cancer.

1. Sentence 1: **People are afraid, angry, and, confused over the news that radon gas may be in their homes.**

   What correction should be made to this sentence?

   (1) insert a comma after people
   (2) remove the comma after afraid
   (3) remove the comma after and
   (4) insert a comma after be
   (5) no correction is necessary

2. Sentence 2: **Radon, a gas from uranium in the soil, can enter homes through cracks in basements, walls, and floors.**

   What correction should be made to this sentence?

   (1) remove the comma after Radon
   (2) remove the comma after soil
   (3) insert a comma after homes
   (4) remove the comma after basements
   (5) no correction is necessary

3. Sentence 3: **According to Floyd Whellan a government official, "There is a definite connection between breathing radon gas and dying from lung cancer."**

   What correction should be made to this sentence?

   (1) insert a comma after Whellan
   (2) remove the comma after official
   (3) insert a comma after connection
   (4) insert a comma after gas
   (5) no correction is necessary

4. Sentence 4: **Radon, a radioactive gas is invisible and has no color or odor.**

   What correction should be made to this sentence?

   (1) remove the comma after Radon
   (2) insert a comma after gas
   (3) insert a comma after color
   (4) insert a comma after or
   (5) no correction is necessary

5. Sentence 5: **We should do more research on the connection between radon gas and cancer.**

   What correction should be made to this sentence?

   (1) insert quotation marks before we and after cancer
   (2) insert commas after radon and gas
   (3) insert a comma after gas
   (4) change radon to Radon
   (5) no correction is necessary

Unit 1: Mechanics

Items 6 to 10 refer to the following paragraph.

(1) Yes there are more jobs available to people with a GED. (2) However, even with a GED, the interview process is important. (3) When Ellen applied for a job, the manager said "You should arrive a few minutes early." (4) Once Ellen arrived, she was greeted by the receptionist. (5) The receptionist said, "Ellen, please complete this application form and return it to me." (6) After Ellen completed the application, the receptionist asked her to return for an interview on Tuesday March 13. (7) Nervous about her chances of getting the job, Ellen was unable to sleep well Sunday, or Monday. (8) As a result of her interview, Ellen got the job.

6. Sentence 1: **Yes there are more jobs available to people with a GED.**

    What correction should be made to this sentence?

    (1) insert a comma after <u>Yes</u>
    (2) insert a comma after <u>available</u>
    (3) change <u>people</u> to <u>People</u>
    (4) insert a comma after <u>people</u>
    (5) no correction is necessary

7. Sentence 3: **When Ellen applied for a job, the manager said "You should arrive a few minutes early."**

    What correction should be made to this sentence?

    (1) insert a comma after <u>manager</u>
    (2) insert a comma after <u>said</u>
    (3) change <u>You</u> to <u>you</u>
    (4) insert a comma after <u>few</u>
    (5) no correction is necessary

8. Sentence 5: **The receptionist said, "Ellen, please complete this application form and return it to me."**

    What correction should be made to this sentence?

    (1) change <u>receptionist</u> to <u>Receptionist</u>
    (2) remove the comma after <u>said</u>
    (3) remove the comma after <u>Ellen</u>
    (4) change <u>Ellen</u> to <u>ellen</u>
    (5) no correction is necessary

9. Sentence 6: **After Ellen completed the application, the receptionist asked her to return for an interview on Tuesday March 13.**

    What correction should be made to this sentence?

    (1) insert a comma after <u>receptionist</u>
    (2) change the period to a question mark
    (3) insert a comma after <u>March</u>
    (4) insert a comma after <u>Tuesday</u>
    (5) no correction is necessary

10. Sentence 7: **Nervous about her chances of getting the job, Ellen was unable to sleep well Sunday, or Monday.**

    What correction should be made to this sentence?

    (1) remove the comma after <u>job</u>
    (2) insert a comma after <u>Ellen</u>
    (3) remove the comma after <u>Sunday</u>
    (4) change <u>Sunday, or Monday</u> to <u>sunday, or monday</u>
    (5) no correction is necessary

Answers are on page 259.

Commas in Complex Sentences

Many sentences express two ideas. If an idea is a complete thought, it is an independent clause. If the idea is an incomplete thought, it is a dependent clause. When a sentence has at least one dependent and one independent clause, it is a complex sentence.

A dependent clause has a subject and a verb but does not express a complete thought; therefore, it is a subordinate idea. A dependent clause cannot stand alone as a sentence. If not joined to an independent clause, it is a fragment and is incorrect.

Rule: Use a comma to separate a part of a sentence that cannot stand alone (a dependent clause) when it comes before the independent clause.

Example: If the back door had been unlocked, I would have left the package inside your house.

Note: A sentence that begins with *if, as,* or *when* probably has an introductory dependent clause.

Rule: If the dependent clause comes at the end of the sentence, a comma is usually not needed.

Example: I would have left the package inside your house if the back door had been unlocked.

Commas in Compound Sentences

When a sentence expresses two or more complete ideas that are related, it is called a compound sentence. Each complete thought is an independent clause that can stand alone as a complete sentence. In other words, an independent clause has a subject and a verb and expresses a complete thought.

Although two independent clauses can be written as two separate sentences, they can also be joined as a compound sentence.

Rule: Use a comma to join the two main parts of a compound sentence connected by a coordinating conjunction, such as *and, but, or, nor, so,* and *for.*

Example: Sam tries to budget his money, but he has never been successful.

Note: Joining two independent clauses with a coordinating conjunction but no comma creates a run-on sentence. Joining two independent clauses with a comma but no coordinating conjunction creates a comma splice.

Rule: If two extremely short sentences are joined by a conjunction, a comma is not needed.

Example: They fished and we swam.

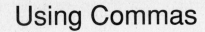

Items 1 to 5 refer to the following paragraph. Choose the best answer to each item.

(1) If our nation did away with television our young people would probably read more books. (2) Young people would, no doubt, read more, if their parents encouraged reading. (3) Reading a good book is a relaxing way to spend an evening but most people simply do not feel they have the time. (4) Because reading has so much more to offer people than watching sports, movies, or videos, it's unfortunate that our children won't read more. (5) Reading can help them learn about places they have never been. (6) Many of us, for example, first learned about our nation's capital, Washington D.C., by reading about it.

1. Sentence 1: **If our nation did away with television our young people would probably read more books.**

   What correction should be made to this sentence?

   (1) change nation to Nation
   (2) insert a comma after television
   (3) change television to Television
   (4) insert a comma after people
   (5) no correction is necessary

2. Sentence 2: **Young people would, no doubt, read more, if their parents encouraged reading.**

   What correction should be made to this sentence?

   (1) change Young to young
   (2) remove the comma after would
   (3) remove the comma after doubt
   (4) remove the comma after more
   (5) no correction is necessary

3. Sentence 3: **Reading a good book is a relaxing way to spend an evening but most people simply do not feel they have the time.**

   What correction should be made to this sentence?

   (1) insert a comma after book
   (2) insert a comma after evening
   (3) change evening to Evening
   (4) insert a comma after but
   (5) no correction is necessary

4. Sentence 4: **Because reading has so much more to offer people than watching sports, movies, or videos, it's unfortunate that our children won't read more.**

   What correction should be made to this sentence?

   (1) remove the comma after sports
   (2) remove the comma after movies
   (3) remove the comma after videos
   (4) change sports, movies, or videos to Sports, Movies, or Videos
   (5) no correction is necessary

5. Sentence 6: **Many of us, for example, first learned about our nation's capital, Washington D.C., by reading about it.**

   What correction should be made to this sentence?

   (1) remove the comma after us
   (2) remove the comma after example
   (3) insert a comma after Washington
   (4) remove the comma after D.C.
   (5) no correction is necessary

Items 6 to 10 refer to the following paragraphs.

(1) Are firefighters, ambulance drivers, and paramedics aware of the importance of good nutrition? (2) Do they realize that their eating habits can affect their reaction time, stamina, and overall, job performance? (3) Mrs. Ruth Lahiff, a county nutritionist decided to find out. (4) After gathering data from more than 500 county employees Lahiff concluded, "Most of them get enough protein. (5) But," she added "about one-third of them should cut down on fats and eat more fruits, vegetables, and fiber."

(6) The president of the local firefighter's union and the leader of the local paramedics agree. (7) "For most of us, it's a macho thing to live on burgers, fries, shakes, and coffee" the union leader chuckled.

(8) "We'd feel silly eating salads and juice in front of the rest of the guys," added one paramedic from station 74.

6. Sentence 2: **Do they realize that their eating habits can affect their reaction time, stamina, and overall, job performance?**

   What correction should be made to this sentence?

   (1) insert a comma after realize
   (2) insert a comma after habits
   (3) remove the comma after time
   (4) remove the comma after overall
   (5) no correction is necessary

7. Sentence 3: **Mrs. Ruth Lahiff, a county nutritionist decided to find out.**

   What correction should be made to this sentence?

   (1) remove the comma after Lahiff
   (2) insert a comma after nutritionist
   (3) insert a comma after decided
   (4) insert a comma after to
   (5) no correction is necessary

8. Sentence 4: **After gathering data from more than 500 county employees Lahiff concluded, "Most of them get enough protein."**

   What correction should be made to this sentence?

   (1) insert a comma after data
   (2) insert a comma after 500
   (3) insert a comma after employees
   (4) remove the comma after concluded
   (5) no correction is necessary

9. Sentence 5: **"But," she added "about one-third of them should cut down on fats and eat more fruits, vegetables, and fiber."**

   What correction should be made to this sentence?

   (1) remove the comma after But
   (2) insert a comma after added
   (3) remove the comma after fruits
   (4) remove the comma after vegetables
   (5) no correction is necessary

10. Sentence 7: **"For most of us, it's a macho thing to live on burgers, fries, shakes, and coffee" the union leader chuckled.**

    What correction should be made to this sentence?

    (1) remove the comma after us
    (2) insert a comma after thing
    (3) remove the comma after burgers
    (4) insert a comma after coffee
    (5) no correction is necessary

tip **Avoid excess commas in a series of items by counting the number of items. If there are only two items, do not use commas. For three or more items, subtract one from the number of items. That's the number of commas you need.**

Answers are on page 260.

Directions: Choose the best answer to each item.

Items 1 to 4 refer to the following paragraphs.

(1) Each state has a Department of Health, which deals with issues of public health and safety. (2) For example, the California Department of Health recently issued an informative up-to-date report on dangerous killer bees, which migrate there from Mexico. (3) State health departments often run free inoculation clinics where vaccines for measles, tetanus, diphtheria, and polio are given, (4) Even with these clinics, four women were hospitalized yesterday with typhoid fever, according to Dr. Susan Yim, a health department representative. (5) Because the symptoms of typhoid include rash, high fever, coughing, and internal bleeding it is easy to diagnose. (6) Dr. Henley, an expert on world health problems, told reporters, "There could be a serious outbreak of typhoid."

1. Sentence 1: **Each state has a Department of Health, which deals with issues of public health and safety.**

   What correction should be made to this sentence?

   (1) change state to State
   (2) insert a comma after state
   (3) change Department of Health to department of health
   (4) remove the comma after Department of Health
   (5) no correction is necessary

2. Sentence 2: **For example, the California Department of Health recently issued an informative up-to-date report on dangerous killer bees, which migrate there from Mexico.**

   What correction should be made to this sentence?

   (1) change Department of Health to department of health
   (2) insert a comma after informative
   (3) insert a comma after dangerous
   (4) remove the comma after bees
   (5) no correction is necessary

3. Sentence 3: **State health departments often run free inoculation clinics where vaccines for measles, tetanus, diphtheria, and polio are given,**

   What correction should be made to this sentence?

   (1) change health departments to Health Departments
   (2) insert a comma after departments
   (3) remove the comma after measles
   (4) change the comma after given to a period
   (5) no correction is necessary

4. Sentence 5: **Because the symptoms of typhoid include rash, high fever, coughing, and internal bleeding it is easy to diagnose.**

   What correction should be made to this sentence?

   (1) change typhoid to Typhoid
   (2) remove the comma after rash
   (3) remove the comma after fever
   (4) insert a comma after bleeding
   (5) no correction is necessary

Items 5 to 9 refer to the following paragraph.

(1) While most people would like to own their own homes many often disregard the advantages of renting. (2) A person who rents a house or an apartment has far fewer worries than a homeowner. (3) If you have a leak in the plumbing, for example in the house you own, you have to pay a plumber. (4) However if you live in an apartment, the landlord is responsible for all maintenance, repairs, and improvements. (5) A leaky faucet may be simple to fix, but do you know how much it costs to replace a boiler or a roof. (6) Property taxes and insurance payments are two other items prospective homeowners often fail to think about. (7) Although mortgage payments may be comparable to your present rent, the cost of your yearly, property tax could be as high as three hundred dollars a month. (8) I'd rather spend the money buying furniture for my apartment.

5. Sentence 1: **While most people would like to own their own homes many often disregard the advantages of renting.**

   What correction should be made to this sentence?

   (1) insert a comma after while
   (2) change the period to a question mark
   (3) insert a comma after homes
   (4) insert a comma after many
   (5) no correction is necessary

6. Sentence 3: **If you have a leak in the plumbing, for example in the house you own, you have to pay a plumber.**

   What correction should be made to this sentence?

   (1) remove the comma after plumbing
   (2) insert a comma after example
   (3) remove the comma after own
   (4) change plumber to Plumber
   (5) no correction is necessary

7. Sentence 4: **However if you live in an apartment, the landlord is responsible for all maintenance, repairs, and improvements.**

   What correction should be made to this sentence?

   (1) insert a comma after However
   (2) change landlord to Landlord
   (3) remove the comma after apartment
   (4) remove the comma after repairs
   (5) no correction is necessary

8. Sentence 5: **A leaky faucet may be simple to fix, but do you know how much it costs to replace a boiler or a roof.**

   What correction should be made to this sentence?

   (1) remove the comma after fix
   (2) insert a comma after but
   (3) replace the period with a question mark
   (4) insert a comma after boiler
   (5) no correction is necessary

9. Sentence 7: **Although mortgage payments may be comparable to your present rent, the cost of your yearly, property tax could be as high as three hundred dollars a month.**

   What correction should be made to this sentence?

   (1) insert a comma after Although
   (2) remove the comma after rent
   (3) remove the comma after yearly
   (4) insert a comma after dollars
   (5) no correction is necessary

Answers are on page 261.

Lesson 4

Avoiding Unnecessary Commas

Unnecessary commas can make writing unclear.

The following paragraph contains unnecessary commas. As you read, find the commas and consider whether they are necessary.

(1) My neighbor, lives in the house at the corner. (2) Every day he jogs swiftly, confidently, and effortlessly, around the neighborhood. (3) A person, who exercises so frequently, must be in good health. (4) Jill, and Lucy are the names of his dogs. (5) They like to jog with him.

Now look at the rules on avoiding unnecessary commas:

Rule: Do not use a comma to separate a subject and a verb.

Example: (Sentence 1) My <u>neighbor, lives</u> in the house at the corner.

Correct: My <u>neighbor lives</u> in the house at the corner.
<u>Neighbor</u> is the subject. <u>Lives</u> is the verb. There should be no comma between them.

Rule: Do not use a comma between the last item in a series and the next word.

Example: (Sentence 2) Every day he jogs swiftly, confidently, and <u>effortlessly, around</u> the neighborhood.

Correct: Every day he jogs swiftly, confidently, and <u>effortlessly around</u> the neighborhood.

Rule: Do not use commas to set off phrases that are essential to the meaning of a sentence.

Example: (Sentence 3) A person, <u>who exercises so frequently,</u> must be in good health.

Correct: A person <u>who exercises so frequently</u> must be in good health.

Rule: Do not use a comma to separate only two items in a series. Be especially careful with compound verbs and compound subjects.

Example: (Sentence 5) <u>Jill, and Lucy</u> are the names of his dogs.

Correct: <u>Jill and Lucy</u> are the names of his dogs.

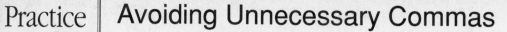

Items 1 to 4 refer to the following paragraph. Choose the best answer to each item.

(1) The recent rainfall, has increased debate about the dangers of building in Arbor Canyon. (2) For two weeks, thunderstorms battered the region. (3) Soil erosion, heavy rains, and strong winds, contributed to mud slides and flooding. (4) Those houses, which were built near the bottom of Arbor Canyon, suffered heavy damage. (5) Other dwellings became submerged in over five feet of water. (6) Residents say they will repair the damage, but some experts think that the area is just not suitable for habitation. (7) Certainly, the level of recent rainfall was unusual. (8) However, if it happened once, it can happen again in the future.

1. Sentence 1: **The recent rainfall, has increased debate about the dangers of building in Arbor Canyon.**

   What correction should be made to this sentence?

   (1) change the period to an exclamation mark
   (2) remove the comma after rainfall
   (3) insert a comma after recent
   (4) change Canyon to canyon
   (5) no correction is necessary

2. Sentence 3: **Soil erosion, heavy rains, and strong winds, contributed to mud slides and flooding.**

   What correction should be made to this sentence?

   (1) remove the comma after erosion
   (2) remove the comma after rains
   (3) remove the comma after winds
   (4) insert a comma after slides
   (5) no correction is necessary

3. Sentence 4: **Those houses, which were built near the bottom of Arbor Canyon, suffered heavy damage.**

   What correction should be made to this sentence?

   (1) remove the comma after houses
   (2) remove the comma after Canyon
   (3) remove the commas after houses and Canyon
   (4) change Arbor Canyon to arbor canyon
   (5) no correction is necessary

4. Sentence 6: **Residents say they will repair the damage, but some experts think that the area is just not suitable for habitation.**

   What correction should be made to this sentence?

   (1) remove the comma after damage
   (2) change experts to Experts
   (3) insert a comma after experts
   (4) change the period to a question mark
   (5) no correction is necessary

>**tip** **Saying a sentence to yourself can help you avoid using unnecessary commas to separate the subject and the verb. If you don't pause while speaking, don't use a comma.**

Items 5 to 9 refer to the following paragraph.

(1) The new bus service has been a real boon to the community. (2) Before the extension of the Hudson avenue line, it was difficult for my neighbors and me to get around. (3) Nurses, doctors, and technicians, who worked at Canetti Hospital used to have an hour-and-a-half commute. (4) Now, they no longer have to transfer between buses three times just to get to work. (5) The Hudson Avenue extension, has also eased congestion on the side streets, boulevards, and public parking areas. (6) When the new service started many people began taking the bus instead of driving. (7) Although the new service is great, there is still room for improvement. (8) Commuters would like to see, for example, trip frequency increased to two, or three times an hour. (9) However, the new service has made a major difference in the lives of area residents.

5. Sentence 2: **Before the extension of the Hudson avenue line, it was difficult for my neighbors and me to get around.**

   What correction should be made to this sentence?

   (1) change avenue to Avenue
   (2) remove the comma after line
   (3) insert a comma after neighbors
   (4) insert a comma after me
   (5) no correction is necessary

6. Sentence 3: **Nurses, doctors, and technicians, who worked at Canetti Hospital used to have an hour-and-a-half commute.**

   What correction should be made to this sentence?

   (1) remove the commas after doctors and technicians
   (2) remove the comma after doctors
   (3) remove the comma after technicians
   (4) insert a comma after Hospital
   (5) no correction is necessary

7. Sentence 5: **The Hudson Avenue extension, has also eased congestion on the side streets, boulevards, and public parking areas.**

   What correction should be made to this sentence?

   (1) remove the comma after extension
   (2) remove the comma after streets
   (3) remove the comma after boulevards
   (4) change public parking to Public Parking
   (5) no correction is necessary

8. Sentence 6: **When the new service started many people began taking the bus instead of driving.**

   What correction should be made to this sentence?

   (1) insert a comma after started
   (2) insert a comma after people
   (3) insert commas after started and people
   (4) change the period to an exclamation mark
   (5) no correction is necessary

9. Sentence 8: **Commuters would like to see, for example, trip frequency increased to two, or three times an hour.**

   What correction should be made to this sentence?

   (1) remove the comma after see
   (2) remove the commas after see and example
   (3) remove the comma after two
   (4) insert a comma after three
   (5) no correction is necessary

Answers are on page 262.

Directions: Choose the best answer to each item.

Items 1 to 4 refer to the following paragraph.

(1) For many people, going to work doesn't mean driving to an office or a factory. (2) Changing technology has made it increasingly easy for people to work in their own homes. (3) For example, writers, editors and graphic artists can work in their home offices and send their completed work to their employers. (4) With the help of a computer or fax machine people who work at home don't even have to travel to the post office. (5) Delivering work to its destination can be as easy as pushing one or two buttons on a computer, a common feature in many home offices. (6) Working at home has advantages and disadvantages. (7) On the one hand, parents who work at home, don't have to worry about finding reliable, affordable day care. (8) They also have more flexibility than those who work from nine to five. (9) On the other hand, many who work in a home office miss the human interaction of working with other people.

1. Sentence 1: **For many people, going to work doesn't mean driving to an office or a factory.**

   What correction should be made to this sentence?

   (1) change people to People
   (2) remove the comma after people
   (3) insert a comma after work
   (4) insert a comma after office
   (5) no correction is necessary

2. Sentence 3: **For example, writers, editors and graphic artists can work in their home offices and send their completed work to their employers.**

   What correction should be made to this sentence?

   (1) remove the comma after example
   (2) remove the comma after writers
   (3) insert a comma after editors
   (4) insert a comma after artists
   (5) no correction is necessary

3. Sentence 4: **With the help of a computer or fax machine people who work at home don't even have to travel to the post office.**

   What correction should be made to this sentence?

   (1) insert a comma after computer
   (2) insert a comma after machine
   (3) insert commas after computer and machine
   (4) change the period to a question mark
   (5) no correction is necessary

4. Sentence 7: **On the one hand, parents who work at home, don't have to worry about finding reliable, affordable day care.**

   What correction should be made to this sentence?

   (1) remove the comma after hand
   (2) insert a comma after parents
   (3) remove the comma after home
   (4) remove the comma after reliable
   (5) no correction is necessary

Unit 1: Mechanics

Items 5 to 9 refer to the following paragraph.

(1) I like to listen to most music, especially jazz, at a reasonably loud volume. (2) Saxophones, drums, guitars, and other instruments, just seem to sound better at a higher volume. (3) My mother, however, refuses to let me play the stereo, without using headphones. (4) She makes me use headphones because loud music disturbs her peace, and quiet. (5) I mind only when I am cleaning the apartment. (6) I find that cleaning is less boring with music playing but it's hard to mop or vacuum with headphones on. (7) Trying to manipulate vacuum attachments and other equipment is impossible while connected to the amplifier by a cord. (8) When my mother is not at home, of course, I can listen to jazz as loud as I like.

5. Sentence 1: **I like to listen to most music, especially jazz, at a reasonably loud volume.**

   What correction should be made to this sentence?

   (1) remove the comma after music
   (2) remove the comma after jazz
   (3) remove the commas after music and jazz
   (4) insert a comma after reasonably
   (5) no correction is necessary

6. Sentence 2: **Saxophones, drums, guitars, and other instruments, just seem to sound better at a higher volume.**

   What correction should be made to this sentence?

   (1) remove the comma after Saxophones
   (2) remove the comma after guitars
   (3) remove the comma after instruments
   (4) insert a comma after better
   (5) no correction is necessary

7. Sentence 3: **My mother, however, refuses to let me play the stereo, without using headphones.**

   What correction should be made to this sentence?

   (1) change mother to Mother
   (2) remove the comma after mother
   (3) remove the comma after however
   (4) remove the comma after stereo
   (5) no correction is necessary

8. Sentence 4: **She makes me use headphones because loud music disturbs her peace, and quiet.**

   What correction should be made to this sentence?

   (1) insert a comma after She
   (2) insert a comma after headphones
   (3) insert a comma after music
   (4) remove the comma after peace
   (5) no correction is necessary

9. Sentence 6: **I find that cleaning is less boring with music playing but it's difficult to mop or vacuum with headphones on.**

   What correction should be made to this sentence?

   (1) insert a comma after boring and playing
   (2) insert a comma after playing
   (3) insert a comma after mop
   (4) insert a comma after vacuum
   (5) no correction is necessary

Answers are on page 263.

Lesson 5

Using Semicolons

Use semicolons in compound sentences to separate independent clauses. To decide if the clauses are independent, ask yourself whether each clause can stand alone as a separate sentence.

Read the paragraph. Note the semicolons and commas.

(1) Nuclear weapons are a serious issue; failure to solve this problem could have very serious consequences. (2) People are interested in avoiding nuclear war; however, they do not always agree on the best way to do so. (3) Is the answer to build up a supply of arms and prevent war through strength, or is the answer to work for disarmament? (4) World leaders, thinkers, and ordinary people have thought, of course, about these questions; but none has solved this crisis.

In the paragraph, all of the sentences contain at least two ideas and use commas and/or semicolons. Look at the following rules to see when semicolons should be used.

Rule:	Use a semicolon to join clauses that can stand alone (independent clauses) and that are not joined by a connecting word.
Example:	(Sentence 1) Nuclear weapons are a serious issue; failure to solve this problem could have very serious consequences.
Note:	In joining these two clauses, you have the option of using the semicolon or of eliminating the semicolon and using a conjunction and a comma. Either is correct.
Rule:	Use a semicolon to join two clauses that could stand alone but are joined by such linking words as *however* or *therefore*. Always use a comma following the linking word.
Example:	(Sentence 2) People are interested in avoiding nuclear war; however, they do not always agree on the best way to do so.
Rule:	Sometimes it is necessary to use a semicolon instead of a comma to connect two independent clauses joined with a conjunction. When there are other commas in the independent clauses that may cause the reader confusion, use a semicolon.
Example:	(Sentence 4) World leaders, thinkers, and ordinary people have thought, of course, about these questions; but none has solved this crisis.
Note:	Since there are several other commas in the first clause, a semicolon is used instead of a comma to separate the clauses.

ged Practice | Using Semicolons

Items 1 to 5 refer to the following paragraph. Choose the best answer to each item.

(1) Newborn babies are tiny and helpless they need very special care. (2) Family members and friends usually want to hold your baby, however, your baby should have some quiet time. (3) You will need to take time to consider the benefits of nursing your baby, and you will need a large supply of diapers. (4) It is the hope, dream, and wish of every parent, of course, to have a healthy baby; and it is the goal of every parent to provide the best possible life for the child. (5) First-time parents are often nervous about how to care for their newborn; therefore they often ask friends, relatives, and doctors for advice.

1. Sentence 1: **Newborn babies are tiny and helpless they need very special care.**

   Which of the following is the best way to write the underlined portion of this sentence? If you think the original is the best way, choose option (1).

   (1) and helpless they
   (2) and helpless, they
   (3) and helpless; they
   (4) and helpless; and they
   (5) and helpless, however, they

2. Sentence 2: **Family members and friends usually want to hold your baby, however, your baby should have some quiet time.**

   Which of the following is the best way to write the underlined portion of this sentence? If you think the original is the best way, choose option (1).

   (1) baby, however, your
   (2) baby however, your
   (3) baby, however; your
   (4) baby, however your
   (5) baby; however, your

3. Sentence 3: **You will need to take time to consider the benefits of nursing your baby, and you will need a large supply of diapers.**

   Which of the following is the best way to write the underlined portion of this sentence? If you think the original is the best way, choose option (1).

   (1) baby, and you
   (2) baby and you
   (3) baby; and, you
   (4) baby; and you
   (5) baby and, you

4. Sentence 4: **It is the hope, dream, and wish of every parent, of course, to have a healthy baby; and it is the goal of every parent to provide the best possible life for the child.**

   Which of the following is the best way to write the underlined portion of this sentence? If you think the original is the best way, choose option (1).

   (1) baby; and it
   (2) baby and it
   (3) baby; and, it
   (4) baby, and, it
   (5) baby, and; it

5. Sentence 5: **First-time parents are often nervous about how to care for their newborn; therefore they often ask friends, relatives, and doctors for advice.**

   What correction should be made to this sentence?

   (1) change the semicolon to a comma
   (2) insert a comma after therefore
   (3) remove the comma after relatives
   (4) insert a comma after doctors
   (5) no correction is necessary

Items 6 to 15 refer to the following paragraph.

(1) You say you are bored at your job but it may be your own fault. (2) You, your coworkers, and your boss may have given up and all of you may have stopped trying to make your jobs interesting. (3) Job burnout happens when a person works too hard under stressful conditions; job boredom is a far more common problem. (4) A person who finds work boring is likely to take that same problem on to the next job, therefore, changing jobs is not usually the answer. (5) Most people who enjoy their jobs do their jobs well perhaps pride in their work is the solution to job boredom. (6) Many who have tried enriching their jobs and raising their performance standards have found that their job boredom has decreased. (7) What can you do to increase your job satisfaction, raise your performance standard, and decrease your boredom. (8) There are many possible solutions. (9) First, concentrate on the problem, decide which areas of your daily work induce boredom. (10) By figuring out ways to improve your performance in those areas; you may find that your boredom will decrease. (11) Although employees may be eager for new challenges, some bosses are hesitant to overload their employees. (12) Don't be afraid to ask for increased responsibilities, indeed, a new challenge may be just what you need.

6. Sentence 1: **You say you are bored at your job but it may be your own fault.**

   What correction should be made to this sentence?

   (1) insert commas after bored and job
   (2) insert a comma after job
   (3) insert a comma after say and a semicolon after job
   (4) insert a comma after job and a semicolon after but
   (5) no correction is necessary

7. Sentence 2: **You, your coworkers, and your boss may have given up and all of you may have stopped trying to make your jobs interesting.**

   What correction should be made to this sentence?

   (1) remove the comma after You
   (2) insert a comma after boss
   (3) insert a semicolon after up
   (4) insert a semicolon after trying
   (5) no correction is necessary

8. Sentence 3: **Job burnout happens when a person works too hard under stressful conditions; job boredom is a far more common problem.**

   What correction should be made to this sentence?

   (1) insert a comma after happens
   (2) insert commas after burnout and happens
   (3) change the semicolon after conditions to a comma
   (4) remove the semicolon after conditions
   (5) no correction is necessary

9. Sentence 4: **A person who finds work boring is likely to take that same problem on to the next job, therefore, changing jobs is not usually the answer.**

   What correction should be made to this sentence?

   (1) insert commas after person and boring
   (2) change the comma after job to a semicolon
   (3) change both commas in the sentence to semicolons
   (4) insert a comma after jobs
   (5) no correction is necessary

10. Sentence 5: **Most people who enjoy their jobs do their jobs well perhaps pride in their work is the solution to job boredom.**

What correction should be made to this sentence?

(1) insert commas after people and jobs
(2) insert commas after people, jobs, and well
(3) insert a comma after well
(4) insert a semicolon after well
(5) no correction is necessary

11. Sentence 6: **Many who have tried enriching their jobs and raising their performance standards have found that their job boredom has decreased.**

What correction should be made to this sentence?

(1) insert commas after Many and jobs
(2) insert a semicolon after jobs
(3) insert commas after jobs and standards
(4) insert a comma after standards
(5) no correction is necessary

12. Sentence 7: **What can you do to increase your job satisfaction, raise your performance standard, and decrease your boredom.**

What correction should be made to this sentence?

(1) remove the comma after satisfaction
(2) change the comma after satisfaction to a semicolon
(3) change the comma after standard to a semicolon
(4) change the period to a question mark
(5) no correction is necessary

13. Sentence 9: **First, concentrate on the problem, decide which areas of your daily work induce boredom.**

What correction should be made to this sentence?

(1) remove the comma after First
(2) remove the comma after problem
(3) change the comma after problem to a semicolon
(4) change both commas in the sentence to semicolons
(5) no correction is necessary

14. Sentence 10: **By figuring out ways to improve your performance in those areas; you may find that your boredom will decrease.**

Which of the following is the best way to rewrite the underlined portion of this sentence? If you think the original is the best way, choose option (1).

(1) areas; you
(2) areas; and you
(3) areas, you
(4) areas; you,
(5) areas you

15. Sentence 12: **Don't be afraid to ask for increased responsibilities, indeed, a new challenge may be just what you need.**

Which of the following is the best way to rewrite the underlined portion of this sentence? If you think the original is the best way, choose option (1).

(1) responsibilities, indeed, a new
(2) responsibilities, indeed; a new
(3) responsibilities; indeed, a new
(4) responsibilities; indeed a new
(5) responsibilities indeed a new

Answers are on page 264.

Directions: Choose the best answer to each item.

Items 1 to 5 refer to the following paragraph.

(1) Deer hunting is considered a sport, but, if it is done out of season, or if the hunter uses illegal methods, deer hunting is a crime. (2) Max McGarrity found that out when he was caught and arrested Thursday at 2:00 A.M.; he was gutting a 200-pound buck at the time. (3) McGarrity's arrest was, the result of complaints from residents near the woods where he often hunted during early morning hours. (4) According to Game Commissioner Dave Peebles, McGarrity is charged with "jacklighting," the illegal practice of shining a light in a deer's eyes. (5) Max plans to go hunting again next year and he promises to follow the rules.

1. Sentence 1: **Deer hunting is considered a sport, but, if it is done out of season, or if the hunter uses illegal methods, deer hunting is a crime.**

   Which of the following is the best way to write the underlined portion of this sentence? If you think the original is the best way, choose option (1).

   (1) considered a sport, but,
   (2) considered. a sport, but
   (3) considered a sport; but
   (4) considered a sport. but
   (5) considered a sport, but.

2. Sentence 2: **Max McGarrity found that out when he was caught and arrested Thursday at 2:00 A.M.; he was gutting a 200-pound buck at the time.**

   Which of the following is the best way to write the underlined portion of this sentence? If you think the original is the best way, choose option (1).

   (1) at 2:00 A.M.; he was
   (2) at, 2:00 A.M.; he was
   (3) at 2:00, A.M.; he was
   (4) at 2:00 A.M., he was
   (5) at 2:00 A.M. he was

3. Sentence 3: **McGarrity's arrest was, the result of complaints from residents near the woods where he often hunted during early morning hours.**

   Which of the following is the best way to write the underlined portion of this sentence? If you think the original is the best way, choose option (1).

   (1) McGarrity's arrest was,
   (2) McGarrity's arrest; was
   (3) McGarrity's arrest. was
   (4) McGarrity's arrest, was
   (5) McGarrity's arrest was

4. Sentence 4: **According to Game Commissioner Dave Peebles, McGarrity is charged with "jacklighting," the illegal practice of shining a light in a deer's eyes.**

   What correction should be made to this sentence?

   (1) change Game Commissioner to game commissioner
   (2) remove the comma after Peebles
   (3) insert a comma after light
   (4) change the period to a question mark
   (5) no correction is necessary

5. Sentence 5: **Max plans to go hunting again next year and he promises to follow the rules.**

   What correction should be made to this sentence?

   (1) insert commas after again and year
   (2) insert a comma after year
   (3) insert a semicolon after year
   (4) insert a period after year
   (5) no correction is necessary

Items 6 to 10 refer to the following paragraph.

(1) Most people who quit school regret it later, that has been my observation. (2) One reason is that our high schools, are geared too much to the college bound; other students are being ignored. (3) Formal education does not always adequately prepare a person to find a job; some people attend special training programs for that. (4) As a matter of fact, every Fall our local community college has a program on how to write résumés and go through interviews. (5) Academic knowledge is important, however, people need more training in real-life skills.

6. Sentence 1: **Most people who quit school regret it later, that has been my observation.**

   What correction should be made to this sentence?

   (1) insert commas after people and school
   (2) remove the comma after later
   (3) replace the comma after later with a semicolon
   (4) insert a comma after that
   (5) no correction is necessary

7. Sentence 2: **One reason is that our high schools, are geared too much to the college bound; other students are being ignored.**

   What correction should be made to this sentence?

   (1) remove the comma after schools
   (2) insert a comma after much
   (3) change the semicolon after bound to a comma
   (4) remove the semicolon after bound
   (5) no correction is necessary

8. Sentence 3: **Formal education does not always adequately prepare a person to find a job; some people attend special training programs for that.**

   What correction should be made to this sentence?

   (1) change education to Education
   (2) insert a comma after person
   (3) change the semicolon after job to a comma
   (4) insert a comma after people
   (5) no correction is necessary

9. Sentence 4: **As a matter of fact, every Fall our local community college has a program on how to write résumés and go through interviews.**

   What correction should be made to this sentence?

   (1) change Fall to fall
   (2) change community college to Community College
   (3) insert a comma after program
   (4) insert a comma after résumés
   (5) no correction is necessary

10. Sentence 5: **Academic knowledge is important, however, people need more training in real-life skills.**

    Which of the following is the best way to rewrite the underlined portion of this sentence? If you think the original is the best way, choose option (1).

    (1) important, however, people need
    (2) important; however, people need
    (3) important; however people need
    (4) important; however, people, need
    (5) important, however, people, need

Answers are on page 266.

Using Apostrophes and Quotation Marks

Read the paragraph. Pay attention to how apostrophes are used.

(1) My sister's idea of the ideal job is one with good wages, insurance, and an opportunity for promotion. (2) You can find many jobs with these benefits by contacting several employment agencies. (3) The agencies' fees can be quite expensive, so be careful what you sign. (4) The Success Agency takes care of its clients. (5) I'd like a better job because my current job doesn't pay enough money. (6) I'd like a job with a children's day-care program.

In the paragraph above, the apostrophes are correctly used to form contractions and possessives. You can learn how to use apostrophes correctly by observing a few simple rules.

Rule: A contraction combines two words, one of which is usually a verb. The apostrophe takes the place of any missing letters.

Example: (Sentence 5) I'd like a better job because my current job doesn't pay enough money. (I'd = I would; doesn't = does not)

Rule: An apostrophe shows that an object or a characteristic belongs to a particular person or thing. The possessive of most singular nouns is formed by adding an apostrophe and s ('s).

Example: (Sentence 1) My sister's idea of the ideal job is one with good wages, insurance, and an opportunity for promotion.

Note: If a singular noun ends in -s, form the possessive by adding 's (witness's, boss's).

Rule: The possessive of most plural nouns that end in -s is formed by adding an apostrophe (').

Example: (Sentence 3) The agencies' fees can be quite expensive, so be careful what you sign.

Rule: The possessive of plural nouns that do not end in -s is formed by adding an apostrophe and s ('s).

Example: (Sentence 6) I'd like a job with a children's day-care program.

 Use apostrophes to show possession and to replace missing letters in contractions.

Items 1 to 7 refer to the following paragraph. Choose the best answer to each item.

(1) I'd like to have a pet because I dont want to be alone. (2) Helen's favorite animals are cats. (3) The womens group is helping the animal shelter find homes for its cats and dogs. (4) Last month, the boys' club was successful in its program to help lost animals find their owner's. (5) The shelter takes good care of it's animals. (6) I'd say its about time for our club to do something. (7) Meanwhile, maybe Ill adopt a puppy!

1. Sentence 1: **I'd like to have a pet because I dont want to be alone.**

   What correction should be made to this sentence?

   (1) change I'd to Id
   (2) replace dont with don't
   (3) change dont to do'nt
   (4) replace dont with donot
   (5) no correction is necessary

2. Sentence 2: **Helen's favorite animals are cats.**

   What correction should be made to this sentence?

   (1) change Helen's to Helens'
   (2) change Helen's to Helens
   (3) change animals to animal's
   (4) change cats to cat's
   (5) no correction is necessary

3. Sentence 3: **The womens group is helping the animal shelter find homes for its cats and dogs.**

   What correction should be made to this sentence?

   (1) change womens to womens'
   (2) change womens to women's
   (3) replace homes with homes'
   (4) replace cats and dogs with cat's and dog's
   (5) no correction is necessary

4. Sentence 4: **Last month, the boys' club was successful in its program to help lost animals find their owner's.**

   What correction should be made to this sentence?

   (1) replace boys' with boys
   (2) replace boys' with boy's
   (3) change animals to animals'
   (4) change owner's to owners
   (5) no correction is necessary

5. Sentence 5: **The shelter takes good care of it's animals.**

   What correction should be made to this sentence?

   (1) replace takes with take's
   (2) change it's to its'
   (3) change it's to its
   (4) replace animals with animals'
   (5) no correction is necessary

6. Sentence 6: **I'd say its about time for our club to do something.**

   What correction should be made to this sentence?

   (1) change I'd to I had
   (2) change its to its'
   (3) replace its with it's
   (4) replace our with our'
   (5) no correction is necessary

7. Sentence 7: **Meanwhile, maybe Ill adopt a puppy!**

   What correction should be made to this sentence?

   (1) remove the comma after Meanwhile
   (2) change Ill to I'll
   (3) change Ill to Il'l
   (4) change the exclamation mark to a question mark
   (5) no correction is necessary

Answers are on page 267.

Use quotation marks to set off a person's exact words or a special term.

Read the passage and note how quotation marks are used.

(1) Mark said, "What kind of job are you looking for?"
(2) Mary replied, "I want a sales job in a retail store."
(3) "Are you willing to work on weekends?" asked Mark.
(4) Mary answered, "No, I'm not. I want a supervisory position."
(5) "Oh," Mark said, "you want to get into management." (6) Mark explained that one of management's biggest headaches is dealing with "lazy employees." (7) He also explained in detail to Mary that most management positions require more education as well as experience.

Here are some rules to help you use quotation marks correctly.

Rule:	Use quotation marks to set off someone's exact words. Notice that quotation marks are always used in pairs.
Examples:	(Sentence 2) Mary replied, "I want a sales job in a retail store." (Sentence 5) "Oh," Mark said, "you want to get into management."
Rule:	A punctuation mark—such as a period, comma, exclamation point, or question mark—that is part of the quote is always placed before, or inside, the second quotation mark.
Example:	(Sentence 3) "Are you willing to work on weekends?" asked Mark.
Rule:	Quotation marks should not be used unless someone's exact words are given. An indirect quotation is not set off by quotation marks.
Example:	(Sentence 7) He also explained in detail to Mary that most management positions require more education as well as experience.
Rule:	Use quotation marks to set off an unusual term or an exact phrase used by a specific person.
Example:	(Sentence 6) Mark explained that one of management's biggest headaches is dealing with "lazy employees."

Items 1 to 5 refer to the following paragraph. Choose the best answer to each item.

(1) The restaurant employees were discussing the importance of serving food while it's "hot." (2) "It's always better to have hot food," said Tim. (3) "I'm in agreement with that statement, said Bill. (4) Tim indicated that "his feelings are shared by the manager, the head cook, the head server, and the cashier." (5) The head cook said, "Kitchen workers should try to notify servers promptly when the food is hot." (6) "Why don't we give each waiter a beeper"? asked a kitchen worker. (7) The "beeper system" will alert each server promptly when a food order is ready.

1. Sentence 1: **The restaurant employees were discussing the importance of serving food while it's "hot."**

   What correction should be made to this sentence?

   (1) change employees to employee's
   (2) change it's to its'
   (3) change it's to its
   (4) remove both quotation marks
   (5) no correction is necessary

2. Sentence 3: **"I'm in agreement with that statement, said Bill.**

   What correction should be made to this sentence?

   (1) remove the quotation mark before I'm
   (2) remove the apostrophe from I'm
   (3) remove the comma after statement
   (4) insert a quotation mark after statement,
   (5) no correction is necessary

3. Sentence 4: **Tim indicated that "his feelings are shared by the manager, the head cook, the head server, and the cashier."**

   What correction should be made to this sentence?

   (1) remove the quotation mark before his
   (2) change that "his to "that his
   (3) remove the quotation mark after cashier.
   (4) remove both quotation marks
   (5) no correction is necessary

4. Sentence 6: **"Why don't we give each waiter a beeper"? asked a kitchen worker.**

   What correction should be made to this sentence?

   (1) remove the quotation mark before Why
   (2) change don't to dont
   (3) replace beeper"? with beeper?"
   (4) remove both quotation marks
   (5) no correction is necessary

5. Sentence 7: **The "beeper system" will alert each server promptly when a food order is ready.**

   What correction should be made to this sentence?

   (1) remove the quotation mark before beeper
   (2) remove the quotation mark after system
   (3) remove both quotation marks
   (4) change server to server's
   (5) no correction is necessary

Items 6 to 16 refer to the following paragraphs.

(1) A local group of veterinarians recently commissioned a study to find out if dogs are still man's best friend." (2) Dick Grover, group spokesman, said "One surprise in the study is that cats are becoming more popular, while dogs' popularity is declining." (3) "Dogs will never lose their popularity as pets, especially as children's companions, predicted Grover. (4) When a dog dies, it's like a member of the family has passed away," added Grover's sister.
(5) Some people have requested a cemetery in which they can be buried alongside their pets, and Brookville's cemetery, because of its vast unused space, could someday offer that option. (6) For the past 25 years, the cemetery's grounds have been available only for human burials; last month, however, its southeastern corner became a graveyard for cats' and dogs. (7) Cat owners are not hesitant to explain "why they like their favorite pets." (8) "Cats have fewer needs than dogs," said Helen Marcus pet owner. (9) "Dog's need to be exercised, bathed, and house trained." (10) Jeanine, Helen's roommate, agreed, Even if you are away from home all day, taking care of a cat is easy." (11) Cat care may be easy, but a cat owners expenses may be as high as hundreds of dollars a year.

6. Sentence 1: **A local group of veterinarians recently commissioned a study to find out if dogs are still man's best friend."**

   What correction should be made to this sentence?

   (1) change veterinarians to veterinarians'
   (2) insert a quotation mark before man's
   (3) change man's to mans'
   (4) insert a period after out
   (5) no correction is necessary

7. Sentence 2: **Dick Grover, group spokesman, said "One surprise in the study is that cats are becoming more popular, while dogs' popularity is declining."**

   What correction should be made to this sentence?

   (1) remove the comma after Grover
   (2) insert a comma after said
   (3) insert a comma after is
   (4) change cats to cats'
   (5) no correction is necessary

8. Sentence 3: **"Dogs will never lose their popularity as pets, especially as children's companions, predicted Grover.**

   What correction should be made to this sentence?

   (1) remove the quotation mark before Dogs
   (2) change Dogs to Dogs'
   (3) change children's to childrens'
   (4) insert a quotation mark after companions,
   (5) no correction is necessary

9. Sentence 4: **When a dog dies, it's like a member of the family has passed away," added Grover's sister.**

   What correction should be made to this sentence?

   (1) insert a quotation mark before When
   (2) change it's to its
   (3) remove the comma after away
   (4) change Grover's to Grovers
   (5) no correction is necessary

10. Sentence 5: **Some people have requested a cemetery in which they can be buried alongside their pets, and Brookville's cemetery, because of its vast unused space, could someday offer that option.**

    What correction should be made to this sentence?

    (1) insert a comma after <u>which</u>
    (2) change <u>pets</u> to <u>pets'</u>
    (3) change the comma after <u>pets</u> to a semicolon
    (4) remove the apostrophe in <u>Brookville's</u>
    (5) no correction is necessary

11. Sentence 6: **For the past 25 years, the cemetery's grounds have been available only for human burials; last month, however, its southeastern corner became a graveyard for cats' and dogs.**

    What correction should be made to this sentence?

    (1) change <u>cemetery's</u> to <u>cemeterys'</u>
    (2) change <u>grounds</u> to <u>grounds'</u>
    (3) change the semicolon after <u>burials</u> to a comma
    (4) change <u>cats'</u> to <u>cats</u>
    (5) no correction is necessary

12. Sentence 7: **Cat owners are not hesitant to explain "why they like their favorite pets."**

    What correction should be made to this sentence?

    (1) change <u>owners</u> to <u>owners'</u>
    (2) change <u>explain</u> to <u>explains</u>
    (3) remove both quotation marks
    (4) change <u>pets</u> to <u>pet's</u>
    (5) no correction is necessary

13. Sentence 8: **"Cats have fewer needs than dogs," said Helen Marcus pet owner.**

    What correction should be made to this sentence?

    (1) change <u>Cats</u> to <u>Cat's</u>
    (2) remove the quotation mark after <u>dogs,</u>
    (3) insert a semicolon after <u>Marcus</u>
    (4) insert a comma after <u>Marcus</u>
    (5) no correction is necessary

14. Sentence 9: **"Dog's need to be exercised, bathed, and house trained."**

    What correction should be made to this sentence?

    (1) change <u>Dog's</u> to <u>Dogs'</u>
    (2) change <u>Dog's</u> to <u>Dogs</u>
    (3) insert a comma after <u>Dog's</u>
    (4) remove the comma after <u>bathed</u>
    (5) no correction is necessary

15. Sentence 10: **Jeanine, Helen's roommate, agreed, Even if you are away from home all day, taking care of a cat is easy."**

    What correction should be made to this sentence?

    (1) change <u>Helen's</u> to <u>Helens'</u>
    (2) remove the commas after <u>Jeanine</u> and <u>roommate</u>
    (3) insert a quotation mark before <u>Even</u>
    (4) change the comma after <u>day</u> to a semicolon
    (5) no correction is necessary

16. Sentence 11: **Cat care may be easy, but a cat owners expenses may be as high as hundreds of dollars a year.**

    What correction should be made to this sentence?

    (1) change the comma after <u>easy</u> to a semicolon
    (2) change <u>owners</u> to <u>owners'</u>
    (3) change <u>owners</u> to <u>owner's</u>
    (4) change <u>expenses</u> to <u>expenses'</u>
    (5) no correction is necessary

Answers are on page 267.

Directions: Choose the best answer to each item.

Items 1 to 11 refer to the following paragraph.

(1) If being a game-show contestant is a secret dream of your's, you might be interested in Bob's recent experience. (2) "I've tried out before," says Bob, and I don't know why I didn't give up hope." (3) These three things helped him: his intelligence, his enthusiasm and his experience. (4) The tryouts aren't easy," according to the lucky ones who've been there. (5) Would-be contestants sometimes have to take a written test; only a few get to audition with these shows producers. (6) Competition may be steep during these auditions. (7) Game-show producers rate contestants on their knowledge and on-air poise. (8) "Everyone's nerves' were on edge," said Bob, "during those auditions." (9) However, the results can be worth the efforts; Bob won $9,000 in one appearance on a show he'd never even watched. (10) "So, in addition," says Bob, it helps to be lucky." (11) Bob is already planning his next game-show appearance. (12) "Even if he doesn't win," Bob says that it is still fun.

1. Sentence 1: **If being a game-show contestant is a secret dream of your's, you might be interested in Bob's recent experience.**

   What correction should be made to this sentence?

   (1) change your's to yours
   (2) change the comma after your's to a semicolon
   (3) remove the comma after your's
   (4) change Bob's to Bobs
   (5) no correction is necessary

2. Sentence 2: **"I've tried out before," says Bob, and I don't know why I didn't give up hope."**

   What correction should be made to this sentence?

   (1) change I've to Iv'e
   (2) remove the quotation mark after before
   (3) insert a quotation mark before and
   (4) change don't to do'nt
   (5) no correction is necessary

3. Sentence 3: **These three things helped him: his intelligence, his enthusiasm and his experience.**

   What correction should be made to this sentence?

   (1) change things to thing's
   (2) change things to things'
   (3) remove the comma after intelligence
   (4) insert a comma after enthusiasm
   (5) no correction is necessary

4. Sentence 4: **The tryouts aren't easy," according to the lucky ones who've been there.**

   What correction should be made to this sentence?

   (1) insert a quotation mark before The
   (2) change aren't to are'nt
   (3) remove the quotation mark after easy
   (4) change ones to one's
   (5) no correction is necessary

5. Sentence 5: **Would-be contestants sometimes have to take a written test; only a few get to audition with these shows producers.**

   What correction should be made to this sentence?

   (1) change contestants to contestant's
   (2) change contestants to contestants'
   (3) change the semicolon after test to a comma
   (4) change shows to shows'
   (5) no correction is necessary

6. Sentence 7: **Game-show producers rate contestants on their knowledge and on-air poise.**

   What correction should be made to this sentence?

   (1) change producers to producers'
   (2) change producers to producer's
   (3) change their to their'
   (4) insert a comma after knowledge
   (5) no correction is necessary

7. Sentence 8: **"Everyone's nerves' were on edge," said Bob, "during those auditions."**

   What correction should be made to this sentence?

   (1) change Everyone's to Everyones
   (2) change nerves' to nerves
   (3) remove the quotation marks before Everyone's and after edge,
   (4) change auditions to auditions'
   (5) no correction is necessary

tip Quotation marks come in pairs. If you find only one set of quotation marks in a test item, it's probably an error. Remove the set if there is no direct quotation in the sentence; add another set if there is a direct quotation.

8. Sentence 9: **However, the results can be worth the efforts; Bob won $9,000 in one appearance on a show he'd never even watched.**

   What correction should be made to this sentence?

   (1) remove the comma after However
   (2) change results to results'
   (3) change efforts to effort's
   (4) change he'd to hed
   (5) no correction is necessary

9. Sentence 10: **"So, in addition," says Bob, it helps to be lucky."**

   What correction should be made to this sentence?

   (1) remove the comma after So
   (2) remove the comma after addition
   (3) change in addition," to in addition",
   (4) insert a quotation mark before it
   (5) no correction is necessary

10. Sentence 11: **Bob is already planning his next game-show appearance.**

    What correction should be made to this sentence?

    (1) change Bob to Bobs'
    (2) change Bob to bob
    (3) change his to his'
    (4) insert quotation marks around game-show
    (5) no correction is necessary

11. Sentence 12: **"Even if he doesn't win," Bob says that it is still fun.**

    What correction should be made to this sentence?

    (1) remove both quotation marks
    (2) change doesn't to doesnt
    (3) insert a comma after says
    (4) insert quotation marks before that and after fun
    (5) no correction is necessary

Answers are on page 269.

Basic Spelling Rules and Contractions

Spelling errors often occur in words that contain the letter combinations *ie* or *ei,* words that have special endings called **suffixes,** and words that have special beginnings called **prefixes.**

Rule: Use *i* before *e,* except after *c,* or where sounded as *a,* as in *neighbor* and *weigh.*

Examples:
pie	friend	believe
receive	deceit	weight

Exceptions:
either	height	science
neither	seize	conscience
foreign	weird	leisure

Rule: When adding a suffix that starts with a vowel—such as *-ed, -ing, -er,* or *-est*—to a word, the spelling of most words doesn't change.

Examples:
small	+	-est	= smallest
find	+	-ing	= finding

Rule: If the word ends in *e,* drop the *e* before adding a suffix that starts with a vowel.

Examples:
nice	+	-er	= nicer
large	+	-est	= largest
make	+	-ing	= making
please	+	-ed	= pleased

Exception: If a word ends in *ce* or *ge,* keep the final *e* when adding a suffix that begins with *a* or *o.*

Examples:
notice	+	-able	= noticeable
courage	+	-ous	= courageous

Rule: If a word ends in a consonant-vowel-consonant combination *(r-o-l* in *control),* double the consonant before adding a suffix beginning with a vowel.

Examples:
fat	+	-er	= fatter
flat	+	-est	= flattest
stop	+	-ing	= stopping
admit	+	-ed	= admitted

Exception: In two-syllable words, do not double the final consonant if the first syllable is the one stressed when spoken.

Examples:
TRAVel	+	-ed	= traveled
BOTHer	+	-ing	= bothering

Rule:	If a word ends in *y* preceded by a consonant, change the *y* to *i* before adding the suffix.
Examples:	happy	+	-er	=	happier
	hurry	+	-ed	=	hurried
	pretty	+	-est	=	prettiest

| Exception: | If the suffix begins with an *i*, do not change the *y* to an *i*. |
| Example: | hurry | + | -ing | = | hurrying |

Rule:	When adding a suffix that begins with a consonant to a word that ends in *e* or in a consonant, just add the suffix.
Examples:	help	+	-ful	=	helpful
	cool	+	-ly	=	coolly
	agree	+	-ment	=	agreement

| Exceptions: | true | + | -ly | = | truly |
| | judge | + | -ment | = | judgment |

Rule:	When a prefix is added to a word, the spelling of the word is not changed.
Examples:	un	+	necessary	=	unnecessary
	mis	+	spell	=	misspell
	co	+	operate	=	cooperate

 Memorize one example for each spelling rule. You can remember the rules and apply them to test items by recalling your examples.

Contractions

A contraction combines two words. An apostrophe takes the place of the missing letter or letters.

Most contractions combine a personal pronoun and verb:

I'm	=	I am		you're	=	you are
I've	=	I have		you've	=	you have
I'd	=	I had		you'll	=	you will
I'd	=	I would		you'd	=	you would

Other contractions combine a verb and the word *not:*

isn't	=	is not		aren't	=	are not
don't	=	do not		didn't	=	did not
won't	=	will not		hasn't	=	has not
wasn't	=	was not		weren't	=	were not
couldn't	=	could not		shouldn't	=	should not

Directions: Choose the <u>best answer</u> to each item.

Items 1 to 12 refer to the following paragraph.

(1) This winter a new strain of flu is goeing around. (2) Its worse than other flus, and people are sicker than ever. (3) The flu victims suffer from noticable symptoms, including runny noses, watery eyes, and coughing. (4) Theyr'e also experiencing muscle aches, chills, and high fevers. (5) Visiting the emergency room is unecessary, say many doctors. (6) Yo'ud be better off staying in bed, resting, and drinking a variety of liquids. (7) Youll be making steps toward a full recovery within a week. (8) Next year, show good judgment by geting a flu shot in November. (9) Don't wait until you already have the flu; the shot will be useless. (10) The flu is especially dangerous for children and senior citizens. (11) Start encourageing your grandparents and elderly neighbors to go to the clinic early. (12) Hurrying to get vaccinated in November means being healthyer during the flu season.

1. Sentence 1: **This winter a new strain of flu is goeing around.**

   What correction should be made to this sentence?

   (1) change <u>winter</u> to <u>Winter</u>
   (2) change <u>is</u> to <u>are</u>
   (3) change <u>is</u> to <u>be</u>
   (4) change the spelling of <u>goeing</u> to <u>going</u>
   (5) no correction is necessary

2. Sentence 2: **Its worse than other flus, and people are sicker than ever.**

   What correction should be made to this sentence?

   (1) change <u>Its</u> to <u>It's</u>
   (2) change the comma after <u>flus</u> to a semicolon
   (3) change the spelling of <u>sicker</u> to <u>sickker</u>
   (4) change the first <u>than</u> to <u>then</u>
   (5) no correction is necessary

3. Sentence 3: **The flu victims suffer from noticable symptoms, including runny noses, watery eyes, and coughing.**

   What correction should be made to this sentence?

   (1) change the spelling of <u>noticable</u> to <u>noticeable</u>
   (2) change <u>victims</u> to <u>victim's</u>
   (3) change the spelling of <u>including</u> to <u>includeing</u>
   (4) change the spelling of <u>coughing</u> to <u>coffing</u>
   (5) no correction is necessary

4. Sentence 4: **Theyr'e also experiencing muscle aches, chills, and high fevers.**

   What correction should be made to this sentence?

   (1) change <u>Theyr'e</u> to <u>They're</u>
   (2) change the spelling of <u>experiencing</u> to <u>experienceing</u>
   (3) change the spelling of <u>experiencing</u> to <u>expereincing</u>
   (4) remove the comma after <u>chills</u>
   (5) no correction is necessary

5. Sentence 5: **Visiting the emergency room is unecessary, say many doctors.**

   What correction should be made to this sentence?

   (1) change the spelling of <u>Visiting</u> to <u>Visitting</u>
   (2) replace the comma after <u>unecessary</u> with a semicolon
   (3) change the spelling of <u>unecessary</u> to <u>unnecessary</u>
   (4) change <u>doctors</u> to <u>Doctors</u>
   (5) no correction is necessary

6. Sentence 6: **Yo'ud be better off staying in bed, resting, and drinking a variety of liquids.**

What correction should be made to this sentence?

(1) change Yo'ud to Youd
(2) change Yo'ud to You'd
(3) change off to of
(4) change the spelling of variety to vareity
(5) no correction is necessary

7. Sentence 7: **Youll be making steps toward a full recovery within a week.**

What correction should be made to this sentence?

(1) change Youll to You'll
(2) change the spelling of making to makeing
(3) change steps to step's
(4) change week to Week
(5) no correction is necessary

8. Sentence 8: **Next year, show good judgment by geting a flu shot in November.**

What correction should be made to this sentence?

(1) change judgment to judgement
(2) change geting to getting
(3) change shot to shots
(4) change November to november
(5) no correction is necessary

9. Sentence 9: **Don't wait until you already have the flu; the shot will be useless.**

What correction should be made to this sentence?

(1) change Don't to Dont
(2) change Don't to Do'nt
(3) change the spelling of useless to usless
(4) change the semicolon after flu to a comma
(5) no correction is necessary

10. Sentence 10: **The flu is especially dangerous for children and senior citizens.**

What correction should be made to this sentence?

(1) change the spelling of especially to especialy
(2) change the spelling of dangerous to dangeress
(3) change children to childs
(4) change senior citizens to senior Citizens
(5) no correction is necessary

11. Sentence 11: **Start encourageing your grandparents and elderly neighbors to go to the clinic early.**

What correction should be made to this sentence?

(1) change the spelling of encourageing to encouraging
(2) change grandparents to Grandparents
(3) change the spelling of elderly to elderrly
(4) change the spelling of neighbors to nieghbors
(5) no correction is necessary

12. Sentence 12: **Hurrying to get vaccinated in November means being healthyer during the flu season.**

What correction should be made to this sentence?

(1) change the spelling of Hurrying to Hurriing
(2) change means to mean's
(3) change the spelling of healthyer to healthier
(4) change season to Season
(5) no correction is necessary

Answers are on page 270.

Directions: Choose the <u>best answer</u> to each item.

Items 1 to 4 refer to the following paragraph.

(1) George, my next-door neighbor, noticed that I've frequently been missplacing my keys. (2) We drive together to work, and he's had to wait impatiently in the car several times while I search the apartment for the missing keys. (3) I hate to keep my friend waiting, and he gets worryed that we'll be late. (4) On Thursday, locateing the keys took me forty-five minutes; they were sitting on top of the refrigerator. (5) The day before that, they mischievously concealed themselves in the dishwasher. (6) Sometimes it seems as if my keys have a mind of their own. (7) The problem is becoming unbelievable; it would be funny if it were'nt so frustrating. (8) George has suggested that if I place my keys on the table next to the door immediately upon entering the house, our mornings would become less adventurous.

1. Sentence 1: **George, my next-door neighbor, noticed that I've frequently been missplacing my keys.**

   What correction should be made to this sentence?

   (1) remove the comma after <u>neighbor</u>
   (2) change the spelling of <u>neighbor</u> to <u>nieghbor</u>
   (3) change the spelling of <u>noticed</u> to <u>noticeed</u>
   (4) change the spelling of <u>missplacing</u> to <u>misplacing</u>
   (5) no correction is necessary

2. Sentence 3: **I hate to keep my friend waiting, and he gets worryed that we'll be late.**

   What correction should be made to this sentence?

   (1) change the spelling of <u>friend</u> to <u>freind</u>
   (2) change the spelling of <u>waiting</u> to <u>waitting</u>
   (3) change the spelling of <u>worryed</u> to <u>worried</u>
   (4) change <u>we'll</u> to <u>w'ell</u>
   (5) no correction is necessary

3. Sentence 4: **On Thursday, locateing the keys took me forty-five minutes; they were sitting on top of the refrigerator.**

   What correction should be made to this sentence?

   (1) change <u>Thursday</u> to <u>thursday</u>
   (2) change the spelling of <u>locateing</u> to <u>locating</u>
   (3) change the spelling of <u>sitting</u> to <u>siting</u>
   (4) replace the semicolon with a comma
   (5) no correction is necessary

4. Sentence 7: **The problem is becoming unbelievable; it would be funny if it were'nt so frustrating.**

   What correction should be made to this sentence?

   (1) change the spelling of <u>becoming</u> to <u>becomeing</u>
   (2) change the spelling of <u>unbelievable</u> to <u>unbeleivable</u>
   (3) change <u>were'nt</u> to <u>weren't</u>
   (4) change the spelling of <u>frustrating</u> to <u>frustrateing</u>
   (5) no correction is necessary

Items 5 to 9 refer to the following paragraph.

(1) Many of us like the idea of traveling to a foriegn country but cannot afford to do so; airplane tickets are often prohibitively expensive. (2) If a person doesn't travel with a great deal of luggage, however, air courier travel may be one way of avoiding outrageous fares. (3) A tourist, flying as an air courier, is permitted to travel with only a single carry-on bag. (4) The companys that issue courier tickets use that passenger's baggage allowance for shipping items to overseas customers. (5) In return, the passenger is able to purchase the airline ticket at a great discount. (6) Theres often an extra discount available to people who are able to accept last-minute travel arrangements. (7) For people who have that kind of flexibility, courier travel can be a very affordable way to see the world.

5. Sentence 1: **Many of us like the idea of traveling to a foriegn country but cannot afford to do so; airplane tickets are often prohibitively expensive.**

   What correction should be made to this sentence?

   (1) insert a comma after us
   (2) change the spelling of foriegn to foreign
   (3) change the semicolon after so to a comma
   (4) change the spelling of prohibitively to prohibitivly
   (5) no correction is necessary

6. Sentence 2: **If a person doesn't travel with a great deal of luggage, however, air courier travel may be one way of avoiding outrageous fares.**

   What correction should be made to this sentence?

   (1) change doesn't to does'nt
   (2) remove the comma after however
   (3) change the spelling of avoiding to avoidding
   (4) change the spelling of outrageous to outragous
   (5) no correction is necessary

7. Sentence 3: **A tourist, flying as an air courier, is permitted to travel with only a single carry-on bag.**

   What correction should be made to this sentence?

   (1) change tourist to Tourist
   (2) change the spelling of flying to fliing
   (3) remove the commas after tourist and courier
   (4) change the spelling of permitted to permited
   (5) no correction is necessary

8. Sentence 4: **The companys that issue courier tickets use that passenger's baggage allowance for shipping items to overseas customers.**

   What correction should be made to this sentence?

   (1) insert a comma after companys
   (2) change the spelling of companys to companies
   (3) change passenger's to passengers
   (4) change the spelling of shipping to shiping
   (5) no correction is necessary

9. Sentence 6: **Theres often an extra discount available to people who are able to accept last-minute travel arrangements.**

   What correction should be made to this sentence?

   (1) change Theres to There's
   (2) change Theres to Ther'es
   (3) insert a comma after people
   (4) change the spelling of arrangements to arrangments
   (5) no correction is necessary

Answers are on page 271.

Lesson 8

GED Master Spelling List

With some practice and concentration you can improve your spelling ability. Study the words on the GED Master Spelling List. These are the most commonly misspelled words. Write the words as someone reads them to you. Make a list of the ones you spelled incorrectly. You may find it easier to master the ones you missed if you learn the correct spelling of ten to twelve words at a time.

The spelling rules you have learned will help you with many difficult-to-spell words. When you come to a difficult word in a test item, recall the spelling rules and decide whether they apply to the item.

GED Master Spelling List

a lot ☐	agree ☐	arouse ☐	between ☐
ability ☐	aisle ☐	arrange ☐	bicycle ☐
absence ☐	all right ☐	arrangement ☐	board ☐
absent ☐	almost ☐	article ☐	bored ☐
abundance ☐	already ☐	artificial ☐	borrow ☐
accept ☐	although ☐	ascend ☐	bottle ☐
acceptable ☐	altogether ☐	assistance ☐	bottom ☐
accident ☐	always ☐	assistant ☐	boundary ☐
accommodate ☐	amateur ☐	associate ☐	brake ☐
accompanied ☐	American ☐	association ☐	breadth ☐
accomplish ☐	among ☐	attempt ☐	break ☐
accumulation ☐	amount ☐	attendance ☐	breath ☐
accuse ☐	analysis ☐	attention ☐	breathe ☐
accustomed ☐	analyze ☐	audience ☐	brilliant ☐
ache ☐	angel ☐	August ☐	building ☐
achieve ☐	angle ☐	author ☐	bulletin ☐
achievement ☐	annual ☐	automobile ☐	bureau ☐
acknowledge ☐	another ☐	autumn ☐	burial ☐
acquaintance ☐	answer ☐	auxiliary ☐	buried ☐
acquainted ☐	antiseptic ☐	available ☐	bury ☐
acquire ☐	anxious ☐	avenue ☐	bushes ☐
address ☐	apologize ☐	awful ☐	business ☐
addressed ☐	apparatus ☐	awkward ☐	
adequate ☐	apparent ☐		cafeteria ☐
advantage ☐	appear ☐	bachelor ☐	calculator ☐
advantageous ☐	appearance ☐	balance ☐	calendar ☐
advertise ☐	appetite ☐	balloon ☐	campaign ☐
advertisement ☐	apply ☐	bargain ☐	capital ☐
advice ☐	appreciate ☐	basic ☐	capitol ☐
advisable ☐	appreciation ☐	beautiful ☐	captain ☐
advise ☐	approach ☐	because ☐	career ☐
aerial ☐	appropriate ☐	become ☐	careful ☐
affect ☐	approval ☐	before ☐	careless ☐
affectionate ☐	approve ☐	beginning ☐	carriage ☐
again ☐	approximate ☐	being ☐	carrying ☐
against ☐	argue ☐	believe ☐	category ☐
aggravate ☐	arguing ☐	benefit ☐	ceiling ☐
aggressive ☐	argument ☐	benefited ☐	cemetery ☐

cereal	☐	corroborate	☐	disastrous	☐	exercise	☐
certain	☐	council	☐	discipline	☐	exhausted	☐
changeable	☐	counsel	☐	discover	☐	exhaustion	☐
characteristic	☐	counselor	☐	discriminate	☐	exhilaration	☐
charity	☐	courage	☐	disease	☐	existence	☐
chief	☐	courageous	☐	dissatisfied	☐	exorbitant	☐
choose	☐	course	☐	dissection	☐	expense	☐
chose	☐	courteous	☐	dissipate	☐	experience	☐
cigarette	☐	courtesy	☐	distance	☐	experiment	☐
circumstance	☐	criticism	☐	distinction	☐	explanation	☐
citizen	☐	criticize	☐	division	☐	extreme	☐
clothes	☐	crystal	☐	doctor	☐		
clothing	☐	curiosity	☐	dollar	☐	facility	☐
coarse	☐	cylinder	☐	doubt	☐	factory	☐
coffee	☐			dozen	☐	familiar	☐
collect	☐	daily	☐	dyed	☐	farther	☐
college	☐	daughter	☐			fascinate	☐
column	☐	daybreak	☐	earnest	☐	fascinating	☐
comedy	☐	death	☐	easy	☐	fatigue	☐
comfortable	☐	deceive	☐	ecstasy	☐	February	☐
commitment	☐	December	☐	ecstatic	☐	financial	☐
committed	☐	deception	☐	education	☐	financier	☐
committee	☐	decide	☐	effect	☐	flourish	☐
communicate	☐	decision	☐	efficiency	☐	forcibly	☐
company	☐	decisive	☐	efficient	☐	forehead	☐
comparative	☐	deed	☐	eight	☐	foreign	☐
compel	☐	definite	☐	either	☐	formal	☐
competent	☐	delicious	☐	eligibility	☐	former	☐
competition	☐	dependent	☐	eligible	☐	fortunate	☐
complement	☐	deposit	☐	eliminate	☐	fourteen	☐
compliment	☐	derelict	☐	embarrass	☐	fourth	☐
conceal	☐	descend	☐	embarrassment	☐	frequent	☐
conceit	☐	descent	☐	emergency	☐	friend	☐
conceivable	☐	describe	☐	emphasis	☐	frightening	☐
conceive	☐	description	☐	emphasize	☐	fundamental	☐
concentration	☐	desert	☐	enclosure	☐	further	☐
conception	☐	desirable	☐	encouraging	☐		
condition	☐	despair	☐	endeavor	☐	gallon	☐
conference	☐	desperate	☐	engineer	☐	garden	☐
confident	☐	dessert	☐	English	☐	gardener	☐
congratulate	☐	destruction	☐	enormous	☐	general	☐
conquer	☐	determine	☐	enough	☐	genius	☐
conscience	☐	develop	☐	entrance	☐	government	☐
conscientious	☐	development	☐	envelope	☐	governor	☐
conscious	☐	device	☐	environment	☐	grammar	☐
consequence	☐	devise	☐	equipment	☐	grateful	☐
consequently	☐	dictator	☐	equipped	☐	great	☐
considerable	☐	died	☐	especially	☐	grievance	☐
consistency	☐	difference	☐	essential	☐	grievous	☐
consistent	☐	different	☐	evening	☐	grocery	☐
continual	☐	dilemma	☐	evident	☐	guarantee	☐
continuous	☐	dinner	☐	exaggerate	☐	guard	☐
controlled	☐	direction	☐	exaggeration	☐	guess	☐
controversy	☐	disappear	☐	examine	☐	guidance	☐
convenience	☐	disappoint	☐	exceed	☐		
convenient	☐	disappointment	☐	excellent	☐	half	☐
conversation	☐	disapproval	☐	except	☐	hammer	☐
corporal	☐	disapprove	☐	exceptional	☐	handkerchief	☐

happiness ☐	jealous ☐	monkey ☐	pastime ☐
healthy ☐	judgment ☐	monotonous ☐	patience ☐
heard ☐	journal ☐	moral ☐	patients ☐
heavy ☐		morale ☐	peace ☐
height ☐	kindergarten ☐	mortgage ☐	peaceable ☐
herd ☐	kitchen ☐	mountain ☐	pear ☐
heroes ☐	knew ☐	mournful ☐	peculiar ☐
heroine ☐	knock ☐	muscle ☐	pencil ☐
hideous ☐	know ☐	mysterious ☐	people ☐
himself ☐	knowledge ☐	mystery ☐	perceive ☐
hoarse ☐			perception ☐
holiday ☐	labor ☐	narrative ☐	perfect ☐
hopeless ☐	laboratory ☐	natural ☐	perform ☐
horse ☐	laid ☐	necessary ☐	performance ☐
hospital ☐	language ☐	needle ☐	perhaps ☐
humorous ☐	later ☐	negligence ☐	period ☐
hurried ☐	latter ☐	neighbor ☐	permanence ☐
hurrying ☐	laugh ☐	neither ☐	permanent ☐
	leisure ☐	newspaper ☐	perpendicular ☐
ignorance ☐	length ☐	newsstand ☐	perseverance ☐
imaginary ☐	lesson ☐	niece ☐	persevere ☐
imbecile ☐	library ☐	noticeable ☐	persistent ☐
imitation ☐	license ☐		persuade ☐
immediately ☐	light ☐	o'clock ☐	personality ☐
incidental ☐	lightning ☐	obedient ☐	personal ☐
increase ☐	likelihood ☐	obstacle ☐	personnel ☐
independence ☐	likely ☐	occasion ☐	persuade ☐
independent ☐	literal ☐	occasional ☐	persuasion ☐
indispensable ☐	literature ☐	occur ☐	pertain ☐
inevitable ☐	livelihood ☐	occurred ☐	picture ☐
influence ☐	loaf ☐	occurrence ☐	piece ☐
influential ☐	loneliness ☐	ocean ☐	plain ☐
initiate ☐	loose ☐	offer ☐	plane ☐
innocence ☐	lose ☐	often ☐	playwright ☐
inoculate ☐	losing ☐	omission ☐	pleasant ☐
inquiry ☐	loyal ☐	omit ☐	please ☐
insistent ☐	loyalty ☐	once ☐	pleasure ☐
instead ☐		operate ☐	pocket ☐
instinct ☐	magazine ☐	opinion ☐	poison ☐
integrity ☐	maintenance ☐	opportune ☐	policeman ☐
intellectual ☐	maneuver ☐	opportunity ☐	political ☐
intelligence ☐	marriage ☐	optimist ☐	population ☐
intercede ☐	married ☐	optimistic ☐	portrayal ☐
interest ☐	marry ☐	origin ☐	positive ☐
interfere ☐	match ☐	original ☐	possess ☐
interference ☐	mathematics ☐	oscillate ☐	possession ☐
interpreted ☐	measure ☐	ought ☐	possessive ☐
interrupt ☐	medicine ☐	ounce ☐	possible ☐
invitation ☐	million ☐	overcoat ☐	post office ☐
irrelevant ☐	miniature ☐		potatoes ☐
irresistible ☐	minimum ☐	paid ☐	practical ☐
irritable ☐	miracle ☐	pamphlet ☐	prairie ☐
island ☐	miscellaneous ☐	panicky ☐	precede ☐
its ☐	mischief ☐	parallel ☐	preceding ☐
it's ☐	mischievous ☐	parallelism ☐	precise ☐
itself ☐	misspelled ☐	pare ☐	predictable ☐
	mistake ☐	particular ☐	prefer ☐
January ☐	momentous ☐	partner ☐	preference ☐

preferential ☐	renovate ☐	specified ☐	university ☐
preferred ☐	repeat ☐	specimen ☐	unnecessary ☐
prejudice ☐	repetition ☐	speech ☐	unusual ☐
preparation ☐	representative ☐	stationary ☐	useful ☐
prepare ☐	requirements ☐	stationery ☐	usual ☐
prescription ☐	resemblance ☐	statue ☐	
presence ☐	resistance ☐	stockings ☐	vacuum ☐
president ☐	resource ☐	stomach ☐	vain ☐
prevalent ☐	respectability ☐	straight ☐	valley ☐
primitive ☐	responsibility ☐	strength ☐	valuable ☐
principal ☐	restaurant ☐	strenuous ☐	variety ☐
principle ☐	rhythm ☐	stretch ☐	vegetable ☐
privilege ☐	rhythmical ☐	striking ☐	vein ☐
probably ☐	ridiculous ☐	studying ☐	vengeance ☐
procedure ☐	right ☐	substantial ☐	versatile ☐
proceed ☐	role ☐	succeed ☐	vicinity ☐
produce ☐	roll ☐	successful ☐	vicious ☐
professional ☐	roommate ☐	sudden ☐	view ☐
professor ☐		superintendent ☐	village ☐
profit ☐	sandwich ☐	suppress ☐	villain ☐
profitable ☐	Saturday ☐	surely ☐	visitor ☐
prominent ☐	scarcely ☐	surprise ☐	voice ☐
promise ☐	scene ☐	suspense ☐	volume ☐
pronounce ☐	schedule ☐	sweat ☐	
pronunciation ☐	science ☐	sweet ☐	waist ☐
propeller ☐	scientific ☐	syllable ☐	ware ☐
prophet ☐	scissors ☐	symmetrical ☐	waste ☐
prospect ☐	season ☐	sympathy ☐	weak ☐
psychology ☐	secretary ☐	synonym ☐	wear ☐
pursue ☐	seize ☐		weather ☐
pursuit ☐	seminar ☐	technical ☐	Wednesday ☐
	sense ☐	telegram ☐	week ☐
quality ☐	separate ☐	telephone ☐	weigh ☐
quantity ☐	service ☐	temperament ☐	weird ☐
quarreling ☐	several ☐	temperature ☐	whether ☐
quart ☐	severely ☐	tenant ☐	which ☐
quarter ☐	shepherd ☐	tendency ☐	while ☐
quiet ☐	sheriff ☐	tenement ☐	whole ☐
quite ☐	shining ☐	therefore ☐	wholly ☐
	shoulder ☐	thorough ☐	whose ☐
raise ☐	shriek ☐	through ☐	witch ☐
realistic ☐	siege ☐	title ☐	wretched ☐
realize ☐	sight ☐	together ☐	
reason ☐	signal ☐	tomorrow ☐	
rebellion ☐	significance ☐	tongue ☐	
recede ☐	significant ☐	toward ☐	
receipt ☐	similar ☐	tragedy ☐	
receive ☐	similarity ☐	transferred ☐	
recipe ☐	since ☐	treasury ☐	
recognize ☐	sincerely ☐	tremendous ☐	
recommend ☐	site ☐	tries ☐	
recuperate ☐	soldier ☐	truly ☐	
referred ☐	solemn ☐	twelfth ☐	
rehearsal ☐	sophomore ☐	twelve ☐	
reign ☐	soul ☐	tyranny ☐	
relevant ☐	source ☐		
relieve ☐	souvenir ☐	undoubtedly ☐	
remedy ☐	special ☐	United States ☐	

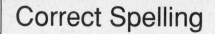

Items 1 to 8 refer to the following paragraph. Choose the best answer to each item.

(1) Yesterday, Adam, my oldest son, was admitted to kindergarten, and I carefully controlled my own anxiety about this big step in Adam's life. (2) He has eight friends and nieghbors beginning kindergarten in the same school, but none of them is in his class. (3) This morning he awakened befour anyone else in the family; worried about being late, he did not believe my reassurances that he would be on time. (4) I tried not to show my own misgivings, but watching Adam's nervousness mount, I decided it was unecessary to be so virtuous and conceal my own feelings. (5) "Oh, Adam," I said, "it's so exciting and scary to send you off to a new place," and I saw the weight of his worry lift immediately. (6) He went to kindergarten this morning a little frightened, but couragous, because I had let him see that his mother was feeling somewhat unsure, too. (7) That helped ease his fear, which had seemed unnacceptable to him, and made him feel more comfortable. (8) This experience has caused me to doubt the wisdom of concealing our feelings from children in hopes of increasing their coping ability.

1. Sentence 1: **Yesterday, Adam, my oldest son, was admitted to kindergarten, and I carefuly controlled my own anxiety about this big step in Adam's life.**

   What spelling correction should be made to this sentence?

   (1) change admitted to admited
   (2) change kindergarten to kintergarden
   (3) change carefuly to carefully
   (4) change controlled to controled
   (5) no correction is necessary

2. Sentence 2: **He has eight friends and nieghbors beginning kindergarten in the same school, but none of them is in his class.**

   What spelling correction should be made to this sentence?

   (1) change eight to eght
   (2) change friends to freinds
   (3) change nieghbors to neighbors
   (4) change beginning to begining
   (5) no correction is necessary

3. Sentence 3: **This morning he awakened befour anyone else in the family; worried about being late, he did not believe my reassurances that he would be on time.**

   What spelling correction should be made to this sentence?

   (1) change befour to before
   (2) change being to beng
   (3) change believe to bilieve
   (4) change reassurances to reassurrances
   (5) no correction is necessary

4. Sentence 4: **I tried not to show my own misgivings, but watching Adam's nervousness mount, I decided it was unecessary to be so virtuous and conceal my own feelings.**

   What spelling correction should be made to this sentence?

   (1) change decided to desided
   (2) change unecessary to unnecessary
   (3) change virtuous to vertuous
   (4) change conceal to conseal
   (5) no correction is necessary

5. Sentence 5: **"Oh, Adam," I said, "it's so exciting and scary to send you off to a new place," and I saw the weight of his worry lift immediately.**

   What spelling correction should be made to this sentence?

   (1) change it's to its
   (2) change weight to wieght
   (3) change worry to werry
   (4) change immediately to immediatly
   (5) no correction is necessary

6. Sentence 6: **He went to kindergarten this morning a little frightened, but couragous, because I had let him see that his mother was feeling somewhat unsure, too.**

   What spelling correction should be made to this sentence?

   (1) change kindergarten to kintergarten
   (2) change frightened to fritened
   (3) change couragous to courageous
   (4) change because to becuase
   (5) no correction is necessary

7. Sentence 7: **That helped ease his fear, which had seemed unnacceptable to him, and made him feel more comfortable.**

   What spelling correction should be made to this sentence?

   (1) change which to wich
   (2) change seemed to seemmed
   (3) change unnacceptable to unacceptable
   (4) change comfortable to comforteble
   (5) no correction is necessary

8. Sentence 8: **This experience has caused me to doubt the wisdom of concealing our feelings from children in hopes of increasing their coping ability.**

   What spelling correction should be made to this sentence?

   (1) change experience to experence
   (2) change concealing to consealing
   (3) change increasing to incresing
   (4) change ability to abilaty
   (5) no correction is necessary

Items 9 to 12 refer to the following paragraph.

(1) Mary believes she will receive formal approval from the personel office for her promotion. (2) Her chief strength is her consceintious effort and attendance. (3) Mary also has adequate work experience and the appropreate education for the available position. (4) In her previous position, she initiated several new policies that gave her the oportunity to get this great new job.

9. Sentence 1: **Mary believes she will receive formal approval from the personel office for her promotion.**

   What spelling correction should be made to this sentence?

   (1) change believes to beleives
   (2) change receive to recieve
   (3) change approval to aproval
   (4) change personel to personnel
   (5) no correction is necessary

10. Sentence 2: **Her chief strength is her consceintious effort and attendance.**

    What spelling correction should be made to this sentence?

    (1) change chief to cheif
    (2) change strength to strenth
    (3) change consceintious to conscientious
    (4) change attendance to attendence
    (5) no correction is necessary

11. Sentence 3: **Mary also has adequate work experience and the appropreate education for the available position.**

What spelling correction should be made to this sentence?

(1) change adequate to adequit
(2) change experience to experiance
(3) change appropreate to appropriate
(4) change education to edacation
(5) change available to availible

12. Sentence 4: **In her previous position, she initiated several new policies that gave her the oportunity to get this great new job.**

What spelling correction should be made to this sentence?

(1) change initiated to inisheated
(2) change several to sevral
(3) change oportunity to opportunity
(4) change great to graet
(5) no correction is necessary

Items 13 to 17 refer to the following paragraph.

(1) The week of the anual tax deadline was always a stressful period for Horace. (2) He never suceeded in beginning to prepare his receipts before April. (3) As the deadline approached, he grew panicky and scrambled to collect his finanshal records. (4) Sweat appeared on his forhead as he searched through a mountain of receipts. (5) Saturday evening Horace finished and felt tremendous exhilaration.

13. Sentence 1: **The week of the anual tax deadline was always a stressful period for Horace.**

What spelling correction should be made to this sentence?

(1) change week to weak
(2) change anual to annual
(3) change always to allways
(4) change period to periad
(5) no correction is necessary

14. Sentence 2: **He never suceeded in beginning to prepare his receipts before April.**

What spelling correction should be made to this sentence?

(1) change suceeded to succeeded
(2) change beginning to begining
(3) change receipts to reciepts
(4) change April to april
(5) no correction is necessary

15. Sentence 3: **As the deadline approached, he grew panicky and scrambled to collect his finanshal records.**

What spelling correction should be made to this sentence?

(1) change approached to aproached
(2) change panicky to pannicky
(3) change collect to colect
(4) change finanshal to financial
(5) no correction is necessary

16. Sentence 4: **Sweat appeared on his forhead as he searched through a mountain of receipts.**

What spelling correction should be made to this sentence?

(1) change appeared to appeered
(2) change forhead to forehead
(3) change mountain to mounten
(4) change receipts to reciepts
(5) no correction is necessary

17. Sentence 5: **Saturday evening Horace finished and felt tremendous exhilaration.**

What spelling correction should be made to this sentence?

(1) change Saturday to saturday
(2) change evening to evning
(3) change tremendous to tremendus
(4) change exhilaration to exhileration
(5) no correction is necessary

Answers are on page 271.

Unit 1: Mechanics

Possessives and Homonyms

Possessives are used to show ownership. Homonyms are words that sound alike but have different spellings or different meanings.

The following note uses several possessives and homonyms.

Hi,

(1) Is it true that Bob's sisters overheard a conversation about their jobs? (2) It's too bad if it's true that the management will fire its two most experienced employees. (3) Everybody knew they intended to hire new employees, but are dismissals necessary? (4) Who's the person who told your brother it's true? (5) I guess you can't be too sure that your job is going to last more than two years.

Your friend,
Allan

Rule: Form the possessive of a noun by adding *'s* (or just an apostrophe if the noun is a plural and ends in -*s*).

Example: (Sentence 1) Is it true that <u>Bob's</u> sisters overheard a conversation about their jobs?

Rule: Do not confuse words that are homonyms. Be sure of the spelling and the meaning.

Example: (Sentence 3) Everybody <u>knew</u> they intended to hire new employees, but are dismissals necessary?
The homonyms are <u>knew</u>, the past tense of the verb <u>know</u>, and <u>new</u>, meaning "latest" or "additional."

Example: (Sentence 5) I guess you can't be <u>too</u> sure that your job is going <u>to</u> last more than <u>two</u> years.
The homonyms are <u>too</u>, meaning "very" or "also"; <u>to</u>, a preposition or part of an infinitive verb form; and <u>two</u>, a number.

Rule: Do not confuse possessive pronouns with contractions that sound the same.

Example: (Sentence 2) <u>It's</u> too bad if <u>it's</u> true that the management will fire <u>its</u> two most experienced employees.
<u>It's</u> is a contraction meaning "it is"; <u>its</u> is a possessive pronoun.

Note: Most pronouns that show possession are <u>not</u> spelled with an apostrophe. The possessive pronouns are *my, mine, your, yours, his, her, hers, its, our, ours, their, theirs, whose.*

To avoid errors with homonyms, read the entire sentence before you decide how to spell the word. That way, you will know the intended meaning of the word.

The most commonly confused homonyms are contractions and possessives: it's/its, you're/your, they're/their, who's/whose.

Here are some other commonly confused words:

accept (to receive)
except (to exclude)

pane (window glass)
pain (hurt)

affect (to influence)
effect (a result)

passed (went by)
past (a time before)

be (to exist)
bee (an insect)

plane (flat surface; airplane)
plain (simple, ordinary)

board (piece of wood)
bored (uninterested)

principal (main)
principle (rule, belief)

brake (to stop)
break (rest period; to damage or destroy)

right (correct; opposite of left)
write (to form words)

course (path, track)
coarse (rough, textured)

some (a few)
sum (total amount)

feet (plural of foot)
feat (achievement)

too (also, very)
two (2)
to (part of infinitive verb form; in the direction of)

grate (shred)
great (very good)

way (path, direction)
weigh (to measure the heaviness of something)

hear (to listen)
here (in this place)

weak (not strong)
week (seven days)

knew (past tense of know)
new (latest, additional)

where (what place)
wear (to have on clothing)

know (to be certain of)
no (negative)

whether (if)
weather (climate)

lessen (to decrease)
lesson (something taught)

whole (entire)
hole (opening)

made (created)
maid (cleaning person)

wood (what trees are made of)
would (verb expressing a wish)

one (1)
won (past tense of win)

Items 1 to 5 refer to the following paragraph. Choose the best answer to each item.

(1) John and his two sons are planning to go on a fishing trip next week. (2) John's sons are planning to bring there swim trunks for swimming at the lake. (3) The whether report says that the temperature is going to be low, and it might rain, too. (4) I hope the weather report is wrong; it could spoil the whole trip four them. (5) The cold weather and rain would probably ruin the boy's plans for a great vacation.

1. Sentence 1: **John and his two sons are planning to go on a fishing trip next week.**

   What correction should be made to this sentence?

   (1) change two to to
   (2) change sons to suns
   (3) change to to too
   (4) change week to weak
   (5) no correction is necessary

2. Sentence 2: **John's sons are planning to bring there swim trunks for swimming at the lake.**

   What correction should be made to this sentence?

   (1) change John's to Johns
   (2) change to to two
   (3) change there to their
   (4) change for to four
   (5) no correction is necessary

3. Sentence 3: **The whether report says that the temperature is going to be low, and it might rain, too.**

   What correction should be made to this sentence?

   (1) change whether to weather
   (2) change to to two
   (3) change might to mite
   (4) change too to to
   (5) no correction is necessary

4. Sentence 4: **I hope the weather report is wrong; it could spoil the whole trip four them.**

   What correction should be made to this sentence?

   (1) change weather to whether
   (2) replace it with its
   (3) change whole to hole
   (4) change four to for
   (5) no correction is necessary

5. Sentence 5: **The cold weather and rain would probably ruin the boy's plans for a great vacation.**

   What correction should be made to this sentence?

   (1) replace would with wood
   (2) change boy's to boys'
   (3) change plans to plans'
   (4) replace great with grate
   (5) no correction is necessary

Items 6 to 10 refer to the following paragraph.

(1) When I came hear four years ago, everyone said Mr. Patterson was on his way out. (2) As head of the department for the passed twenty-five years, he had made great changes. (3) Newspaper circulation had nearly doubled, and the publisher always felt Mr. Patterson deserved credit for that feet. (4) He's a genius who knows people, production, and politics; know one will ever be able to fill his shoes. (5) Most of the reporters here were personally taught how to write by Mr. Patterson. (6) Even though Mr. Patterson's style of instruction was very plain, no one ever became board while listening to him.

6. Sentence 1: **When I came hear four years ago, everyone said Mr. Patterson was on his way out.**

What correction should be made to this sentence?

(1) replace hear with here
(2) replace four with for
(3) replace his with hi's
(4) replace way with weigh
(5) no correction is necessary

7. Sentence 2: **As head of the department for the passed twenty-five years, he had made great changes.**

What correction should be made to this sentence?

(1) replace passed with past
(2) remove the comma after years
(3) replace made with maid
(4) replace great with grate
(5) no correction is necessary

8. Sentence 3: **Newspaper circulation had nearly doubled, and the publisher always felt Mr. Patterson deserved credit for that feet.**

What correction should be made to this sentence?

(1) change the comma after doubled to a semicolon
(2) change publisher to Publisher
(3) replace for with four
(4) replace feet with feat
(5) no correction is necessary

9. Sentence 4: **He's a genius who knows people, production, and politics; know one will ever be able to fill his shoes.**

What correction should be made to this sentence?

(1) replace knows with nose
(2) replace know with no
(3) replace one with won
(4) replace will with we'll
(5) no correction is necessary

10. Sentence 6: **Even though Mr. Patterson's style of instruction was very plain, no one ever became board while listening to him.**

What correction should be made to this sentence?

(1) change Patterson's to Pattersons'
(2) replace plain with plane
(3) replace board with bored
(4) remove the comma after plain
(5) no correction is necessary

Answers are on page 272.

Unit 1: Mechanics

Directions: Choose the best answer to each item.

Items 1 to 5 refer to the following paragraph.

(1) Deciding whether to join a union isn't easy, especially sense the choice is such an important one. (2) Some say you'll make the right choice if you're answer to the question "Can the union live up to its promises?" is considered carefully. (3) Unions are allowed to make promises to potential members, just as politicians have always made promises to they're supporters. (4) Before joining, you would probably want to find out as much as you can about the union's reputation in your community. (5) Your final decision may be based largely on who's promises you are most likely to believe, the union's or management's. (6) As you consider witch choice to make, think carefully about the long-term effects of your decision.

1. Sentence 1: **Deciding whether to join a union isn't easy, especially sense the choice is such an important one.**

   What correction should be made to this sentence?

   (1) replace whether with weather
   (2) change isn't to is'nt
   (3) replace sense with since
   (4) replace one with won
   (5) no correction is necessary

2. Sentence 2: **Some say you'll make the right choice if you're answer to the question "Can the union live up to its promises?" is considered carefully.**

   What correction should be made to this sentence?

   (1) change you'll to youll
   (2) change right to write
   (3) change you're to your
   (4) change its to it's
   (5) no correction is necessary

3. Sentence 3: **Unions are allowed to make promises to potential members, just as politicians have always made promises to they're supporters.**

   What correction should be made to this sentence?

   (1) change members to member's
   (2) replace made with maid
   (3) replace they're with there
   (4) replace they're with their
   (5) no correction is necessary

4. Sentence 5: **Your final decision may be based largely on who's promises you are most likely to believe, the union's or management's.**

   What correction should be made to this sentence?

   (1) replace Your with You're
   (2) replace be with bee
   (3) replace who's with whose
   (4) replace union's with unions
   (5) no correction is necessary

5. Sentence 6: **As you consider witch choice to make, think carefully about the long-term effects of your decision.**

   What correction should be made to this sentence?

   (1) replace witch with which
   (2) replace effects with affects
   (3) change effects to effect's
   (4) change your to you're
   (5) no correction is necessary

Items 6 to 16 refer to the following paragraphs.

(1) Getting credit seems easy when you don't want it, I even received a credit card in the mail that I hadn't asked for. (2) Getting credit threw major credit card companies can be difficult, however, for those who have no credit rating or those who have a bad one. (3) Bank cards usually cost you something, but department stores don't charge a yearly fee for the use of there credit cards.

(4) Our experience with department store cards has been good, as long as we remember to pay our balance each month. (5) Anyone, who's ever lost a credit card knows the importance of keeping track of card numbers and information about how to report the loss. (6) There are insurance programs available to protect people who mite be likely to lose their credit cards. (7) If your credit card is stolen, you should immediately call the store or company whose card was taken.

(8) One principle thing to remember about credit cards is that having a credit line doesn't mean you have access to "free money." (9) I have friends, new credit card holders, whose credit card purchases add up to a huge some every month. (10) Since they can't afford to pay for the purchases they have maid, high interest charges add up on their accounts. (11) Often, people find that it's difficult to brake the cycle of purchasing too much and paying interest fees. (12) It would be better if they didn't use their cards but always paid cash instead.

6. Sentence 1: **Getting credit seems easy when you don't want it, I even received a credit card in the mail that I hadn't asked for.**

What correction should be made to this sentence?

(1) replace seems with seams
(2) change don't to dont
(3) replace the comma after it with a semicolon
(4) change hadn't to hadnt
(5) no correction is necessary

7. Sentence 2: **Getting credit threw major credit card companies can be difficult, however, for those who have no credit rating or those who have a bad one.**

What correction should be made to this sentence?

(1) change threw to through
(2) replace the comma before however with a semicolon
(3) replace for with four
(4) replace no with know
(5) no correction is necessary

8. Sentence 3: **Bank cards usually cost you something, but department stores don't charge a yearly fee for the use of there credit cards.**

What correction should be made to this sentence?

(1) change cards to Cards
(2) change the comma after something to a semicolon
(3) change department stores to Department Stores
(4) change there to their
(5) no correction is necessary

9. Sentence 5: **Anyone, who's ever lost a credit card knows the importance of keeping track of card numbers and information about how to report the loss.**

What correction should be made to this sentence?

(1) remove the comma after Anyone
(2) replace who's with whose
(3) insert a comma after credit card
(4) insert a comma after information
(5) no correction is necessary

10. Sentence 6: **There are insurance programs available to protect people who mite be likely to lose their credit cards.**

What correction should be made to this sentence?

(1) replace There with Their
(2) replace to with too
(3) replace mite with might
(4) replace their with there
(5) no correction is necessary

11. Sentence 7: **If your credit card is stolen, you should immediately call the store or company whose card was taken.**

What correction should be made to this sentence?

(1) change your to you're
(2) insert a semicolon after should
(3) change store or company to Store or Company
(4) change whose to who's
(5) no correction is necessary

12. Sentence 8: **One principle thing to remember about credit cards is that having a credit line doesn't mean you have access to "free money."**

What correction should be made to this sentence?

(1) replace One with Won
(2) replace principle with principal
(3) change cards to card's
(4) change the spelling of having to haveing
(5) no correction is necessary

 To decide whether to use *its* or *it's* in a sentence, replace the word with *it is*. If the sentence makes sense, use the contraction *it's;* if it doesn't, use the possessive *its.*

13. Sentence 9: **I have friends, new credit card holders, whose credit card purchases add up to a huge some every month.**

What correction should be made to this sentence?

(1) change the spelling of friends to freinds
(2) replace new with knew
(3) replace whose with who's
(4) replace some with sum
(5) no correction is necessary

14. Sentence 10: **Since they can't afford to pay for the purchases they have maid, high interest charges add up on their accounts.**

What correction should be made to this sentence?

(1) remove the comma after maid
(2) replace maid with made
(3) replace their with there
(4) replace their with they're
(5) no correction is necessary

15. Sentence 11: **Often, people find that it's difficult to brake the cycle of purchasing too much and paying interest fees.**

What correction should be made to this sentence?

(1) replace it's with its
(2) replace brake with break
(3) change the spelling of purchasing to purchaseing
(4) replace too with to
(5) no correction is necessary

16. Sentence 12: **It would be better if they didn't use their cards but always paid cash instead.**

What correction should be made to this sentence?

(1) change would with wood
(2) change didn't with did'nt
(3) change their to there
(4) replace paid with payed
(5) no correction is necessary

Answers are on page 273.

Directions: Choose the best answer to each item.

Items 1 to 5 refer to the following paragraph.

(1) Managers have become interested in the veiws of their employees. (2) One new way employees can communicate with management is through an attitude survey. (3) Such surveys are usually designed and processed by experts? (4) Their purpose is to give employees a chance to tell their bosses how they feel about their jobs and the Company, while ensuring confidentiality. (5) Some questions such as those related to satisfaction with salary may receive fairly low ratings from even the most satisfied employees; few will admit that they're satisfied with their pay.

1. Sentence 1: **Managers have become interested in the veiws of their employees.**

   Which of the following is the best way to write the underlined portion of this sentence? If you think the original is the best way, choose option (1).

   (1) veiws of their employees
   (2) views of their employees
   (3) views, of their employees
   (4) views of there employees
   (5) views of their employees'

2. Sentence 2: **One new way employees can communicate with management is through an attitude survey.**

   Which of the following is the best way to write the underlined portion of this sentence? If you think the original is the best way, choose option (1).

   (1) communicate with management is
   (2) comunicate with management is
   (3) communicate with managment is,
   (4) communicate with management, is
   (5) communicate with management is;

3. Sentence 3: **Such surveys are usually designed and processed by experts?**

   What correction should be made to this sentence?

   (1) change surveys to survey's
   (2) change the spelling of usually to usualy
   (3) change experts to expert's
   (4) change the question mark to a period
   (5) no correction is necessary

4. Sentence 4: **Their purpose is to give employees a chance to tell their bosses how they feel about their jobs and the Company, while ensuring confidentiality.**

   What correction should be made to this sentence?

   (1) change Their to There
   (2) replace bosses with bosses'
   (3) change Company to company
   (4) replace confidentiality with Confidentiality
   (5) no correction is necessary

5. Sentence 5: **Some questions such as those related to satisfaction with salary may receive fairly low ratings from even the most satisfied employees; few will admit that they're satisfied with their pay.**

   What correction should be made to this sentence?

   (1) insert commas after questions and salary
   (2) change receive to recieve
   (3) change the semicolon to a comma
   (4) change they're to there
   (5) no correction is necessary

Items 6 to 10 refer to the following paragraph.

(1) Department managers receive tabulated results of the surveys, then they hold meetings with their employees and present the data. (2) During each meeting; certain problem areas are defined and employee task groups may be formed to recommend solutions. (3) Surveys can never take the place of face-to-face communication, but as one worker stated, I liked being able to tell the boss what I would change about my job if I had the chance." (4) Managers sometimes find that their employees' suggestions are workable their suggestions often improve productivity. (5) Worker morale also may be improved, along with company profits.

6. Sentence 1: **Department managers receive tabulated results of the surveys, then they hold meetings with their employees and present the data.**

Which of the following is the best way to write the underlined portion of this sentence? If you think the original is the best way, choose option (1).

(1) surveys, then
(2) surveys! then
(3) surveys. then
(4) surveys. Then
(5) surveys? Then

7. Sentence 2: **During each meeting; certain problem areas are defined and employee task groups may be formed to recommend solutions.**

What correction should be made to this sentence?

(1) change the semicolon to a comma
(2) change areas to areas'
(3) replace to with too
(4) change the spelling of recommend to recomend
(5) no correction is necessary

8. Sentence 3: **Surveys can never take the place of face-to-face communication, but as one worker stated, I liked being able to tell the boss what I would change about my job if I had the chance."**

Which of the following is the best way to write the underlined portion of this sentence? If you think the original is the best way, choose option (1).

(1) but as one worker stated, I liked
(2) but as one worker stated I liked
(3) but, "as one worker stated, I liked
(4) but as one worker stated, "I liked
(5) but, as one worker stated, "I liked

9. Sentence 4: **Managers sometimes find that their employees' suggestions are workable their suggestions often improve productivity.**

What correction should be made to this sentence?

(1) replace their employees' with there employees'
(2) change employees' to employee's
(3) insert a semicolon after workable
(4) replace suggestions with suggestions'
(5) no correction is necessary

10. Sentence 5: **Worker morale also may be improved, along with company profits.**

Which of the following is the best way to rewrite the underlined portion of this sentence? If you think the original is the best way, choose option (1).

(1) improved, along
(2) improved along
(3) improved; along
(4) improved. along
(5) improved. Along

Items 11 to 21 refer to the following paragraphs.

(1) Much has been written about "displaced homemakers" and "children of divorce." (2) According to a recent publication, "Depression, Divorce, And Death," little research has been done on how divorce relates to depression. (3) "Depression probably precedes divorce," according to Dr. Stanley Livingood author of a recent book on the subject. (4) "But, he added, "we are just beginning to discover to what extent depression also follows divorce and what its effects are." (5) Teenage suicide, a growing problem is being linked to the increasing divorce rate. (6) "Being able to talk out your problems and feelings with someone who will really listen to you is very important during this time," says Dr. Livingood. (7) "Fear of the unknown is the biggest part of the problem, concludes Dr. Livingood. (8) "We don't function very well when we can't control what's going to happen next in our lives." (9) Support groups, free counseling programs, and suicide prevention programs are all part of the Solution to this growing problem.

(10) People, who suffer from depression, can benefit from the great body of knowledge that exists on the subject. (11) Unfortunately, millions of Americans who's lives are made miserable by depression go untreated. (12) The outlook for those who do seek help has never been better, indeed, the majority of depressive disorders are easily treatable.

11. Sentence 1: **Much has been written about "displaced homemakers" and "children of divorce."**

    What correction should be made to this sentence?

    (1) change written to Written
    (2) insert a semicolon after written
    (3) remove the quotation mark before displaced
    (4) change children to children's
    (5) no correction is necessary

12. Sentence 2: **According to a recent publication, "Depression, Divorce, And Death," little research has been done on how divorce relates to depression.**

    What correction should be made to this sentence?

    (1) change to to too
    (2) remove the comma after publication
    (3) change And to and
    (4) change Death," to Death",
    (5) no correction is necessary

13. Sentence 3: **"Depression probably precedes divorce," according to Dr. Stanley Livingood author of a recent book on the subject.**

    What correction should be made to this sentence?

    (1) remove the quotation mark before Depression
    (2) replace to with too
    (3) insert a comma after Livingood
    (4) insert a comma after book
    (5) no correction is necessary

14. Sentence 4: **"But, he added, "we are just beginning to discover to what extent depression also follows divorce and what its effects are."**

    What correction should be made to this sentence?

    (1) insert a quotation mark after But,
    (2) remove the quotation mark before we
    (3) change the spelling of beginning to begining
    (4) change its to it's
    (5) no correction is necessary

15. Sentence 5: **Teenage suicide, a growing problem is being linked to the increasing divorce rate.**

What correction should be made to this sentence?

(1) change Teenage to teenage
(2) remove the comma after suicide
(3) insert a comma after problem
(4) change the spelling of increasing to incresing
(5) no correction is necessary

16. Sentence 6: **"Being able to talk out your problems and feelings with someone who will really listen to you is very important during this time," says Dr. Livingood.**

What correction should be made to this sentence?

(1) remove the quotation marks before Being and after time,
(2) change your to you're
(3) change someone to Someone
(4) insert a comma after important
(5) no correction is necessary

17. Sentences 7 and 8: **"Fear of the unknown is the biggest part of the problem, concludes Dr. Livingood. "We don't function very well when we can't control what's going to happen next in our lives."**

What correction should be made to these sentences?

(1) change biggest to Biggest
(2) insert a quotation mark after problem,
(3) change the period after Livingood to a comma
(4) change what's to whats
(5) no correction is necessary

18. Sentence 9: **Support groups, free counseling programs, and suicide prevention programs are all part of the Solution to this growing problem.**

What correction should be made to this sentence?

(1) remove the comma after groups
(2) remove the comma after programs
(3) change the spelling of counseling to counsiling
(4) change Solution to solution
(5) no correction is necessary

19. Sentence 10: **People, who suffer from depression, can benefit from the great body of knowledge that exists on the subject.**

What correction should be made to this sentence?

(1) remove the commas after People and depression
(2) change the comma after depression to a semicolon
(3) replace great with grate
(4) change the spelling of knowledge to knowlege
(5) no correction is necessary

20. Sentence 11: **Unfortunately, millions of Americans who's lives are made miserable by depression go untreated.**

What correction should be made to this sentence?

(1) change the spelling of Unfortunately to Unfortunatly
(2) change millions to millions'
(3) change Americans to americans
(4) replace who's with whose
(5) no correction is necessary

21. Sentence 12: **The outlook for those who do seek help has never been <u>better, indeed, the</u> majority of depressive disorders are easily treatable.**

Which of the following is the best way to write the underlined portion of this sentence? If you think the original is the best way, choose option (1).

(1) better, indeed, the
(2) better; indeed, the
(3) better indeed; the
(4) better indeed the
(5) better, indeed the

Items 22 to 25 refer to the following paragraph.

(1) Going to a new country, learning to communicate every day in a new language, and getting used to new customs can be difficult. (2) As Keiko Shimuzu discovered last summer, when she moved to the Washington, D.C., area, it can also be challenging and rewarding. (3) Her husband, a television reporter was offered a two-year job that mostly involved covering the White House and national politics. (4) When he traveled, he often left Keiko alone with their five-year-old son and two-year-old daughter. (5) Keiko knew a lot of English, but her children knew almost none she worried that it would be hard for them to make friends and enjoy their new neighborhood. (6) She was happy when, after two week's in his new kindergarten, her son was invited to another boy's house for lunch.

22. Sentence 1: **Going to a new country, learning to communicate every day in a new language, and getting used to new customs can be difficult.**

What correction should be made to this sentence?

(1) remove the comma after <u>country</u>
(2) change <u>learning</u> to <u>Learning</u>
(3) change the spelling of <u>communicate</u> to <u>comunicate</u>
(4) change the spelling of <u>getting</u> to <u>geting</u>
(5) no correction is necessary

23. Sentence 3: **Her husband, a television reporter was offered a two-year job that mostly involved covering the White House and national politics.**

What correction should be made to this sentence?

(1) remove the comma after <u>husband</u>
(2) insert a comma after <u>reporter</u>
(3) change <u>White House</u> to <u>white house</u>
(4) change <u>national</u> to <u>National</u>
(5) no correction is necessary

24. Sentence 5: **Keiko knew a lot of English, but her children knew almost none she worried that it would be hard for them to make friends and enjoy their new neighborhood.**

What correction should be made to this sentence?

(1) change <u>English</u> to <u>english</u>
(2) change the spelling of <u>almost</u> to <u>allmost</u>
(3) insert a semicolon after <u>none</u>
(4) change the spelling of <u>neighborhood</u> to <u>nieghborhood</u>
(5) no correction is necessary

25. Sentence 6: **She was happy when, after two week's in his new kindergarten, her son was invited to another boy's house for lunch.**

What correction should be made to this sentence?

(1) remove the comma after <u>when</u>
(2) change <u>week's</u> to <u>weeks</u>
(3) change the spelling of <u>kindergarten</u> to <u>kindergarden</u>
(4) change <u>boy's</u> to <u>boys</u>
(5) no correction is necessary

Performance Analysis
Unit 1 Cumulative Review: Mechanics

Name: _____ **Class:** _____ **Date:** _____

Use the Answer Key on pages 275–277 to check your answers to the GED Unit 1 Cumulative Review: Mechanics. Then use the chart to figure out the skill areas in which you need additional review. Circle on the chart the numbers of the test items you answered correctly. Then go back and review the lessons for the skill areas that are difficult for you. For additional review, see the *Steck-Vaughn GED Writing Skills Exercise Book,* Unit 1: Mechanics.

Skill	Question	Lessons for Review
Capitalization	4 12 18	1
End Punctuation	3 6	2
Commas	5 7 10 13 15 19 22 23	3 and 4
Semicolons	9 21 24	5
Apostrophes **Quotation Marks**	25 8 11 14 16 17	6 6
Spelling	1 2	7 and 8
Possessives and Homonyms	20	9

Unit 2 USAGE

Usage shows us how to use words in sentences.

Your study of mechanics in Unit 1 gave you an understanding of how words are spelled, when they are capitalized, and how sentences are punctuated. This unit, on usage and grammar, will show you how words are applied in sentences.

Grammar is the rules of our language. **Usage** pertains to the standard ways we construct ideas and use our language. In Unit 2, grammar rules and usage concepts are organized so that you can study them efficiently and refer to them quickly.

The focus of lesson 10 is parts of speech. You will review the different kinds of words and groups of words that make up a sentence.

In lesson 11, you will learn how the two basic parts of the sentence, the **subject** and **verb**, relate to each other. The subject and the verb of a sentence must match, or agree with, each other.

In lesson 12, you will learn that every verb has three principal forms: present, past, and past participle. To construct these forms, verbs change. In the lesson, you will learn the normal way to form the three parts of a verb; you will also learn how **irregular verbs** are formed.

parts of speech
the different kinds of words that make up a sentence

subject
the noun or pronoun a sentence is about

verb
the state of being or action of the subject in a sentence

irregular verb
a verb that changes its spelling to form its principal parts

Lesson 13 covers **verb tenses.** Verb tenses communicate how the action of a sentence relates to the passage of time. Present, past, and future tenses tell when an action takes place. The three perfect tenses show the time relationship of one event to another. You will learn how to form each tense and when it is correct to use each tense.

In lesson 14, you will learn about the kinds of **pronouns** and when to use them as subjects or objects. Pronouns take the place of **nouns.** Subject pronouns are used as subjects, and object pronouns take the place of noun objects. You will also learn when to use possessive pronouns.

The focus of lesson 15 is agreement between pronouns and their **antecedents,** the nouns to which they refer. Just as subjects and verbs must agree, pronouns must match the nouns they represent.

In lesson 16, you will learn more about handling the special problems that arise with pronoun usage. You will learn when to use *who* and *whom,* how to handle double negatives, and how to distinguish between possessive pronouns and other words that are similar.

Lesson 17, the last lesson in this unit, covers correct usage of **adjectives** and **adverbs.** This lesson will show you how to distinguish between confusing adjectives and adverbs. Also, you will learn how to use adjectives and adverbs to make comparisons.

By studying the rules and examples in this unit, your understanding of grammar and usage will be greatly improved.

verb tense
a time frame that is expressed by the verb form

noun
a word that names a person, place, thing, or quality

pronoun
a word that takes the place of a noun

antecedent
the particular noun or group of words to which a pronoun refers

adjective
a word that describes or modifies a noun or a pronoun

adverb
a word that describes or modifies an action verb, an adjective, or another adverb

SEE ALSO: Steck-Vaughn Writing Skills Exercise Book, Unit 2: Usage.

Lesson 10

Parts of Speech

There are eight parts of speech in the English language: nouns, pronouns, verbs, adjectives, adverbs, prepositions, conjunctions, and interjections. Each part of speech has a separate function.

Read the paragraphs. Try to identify the different parts of speech.

(1) My family is very active. (2) Darlene, my daughter, plays baseball in the park. (3) Horace, Randall, and Jenny are great swimmers. (4) Horace, my oldest son, is a member of the all-state swimming team. (5) Randall is an equally strong swimmer, but he doesn't swim competitively. (6) Even my father still plays tennis once or twice a week.

(7) In fact, I am the only nonathlete in the family. (8) Am I unhappy about this? (9) Does it bother me to be unathletic in such an athletic family? (10) It doesn't bother me in the least. (11) There is enough activity in the family without me. (12) For me, the recliner in the living room is a very comfortable place. (13) I recline happily while my energetic children exercise. (14) Wow! I think it's time for my favorite television program.

Nouns

Nouns name people, places, things, or ideas. Concrete nouns name objects that can be perceived by the senses (*wall, house, teacher*). Abstract nouns name feelings or ideas (*freedom, justice, happiness*).

Rule: A noun can be the subject of a sentence, the object of a verb, the object of a preposition, or the modifier of another noun.

Example: (Sentence 2) Darlene, my daughter, plays baseball in the park.

There are four nouns in the sentence. Darlene is the subject, the doer of the action. Daughter is a noun modifying the noun Darlene as part of the appositive phrase my daughter. Baseball is a direct object; it receives the action of the verb plays. Park is the object of the preposition in.

 tip   **Certain words can be used as more than one part of speech. For example: Voting is an important responsibility. (noun)**
I stepped into the voting booth. (adjective)
Marcia is voting today. (verb)

Rule:	A sentence can have a compound subject made up of several nouns. Two nouns forming a compound subject are linked by a conjunction; three or more nouns are separated by commas.
Example:	(Sentence 3) Horace, Randall, and Jenny are great swimmers. The three nouns forming the compound subject are <u>Horace</u>, <u>Randall</u>, and <u>Jenny</u>.

Rule:	A noun can also function as an appositive. When a noun functions as an appositive it modifies another noun. Set off the appositive word or phrase with commas.
Example:	(Sentence 4) Horace, my oldest son, is a member of the all-state swimming team.

▤Pronouns

A pronoun refers to or takes the place of a noun or nouns. Like nouns, pronouns can be used as subjects or objects. Using pronouns makes writing less repetitious by avoiding the need to repeat a specific noun.

Rule:	Use a pronoun in a sentence to substitute for a noun that has already been named.
Example:	(Sentence 5) Randall is an equally strong swimmer, but he doesn't swim competitively. The pronoun <u>he</u> has been substituted for the noun <u>Randall</u>.

For more discussion of pronoun use, see lessons 14, 15, and 16.

▤Verbs

Every sentence must have a verb. A verb is the word or group of words that expresses the action or state of being in the sentence.

Rule:	An action verb expresses the action of the subject.
Example:	(Sentence 6) Even my father still <u>plays</u> tennis once or twice a week.

Rule:	A linking verb expresses a state or condition by linking the subject to words that describe the subject. Common linking verbs include the forms of *be* and verbs such as *seem, become,* and *appear.*
Example:	(Sentence 7) In fact, I am the only nonathlete in the family. The verb <u>am</u> links the subject <u>I</u> to words that describe the subject.

Prepositions

A preposition shows direction or location. Common prepositions are *with, under, for, in,* and *between.* A prepositional phrase is a group of words that starts with a preposition, includes a noun—the object of the preposition—and any words modifying the noun.

Rule: Prepositional phrases may separate the subject and the verb in a sentence.

Example: (Sentence 12) For me, the recliner in the living room is a very comfortable place.

The prepositional phrase <u>in the living room</u> separates the subject <u>recliner</u> from the verb <u>is</u>; <u>living room</u> is the object of the preposition <u>in</u>.

Adjectives and Adverbs

Adjectives modify or describe nouns. Adverbs modify verbs, adjectives, or other adverbs.

Rule: Modifiers are generally placed near the words they modify.

Example: (Sentence 13) I recline happily while my energetic children exercise.

In this sentence the adverb <u>happily</u> modifies the verb <u>recline</u>. The adjective <u>energetic</u> modifies the noun <u>children</u>.

For more discussion of adjectives and adverbs, see lesson 17.

Conjunctions

Conjunctions show connections between two words or groups of words. The most common conjunctions are *and, or,* and *but.*

Example: (Sentence 3) Horace, Randall, <u>and</u> Jenny are great swimmers.

For more discussion of conjunction use, see lessons 19 and 20.

Interjections

Interjections such as *wow, oh no, my goodness,* and *alas* display extreme emotion or excitement. They are usually followed by an exclamation mark.

Example: (Sentence 14) Wow! I think it's time for my favorite television program.

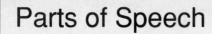

Items 1 to 5 refer to the following paragraph. Choose the <u>best answer</u> to each item.

(1) Athletes do deserve to be paid millions of dollars a year for playing professional sports? (2) I certainly don't think so. (3) Health and safety workers real role models don't earn nearly enough money. (4) Firefighters, police officers, ambulance drivers, and nurses more deserving of large salaries than athletes. (5) A baseball player doesn't save anyone's life when a baseball player hits a home run or steals second base. (6) There should be a limit to how much money athletes receive.

1. Sentence 1: **Athletes do deserve to be paid millions of dollars a year for playing professional sports?**

   Which of the following is the best way to write the underlined portion of this sentence? If you think the original is the best way, choose option (1).

   (1) Athletes do deserve to
   (2) Athletes do deserve two
   (3) Athlete's do deserve to
   (4) Athletes, do deserve to
   (5) Do athletes deserve to

2. Sentence 3: **Health and safety workers real role models don't earn nearly enough money.**

   What correction should be made to this sentence?

   (1) change <u>safety</u> to <u>Safety</u>
   (2) insert a comma after <u>workers</u>
   (3) insert commas after <u>workers</u> and <u>models</u>
   (4) change the spelling of <u>nearly</u> to <u>nearrly</u>
   (5) no correction is necessary

3. Sentence 4: **Firefighters, police officers, ambulance drivers, and nurses more deserving of large salaries than athletes.**

   Which of the following is the best way to write the underlined portion of this sentence? If you think the original is the best way, choose option (1).

   (1) Firefighters, police officers, ambulance drivers, and nurses more
   (2) Firefighters, police officers, ambulance drivers, and nurses, more
   (3) Firefighters, police officers, ambulance drivers, and nurses are more
   (4) Firefighters, police officers, ambulance drivers, and nurses, are more
   (5) Firefighters, Police Officers, Ambulance Drivers, and Nurses are more

4. Sentence 5: **A baseball player doesn't save anyone's life when a baseball player hits a home run or steals second base.**

   What correction should be made to this sentence?

   (1) change <u>doesn't</u> to <u>does'nt</u>
   (2) insert a comma before <u>doesn't</u>
   (3) replace the second <u>a baseball player</u> with <u>he</u>
   (4) change <u>home run</u> to <u>Home Run</u>
   (5) no correction is necessary

5. Sentence 6: **There should be a limit to how much money athletes receive.**

   Which of the following is the best way to write the underlined portion of this sentence? If you think the original is the best way, choose option (1).

   (1) There should be a limit
   (2) Their should be a limit
   (3) They're should be a limit
   (4) There a limit should be
   (5) Their a limit should be

Answers are on page 277.

Choose the best answer to each item.

Items 1 to 5 refer to the following paragraph.

(1) The Sahara the best-known desert on the planet. (2) This desert covers some 80,000 square kilometers of North and West Africa enormous. (3) For many people, inspires visions of a wasteland filled with towering sand dunes. (4) The temperature is extreme; the temperature can reach over 120 degrees in the shade. (5) Even so, a visitor may be surprised by the great variety of plants' and animals in the Sahara. (6) The Sahara wasn't always such a harsh environment; severe climate changes thousands of years ago turned the area into a desert. (7) The process of desertification is ongoing; the Sahara continues to grow larger every year.

1. Sentence 1: **The Sahara the best-known desert on the planet.**

   What correction should be made to this sentence?

   (1) change the period to an exclamation mark.
   (2) change Sahara to sahara
   (3) insert is after Sahara
   (4) insert a semicolon after Sahara
   (5) no correction is necessary

2. Sentence 2: **This desert covers some 80,000 square kilometers of North and West Africa enormous.**

   What correction should be made to this sentence?

   (1) insert a comma after desert
   (2) change North and West to north and west
   (3) move enormous after This
   (4) change kilometers to kilometer's
   (5) no correction is necessary

3. Sentence 3: **For many people, inspires visions of a wasteland filled with towering sand dunes.**

   What correction should be made to this sentence?

   (1) change for to four
   (2) insert the desert before inspires
   (3) remove the comma after people
   (4) change the period to a question mark
   (5) no correction is necessary

4. Sentence 4: **The temperature is extreme; the temperature can reach over 120 degrees in the shade.**

   What correction should be made to this sentence?

   (1) replace is with very
   (2) change the semicolon to a comma
   (3) replace the second the temperature with it
   (4) insert a comma after degrees
   (5) no correction is necessary

5. Sentence 5: **Even so, a visitor may be surprised by the great variety of plants' and animals in the Sahara.**

   What correction should be made to this sentence?

   (1) replace great with grate
   (2) remove surprised
   (3) change the spelling of variety to vareity
   (4) change plants' to plants
   (5) no correction is necessary

Items 6 to 11 refer to the following paragraph.

(1) There few tasks are more complicated than trying to decide which life insurance policy to buy. (2) Although some people compare the process to choosing a new car, there are only about a dozen companies selling cars in this country. (3) By comparison, over sell two thousand companies life insurance. (4) Whole life, term life and universal life are just three of the products these companies offer. (5) The main purpose of life insurance to provide security if a family loses its source of income due to a family member's death. (6) How people can decide which product will best protect them if tragedy occurs? (7) They should pick up a consumer guide to life insurance and learn about themselves with the types of products available.

6. Sentence 1: **There few tasks are more complicated than trying to decide which life insurance policy to buy.**

   What correction should be made to this sentence?

   (1) move are after There
   (2) remove are
   (3) change the spelling of decide to deside
   (4) change which to witch
   (5) no correction is necessary

7. Sentence 2: **Although some people compare the process to choosing a new car, there are only about a dozen companies selling cars in this country.**

   What correction should be made to this sentence?

   (1) remove the comma after car
   (2) change the spelling of choosing to chooseing
   (3) change there to they're
   (4) change cars to car's
   (5) no correction is necessary

8. Sentence 3: **By comparison, over sell two thousand companies life insurance.**

   What correction should be made to this sentence?

   (1) remove the comma after comparison
   (2) move sell after companies
   (3) change two to too
   (4) change companies to companies'
   (5) no correction is necessary

9. Sentence 4: **Whole life, term life and universal life are just three of the products these companies offer.**

   What correction should be made to this sentence?

   (1) remove the comma after Whole life
   (2) insert a comma after term life
   (3) remove are
   (4) change the spelling of offer to ofer
   (5) no correction is necessary

10. Sentence 5: **The main purpose of life insurance to provide security if a family loses its source of income due to a family member's death.**

    What correction should be made to this sentence?

    (1) insert is after insurance
    (2) insert a semicolon after insurance
    (3) change its to it's
    (4) change member's to members
    (5) no correction is necessary

11. Sentence 6: **How people can decide which product will best protect them if tragedy occurs?**

    What correction should be made to this sentence?

    (1) move can after How
    (2) move can decide after How
    (3) replace them with people
    (4) change the question mark to an exclamation mark
    (5) no correction is necessary

Answers are on page 278.

Lesson 11

Subject-Verb Agreement

Subject-verb agreement means that the two parts of a sentence—the subject and the verb—match or agree.

Read the company bulletin. Notice how the subjects and verbs agree in each sentence.

(1) Once again, Ms. Lopez is busy planning the annual company party. (2) The Garrisons have offered the use of their home for the event. (3) There is a map on the bulletin board showing the way to their house. (4) If you have any questions, Pauline and Ray know what activities are planned. (5) The tug-of-war should certainly be more fun this year since neither the shipping clerks nor Mr. Paulson is planning to attend. (6) The budget committee has finally reached a decision about bringing spouses and children. (7) Everyone is welcome!

To make a subject and verb agree, decide whether the subject is singular or plural, then make the verb form match the subject.

> **tip**
>
> Most verb forms ending in *s* are singular: *she walks, he sings.* Most verb forms not ending in *s* are plural: *we were, they have.* Verbs following the pronouns *I* and singular *you* are exceptions: *I am, I walk, you are, you sing.*

Rule: A singular subject (one person or thing) takes a singular verb. Many singular verb forms end in *-s: talks, is, was, has.*

Example: (Sentence 1) Once again, Ms. Lopez is busy planning the annual company party.
The singular subject, Ms. Lopez, requires a singular verb form. The word is is a singular form of the verb be.

Rule: A plural subject (more than one person or thing) takes a plural verb. Plural forms of some commonly used verbs are *have, were,* and *are.* The plural forms of verbs do not end in *-s.*

Example: (Sentence 2) The Garrisons have offered the use of their home for the event.
The subject in this sentence, Garrisons, refers to more than one person. The plural verb have offered agrees with the plural subject.

Rule: When a sentence starts with *here* or *there,* the subject usually comes after the verb. The subject and verb must still agree.

Example: (Sentence 3) There is a map on the bulletin board showing the way to their house.
The subject of this sentence is map. Since map is singular, the verb is is correct.

Compound subjects can cause confusion in determining subject-verb agreement. Study the following rules to avoid errors.

Rule: Most compound subjects joined by *and* take a plural verb.

Example: (Sentence 4) If you have any questions, Pauline and Ray know what activities are planned.

The subject <u>Pauline and Ray</u> refers to two people. The plural verb form <u>know</u> agrees with the subject.

Rule: When a singular subject and a plural subject are joined by *or, either-or, neither-nor,* or *not only–but also,* the verb agrees with the nearest subject.

Example: (Sentence 5) The tug-of-war should certainly be more fun this year since <u>neither the shipping clerks nor Mr. Paulson</u> is planning to attend.

The subject in the second part of the sentence is made up of two parts joined by <u>neither-nor</u>. The first part, <u>the shipping clerks</u>, is plural; the second part, <u>Mr. Paulson</u>, is singular. The singular verb <u>is</u> is closest to the second part and so agrees with <u>Mr. Paulson</u>.

Rule: A word that refers to a group of people is usually considered singular.

Example: (Sentence 6) The budget committee has finally reached a decision about bringing spouses and children.

Although a <u>committee</u> is made up of more than one person, there is only one committee. The singular verb <u>has reached</u> agrees with the singular subject <u>committee</u>.

Rule: Some pronouns may not seem clearly singular or plural. The following list will help you in determining subject-verb agreement.

Always Singular			Always Plural	Either Singular or Plural	
one	either	anything	several	all	any
each	neither	everything	few	some	part
much	anybody	something	both	none	half
other	everybody	nothing	many	most	
another	somebody	someone			
anyone	nobody				
everyone	no one				

Example: (Sentence 7) Everyone is welcome!
The singular verb form <u>is</u> agrees with the singular pronoun <u>everyone</u>.

Items 1 to 7 refer to the following paragraph. Choose the best answer to each item.

(1) Vince hope to sign a contract with a major league baseball team. (2) The Firebirds have offered him a tryout during spring training. (3) There are a good opportunity for a spot on the team as a relief pitcher. (4) Vince and his two friends, Raul and Al, plays sandlot ball. (5) Neither Vince nor his friends have any professional experience. (6) However, the team are very positive about Vince. (7) With work, someone with his talent are bound to succeed.

1. Sentence 1: **Vince hope to sign a contract with a major league baseball team.**

   What correction should be made to this sentence?

   (1) change Vince to Vince's
   (2) change hope to hopes
   (3) change sign to signs
   (4) change baseball to Baseball
   (5) no correction is necessary

2. Sentence 2: **The Firebirds have offered him a tryout during spring training.**

   What correction should be made to this sentence?

   (1) change Firebirds to Firebird
   (2) change have to has
   (3) change offered to offers
   (4) change spring to Spring
   (5) no correction is necessary

3. Sentence 3: **There are a good opportunity for a spot on the team as a relief pitcher.**

   What correction should be made to this sentence?

   (1) change are to is
   (2) change are to be
   (3) change are to were
   (4) change the spelling of opportunity to oportunity
   (5) no correction is necessary

4. Sentence 4: **Vince and his two friends, Raul and Al, plays sandlot ball.**

   What correction should be made to this sentence?

   (1) change two to too
   (2) remove the comma after Al
   (3) change plays to play
   (4) change sandlot to Sandlot
   (5) no correction is necessary

5. Sentence 5: **Neither Vince nor his friends have any professional experience.**

   What correction should be made to this sentence?

   (1) change Vince to vince
   (2) change nor to or
   (3) change have to has
   (4) change friends to friend's
   (5) no correction is necessary

6. Sentence 6: **However, the team are very positive about Vince.**

   What correction should be made to this sentence?

   (1) change team to Team
   (2) change team to team's
   (3) change are to were
   (4) change are to is
   (5) no correction is necessary

7. Sentence 7: **With work, someone with his talent are bound to succeed.**

   What correction should be made to this sentence?

   (1) change are to is
   (2) change are to were
   (3) change are to be
   (4) change bound to bounds
   (5) no correction is necessary

Items 8 to 14 refer to the following paragraph.

(1) Anna want to go to a movie with Mike and Sonia Hahn. (2) The Hahns has decided against going to a movie for the fourth weekend in a row. (3) There is many other things to do besides watching a movie. (4) Jim, Anna's husband, do not want to go to a movie either. (5) He prefers to go bowling in his spare time. (6) Jim pursuades Anna to compromise. (7) If Anna go bowling this weekend, Jim will go to the movies next weekend.

8. Sentence 1: **Anna want to go to a movie with Mike and Sonia Hahn.**

    What correction should be made to this sentence?

    (1) change want to wants
    (2) change want to want's
    (3) insert a comma after movie
    (4) change movie to Movie
    (5) no correction is necessary

9. Sentence 2: **The Hahns has decided against going to a movie for the fourth weekend in a row.**

    What correction should be made to this sentence?

    (1) change Hahns to Hahn's
    (2) change has to have
    (3) change the spelling of against to aganst
    (4) change fourth to forth
    (5) no correction is necessary

10. Sentence 3: **There is many other things to do besides watching a movie.**

    What correction should be made to this sentence?

    (1) change There to They're
    (2) change There to Their
    (3) change is to are
    (4) change is to be
    (5) no correction is necessary

11. Sentence 4: **Jim, Anna's husband, do not want to go to a movie either.**

    What correction should be made to this sentence?

    (1) remove the comma after Jim
    (2) change husband to Husband
    (3) remove the comma after husband
    (4) change do to does
    (5) no correction is necessary

12. Sentence 5: **He prefers to go bowling in his spare time.**

    What correction should be made to this sentence?

    (1) change prefers to prefer
    (2) change go to goes
    (3) change go to went
    (4) insert a comma after bowling
    (5) no correction is necessary

13. Sentence 6: **Jim pursuades Anna to compromise.**

    What correction should be made to this sentence?

    (1) change pursuades to pursuade
    (2) change the spelling of pursuades to persuades
    (3) change the spelling of pursuades to purswades
    (4) change the period to an exclamation mark
    (5) no correction is necessary

14. Sentence 7: **If Anna go bowling this weekend, Jim will go to the movies next weekend.**

    What correction should be made to this sentence?

    (1) change the first go to goes
    (2) remove the comma after weekend
    (3) change the comma to a semicolon
    (4) change the second go to goes
    (5) no correction is necessary

Items 15 to 19 refer to the following paragraph.

(1) Ms. Boles, the warehouse manager, are organizing the holiday schedule. (2) She decides that a Veterans Day holiday and a two-day Thanksgiving holiday is too many days off in November. (3) The union at the warehouse disagree with her decision to cancel the Veterans Day holiday. (4) Ms. Cervantes and Mr. Murray points out that the company always has had the three days off in November. (5) Neither Ms. Boles nor the workers is willing to discuss the issue.

15. Sentence 1: **Ms. Boles, the warehouse manager, are organizing the holiday schedule.**

    What correction should be made to this sentence?

    (1) remove the comma after Boles
    (2) change Ms. Boles to Ms. boles
    (3) change manager to Manager
    (4) change are to is
    (5) no correction is necessary

16. Sentence 2: **She decides that a Veterans Day holiday and a two-day Thanksgiving holiday is too many days off in November.**

    What correction should be made to this sentence?

    (1) change decides to decide
    (2) change Day to day
    (3) change holiday to Holiday
    (4) change is to are
    (5) no correction is necessary

17. Sentence 3: **The union at the warehouse disagree with her decision to cancel the Veterans Day holiday.**

    What correction should be made to this sentence?

    (1) change union to Union
    (2) change disagree to disagrees
    (3) insert a comma after decision
    (4) change holiday to holidays
    (5) no correction is necessary

18. Sentence 4: **Ms. Cervantes and Mr. Murray points out that the company always has had the three days off in November.**

    What correction should be made to this sentence?

    (1) change points to point
    (2) insert a comma after out
    (3) change has to have
    (4) change days to day's
    (5) no correction is necessary

19. Sentence 5: **Neither Ms. Boles nor the workers is willing to discuss the issue.**

    What correction should be made to this sentence?

    (1) change the spelling of neither to niether
    (2) change workers to Workers
    (3) change is to are
    (4) change is to was
    (5) no correction is necessary

tip To check subject-verb agreement in a sentence with a prepositional phrase between the subject and verb, read the sentence without the prepositional phrase. For example, *The shed next to the apartments (is) (are) painted red.* Read the sentence without the prepositional phrase. *The shed (is) (are) painted red.* Now it's easy to see that the subject *shed* requires the singular verb *is*.

Answers are on page 279.

Unit 2: Usage

Directions: Choose the best answer to each item.

Items 1 to 5 refer to the following paragraph.

(1) Levi and his partners is trying to decide the best way to advertise their new company. (2) Evie and John feels they should put all of the money into billboard publicity. (3) Corey thinks advertising in the Yellow Pages is more effective. (4) Also, Corey and Levi believes that a combination of strategies is the best idea. (5) Neither Levi nor his partners wants to waste any money. (6) Everyone agrees to hire a consultant for advice. (7) Several have already been interviewed; Levi is making the decision about which consultant to hire. (8) He hopes the consultant will be able to come up with an efficient plan for the advertising budget.

1. Sentence 1: **Levi and his partners is trying to decide the best way to advertise their new company.**

   What correction should be made to this sentence?

   (1) change partners to Partners
   (2) change is to are
   (3) change the spelling of advertise to advertize
   (4) change their to there
   (5) no correction is necessary

2. Sentence 2: **Evie and John feels they should put all of the money into billboard publicity.**

   What correction should be made to this sentence?

   (1) change feels to feel
   (2) insert a comma after feels
   (3) change money to Money
   (4) insert a comma after money
   (5) no correction is necessary

3. Sentence 4: **Also, Corey and Levi believes that a combination of strategies is the best idea.**

   What correction should be made to this sentence?

   (1) change Also to also
   (2) change believes to believe
   (3) insert a comma after believes
   (4) change is to are
   (5) no correction is necessary

4. Sentence 5: **Neither Levi nor his partners wants to waste any money.**

   What correction should be made to this sentence?

   (1) change nor to or
   (2) change partners to partner
   (3) change wants to want
   (4) change waste to waist
   (5) no correction is necessary

5. Sentence 7: **Several have already been interviewed; Levi is making the decision about which consultant to hire.**

   What correction should be made to this sentence?

   (1) change have to has
   (2) change the spelling of interviewed to interveiwed
   (3) replace the semicolon with a comma
   (4) replace is with are
   (5) no correction is necessary

Answers are on page 280.

Lesson 12

Irregular Verbs

Every verb has three principal parts: present, past, and past participle. An irregular verb usually changes its spelling to make the past and past participle forms.

Read the paragraph. Notice how verbs are used.

(1) In the past decade, the recycling business has grown into a multimillion-dollar industry. (2) Scientists have known for some time that we face a tremendous waste disposal problem. (3) In addition, the amount of garbage produced by the average American has risen sharply. (4) In the past, corporations often shrank from their responsibilities in waste management. (5) They gave us plastic containers and packing materials despite the growing threat to the environment. (6) They chose to ignore the problem before; now they must look for solutions.

With regular verbs, the past and past participle forms are made by adding *-d* or *-ed* to the present form. For example, the principal parts of the verb *ask* are *ask, asked,* and *asked.* Irregular verbs do not follow this pattern. The *to . . .* form of the verb is called the **infinitive.** The infinitive is formed by adding *to* in front of the present part of a verb.

The following rules will help you correctly use the present, past, and past participle forms of all verbs, including the irregular ones.

Rule: The past participle form always uses a helping verb, such as *has, have, had, is, are, was,* or *were.*

Study these sentences. The past participle form is underlined once. The helping verb in each case is underlined twice.

Examples: (Sentence 1) In the past decade, the recycling business <u><u>has</u></u> <u>grown</u> into a multimillion-dollar industry.
(Sentence 2) Scientists <u><u>have</u></u> <u>known</u> for some time that we face a tremendous waste disposal problem.
(Sentence 3) In addition, the amount of garbage produced by the average American <u><u>has</u></u> <u>risen</u> sharply.

Rule: The past form never uses a helping verb.
Examples: (Sentence 4) In the past, corporations often <u>shrank</u> from their responsibilities in waste management.
(Sentence 5) They <u>gave</u> us plastic containers and packing materials despite the growing threat to the environment.
(Sentence 6) They <u>chose</u> to ignore the problem before; now they must look for solutions.

Some irregular verbs can be grouped according to the patterns by which they change. Study the verbs in the charts below. Notice how -n or -en is added to the past form to make the past participle. (When the past form ends in a consonant, as in *bit,* the consonant is doubled before -en is added.)

Present	Past	Past Participle
break	broke	broken
bite	bit	bitten
choose	chose	chosen
freeze	froze	frozen

Present	Past	Past Participle
speak	spoke	spoken
steal	stole	stolen
swear	swore	sworn
wear	wore	worn

Here is another group of irregular verbs. Notice how the middle vowel changes from *i* in the present form to *a* in the past and to *u* in the past participle.

Present	Past	Past Participle
begin	began	begun
drink	drank	drunk
ring	rang	rung

Present	Past	Past Participle
sing	sang	sung
sink	sank	sunk
swim	swam	swum

In the irregular verbs that follow, notice how the vowels change to make the past form. To make the past participle, -n or -en is added to the present form. (In some verbs, such as *ridden* and *written,* the last consonant must be doubled in forming the past participle.)

Present	Past	Past Participle
blow	blew	blown
drive	drove	driven
eat	ate	eaten
give	gave	given
grow	grew	grown
know	knew	known

Present	Past	Past Participle
ride	rode	ridden
rise	rose	risen
see	saw	seen
shake	shook	shaken
take	took	taken
write	wrote	written

The irregular verbs in this chart do not follow a pattern.

Present	Past	Past Participle
come	came	come
run	ran	run
go	went	gone
make	made	made

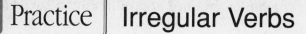

Items 1 to 6 refer to the following paragraph. Choose the best answer to each item.

(1) Hiroko was shaked to see the empty office building. (2) She could have swear the receptionist told her the appointment was at 9 A.M. (3) Perhaps she had wrote down the wrong address. (4) Hiroko went around to the back door of the building. (5) There she sawed a sign with the company's new address. (6) Quickly, she drived to the new location.

1. Sentence 1: **Hiroko was shaked to see the empty office building.**

   What correction should be made to this sentence?

   (1) change was to were
   (2) change shaked to shooked
   (3) change shaked to shaken
   (4) change shaked to shakes
   (5) no correction is necessary

2. Sentence 2: **She could have swear the receptionist told her the appointment was at 9 A.M.**

   What correction should be made to this sentence?

   (1) change swear to sweared
   (2) change swear to sworn
   (3) change swear to swored
   (4) change was to were
   (5) no correction is necessary

3. Sentence 3: **Perhaps she had wrote down the wrong address.**

   What correction should be made to this sentence?

   (1) change wrote to write
   (2) change wrote to wroted
   (3) change wrote to written
   (4) change the spelling of address to adress
   (5) no correction is necessary

4. Sentence 4: **Hiroko went around to the back door of the building.**

   What correction should be made to this sentence?

   (1) change went to gone
   (2) change went to had went
   (3) change went to go
   (4) change building to Building
   (5) no correction is necessary

5. Sentence 5: **There she sawed a sign with the company's new address.**

   What correction should be made to this sentence?

   (1) change There to Their
   (2) change sawed to seen
   (3) change sawed to see
   (4) change sawed to saw
   (5) no correction is necessary

6. Sentence 6: **Quickly, she drived to the new location.**

   What correction should be made to this sentence?

   (1) change drived to drove
   (2) change drived to driven
   (3) change drived to droved
   (4) insert a comma after drived
   (5) no correction is necessary

Items 7 to 13 refer to the following paragraph.

(1) Ava knowed she would be ready for the triathlon in the spring. (2) Every morning, she eaten breakfast at 6 o'clock to start her training. (3) For comfort, Ava weared loose-fitting jogging clothes. (4) She drive to the beach about five miles away. (5) There she run for one hour. (6) For the next hour she swum. (7) To finish her training, she rode her bike the length of the beach.

7. Sentence 1: **Ava knowed she would be ready for the triathlon in the spring.**

What correction should be made to this sentence?

(1) change knowed to knew
(2) change knowed to known
(3) change for to four
(4) change spring to Spring
(5) no correction is necessary

8. Sentence 2: **Every morning, she eaten breakfast at 6 o'clock to start her training.**

What correction should be made to this sentence?

(1) change eaten to eat
(2) change eaten to ate
(3) change eaten to eats
(4) change eaten to eated
(5) no correction is necessary

9. Sentence 3: **For comfort, Ava weared loose-fitting jogging clothes.**

What correction should be made to this sentence?

(1) change weared to wear
(2) change weared to wore
(3) insert had before weared
(4) change jogging to Jogging
(5) no correction is necessary

10. Sentence 4: **She drive to the beach about five miles away.**

What correction should be made to this sentence?

(1) change drive to drived
(2) change drive to drove
(3) change drive to driven
(4) insert had before drive
(5) no correction is necessary

11. Sentence 5: **There she run for one hour.**

What correction should be made to this sentence?

(1) change There to Their
(2) change There to They're
(3) change run to runned
(4) change run to ran
(5) no correction is necessary

12. Sentence 6: **For the next hour she swum.**

What correction should be made to this sentence?

(1) change swum to swimmed
(2) change swum to swims
(3) change swum to swam
(4) insert was before swum
(5) no correction is necessary

13. Sentence 7: **To finish her training, she rode her bike the length of the beach.**

What correction should be made to this sentence?

(1) change rode to ride
(2) change rode to rided
(3) change rode to ridden
(4) change rode to had ridden
(5) no correction is necessary

Items 14 to 20 refer to the following paragraph.

(1) Sean had never been knew for his green thumb. (2) The plant the office staff had gave him for his birthday was clearly dying. (3) It had not grew much in the past year. (4) On one occasion, a breeze from the air conditioner blown off most of its leaves. (5) Gradually, opening and closing the door had shook off its remaining leaves. (6) Sean once heard that plants like music. (7) So he begun singing to the plant during his breaks. (8) Sean says the plant will be looking healthier already.

14. Sentence 1: **Sean had never been knew for his green thumb.**

   What correction should be made to this sentence?

   (1) change knew to knewn
   (2) change knew to known
   (3) change knew to knowed
   (4) change knew to knows
   (5) no correction is necessary

15. Sentence 2: **The plant the office staff had gave him for his birthday was clearly dying.**

   What correction should be made to this sentence?

   (1) change gave to gaved
   (2) change gave to given
   (3) change birthday to Birthday
   (4) change was to were
   (5) no correction is necessary

16. Sentence 3: **It had not grew much in the past year.**

   What correction should be made to this sentence?

   (1) change grew to grown
   (2) change grew to growed
   (3) change grew to grow
   (4) change past to passed
   (5) no correction is necessary

17. Sentence 4: **On one occasion, a breeze from the air conditioner blown off most of its leaves.**

   What correction should be made to this sentence?

   (1) change the spelling of occasion to occassion
   (2) change blown to blowed
   (3) change blown to blew
   (4) change blown to was blew
   (5) no correction is necessary

18. Sentence 5: **Gradually, opening and closing the door had shook off its remaining leaves.**

   What correction should be made to this sentence?

   (1) change shook to shaken
   (2) change shook to shaked
   (3) change its to it's
   (4) change its to its'
   (5) no correction is necessary

19. Sentence 6: **Sean once heard that plants like music.**

   What correction should be made to this sentence?

   (1) change heard to hear
   (2) change heard to heared
   (3) change like to likes
   (4) change like to liked
   (5) no correction is necessary

20. Sentence 7: **So he begun singing to the plant during his breaks.**

   What correction should be made to this sentence?

   (1) change begun to beginned
   (2) change begun to began
   (3) change singing to sanging
   (4) change his to his'
   (5) no correction is necessary

Answers are on page 281.

Unit 2: Usage

Directions: Choose the best answer to each question.

Items 1 to 5 refer to the following paragraph.

(1) Consumers have know for many years that growers treat produce with pesticides. (2) Recently, the public has began to express deep concern. (3) Nationally, consumers grown angry about the use of Alar, a chemical with which apples and grapes are treated to make them larger and more colorful. (4) The problem is that consumers have choose produce that looks appealing. (5) So produce growers continue to use chemicals in order to sell more fruits and vegetables. (6) The Alar scandal may have drove some consumers away from conventional supermarkets; many people are shopping for produce at organic groceries and farmer's markets. (7) As consumer demand for pesticide-free produce increases, more produce growers may focus their attention on organic growing methods.

1. Sentence 1: **Consumers have know for many years that growers treat produce with pesticides.**

   What correction should be made to this sentence?

   (1) change have to has
   (2) change have to had
   (3) change know to known
   (4) change know to knew
   (5) no correction is necessary

2. Sentence 2: **Recently, the public has began to express deep concern.**

   What correction should be made to this sentence?

   (1) change has to were
   (2) change began to begin
   (3) change began to beginned
   (4) change began to begun
   (5) no correction is necessary

3. Sentence 3: **Nationally, consumers grown angry about the use of Alar, a chemical with which apples and grapes are treated to make them larger and more colorful.**

   What correction should be made to this sentence?

   (1) insert have before grown
   (2) change grown to grewed
   (3) change grown to grows
   (4) change grown to grews
   (5) no correction is necessary

4. Sentence 4: **The problem is that consumers have choose produce that looks appealing.**

   What correction should be made to this sentence?

   (1) change is to are
   (2) change choose to choosed
   (3) take out have
   (4) change looks to look
   (5) no correction is necessary

5. Sentence 6: **The Alar scandal may have drove some consumers away from conventional supermarkets; many people are shopping for produce at organic groceries and farmer's markets.**

   What correction should be made to this sentence?

   (1) change drove to driven
   (2) change drove to drive
   (3) replace the semicolon with a comma
   (4) insert a comma after groceries
   (5) no correction is necessary

Answers are on page 282.

Verb Tenses

The *tense* of a verb tells when an action takes place or when a condition is true.

Read the memorandum.

> Date: February 15
> To: Sofia Oveson
> From: Susan Epstein
> Re: Job Openings
>
>   (1) Mr. Minjarez recommends Paula Hardy for the opening in Inventory Control. (2) Mr. Minjarez worked with Paula on the Raskin project last year. (3) Paula will need to bring her résumé to the company office by Thursday. (4) I have passed along the rest of her application materials to Ms. Randolph.
>   (5) Previously, Ms. Randolph had refused to consider applicants without bookkeeping experience. (6) However, Paula will have completed a class in bookkeeping by the end of the month.
>   (7) I wish Michael Rodriguez were available for the job. (8) We are planning to open another position in the Personnel Department in March. (9) The previous employee was transferred to Purchasing last week. (10) It is essential that the job be filled by someone with Michael's experience.

Rule: The present tense expresses that an action takes place now or that a condition is true now. The present tense of any action verb is the same as the verb's present form.

	I work.		We work.
Singular	You work.	**Plural**	You work.
	He, she, or it works.		They work.

Example: (Sentence 1) Mr. Minjarez recommends Paula Hardy for the opening in Inventory Control.
The present-tense verb <u>recommends</u> indicates that the action of this sentence takes place now.

Rule: The past tense expresses that an action took place or that a condition was true in the past. The past tense of a regular verb is formed by adding *-ed* or *-d* to the verb's present form.

	I worked.		We worked.
Singular	You worked.	**Plural**	You worked.
	He, she, or it worked.		They worked.

Example: (Sentence 2) Mr. Minjarez worked with Paula on the Raskin project last year.
The past-tense verb <u>worked</u> indicates that this action happened in the past.

Rule: The future tense expresses that an action will take place or that a condition will be true in the future. The future tense of any verb is formed by writing *shall* or *will* before the verb's present form.

| **Singular** | I shall/will work. You shall/will work. He, she, or it shall/ will work. | **Plural** | We shall/will work. You shall/will work. They shall/will work. |

Example: (Sentence 3) Paula will need to bring her résumé to the company office by Thursday.
The future-tense verb <u>will need</u> indicates that this action will take place in the future.

Rule: The present perfect tense expresses that an action has been completed or that a condition was true at some indefinite time in the past. The present perfect tense of a verb is formed using the helping verbs *have* or *has* with the verb's past participle.

| **Singular** | I have worked. You have worked. He, she, or it has worked. | **Plural** | We have worked. You have worked. They have worked. |

Example: (Sentence 4) I have passed along the rest of her application materials to Ms. Randolph.
The verb <u>have passed</u> is in present perfect tense. It expresses that the action (passing along materials) was completed at some indefinite time in the past.

Rule: The past perfect tense expresses that an action began and ended before another past action began. The past perfect tense of a verb is formed using the helping verb *had* with the verb's past participle.

| **Singular** | I had worked. You had worked. He, she, or it had worked. | **Plural** | We had worked. You had worked. They had worked. |

Example: (Sentence 5) Previously, Ms. Randolph had refused to consider applicants without bookkeeping experience.
The verb <u>had refused</u> is in past perfect tense. It expresses that the action (refusing to consider) happened in the past before the implied second action (considering applicants) took place.

Rule: The future perfect tense expresses that a future action will begin and end before another definite future action begins. The future perfect tense of a verb is formed using the helping verbs *shall have* or *will have* with the verb's past participle.

Singular
I shall have/will have worked.
You shall have/will have worked.
He, she, or it shall have/will have worked.

Plural
We shall have/will have worked.
You shall have/will have worked.
They shall have/will have worked.

Example: (Sentence 6) However, Paula will have completed a class in bookkeeping by the end of the month.
The verb <u>will have completed</u> expresses that the action of the first part of the sentence will be completed by the end of the month. Both the action and the end of the month are future events.

The Verb Be

The verb *be* is the most frequently used verb. It is an irregular verb.

Present Tense		Past Tense		Future Tense	
Singular	Plural	Singular	Plural	Singular	Plural
I <u>am</u>	we <u>are</u>	I <u>was</u>	we <u>were</u>	I <u>shall/will be</u>	we <u>shall/will be</u>
you <u>are</u>	you <u>are</u>	you <u>were</u>	you <u>were</u>	you <u>shall/will be</u>	you <u>shall/will be</u>
he, she, it <u>is</u>	they <u>are</u>	he, she, it <u>was</u>	they <u>were</u>	he, she, it <u>shall/will be</u>	they <u>shall/will be</u>

Present Perfect		Past Perfect		Future Perfect	
I		I		I	
you		you		you	
we	<u>have been</u>	he/she/it	<u>had been</u>	he/she/it	<u>shall/will/have been</u>
they		we		we	
he		you		you	
she	<u>has been</u>	they		they	
it					

Study these rules about the use of the verb *be*.

Rule: Use *were* when a sentence expresses either a wish or a thought contrary to fact.

Example: (Sentence 7) I wish Michael Rodriguez were available for the job.

Rule: Use a form of *be* and the present participle to create the progressive forms of verbs.

Example: (Sentence 8) We are planning to open another position in the Personnel Department in March.
Are planning is the present progressive form of plan.

Rule: Use a form of *be* and the past participle when a subject receives the action of the verb.

Example: (Sentence 9) The previous employee was transferred to Purchasing last week.

Rule: Use *be* with clauses beginning with *that* which come after the verb and express a request or recommendation.

Example: (Sentence 10) It is essential that the job be filled by someone with Michael's experience.

≡Troublesome Verb Pairs

Several verb pairs are commonly confused. Learn the meaning of the following verbs and their past and past participle forms.

Present	Past	Past Participle
borrow (to receive on loan)	borrowed	borrowed
lend (to loan)	lent	lent
bring (to carry to or with)	brought	brought
take (to carry away)	took	taken
lay (to place)	laid	laid
lie (to recline or to rest)	lay	lain
learn (to gain knowledge)	learned	learned
teach (to give knowledge)	taught	taught
precede (to go or come before)	preceded	preceded
proceed (to continue)	proceeded	proceeded
rise (to go up or get up)	rose	risen
raise (to lift up)	raised	raised
set (to put in place)	set	set
sit (to take a set)	sat	sat

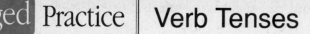

Items 1 to 5 refer to the following paragraph. Choose the best answer to each item.

(1) Rita Hauser encourages others to follow their dreams. (2) Rita begun a successful trucking business at age 52. (3) "I will drived my way to financial success," she said. (4) Indeed, Ms. Hauser have earned the admiration of her family and peers. (5) Before starting her company, she had being "only" a housewife, without even a driver's license. (6) Her decision to go into trucking was maked after careful consideration. (7) Considering Rita's positive experience, it is essential that others be given the chance to live their dreams.

1. Sentence 2: **Rita begun a successful trucking business at age 52.**

   What correction should be made to this sentence?

   (1) change begun to have begun
   (2) change begun to begins
   (3) change begun to began
   (4) change begun to beginning
   (5) no correction is necessary

2. Sentence 3: **"I will drived my way to financial success," she said.**

   What correction should be made to this sentence?

   (1) change will to shall
   (2) change drived to have drived
   (3) change drived to drive
   (4) insert a comma after way
   (5) no correction is necessary

3. Sentence 4: **Indeed, Ms. Hauser have earned the admiration of her family and peers.**

   What correction should be made to this sentence?

   (1) change Ms. to ms.
   (2) insert a comma after Hauser
   (3) change have to was
   (4) change have to has
   (5) no correction is necessary

4. Sentence 5: **Before starting her company, she had being "only" a housewife, without even a driver's license.**

   What correction should be made to this sentence?

   (1) remove the comma after company
   (2) change had to has
   (3) change being to been
   (4) change the spelling of license to lisence
   (5) no correction is necessary

5. Sentence 6: **Her decision to go into trucking was maked after careful consideration.**

   What correction should be made to this sentence?

   (1) change was to been
   (2) change maked to made
   (3) change maked to makes
   (4) change careful to carefull
   (5) no correction is necessary

Items 6 to 11 refer to the following paragraph.

(1) In past years Jim Seus trains many kinds of animals. (2) Seus recently will train Bart, a male Kodiak bear. (3) To teach Bart a trick, Seus touched the bear's foot near the ankle and says "limp." (4) Bart automatically have shifted his weight off the foot. (5) Eventually, Bart learned to shift his weight whenever he has heard the word "limp." (6) Jim Seus had learned Bart the trick.

6. Sentence 1: **In past years Jim Seus trains many kinds of animals.**

   Which of the following is the best way to write the underlined portion of this sentence? If you think the original is the best way, choose option (1).

   (1) trains
   (2) did trained
   (3) will train
   (4) is training
   (5) has trained

7. Sentence 2: **Seus recently will train Bart, a male Kodiak bear.**

   What correction should be made to this sentence?

   (1) replace will train with train
   (2) replace will train with trained
   (3) change train to trane
   (4) change male to mail
   (5) no correction is necessary

8. Sentence 3: **To teach Bart a trick, Seus touched the bear's foot near the ankle and says "limp."**

   Which of the following is the best way to write the underlined portion of this sentence? If you think the original is the best way, choose option (1).

   (1) says
   (2) will have said
   (3) sayed
   (4) said
   (5) will say

9. Sentence 4: **Bart automatically have shifted his weight off the foot.**

   Which of the following is the best way to write the underlined portion of this sentence? If you think the original is the best way, choose option (1).

   (1) have shifted
   (2) will shifted
   (3) will have shifted
   (4) shifted
   (5) is shifted

10. Sentence 5: **Eventually, Bart learned to shift his weight whenever he has heard the word "limp."**

    What correction should be made to this sentence?

    (1) remove has
    (2) replace weight with wait
    (3) replace has heard with is hearing
    (4) replace has heard with are hearing
    (5) no correction is necessary

11. Sentence 6: **Jim Seus had learned Bart the trick.**

    What correction should be made to this sentence?

    (1) change had to was
    (2) replace had with will have
    (3) change learned to taught
    (4) change learned to teaching
    (5) no correction is necessary

tip **Do not switch verb tenses unnecessarily. Use different verb tenses only to show that an action or state of being occurred in a different time frame.**

Answers are on page 283.

Directions: Choose the best answer to each item.

Items 1 to 6 refer to the following paragraph.

(1) Recently, Ms. Barlow has forgetting details about her work tasks. (2) She wishes she was more organized. (3) Ms. Barlow decide her old time-management system is not working out. (4) So she writes down everything she was needed to do during the month. (5) Then she proceeds to divide her work into daily and weekly tasks. (6) Finally, she has created a form to record her telephone messages. (7) She already feels more organized and decides she will have used this new plan next month too.

1. Sentence 1: **Recently, Ms. Barlow has forgetting details about her work tasks.**

    Which of the following is the best way to write the underlined portion of this sentence? If you think the original is the best way, choose option (1).

    (1) has forgetting
    (2) will be forgetting
    (3) has been forgetting
    (4) has forgot
    (5) had forgetting

2. Sentence 2: **She wishes she was more organized.**

    What correction should be made to this sentence?

    (1) change wishes to wish
    (2) change was to is
    (3) change was to were
    (4) change was to has been
    (5) no correction is necessary

3. Sentence 3: **Ms. Barlow decide her old time-management system is not working out.**

    What correction should be made to this sentence?

    (1) change decide to decides
    (2) change decide to will have decide
    (3) change decide to have decided
    (4) change is to are
    (5) no correction is necessary

4. Sentence 4: **So she writes down everything she was needed to do during the month.**

    What correction should be made to this sentence?

    (1) change writes to written
    (2) change writes to had wrote
    (3) change was to were
    (4) change was needed to needs
    (5) no correction is necessary

5. Sentence 5: **Then she proceeds to divide her work into daily and weekly tasks.**

    Which of the following is the best way to write the underlined portion of this sentence? If you think the original is the best way, choose option (1).

    (1) proceeds
    (2) has proceeded
    (3) procedes
    (4) will have proceeded
    (5) proceed

6. Sentence 7: **She already feels more organized and decides she will have used this new plan next month too.**

   What correction should be made to this sentence?

   (1) change feels to feeled
   (2) change will have used to will use
   (3) change month to month's
   (4) change too to to
   (5) no correction is necessary

Items 7 to 11 refer to the following paragraph.

   (1) Jim has been working in the bookstore for one month. (2) When he has completed his probation period, he will have receive a promotion with a salary increase. (3) His favorite part of the job is helped customers locate books. (4) Today he are scheduled to stock shelves and to work the cash register. (5) When his shift is over, the manager will taught him to operate the microfilm machine.

7. Sentence 1: **Jim has been working in the bookstore for one month.**

   What correction should be made to this sentence?

   (1) remove has
   (2) change working to worked
   (3) change bookstore to Bookstore
   (4) change one to won
   (5) no correction is necessary

8. Sentence 2: **When he has completed his probation period, he will have receive a promotion with a salary increase.**

   What correction should be made to this sentence?

   (1) remove has
   (2) change has completed to is completing
   (3) remove have
   (4) remove will
   (5) no correction is necessary

9. Sentence 3: **His favorite part of the job is helped customers locate books.**

   What correction should be made to this sentence?

   (1) insert a comma after job
   (2) change is to were
   (3) change helped to help
   (4) change helped to helping
   (5) no correction is necessary

10. Sentence 4: **Today he are scheduled to stock shelves and to work the cash register.**

    What correction should be made to this sentence?

    (1) change are to been
    (2) change are to were
    (3) change are to is
    (4) change work to worked
    (5) no correction is necessary

11. Sentence 5: **When his shift is over, the manager will taught him to operate the microfilm machine.**

    What correction should be made to this sentence?

    (1) change taught to learn
    (2) change taught to teach
    (3) change taught to teached
    (4) change microfilm to Microfilm
    (5) no correction is necessary

tip Use a helping verb with past and present participle forms, but never with simple past-tense forms. Note that the past and past participle forms for some irregular verbs are the same. Examples: *made, sat, laid, kept, told, read.*

Answers are on page 284.

Lesson 14

Personal Pronouns

A personal pronoun is a word that takes the place of a specific person, place, or thing. It can be used as a subject or an object or to show possession.

Read the letter and notice how pronouns are used.

> (1) I am writing about next week's election for union representative. (2) Andy Walker, who was nominated last week, invited me to help with his campaign. (3) After considering the issues listed below, we hope you will cast your vote for him. (4) Donna Fifer and I are surveying the key employee concerns in our company. (5) Consider each issue carefully and return your completed survey to her or me. (6) We need your input.
>
> (7) Mr. Walker assures you that your concerns are his. (8) You will only hurt yourself if you side with his opponents. (9) I myself plan to vote for Andy Walker.

Subject Pronouns	
Singular	Plural
I	we
you	you
she, he, it	they

Object Pronouns	
Singular	Plural
me	us
you	you
her, him, it	them

Rule: A subject pronoun is used as the subject of a sentence.
Example: (Sentence 1) I am writing about next week's election for union representative.
The pronoun I is the subject.

 tip Remember that personal pronouns never use apostrophes to show possession. Add *'s* to a subject pronoun only when forming a contraction (he is = he's). To show possession, use a possessive pronoun.

Rule:	An object pronoun is used as the object of a verb or of a preposition.
Examples:	(Sentence 2) Andy Walker, who was nominated last week, invited me to help with his campaign.
	The pronoun <u>me</u> is the object of the verb <u>invited</u>.
	(Sentence 3) After considering the issues listed below, we hope you will cast your vote for him.
	The pronoun <u>him</u> is the object of the preposition <u>for</u>.
Rule:	In a compound subject or object composed of a noun and a pronoun, the pronoun is always last. When used with another pronoun, *I* or *me* is placed last.
Examples:	(Sentence 4) <u>Donna Fifer and I</u> are surveying the key employee concerns in our company. (a compound subject)
	(Sentence 5) Consider each issue carefully and return your completed survey to <u>her or me</u>. (a compound object)

▦Common Pronoun Errors

Rule:	Use a subject pronoun when a pronoun that refers to the subject follows a linking verb.
Example:	The winner of the election will be he. (not <u>him</u>)
Rule:	When a comparison is made using the words *than* or *as,* words are often omitted from the sentence. To choose the correct pronoun, mentally fill in the missing words.
Examples:	Marc works more hours than <u>he</u>. (. . . <u>than he works</u>)
	A layoff would be harder on Marta than her. (. . . <u>than on her</u>)
Rule:	When a pronoun is used to restate a subject, choose a subject pronoun.
Example:	The election chairpeople, Alice and <u>he</u>, wrote the survey.
	Mentally remove the compound subject to discover if the pronoun "sounds right." (~~Alice and~~ he wrote the survey.)
Rule:	When a pronoun is used to restate an object, choose an object pronoun.
Example:	We voted for the winners, Andy and <u>him</u>.
	Mentally remove the compound object to find out if the pronoun "sounds right." (We voted for ~~Andy and~~ him.)

Rule: A possessive pronoun is used before nouns or alone.

Used Before Nouns		Used Alone	
Singular	Plural	Singular	Plural
my	our	mine	ours
your	your	yours	yours
his, her, its	their	his, hers	theirs

Note: Possessive personal pronouns never contain apostrophes.

Examples: (Sentence 6) We need your input.
The possessive pronoun your precedes the noun input.
(Sentence 7) Mr. Walker assures you that your concerns are his.
The possessive pronoun your precedes the noun concerns, and the possessive pronoun his stands alone (his concerns is implied).

Reflexive and Intensive Pronouns

Singular	Plural
myself	ourselves
yourself	yourselves
himself,	themselves
herself, itself	

Rule: Use a reflexive pronoun when the subject is both the doer and the receiver of the action. Never use a reflexive pronoun as a subject.

Note: The spellings hisself and theirselves are incorrect.

Example: (Sentence 8) You will only hurt yourself if you side with his opponents.
The pronoun you is the subject. The pronoun yourself is the object. Both refer to the same person.

Rule: Use an intensive pronoun to add emphasis to another noun or pronoun. An intensive pronoun often appears immediately after the subject.

Example: (Sentence 9) I myself plan to vote for Andy Walker.
The pronoun myself gives emphasis to the subject I.
However, the sentence could also be correctly written as:
I plan to vote for Andy Walker myself.

Items 1 to 5 refer to the following paragraph. Choose the best answer to each item.

(1) I was involved in a small accident on Tuesday, August 5, at 3:15 P.M. (2) A car backing out of a driveway hit my wife and I while we were driving down the street. (3) Len Morgan and his wife were in the other car, which wasn't their's. (4) Len and she backed into the street without looking. (5) The accident itself did not injure my wife or I. (6) However, my wife hurt her getting out of the car after the accident. (7) Len and his wife didn't hurt theirselves at all, but the accident may cause their insurance premiums to increase.

1. Sentence 2: **A car backing out of a driveway hit my wife and I while we were driving down the street.**

   What correction should be made to this sentence?

   (1) change my to mine
   (2) change I to me
   (3) change I to myself
   (4) change we to us
   (5) no correction is necessary

2. Sentence 3: **Len Morgan and his wife were in the other car, which wasn't their's.**

   What correction should be made to this sentence?

   (1) change his to his'
   (2) change were to was
   (3) change their's to their
   (4) change their's to theirs
   (5) no correction is necessary

3. Sentence 5: **The accident itself did not injure my wife or I.**

   What correction should be made to this sentence?

   (1) change itself to its
   (2) remove itself
   (3) change I to me
   (4) change I to myself
   (5) no correction is necessary

4. Sentence 6: **However, my wife hurt her getting out of the car after the accident.**

   What correction should be made to this sentence?

   (1) change my to mine
   (2) change her to hers
   (3) change her to herself
   (4) change her to her's
   (5) no correction is necessary

5. Sentence 7: **Len and his wife didn't hurt theirselves at all, but the accident may cause their insurance premiums to increase.**

   What correction should be made to this sentence?

   (1) change didn't to did'nt
   (2) change his to his'
   (3) change the comma after all to a semicolon
   (4) replace theirselves with themselves
   (5) no correction is necessary

Items 6 to 11 refer to the following paragraph.

(1) The faculty at Warner Junior High School met with ours parents group last Monday to present an exciting idea. (2) Us are calling it the "homework update line." (3) Warner will provide a phone number for parents to find out there child's homework assignments. (4) They are meeting again next Monday at 7:00 P.M. (5) Please join us if yourself can work out the details. (6) We think this idea will definitely improve us children's educational experience. (7) Neighboring schools have found that similar programs were of great value to their students. (8) We are hoping to have the same success as them.

6. Sentence 1: **The faculty at Warner Junior High School met with ours parents group last Monday to present an exciting idea.**

   What correction should be made to this sentence?

   (1) change met to meeted
   (2) change met to is meeting
   (3) change ours to our
   (4) change ours to your
   (5) no correction is necessary

7. Sentence 2: **Us are calling it the "homework update line."**

   What correction should be made to this sentence?

   (1) change Us to Them
   (2) change Us to Him
   (3) change Us to We
   (4) change calling to called
   (5) no correction is necessary

8. Sentence 3: **Warner will provide a phone number for parents to find out there child's homework assignments.**

   What correction should be made to this sentence?

   (1) change provide to provided
   (2) change parents to Parents
   (3) change there to they're
   (4) change there to their
   (5) no correction is necessary

9. Sentence 5: **Please join us if yourself can work out the details.**

   What correction should be made to this sentence?

   (1) change us to they
   (2) change yourself to yourselves
   (3) change yourself to your
   (4) change yourself to you
   (5) no correction is necessary

10. Sentence 6: **We think this idea will definitely improve us children's educational experience.**

    What correction should be made to this sentence?

    (1) change us to our
    (2) change us to we
    (3) change us to ourselves
    (4) change the spelling of experience to expereince
    (5) no correction is necessary

11. Sentence 8: **We are hoping to have the same success as them.**

    What correction should be made to this sentence?

    (1) replace We with Us
    (2) change the spelling of hoping to hopeing
    (3) replace them with they
    (4) replace them with their
    (5) no correction is necessary

Items 12 to 17 refer to the following memorandum.

Memorandum

To: All Employees
From: Gene McKinney
Re: Car-pooling

(1) Recently, Rick Fredericks informed I that three fourths of our employees drive separately to work. (2) It concern me that this statistic is so high. (3) Rick and me drive from Kirkland every day. (4) Us could take four riders each. (5) Shannon Michaels has offered her car to anyone driving from Bellevue. (6) Please sign you're name and phone number below if you are interested in riding with someone or can offer a ride.

12. Sentence 1: **Recently, Rick Fredericks informed I that three fourths of our employees drive separately to work.**

What correction should be made to this sentence?

(1) change I to we
(2) change I to me
(3) change drive to drived
(4) change drive to driven
(5) no correction is necessary

13. Sentence 2: **It concern me that this statistic is so high.**

What correction should be made to this sentence?

(1) change concern to concerns
(2) change me to I
(3) change is to be
(4) change so to sew
(5) no correction is necessary

14. Sentence 3: **Rick and me drive from Kirkland every day.**

What correction should be made to this sentence?

(1) change me to us
(2) change me to I
(3) insert a comma after me
(4) change drive to drives
(5) no correction is necessary

15. Sentence 4: **Us could take four riders each.**

What correction should be made to this sentence?

(1) change Us to Them
(2) change Us to Him
(3) change Us to We
(4) change take to takes
(5) no correction is necessary

16. Sentence 5: **Shannon Michaels has offered her car to anyone driving from Bellevue.**

What correction should be made to this sentence?

(1) change has to have
(2) change the spelling of offered to offerred
(3) change anyone to any one
(4) change Bellevue to bellevue
(5) no correction is necessary

17. Sentence 6: **Please sign you're name and phone number below if you are interested in riding with someone or can offer a ride.**

What correction should be made to this sentence?

(1) change you're to your
(2) change you're to you are
(3) replace you are with your
(4) change ride to rode
(5) no correction is necessary

Answers are on page 285.

Lesson 14   133

Directions: Choose the <u>best answer</u> to each item.

<u>Items 1 to 7</u> refer to the following letter.

Dear Neighbor:
(1) We live in such a beautiful neighborhood. (2) But lately its has been marred by suggestive, and sometimes frightening, billboards. (3) Judging from the billboards that surround ours apartments, there are no guidelines that advertisers must follow. (4) Many children live in our area, and them are exposed to these offensive pictures daily. (5) Jan Sheridan, Neal Oshiro, and me are forming a committee to look into the situation. (6) If you want to join us to solve this problem, contact me at 555-3358. (7) Us are hoping to eliminate the billboards altogether.

1. Sentence 1: **We live in such a beautiful neighborhood.**

   What correction should be made to this sentence?

   (1) change <u>live</u> to <u>lives</u>
   (2) insert <u>have</u> before <u>live</u>
   (3) insert <u>had</u> before <u>live</u>
   (4) insert a comma after <u>live</u>
   (5) no correction is necessary

2. Sentence 2: **But lately its has been marred by suggestive, and sometimes frightening, billboards.**

   What correction should be made to this sentence?

   (1) change <u>its</u> to <u>they</u>
   (2) change <u>its</u> to <u>it</u>
   (3) change <u>its</u> to <u>them</u>
   (4) remove <u>has</u>
   (5) no correction is necessary

3. Sentence 3: **Judging from the billboards that surround ours apartments, there are no guidelines that advertisers must follow.**

   What correction should be made to this sentence?

   (1) change <u>surround</u> to <u>surrounds</u>
   (2) change <u>ours</u> to <u>our</u>
   (3) change <u>there</u> to <u>their</u>
   (4) change <u>there</u> to <u>they're</u>
   (5) no correction is necessary

4. Sentence 4: **Many children live in our area, and them are exposed to these offensive pictures daily.**

   What correction should be made to this sentence?

   (1) change <u>our</u> to <u>ours</u>
   (2) change <u>our</u> to <u>are</u>
   (3) change <u>them</u> to <u>theirselves</u>
   (4) change <u>them</u> to <u>they</u>
   (5) no correction is necessary

5. Sentence 5: **Jan Sheridan, Neal Oshiro, and me are forming a committee to look into the situation.**

   What correction should be made to this sentence?

   (1) change <u>me</u> to <u>mine</u>
   (2) change <u>me</u> to <u>us</u>
   (3) change <u>me</u> to <u>I</u>
   (4) change the spelling of <u>committee</u> to <u>commitee</u>
   (5) no correction is necessary

6. Sentence 6: **If you want to join us to solve this problem, contact me at 555-3358.**

   What correction should be made to this sentence?

   (1) change you to your
   (2) change us to we
   (3) change us to they
   (4) change me to I
   (5) no correction is necessary

7. Sentence 7: **Us are hoping to eliminate the billboards altogether.**

   What correction should be made to this sentence?

   (1) change Us to We
   (2) change are to is
   (3) change hoping to hoped
   (4) change the spelling of altogether to all together
   (5) no correction is necessary

Items 8 to 12 refer to the following paragraph.

   (1) Joyce Webberly, a postal worker, wanted to improve hers reading speed. (2) She took a course that promised to help herself understand and remember more of what she read. (3) She learned that the average adult reads between 150 and 200 words per minute. (4) A fellow student and herself increased their reading speeds from 175 to 600 words per minute. (5) Now they can read a book in about too hours.

8. Sentence 1: **Joyce Webberly, a postal worker, wanted to improve hers reading speed.**

   What correction should be made to this sentence?

   (1) change wanted to has wanting
   (2) change wanted to will had wanted
   (3) change hers to her
   (4) change hers to herself
   (5) no correction is necessary

9. Sentence 2: **She took a course that promised to help herself understand and remember more of what she read.**

   What correction should be made to this sentence?

   (1) change She to Her
   (2) change herself to her
   (3) change remember to remembered
   (4) insert is before remember
   (5) no correction is necessary

10. Sentence 3: **She learned that the average adult reads between 150 and 200 words per minute.**

    What correction should be made to this sentence?

    (1) change She to Them
    (2) change learned to teached
    (3) change reads to was reading
    (4) change reads to read
    (5) no correction is necessary

11. Sentence 4: **A fellow student and herself increased their reading speeds from 175 to 600 words per minute.**

    What correction should be made to this sentence?

    (1) change herself to her
    (2) change herself to she
    (3) change their to there
    (4) change their to theirselves
    (5) no correction is necessary

12. Sentence 5: **Now they can read a book in about too hours.**

    What correction should be made to this sentence?

    (1) change they to them
    (2) insert a comma after book
    (3) change too to two
    (4) change hours to ours
    (5) no correction is necessary

Answers are on page 286.

Lesson 15

Pronouns and Antecedents

The noun that a pronoun stands for and refers to is the antecedent of that pronoun. Just as a subject and its verb must agree, a pronoun must agree with its antecedent.

Read these notes from a hotel desk clerk's records. As you read, identify the pronouns and their antecedents.

> (1) The Johnsons and their children moved to Room 215. (2) June Aryiku and Lynn Dupay will be meeting their guests in the lobby at 6:30 P.M. (3) Neither Kevin Escalante nor the Livingstons are happy with their room assignments. (4) Jon Maeda, a friend of the Livingstons, is holding a meeting in his room tomorrow at 8:30 A.M.
>
> (5) Anita Vasquez wants her luggage held at the front desk. (6) The airline may deliver it in the middle of the night. (7) We should contact the airline ourselves if the luggage does not come by morning.

Rule: A pronoun must agree with its antecedent in number—singular or plural.

Example: (Sentence 1) The Johnsons and their children moved to Room 215.
The plural pronoun their agrees with the plural antecedent Johnsons.

Rule: Use a plural pronoun with a compound antecedent (two or more nouns joined by *and*).

Example: (Sentence 2) June Aryiku and Lynn Dupay will be meeting their guests in the lobby at 6:30 P.M.
The plural pronoun their agrees with the compound antecedent and subject June Aryiku and Lynn Dupay.

Rule: When a compound antecedent is joined by *or, either-or,* or *neither-nor,* the pronoun should agree in number with the nearest antecedent.

Example: (Sentence 3) Neither Kevin Escalante nor the Livingstons are happy with their room assignments.
The plural pronoun their agrees with the nearest antecedent, the Livingstons.

Note: Do not be fooled by prepositional phrases or by nonessential phrases set off by commas.

Example: (Sentence 4) Jon Maeda, a friend of the Livingstons, is holding a meeting in his room tomorrow at 8:30 A.M.
The singular pronoun <u>his</u> agrees with the antecedent <u>Jon Maeda</u>. The plural noun <u>Livingstons</u> does not affect the pronoun choice.

Rule: A pronoun must agree with its antecedent in gender—masculine, feminine, or neuter.

Examples: (Sentence 5) Anita Vasquez wants her luggage held at the front desk.
<u>Anita Vasquez</u> is a woman's name, so the pronoun <u>her</u> is used.
(Sentence 6) The airline may deliver it in the middle of the night.
The neuter pronoun <u>it</u> refers to the <u>luggage</u>. In a paragraph, the antecedent may be found in an earlier sentence.

Note: When the gender of a singular antecedent naming a person is unclear, use the masculine gender, or use *he or she, his or hers,* or *him or her;* if the unclear antecedent is plural, use *they, their, theirs,* or *them.*

Example: Each hotel guest should return <u>his or her</u> room key by 11 A.M.

Rule: A pronoun must agree with its antecedent in person—first, second, or third.

First person: I, we, me, us, my, mine, our, ours, myself, ourselves
Second person: you, your, yours, yourselves
Third person: he, she, it, they, him, her, them, his, hers, its, their, theirs, himself, herself, themselves

Example: (Sentence 7) We should contact the airline ourselves if the luggage does not come by morning.
The first-person intensive pronoun <u>ourselves</u> agrees with the first-person antecedent and subject <u>We</u>.

To decide which pronoun to use in a sentence, find its antecedent. Ask yourself: What is its number? What is its gender? Then choose a pronoun that agrees with its antecedent on both points.

 Practice **Pronouns and Antecedents**

Items 1 to 6 refer to the following paragraph. Choose the best answer to each item.

(1) I left its list at home, but I think I can remember the assignments for the potluck. (2) The Taylors are making her terrific strawberry punch. (3) Either Rita or Pat offered to bring their punch bowl. (4) Fred Curtis said their wife could make a casserole. (5) Each person should bring her own utensils. (6) My wife and I have enough plates for everybody, including the Wellstons and his eight kids.

1. Sentence 1: **I left its list at home, but I think I can remember the assignments for the potluck.**

   What correction should be made to this sentence?

   (1) change the first I to My
   (2) change its to my
   (3) change its to mine
   (4) change the comma to a semicolon
   (5) no correction is necessary

2. Sentence 2: **The Taylors are making her terrific strawberry punch.**

   What correction should be made to this sentence?

   (1) change Taylors to taylors
   (2) change are to is
   (3) change making to made
   (4) change her to their
   (5) no correction is necessary

3. Sentence 3: **Either Rita or Pat offered to bring their punch bowl.**

   What correction should be made to this sentence?

   (1) change or to nor
   (2) change offered to offers
   (3) change their to her
   (4) change their to his
   (5) no correction is necessary

4. Sentence 4: **Fred Curtis said their wife could make a casserole.**

   Which of the following is the best way to write the underlined portion of this sentence? If you think the original is the best way, choose option (1).

   (1) said their wife
   (2) say his wife
   (3) said his wife
   (4) said her wife
   (5) said his Wife

5. Sentence 5: **Each person should bring her own utensils.**

   What correction should be made to this sentence?

   (1) change person to people
   (2) change bring to brought
   (3) change her to their
   (4) change her to his or her
   (5) no correction is necessary

6. Sentence 6: **My wife and I have enough plates for everybody, including the Wellstons and his eight kids.**

   What correction should be made to this sentence?

   (1) change I to me
   (2) change My wife and I to Me and my wife
   (3) change his to her
   (4) change his to their
   (5) no correction is necessary

Items 7 to 12 refer to the following paragraph.

(1) Mark and I want to compliment every employee on their work last month. (2) The plumbers have never completed so many of his work orders in one month. (3) Mr. Tim Bickel from Weston called to say our plumber arrived within thirty minutes of their company's call. (4) Frank Mendez mentioned he can answer about five more calls per week now. (5) Fran, Dora, and Carol feel her office's rescheduling problems have decreased. (6) Consequently, the company increased his profits over last month's totals. (7) If the plumbers continue to perform at this level, they will earn themselves substantial bonuses at the end of the year.

7. Sentence 1: **Mark and I want to compliment every employee on their work last month.**

   What correction should be made to this sentence?

   (1) change I to me
   (2) change compliment to complement
   (3) change their to they're
   (4) change their to his or her
   (5) no correction is necessary

8. Sentence 2: **The plumbers have never completed so many of his work orders in one month.**

   What correction should be made to this sentence?

   (1) change plumbers to plumber's
   (2) change have to has
   (3) change his to their
   (4) change his to his or her
   (5) no correction is necessary

9. Sentence 3: **Mr. Tim Bickel from Weston called to say our plumber arrived within thirty minutes of their company's call.**

   What correction should be made to this sentence?

   (1) change our to ours
   (2) change their to his
   (3) change their to her
   (4) change company's to companies
   (5) no correction is necessary

10. Sentence 5: **Fran, Dora, and Carol feel her office's rescheduling problems have decreased.**

    What correction should be made to this sentence?

    (1) change her to their
    (2) change her to hers
    (3) change her to herselves
    (4) change have to has
    (5) no correction is necessary

11. Sentence 6: **Consequently, the company increased his profits over last month's totals.**

    What correction should be made to this sentence?

    (1) change his to its
    (2) change his to it's
    (3) change his to their
    (4) change month's to months
    (5) no correction is necessary

12. Sentence 7: **If the plumbers continue to perform at this level, they will earn themselves substantial bonuses at the end of the year.**

    What correction should be made to this sentence?

    (1) change plumbers to plumbers'
    (2) change they to them
    (3) change earn to earned
    (4) change themselves to theirselves
    (5) no correction is necessary

Answers are on page 287.

Directions: Choose the <u>best answer</u> to each item.

<u>Items 1 to 12</u> refer to the following paragraph.

(1) Me and Joan discussed last Tuesday's fire drill. (2) We decided to tell you our views of it. (3) Apparently, the employees on the second floor never left his offices since the alarm did not ring on that floor. (4) I tried to exit through the fire door on the third floor and found they was locked. (5) Jason started down the south stairwell and, feeling the cold, realized he had left her coat upstairs and went back for it. (6) Neither the accountants nor Howard got up from their coffee break to leave. (7) The plant manager and the foreman didn't know which exit was closest to his offices. (8) Jenny has since decided her needs someone assigned to call the fire department. (9) Everyone should improve their knowledge of safety procedures. (10) Let's consider appointing Joan to be our fire marshal because he has such great organizational skills. (11) There's a need for each employee to make it our own responsibility to learn fire safety. (12) Us employees must realize that fire safety is very important and should be taken seriously. (13) We'll try a fire drill again on Friday.

1. Sentence 1: **Me and Joan discussed last Tuesday's fire drill.**

   What correction should be made to this sentence?

   (1) change <u>Me</u> to <u>I</u>
   (2) change <u>Me and Joan</u> to <u>Joan and me</u>
   (3) change <u>Me and Joan</u> to <u>Joan and I</u>
   (4) change <u>Tuesday's</u> to <u>Tuesdays</u>
   (5) no correction is necessary

2. Sentence 2: **We decided to tell you our views of it.**

   What correction should be made to this sentence?

   (1) change <u>We</u> to <u>Us</u>
   (2) change <u>our</u> to <u>our's</u>
   (3) change <u>views</u> to <u>veiws</u>
   (4) change <u>it</u> to <u>them</u>
   (5) no correction is necessary

3. Sentence 3: **Apparently, the employees on the second floor never left his offices since the alarm did not ring on that floor.**

   What correction should be made to this sentence?

   (1) change <u>second</u> to <u>Second</u>
   (2) change <u>his</u> to <u>their</u>
   (3) change <u>his</u> to <u>his or her</u>
   (4) change <u>ring</u> to <u>rang</u>
   (5) no correction is necessary

4. Sentence 4: **I tried to exit through the fire door on the third floor and found they was locked.**

   What correction should be made to this sentence?

   (1) change <u>I</u> to <u>myself</u>
   (2) change <u>through</u> to <u>threw</u>
   (3) change <u>they</u> to <u>it</u>
   (4) replace <u>they</u> with <u>them</u>
   (5) no correction is necessary

5. Sentence 5: **Jason started down the south stairwell and, feeling the cold, realized he had left her coat upstairs and went back for it.**

Which of the following is the best way to write the underlined portion of this sentence? If you think that the original is the best way, choose option (1).

(1) her
(2) his
(3) him
(4) their
(5) hers

6. Sentence 6: **Neither the accountants nor Howard got up from their coffee break to leave.**

What correction should be made to this sentence?

(1) change Neither to Either
(2) change nor to or
(3) change got to get
(4) change their to his
(5) no correction is necessary

7. Sentence 7: **The plant manager and the foreman didn't know which exit was closest to his offices.**

What correction should be made to this sentence?

(1) change didn't to did'nt
(2) change was to were
(3) change his to their
(4) change his to his or her
(5) no correction is necessary

8. Sentence 8: **Jenny has since decided her needs someone assigned to call the fire department.**

What correction should be made to this sentence?

(1) change has to have
(2) change her to his or her
(3) change her to she
(4) replace her needs with she need
(5) no correction is necessary

9. Sentence 9: **Everyone should improve their knowledge of safety procedures.**

What correction should be made to this sentence?

(1) change knowledge to knowlege
(2) change their to our
(3) change their to his or her
(4) change procedures to proceedures
(5) no correction is necessary

10. Sentence 10: **Let's consider appointing Joan to be our fire marshal because he has such great organizational skills.**

What correction should be made to this sentence?

(1) change let's to lets
(2) change he to her
(3) change he to him
(4) change he to she
(5) no correction is necessary

11. Sentence 11: **There's a need for each employee to make it our own responsibility to learn fire safety.**

What correction should be made to this sentence?

(1) change There's to Theirs
(2) insert a comma after responsibility
(3) change our to their
(4) change our to his or her
(5) no correction is necessary

12. Sentence 12: **Us employees must realize that fire safety is very important and should be taken seriously.**

What correction should be made to this sentence?

(1) change is to are
(2) change seriously to serious
(3) change Us to We
(4) change realize to realizes
(5) no correction is necessary

Answers are on page 288.

Lesson 16

Indefinite Pronouns

An indefinite pronoun makes a general reference to a person, place, or thing. Some indefinite pronouns are always singular and some are always plural.

Singular Indefinite Pronouns		Plural Indefinite Pronouns
another	neither	both
anybody	nobody	few
anyone	no one	many
anything	nothing	several
each	one	
either	other	
everybody	somebody	
everyone	someone	
everything	something	
much		

Read the paragraph. Notice how indefinite pronouns are used.

> (1) Ms. Pesky reminded everyone to bring his or her résumé to the job fair. (2) "Each of the available jobs has its own unique requirements," she said. (3) When the applicants had finished listening to her presentation, several raised their hands and asked questions. (4) "Who makes the final decision about hiring?" (5) "Whom have you appointed to discuss salaries?" (6) "To whom should we give our résumés?" (7) Ms. Pesky answered their questions and announced that she would be hiring the applicants whose education and experience best suited them for the jobs.

Rule: Use a singular pronoun when its antecedent is a singular indefinite pronoun.

Examples: (Sentence 1) Ms. Pesky reminded everyone to bring his or her résumé to the job fair.

The pronoun <u>everyone</u> is a singular antecedent. Since the gender is unclear, the singular compound pronoun <u>his or her</u> correctly agrees with it.

(Sentence 2) "Each of the available jobs has its own unique requirements," she said.

The singular indefinite pronoun <u>Each</u> is the subject and antecedent in this sentence. The third-person singular pronoun <u>its</u> correctly agrees with it. Note that the prepositional phrase <u>of the available jobs</u> does not affect the number of the subject <u>Each</u>.

Unit 2: Usage

Rule:	Use a plural pronoun when its antecedent is a plural indefinite pronoun.
Example:	(Sentence 3) When the applicants had finished listening to her presentation, several raised their hands and asked questions.
	The indefinite pronoun <u>several</u> is the subject of the second clause in the sentence. Since <u>several</u> is always plural, the pronoun <u>their</u> correctly agrees with it.

≡Troublesome Pronouns

The pronouns *who, whom,* and *whose* are often misused. These rules will help you use them correctly.

Rule:	Use *who* (or *whoever*) as the subject of a verb.
Example:	(Sentence 4) "Who makes the final decision about hiring?"
	The pronoun <u>Who</u> is the subject of the verb <u>makes</u>.
Hint:	One way to make sure that you have used *who* correctly is to put the subject before the verb and substitute *he* for *who*. If the sentence makes sense, you have used *who* correctly.
Example:	<u>He</u> makes the final decision about hiring.
Rule:	Use *whom* (or *whomever*) as a direct object or the object of a preposition.
Examples:	(Sentence 5) "Whom have you appointed to discuss salaries?"
	<u>Whom</u> is the direct object of the verb <u>have appointed</u>. (You have appointed <u>whom</u>?)
	(Sentence 6) "To whom should we give our résumés?"
	The pronoun <u>whom</u> is the object of the preposition <u>To</u>.
Hint:	To be sure that you have used *whom* correctly, put the subject before the verb and substitute *him* for *whom*. If the sentence makes sense, you have used *whom* correctly.
Examples:	You have appointed <u>him</u> to discuss salaries.
	We should give our résumés to <u>him</u>.

Remember what you know about subject-verb agreement when using an indefinite pronoun as the subject of a sentence. Match a singular verb form with a singular indefinite pronoun, a plural verb form with a plural indefinite pronoun.

Rule:	Use *whose* to show possession.
Example:	(Sentence 7) Ms. Pesky answered their questions and announced that she would be hiring the applicants whose education and experience best suited them for the jobs. The pronoun <u>whose</u> shows that the applicants possess <u>education and experience</u>.
Hint:	Try substituting the word *their* for *whose*. If the pronoun *their* could make sense in the phrase, you have used *whose* correctly.
Example:	<u>their</u> education and experience

▤Common Pronoun Errors

Some pronouns are confused with words that sound like them. Study the spelling and meaning of the following words.

<u>it's</u>: a contraction of <u>it is</u>

<u>its</u>: a third-person singular possessive pronoun

<u>they're</u>: a contraction of <u>they are</u>

<u>there</u>: an adverb that shows direction

<u>their</u>: a third-person plural possessive pronoun

<u>who's</u>: a contraction of <u>who is</u>

<u>whose</u>: a pronoun showing possession

Another common error is using a **double negative.** Such pronouns as *neither, no one,* and *nobody* have a negative meaning. Sentences with two negative words contain a double negative.

Rule:	In order to make a sentence mean "no" or "not," use only one negative.
Example:	(Wrong) No one did not answer the telephone.
	(Right) No one answered the telephone.

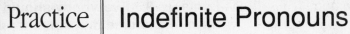

Items 1 to 5 refer to the following paragraph. Choose the best answer to each item.

(1) The Little League coach reminded everybody to wear their uniform to the game, but Elroy and Alvin weren't listening. (2) Neither wore his uniform nor brought their gloves. (3) Both, however, had their mouths stuffed with chewing gum to get that "Big League" look. (4) Later, the coach stepped in a stray wad and shouted, "Who left this gum here? (5) Whoever this gum belongs to is off this team. (6) Whose is it?" (7) Everyone expected Alvin and Elroy to be thrown off the team because of their gum chewing; fortunately for them, the coach decided not to punish nobody.

1. Sentence 1: **The Little League coach reminded everybody to wear their uniform to the game, but Elroy and Alvin weren't listening.**

   Which of the following is the best way to write the underlined portion of this sentence? If you think the original is the best way, choose option (1).

   (1) to wear their uniform
   (2) to wear theirs uniform
   (3) to wear his or her uniform
   (4) to wear his or hers uniform
   (5) to wear its uniform

2. Sentence 2: **Neither wore his uniform nor brought their gloves.**

   What correction should be made to this sentence?

   (1) change his to their
   (2) change his to her
   (3) change their gloves to his glove
   (4) change their to there
   (5) no correction is necessary

3. Sentence 4: **Later, the coach stepped in a stray wad and shouted, "Who left this gum here?"**

   What correction should be made to this sentence?

   (1) change Who to Whom
   (2) change Who to Whose
   (3) change left to leaved
   (4) change here to hear
   (5) no correction is necessary

4. Sentence 5: **Whoever this gum belongs to is off this team.**

   What correction should be made to this sentence?

   (1) change Whoever to Whosever
   (2) change Whoever to Whomever
   (3) change Whoever to Who
   (4) change belongs to belong
   (5) no correction is necessary

5. Sentence 7: **Everyone expected Alvin and Elroy to be thrown off the team because of their gum chewing; fortunately for them, the coach decided not to punish nobody.**

   What correction should be made to this sentence?

   (1) change their to his
   (2) change their to there
   (3) change them to they
   (4) replace nobody with anybody
   (5) no correction is necessary

Items 6 to 11 refer to the following paragraph.

(1) Dr. Merriam of the Northeast Medical Center advises everyone to add some form of exercise to their daily routine. (2) At a recent medical conference, Dr. Merriam suggested that anyone who wants to reduce stress in her life should exercise. (3) "Everybody should choose a form of exercise that suits her lifestyle," he stated. (4) "Most assume jogging and swimming are the best ways to condition theirselves. (5) I see nothing wrong with neither choice." (6) "Too much are made about the type of exercise chosen," Dr. Merriam concluded. (7) "The most important thing is the frequency of the exercise."

6. Sentence 1: **Dr. Merriam of the Northeast Medical Center advises everyone to add some form of exercise to their daily routine.**

   What correction should be made to this sentence?

   (1) change the spelling of advises to advices
   (2) change the spelling of exercise to exersice
   (3) change their to him
   (4) change their to his or her
   (5) no correction is necessary

7. Sentence 2: **At a recent medical conference, Dr. Merriam suggested that anyone who wants to reduce stress in her life should exercise.**

   What correction should be made to this sentence?

   (1) change medical to Medical
   (2) change who to whom
   (3) change wants to want
   (4) change her to his or her
   (5) change her to their

8. Sentence 3: **"Everybody should choose a form of exercise that suits her lifestyle,"** he stated.

   What correction should be made to this sentence?

   (1) change choose to chose
   (2) change her to their
   (3) change her to his or her
   (4) change her to hers
   (5) no correction is necessary

9. Sentence 4: **"Most assume jogging and swimming are the best ways to condition theirselves.**

   What correction should be made to this sentence?

   (1) change are to is
   (2) change are to was
   (3) change theirselves to himself
   (4) change theirselves to themselves
   (5) no correction is necessary

10. Sentence 5: **I see nothing wrong with neither choice."**

   What correction should be made to this sentence?

   (1) change see to sees
   (2) change neither to either
   (3) insert not before neither
   (4) change neither to none
   (5) no correction is necessary

11. Sentence 6: **"Too much are made about the type of exercise chosen,"** Dr. Merriam concluded.

   What correction should be made to this sentence?

   (1) replace Too with Two
   (2) replace are with is
   (3) remove the quotation mark after chosen,
   (4) change Dr. to dr.
   (5) no correction is necessary

Answers are on page 289.

 **Lesson 16**

Directions: Choose the best answer to each item.

Items 1 to 6 refer to the following paragraph.

(1) Anyone who likes a challenge is welcome to add their ideas to the block-party committee. (2) Several have expressed his interest in a scavenger hunt. (3) A few have volunteered his or her yards for the barbecue. (4) Karla, whom is really creative, will help decorate. (5) We need someone to donate her time to plan games. (6) Whomever has time and energy is welcome.

1. Sentence 1: **Anyone who likes a challenge is welcome to add their ideas to the block-party committee.**

   What correction should be made to this sentence?

   (1) change likes to like
   (2) change is to are
   (3) change their to her
   (4) change their to his or her
   (5) no correction is necessary

2. Sentence 2: **Several have expressed his interest in a scavenger hunt.**

   What correction should be made to this sentence?

   (1) change have to has
   (2) change his to his or her
   (3) change his to their
   (4) change his to theirs
   (5) no correction is necessary

3. Sentence 3: **A few have volunteered his or her yards for the barbecue.**

   What correction should be made to this sentence?

   (1) change have to has
   (2) change volunteered to volunteer
   (3) change his or her to their
   (4) change his or her to theirselves
   (5) no correction is necessary

4. Sentence 4: **Karla, whom is really creative, will help decorate.**

   What correction should be made to this sentence?

   (1) remove the comma after Karla
   (2) change whom to who
   (3) change whom to whose
   (4) change is to are
   (5) no correction is necessary

5. Sentence 5: **We need someone to donate her time to plan games.**

   What correction should be made to this sentence?

   (1) change need to needs
   (2) change her to hers
   (3) change her to their
   (4) change her to his or her
   (5) no correction is necessary

6. Sentence 6: **Whomever has time and energy is welcome.**

   What correction should be made to this sentence?

   (1) change Whomever to Whoever
   (2) change Whomever to Whosever
   (3) change is to are
   (4) change is to were
   (5) no correction is necessary

Answers are on page 290.

Lesson 17

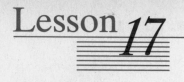

Adjectives and Adverbs

Adjectives and adverbs modify or describe other words.

Read the following advertising copy. Look for adjectives and adverbs as you read.

Many adverbs look the same as adjectives except for the -ly ending. (cautious, cautiously; quiet, quietly) To decide whether to use an adverb or an adjective, look at the word being modified. If the word is a noun or pronoun, use an adjective. If the word is a verb, adjective, or other adverb, use an adverb.

(1) Our new automobile, the XP20 Sedan, is luxurious and affordable. (2) Its powerful V-6 engine has been very carefully engineered for a remarkably smooth ride. (3) In addition, the XP20 is safer and more reliable than the leading competitor. (4) If you want to drive the finest car on the market today, test drive the new XP20—a masterpiece of modern technology.

Rule: Use an adjective to describe a noun or pronoun. Adjectives tell *what kind, which one, how many,* or *how much.*

Example: (Sentence 1) Our new automobile, the XP20 Sedan, is luxurious and affordable.
The adjectives <u>new</u>, <u>luxurious</u>, and <u>affordable</u> modify the noun <u>automobile</u>. Adjectives may come before the word they modify or after a form of the verb <u>be</u>.

Rule: Use an adverb to describe an action verb. Also, use an adverb to describe an adjective or another adverb. Adverbs tell *when, where, how,* or *to what extent.* Many adverbs end in *-ly* but some common ones such as *very* do not.

Example: (Sentence 2) Its powerful V-6 engine has been very carefully engineered for a remarkably smooth ride.
The verb in this sentence is <u>has been engineered</u>. The adverb <u>carefully</u> tells how the car was engineered. The adverb <u>very</u> modifies the adverb <u>carefully</u>, telling *how* carefully. The adjective <u>smooth</u> describes <u>ride</u>. The adverb <u>remarkably</u> modifies the adjective, telling *how* smooth the ride is.

Note: Linking verbs, especially *feel, touch, smell,* and *taste,* are often modified by an adjective.

Example: The garbage smells <u>bad</u>.

Troublesome Adjectives and Adverbs

bad and badly: <u>Bad</u> is an adjective. <u>Badly</u> is always an adverb.

good and well: <u>Good</u> is an adjective; it usually refers to quality or appearance. <u>Well</u> is used as an adjective when referring to satisfactory conditions or to a person's health. <u>Well</u> can also be used as an adverb when describing *how* an action is performed.

Adjectives and adverbs can show degrees of comparison.

fewer and less: Fewer is an adjective used to compare things that can be counted. Less is an adjective used with qualities and quantities that cannot be counted. For example: I had less free time this weekend, so I studied fewer lessons.

Rule: To compare two people, places, or things, use the comparative form of the adjective or adverb. Add -er to one-syllable adjectives and adverbs. Use more or less before adjectives and adverbs of two or more syllables.

Example: (Sentence 3) In addition, the XP20 is safer and more reliable than the leading competitor.
The adjectives safer and more reliable compare the XP20 to the leading competitor.

Rule: To compare more than two people, places, or things, use the superlative form of the adjective or adverb. Add -est to one-syllable adjectives and adverbs. Use most and least before adjectives and adverbs of two or more syllables.

Example: (Sentence 4) If you want to drive the finest car on the market today, test drive the new XP20—a masterpiece of modern technology.
The superlative adjective finest compares the car with all other cars on the market today.

This chart lists some exceptions to the rules for forming comparative and superlative adjectives.

Adjective	Comparative	Superlative
good	better	best
many	more	most
much	more	most
bad	worse	worst
Adverb	**Comparative**	**Superlative**
badly	worse	worst
well	better	best
much	more	most

Rule: Do not make double comparisons. Never use *more, most, less,* or *least* with adjectives or adverbs ending in -er or -est.

Incorrect: The XP20 is the most finest car on the market today.

Items 1 to 6 refer to the following paragraph. Choose the best answer to each item.

(1) The Huggle baby stroller is compactly and durable. (2) The stain-resistant cloth padding is easily washable, but it fades quick in sunlight. (3) Also, the vinyl hood did not hold up good in our tests. (4) The aluminum carriage makes the Huggle much lightest than its leading competitor, the Cuddle Walkmaster. (5) Unfortunately, the Huggle brand is much more expensive. (6) Even so, of the five brands tested, we believe you will get a better value from the Huggle. (7) When it comes to producing the highest quality baby strollers, less companies can compare with Huggle.

1. Sentence 1: **The Huggle baby stroller is compactly and durable.**

   What correction should be made to this sentence?

   (1) change is to are
   (2) change is to were
   (3) change compactly to compacter
   (4) change compactly to compact
   (5) no correction is necessary

2. Sentence 2: **The stain-resistant cloth padding is easily washable, but it fades quick in sunlight.**

   What correction should be made to this sentence?

   (1) change is to was
   (2) change easily to easier
   (3) change it to they
   (4) change quick to quickly
   (5) no correction is necessary

3. Sentence 3: **Also, the vinyl hood did not hold up good in our tests.**

   What correction should be made to this sentence?

   (1) change good to better
   (2) change good to best
   (3) change good to well
   (4) change good to goodest
   (5) no correction is necessary

4. Sentence 4: **The aluminum carriage makes the Huggle much lightest than its leading competitor, the Cuddle Walkmaster.**

   What correction should be made to this sentence?

   (1) change makes to make
   (2) change much to more
   (3) change lightest to lighter
   (4) change lightest to more lighter
   (5) no correction is necessary

5. Sentence 6: **Even so, of the five brands tested, we believe you will get a better value from the Huggle.**

   What correction should be made to this sentence?

   (1) change get to got
   (2) replace a better with the best
   (3) change better to gooder
   (4) change better to more better
   (5) no correction is necessary

6. Sentence 7: **When it comes to producing the highest quality baby strollers, less companies can compare with Huggle.**

   What correction should be made to this sentence?

   (1) change highest to most highest
   (2) change strollers to stroller's
   (3) replace the comma with a semicolon
   (4) replace less with few
   (5) no correction is necessary

Items 7 to 12 refer to the following paragraph.

   (1) Of all the memory techniques, repetition is the more effective of all. (2) This idea might sound too simpler. (3) Still, it is the best helpful way to put facts into your memory. (4) A real good idea is to say the fact aloud many times. (5) The most times you say the information, the more effective it will be. (6) The key is repeating the information enough times so it becomes a part of your long-term memory. (7) Repetition will help you retain new information easy; it's a better technique than any other.

7. Sentence 1: **Of all the memory techniques, repetition is the more effective of all.**

   What correction should be made to this sentence?

   (1) change memory to Memory
   (2) change techniques to technique
   (3) change more to most
   (4) change more to best
   (5) no correction is necessary

8. Sentence 2: **This idea might sound too simpler.**

   What correction should be made to this sentence?

   (1) change sound to sounds
   (2) change simpler to simplest
   (3) change simpler to more simple
   (4) change simpler to simple
   (5) no correction is necessary

9. Sentence 3: **Still, it is the best helpful way to put facts into your memory.**

   What correction should be made to this sentence?

   (1) change best to more
   (2) change best to most
   (3) change helpful to helpfully
   (4) change helpful to helpfuller
   (5) no correction is necessary

10. Sentence 4: **A real good idea is to say the fact aloud many times.**

    Which of the following is the best way to write the underlined portion of this sentence? If you think the original is the best way, choose option (1).

    (1) real good idea
    (2) really good idea
    (3) real best idea
    (4) real better idea
    (5) more real good idea

11. Sentence 5: **The most times you say the information, the more effective it will be.**

    What correction should be made to this sentence?

    (1) change most to more
    (2) change more effective to effectiver
    (3) change more effective to more effect
    (4) change it to it's
    (5) no correction is necessary

12. Sentence 7: **Repetition will help you retain new information easy; it's a better technique than any other.**

    What correction should be made to this sentence?

    (1) replace easy with easily
    (2) replace easy with most easiest
    (3) change better to more better
    (4) change better to best
    (5) no correction is necessary

Answers are on page 291.

 **Lesson 17**

Items 1 to 8 refer to the following paragraph.

(1) More Americans are eating fewer fat in their diets. (2) With so many foods to choose from, we sometimes have difficulty choosing the food with the less fat. (3) Judging by fat content, which is the worst for you, a strip of bacon or a cookie? (4) Although bacon seems to be an obviously fatty food, some cookies are the highest in fat. (5) Tuna is considered to have a lower fat content than red meat. (6) If tuna is packed in oil, however, it becomes the most unhealthful choice. (7) Popcorn that is popped using hot air is best for you than popcorn popped in oil. (8) Of the four food groups, fruits and vegetables have the low fat content.

1. Sentence 1: **More Americans are eating fewer fat in their diets.**

   What correction should be made to this sentence?

   (1) change Americans to americans
   (2) change are to is
   (3) change fewer to less
   (4) change their to his or her
   (5) no correction is necessary

2. Sentence 2: **With so many foods to choose from, we sometimes have difficulty choosing the food with the less fat.**

   What correction should be made to this sentence?

   (1) remove the comma after from
   (2) change have to has
   (3) change less to lessest
   (4) change less to least
   (5) no correction is necessary

3. Sentence 3: **Judging by fat content, which is the worst for you, a strip of bacon or a cookie?**

   What correction should be made to this sentence?

   (1) change is to are
   (2) change the worst to worser
   (3) change the worst to worse
   (4) change the worst to badder
   (5) no correction is necessary

4. Sentence 4: **Although bacon seems to be an obviously fatty food, some cookies are the highest in fat.**

   What correction should be made to this sentence?

   (1) change seems to seem
   (2) remove the comma after food
   (3) change the highest to more high
   (4) change the highest to higher
   (5) no correction is necessary

5. Sentence 5: **Tuna is considered to have a lower fat content than red meat.**

   What correction should be made to this sentence?

   (1) change lower to more low
   (2) change lower to lowlier
   (3) change lower to low
   (4) change a lower to the lowest
   (5) no correction is necessary

6. Sentence 6: **If tuna is packed in oil, however, it becomes the most unhealthful choice.**

   What correction should be made to this sentence?

   (1) change is to were
   (2) change it to they
   (3) change becomes to become
   (4) change most to more
   (5) no correction is necessary

7. Sentence 7: **Popcorn that is popped using hot air is best for you than popcorn popped in oil.**

   What correction should be made to this sentence?

   (1) change that is to that are
   (2) change best to better
   (3) change you to they
   (4) change you to yourself
   (5) no correction is necessary

8. Sentence 8: **Of the four food groups, fruits and vegetables have the low fat content.**

   What correction should be made to this sentence?

   (1) change four to fore
   (2) change have to has
   (3) change low to lower
   (4) change low to lowest
   (5) no correction is necessary

Items 9 to 11 refer to the following paragraph.

   (1) What can you do to stop the most determined criminals from driving quickly away in your car. (2) Auto alarm systems may be one answer to the problem. (3) However, they fared bad in a recent test of security products; the sound of these alarms has become so routine that many people simply ignore them. (4) Even the worse auto thief seems to be able to disconnect an alarm in just a few seconds.

9. Sentence 1: **What can you do to stop the most determined criminals from driving quickly away in your car.**

   What correction should be made to this sentence?

   (1) change most determined to determinedest
   (2) change quickly to quick
   (3) change your to you're
   (4) replace the period with a question mark
   (5) no correction is necessary

10. Sentence 3: **However, they fared bad in a recent test of security products; the sound of these alarms has become so routine that many people simply ignore them.**

    What correction should be made to this sentence?

    (1) replace they with it
    (2) change bad to badly
    (3) change recent to recently
    (4) change the semicolon to a comma
    (5) no correction is necessary

11. Sentence 4: **Even the worse auto thief seems to be able to disconnect an alarm in just a few seconds.**

    What correction should be made to this sentence?

    (1) change worse to worst
    (2) change worse to most worse
    (4) change thief to theif
    (4) replace seems with seams
    (5) no correction is necessary

Answers are on page 292.

Directions: Choose the best answer to each item.

Items 1 to 8 refer to the following paragraph.

(1) Some people thinks that working as a bank teller would be a boring job. (2) Actually, a bank teller's job might be the more challenging job you could have. (3) Since January, Althea worked as a teller at Citizen Bank. (4) Every day, she goes to work early to count the money in their cash drawer. (5) Althea need a good understanding of math. (6) She also tries to be polite and friendly to everyone, even people who are rude to her. (7) At the end of the day, she carefully review all the transactions she made. (8) If she finds a mistake, she stays until her corrects it.

1. Sentence 1: **Some people thinks that working as a bank teller would be a boring job.**

    What correction should be made to this sentence?

    (1) change thinks to thought
    (2) change thinks to think
    (3) insert a comma after thinks
    (4) change bank teller to Bank Teller
    (5) change would be to are

2. Sentence 2: **Actually, a bank teller's job might be the more challenging job you could have.**

    What correction should be made to this sentence?

    (1) remove the apostrophe in teller's
    (2) change teller's to tellers'
    (3) change more to most
    (4) change you to your
    (5) no correction is necessary

3. Sentence 3: **Since January, Althea worked as a teller at Citizen Bank.**

    Which of the following is the best way to write the underlined portion of this sentence? If you think the original is the best way, choose option (1).

    (1) Althea worked as a teller
    (2) Althea work as a teller
    (3) Althea works as a teller
    (4) Althea has been working as a teller
    (5) no correction is necessary

4. Sentence 4: **Every day, she goes to work early to count the money in their cash drawer.**

    What correction should be made to this sentence?

    (1) change goes to go
    (2) change early to earlier
    (3) change their to there
    (4) change their to her
    (5) change their to them

5. Sentence 5: **Althea need a good understanding of math.**

    Which of the following is the best way to write the underlined portion of this sentence? If you think the original is the best way, choose option (1).

    (1) Althea need a good understanding of math
    (2) Althea needs a good understanding of math
    (3) Althea has need a good understanding of math
    (4) Althea have needed a good understanding of math
    (5) no correction is necessary

6. Sentence 6: **She also tries to be polite and friendly to everyone, even people who are rude to her.**

Which of the following is the best way to write the underlined portion of this sentence? If you think the original is the best way, choose option (1).

(1) even people who are rude
(2) even people who had been rude
(3) even people who is rude
(4) even people who will be rude
(5) even people who are ruder

7. Sentence 7: **At the end of the day, she carefully review all the transactions she made.**

What correction should be made to this sentence?

(1) remove the comma after day
(2) change carefully to careful
(3) change review to reviews
(4) change the spelling of review to reveiw
(5) change made to had made

8. Sentence 8: **If she finds a mistake, she stays until her corrects it.**

What correction should be made to this sentence?

(1) change finds to find
(2) remove the comma after mistake
(3) change stays to will have stayed
(4) change stays to stay
(5) change her to she

Items 9 to 11 refer to the following paragraph.

(1) Despite the common belief that only children can learn to play an instrument, many people whom are over sixty have become musicians. (2) Piano, guitar, and keyboard lessons have begun to grow in popularity among the elderly. (3) Many senior citizens will tell you that having time to learn an instrument is one of the most finest aspects of retirement. (4) One musically active group in our town has preceded to form a miniorchestra.

9. Sentence 1: **Despite the common belief that only children can learn to play an instrument, many people whom are over sixty have become musicians.**

What correction should be made to this sentence?

(1) remove the comma after instrument
(2) change whom to who
(3) insert commas after people and sixty
(4) change the spelling of belief to beleif
(5) no correction is necessary

10. Sentence 3: **Many senior citizens will tell you that having time to learn an instrument is one of the more finest aspects of retirement.**

What correction should be made to this sentence?

(1) replace is with are
(2) change more finest to finest
(3) change more finest to most finest
(4) change aspects to aspect's
(5) no correction is necessary

11. Sentence 4: **One musically active group in our town has preceded to form a miniorchestra.**

What correction should be made to this sentence?

(1) change musically to musical
(2) replace our with hour
(3) change has to have
(4) replace preceded with proceeded
(5) no correction is necessary

Items 12 to 16 refer to the following paragraph.

(1) Many changes been made in the American game of baseball since its invention in the 1800s. (2) Games played before the 1930s was scheduled only during daylight. (3) Early professional players wore baggy uniforms, used unpadded gloves to catch balls, and received little or no money for their efforts. (4) A starting pitcher were expected to pitch the entire game. (5) Today baseball is played day and night in such faraway places as Europe, Asia, South America, and Australia. (6) Players wear trim uniforms, collect huge salaries, and enjoy celebrity status. (7) Everyone who watches baseball in this country realize that it has become a big business. (8) Players' salaries, owners' revenues, and concession prices have soared ever upward. (9) There a growing sense is that attending a game costs too much money. (10) Nonetheless, the popularity of baseball continues to grow around the world.

12. Sentence 1: **Many changes been made in the American game of baseball since its invention in the 1800s.**

    What correction should be made to this sentence?

    (1) replace changes with change
    (2) change been made to have been made
    (3) change American to american
    (4) insert a comma after baseball
    (5) change its to it's

13. Sentence 2: **Games played before the 1930s was scheduled only during daylight.**

    What correction should be made to this sentence?

    (1) change played to play
    (2) insert a comma after played
    (3) change was to were
    (4) change was scheduled to have been scheduled
    (5) no correction is necessary

14. Sentence 4: **A starting pitcher were expected to pitch the entire game.**

    Which of the following is the best way to write the underlined portion of this sentence? If you think the original is the best way, choose option (1).

    (1) A starting pitcher were expected
    (2) A starting pitcher have expected
    (3) A starting pitcher was expected
    (4) A Starting Pitcher was expected
    (5) A starting pitched had been expected

15. Sentence 7: **Everyone who watches baseball in this country realize that it has become a big business.**

    What correction should be made to this sentence?

    (1) insert commas after Everyone and country
    (2) change who to whom
    (3) change realize to realizes
    (4) replace it with they
    (5) no correction is necessary

16. Sentence 9: **There a growing sense is that attending a game costs too much money.**

    What correction should be made to this sentence?

    (1) change There to Their
    (2) change a growing sense is to is a growing sense
    (3) change costs to cost's
    (4) change too to to
    (5) no correction is necessary

Items 17 to 21 refer to the following paragraph.

(1) If you had a four-year-old boy, would you let he play with war toys? (2) Would you buy him a toy gun because all of his friends own guns? (3) These be questions that many parents ask themselves when their son or daughter starts asking for Rambo dolls and toy machine guns. (4) Some experts say that watching violent cartoons and playing with war toys increase a child's aggressiveness toward its friends. (5) Other experts say that competition and combat is part of our society. (6) They claim that we can expect children to stop playing war when we do. (7) Everyone agrees that giving a child alternative toys, such as colorful costumes, musical instruments, or sports action figures, opens the door to imaginative play. (8) In recent years, the question of whether toy guns promote violent play has been overshadowed by a news controversy. (9) The spotlight is now focused on violence in video and computer games. (10) Many parents wish that there are rating systems in place to help them decide which video games to purchase.

17. Sentence 1: **If you had a four-year-old boy, would you let he play with war toys?**

    What correction should be made to this sentence?

    (1) change had to has
    (2) change had to was
    (3) remove the comma after boy
    (4) change he to him
    (5) change play to plays

18. Sentence 3: **These be questions that many parents ask themselves when their son or daughter starts asking for Rambo dolls and toy machine guns.**

    What correction should be made to this sentence?

    (1) change be to are
    (2) change be to is
    (3) change themselves to theirselves
    (4) insert a comma after themselves
    (5) change starts to start

19. Sentence 4: **Some experts say that watching violent cartoons and playing with war toys increase a child's aggressiveness toward its friends.**

    What correction should be made to this sentence?

    (1) insert a comma after say
    (2) change cartoons to Cartoons
    (3) change increase to increases
    (4) change its to it's
    (5) change its to his or her

20. Sentence 5: **Other experts say that competition and combat is part of our society.**

    What correction should be made to this sentence?

    (1) change say to says
    (2) change is to are
    (3) change is to was
    (4) change society to Society
    (5) no correction is necessary

21. Sentence 8: **In recent years, the question of whether toy guns promotes violent play has been overshadowed by a new controversy.**

    What correction should be made to this sentence?

    (1) change the comma after years to a semicolon
    (2) replace whether with weather
    (3) change promotes to promote
    (4) change has to have
    (5) no correction is necessary

Items 22 to 26 refer to the following paragraph.

(1) What can be used as a parachute to soften a landing, as an umbrella in a downpour, or as a way to say "hello"? (2) The answer was the bushy tail of a squirrel. (3) About seventy kinds of squirrels live throughout the world in forests, fields, parks, and city backyards. (4) Some squirrels nest in trees, while others live in their colonies underground. (5) Most squirrels store their food, which consists of acorns, nuts, leaf buds, seeds, fruit, berries, mushrooms, pinecones, insects, and bird eggs. (6) Occasionally, squirrels even "plant" new trees by forgetting to uncover them buried nuts. (7) Some people think that the squirrel is a dangerous, disease-carrying menace; others finds squirrels to be intelligent, curious, and very sociable animals. (8) Never try to capture squirrels; despite their cuteness, they should be treated as wild animals. (9) Squirrels are not naturally aggressive animals; however, squirrels may bite when threatened. (10) Although a squirrel's bite can be dangerous, this member of the rodent family plays an important role in our environment.

22. Sentence 2: **The answer was the bushy tail of a squirrel.**

What correction should be made to this sentence?

(1) change was to should have been
(2) change was to is
(3) insert a semicolon after was
(4) insert a comma after was
(5) change squirrel to Squirrel

23. Sentence 4: **Some squirrels nest in trees, while others live in their colonies underground.**

What correction should be made to this sentence?

(1) change their to his
(2) change their to her
(3) change colonies to Colonies
(4) change underground to Underground
(5) no correction is necessary

24. Sentence 6: **Occasionally, squirrels even "plant" new trees by forgetting to uncover them buried nuts.**

What correction should be made to this sentence?

(1) insert a comma after even
(2) change the spelling of forgetting to forgeting
(3) change them to their
(4) change buried to bury
(5) no correction is necessary

25. Sentence 7: **Some people think that the squirrel is a dangerous, disease-carrying menace; others finds squirrels to be intelligent, curious, and very sociable animals.**

What correction should be made to this sentence?

(1) change Some to A lot
(2) change people to peoples
(3) replace the semicolon with a comma
(4) change finds to find
(5) insert a comma after very

26. Sentence 9: **Squirrels are not naturally aggressive animals; however, squirrels may bite when threatened.**

What correction should be made to this sentence?

(1) change are to is
(2) change naturally to natural
(3) change the semicolon to a comma
(4) replace the second squirrels with they
(5) no correction is necessary

Answers are on page 293.

Unit 2: Usage

≡Performance Analysis
Unit 2 Cumulative Review: Usage

Name: _____   Class: _____   Date: _____

Use the Answer Key on pages 293–296 to check your answers to the GED Unit 2 Cumulative Review: Usage. Then use the chart to figure out the skill areas in which you need additional review. Circle on the chart the numbers of the test items you answered correctly. Then go back and review the lessons for the skill areas that are difficult for you. For additional review, see the *Steck-Vaughn GED Writing Skills Exercise Book,* Unit 2: Usage.

Skill	Question	Lessons for Review
Parts of Speech	16 26	10
Subject-Verb Agreement	1 5 7 13 14 20 21 25	11
Irregular Verbs	18	12
Verb Tenses	3 6 11 12 22	13
Personal Pronouns	8 17 24	14
Pronoun and Antecedent Agreement	4 19	15
Indefinite Pronouns	9 15 23	16
Adjectives and Adverbs	2 10	17

Unit 3 SENTENCE STRUCTURE

Correct sentence structure helps you express your ideas clearly.

Part 1 of the Writing Skills GED exam tests your understanding of grammar as well as your ability to construct and revise sentences. In this unit, we turn to sentence structure, the part of writing that deals with correctly expressing related ideas in a sentence and with combining two or more sentences that have related information. This unit focuses on showing you ways to make clear and logical sentences.

In lesson 18, you will review that a **sentence** is a group of words with a subject and a verb that expresses a complete thought. Whenever a subject or a verb or both are missing, what remains is a fragment. You'll also learn about clauses that have both a subject and a verb but do not express a complete idea. These are also fragments. A **fragment** is only part of a sentence. This construction can be corrected either by adding to it the missing part or parts or by joining it to a sentence.

sentence
a group of words that has a subject and a verb and expresses a complete thought

fragment
an incomplete sentence

In lesson 19, you will learn how to identify and correct **run-on sentences.** Run-ons occur when two or more sentences are strung together into one often confusing sentence. This faulty construction can be avoided by separating the ideas into two sentences by using punctuation and conjunctions.

In lesson 20, you will learn about **compound sentence** structures. You will see how sentences with related ideas can be combined into one compound sentence by (1) using a semicolon, (2) using a comma and a coordinating conjunction, such as *and* or *but*, and (3) using a semicolon with a **conjunctive adverb** and a comma.

In lesson 21, you will learn what **parallel structures** within sentences are. You will see how to correct unparallel sentences, in which a series of words, phrases, or clauses are joined by a conjunction but are not written in the same form.

In lesson 22, you will learn about **subordinate** ideas. You will learn the kinds of relationships a lesser idea can have with a sentence's main idea. You will also learn to recognize when a lesser idea is important to understanding a sentence and when it is simply additional information.

In lesson 23, you will learn how to spot and correct **misplaced modifiers.** Modifiers are words or phrases that describe other words or phrases. When they are misplaced, they may seem to describe the wrong thing.

In lesson 24, you will learn how to avoid shifts in focus. When tense, voice, mood, person, or number do not agree, sentences can be confusing.

In lesson 25, you will practice changing the order of the words in a sentence while keeping the main idea the same.

As you work through this unit, you will gain a basic understanding of how sentences can be constructed. You will also learn how to write your ideas in different ways. Once you learn what some common errors are and how to avoid them, your own sentences will improve.

run-on sentence
two or more sentences strung together in one sentence

compound sentence
a sentence that has two or more independent clauses

conjunctive adverb
a word such as therefore, nevertheless, furthermore, *or* however *that shows a connection between main clauses; it is always preceded by a semicolon and followed by a comma*

parallel structure
a series of words, phrases, or clauses in a sentence that all share the same form

phrase
a group of related words that acts as a single part of speech

subordination
secondary ideas related to a sentence's main idea by such subordinating words as because, although, since, *and* while

modifier
a word or phrase describing or referring to another word or phrase

SEE ALSO: Steck-Vaughn GED Writing Skills Exercise Book, Unit 3: Sentence Structure.

Sentence Fragments

Fragments are incomplete sentences. They do not express a complete thought. Many fragments are corrected by just adding a missing subject or verb.

Another kind of fragment contains both a subject and a verb but may begin with a word that makes it dependent upon another sentence for a complete meaning. These fragments are called dependent clauses, and they cannot stand alone. If the fragment is a dependent clause, you can correct it by attaching it to a nearby, related independent clause. Remember to use a comma after the dependent clause if you place it in front of the independent clause. Do not use a comma if the dependent clause is *essential* information needed to understand the meaning of the independent clause. The dependent clause may limit or restrict the meaning of the independent clause in an important way. Without the added information, the thought would not be clearly expressed. Use a comma to separate the dependent clause if it is *nonessential*—that is, not needed to understand the meaning of the independent clause.

Fragments may also happen when a certain kind of pronoun is used as a subject. These pronouns—*who, that, which*—are called **relative pronouns.** They must be part of the sentence containing the noun antecedent to which they refer. Clauses that begin with a relative pronoun are dependent on another related sentence. When making a decision about commas, relative clauses should be treated the same as other dependent clauses.

The following paragraph contains different kinds of fragments. As you read, find them and consider why they are fragments.

(1) Chicken Little was wrong about the sky falling, but once in a while it may seem that he was right. (2) Although the sky itself does not come apart. (3) Rocks sometimes fall to the earth from space. (4) In fact, fall very often. (5) There is a chance that any of us could get hit by one of these rocks. (6) Which are called meteorites. (7) But do not run out and buy a steel umbrella. (8) A group of scientists has figured out that one person will get hit by a meteorite every 180 years. (9) So it's fortunate that a woman in Alabama was only bruised. (10) From being hit by one in 1954. (11) Now the odds going in your favor for another one hundred years.

Identify sentence fragments by asking three questions: Does the sentence have a subject? Does it have a complete verb? Does it express a complete thought? If the answer to one or more of these questions is no, it's a sentence fragment.

Now look at the rules on how to correct fragments.

Rule: A sentence must have a subject.
Example: (Sentence 4) In fact, fall very often.
To correct this fragment, add a subject: In fact, <u>they</u> fall very often.

Rule: A sentence must have a complete verb.
Example: (Sentence 11) Now the odds going in your favor for another one hundred years.
To correct this fragment, make the verb complete: Now the odds <u>are</u> <u>going</u> in your favor for another one hundred years.
Hint: Remember that verbs show action or a condition. The present participle (present form + *-ing*) must be used with a form of the verb *be* in order to be complete.

Rule: A sentence must have both a subject and a verb.
Example: (Sentence 10) From being hit by one in 1954.
To correct this fragment, either add a subject and a verb or treat it like a phrase and combine it with another complete sentence: (Sentences 9 and 10 combined) So it's fortunate that a woman in Alabama was only bruised from being hit by one in 1954.

Rule: A sentence cannot be a dependent clause.

The following words are used to begin dependent clauses:

after	before	though	whenever
although	even though	unless	where
as	if	until	wherever
because	since	when	

Example: (Sentence 2) Although the sky itself does not come apart.
To correct this fragment, join it to another complete sentence, an independent clause: (Sentences 2 and 3 combined) Although the sky itself does not come apart, rocks sometimes fall to the earth from space.
Hint: Remember that an introductory dependent clause is separated from the rest of the sentence by a comma.

Rule: A sentence cannot use a relative pronoun for a subject. The following are relative pronouns: *who, whom, which, that, what, whoever, whatever.*
Example: (Sentence 6) Which are called meteorites.
To correct this fragment, combine it with the sentence containing the noun to which the relative pronoun refers: (Sentences 5 and 6 combined) There is a chance that any of us could be hit by one of these rocks, which are called meteorites.

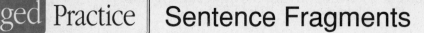

Items 1 to 5 refer to the following paragraph. Choose the best answer to each item.

(1) Recently, an Indiana man received a huge bill from his town's police department for cat care. (2) When he returned home from vacation. (3) Before leaving, he'd turned on his home security system. (4) To inform the local police if a break-in occurred. (5) Also, had left his lonely cat in the house. (6) Soon, the police were going to the house. (7) Several times a day. (8) The cat had quickly learned how to get attention. (9) The man has been asked to pay nearly a thousand dollars to the police. (10) Who had to check out the "cat burglar" every time the cat tripped the alarms.

1. Sentences 1 and 2: **Recently, an Indiana man received a huge bill from his town's police department for cat care. When he returned home from vacation.**

   Which of the following is the best way to write the underlined portion of these sentences? If you think the original is the best way, choose option (1).

   (1) department for cat care. When he
   (2) department for cat care, when he
   (3) department for cat care; when he
   (4) department for cat care when he
   (5) department for cat care. "When he

2. Sentences 3 and 4: **Before leaving, he'd turned on his home security system. To inform the local police if a break-in occurred.**

   Which of the following is the best way to write the underlined portion of these sentences? If you think the original is the best way, choose option (1).

   (1) system. To inform
   (2) system to inform
   (3) system. Informing
   (4) system, to inform
   (5) system; to inform

3. Sentence 5: **Also, had left his lonely cat in the house.**

   What correction should be made to this sentence?

   (1) remove the comma after Also
   (2) insert he after the comma
   (3) change had to has
   (4) change his to him
   (5) insert there after house

4. Sentences 6 and 7: **Soon, the police were going to the house. Several times a day.**

   Which of the following is the best way to write the underlined portion of these sentences? If you think the original is the best way, choose option (1).

   (1) house. Several
   (2) house. several
   (3) house, several
   (4) house several
   (5) house; several

5. Sentences 9 and 10: **The man has been asked to pay nearly a thousand dollars to the police. Who had to check out the "cat burglar" every time the cat tripped the alarms.**

   Which of the following is the best way to write the underlined portion of these sentences? If you think the original is the best way, choose option (1).

   (1) police. Who had to check
   (2) police. Who checking
   (3) police, who had to check
   (4) police; who had to check
   (5) police, whom had to check

Items 6 to 10 refer to the following paragraph.

(1) Previously, we had the choice between gas and electric for cooking. (2) Or wood if one lived far enough away from cities. (3) Now microwave ovens to change all that. (4) Less expensive than gas and electric ranges. (5) Many people prefer microwaves for the speed of cooking. (6) Which is one of their best qualities. (7) Older ovens may have improper shielding. (8) Because of this, businesses must post public signs warning "microwave in use." (9) In fact, are required by law to do so.

6. Sentences 1 and 2: **Previously, we had the choice between gas and electric for cooking. Or wood if one lived far enough away from cities.**

   Which of the following is the best way to write the underlined portion of these sentences? If you think the original is the best way, choose option (1).

   (1) cooking. Or wood
   (2) cooking; or, wood
   (3) cooking; or wood
   (4) cooking, or wood
   (5) cooking or, wood

7. Sentence 3: **Now microwave ovens to change all that.**

   Which of the following is the best way to write the underlined portion of this sentence? If you think the original is the best way, choose option (1).

   (1) ovens to change
   (2) ovens, to change
   (3) ovens are changing
   (4) ovens changing
   (5) ovens changes

8. Sentence 4: **Less expensive than gas and electric ranges.**

   What correction should be made to this sentence?

   (1) change Less expensive to Their less expensive
   (2) change Less expensive to They're less expensive
   (3) replace than with then
   (4) insert a comma after and
   (5) change ranges to range's

9. Sentences 5 and 6: **Many people prefer microwaves for the speed of cooking. Which is one of their best qualities.**

   Which of the following is the best way to write the underlined portion of these sentences? If you think the original is the best way, choose option (1).

   (1) cooking. Which is one
   (2) cooking; which is one
   (3) cooking, which one
   (4) cooking. Being one
   (5) cooking, which is one

10. Sentence 9: **In fact, are required by law to do so.**

    Which of the following is the best way to write the underlined portion of this sentence? If you think the original is the best way, choose option (1).

    (1) In fact, are required
    (2) In fact, it are required
    (3) In fact, they are required
    (4) in fact, they are required
    (5) In fact are required

Items 11 to 14 refer to the following paragraphs.

(1) More older Americans read comic books now than at any time in the past. (2) Part of this trend due to the comic book companies' recent focus on gaining a larger adult audience. (3) Older readers are still happy to read the comics. (4) That they grew up with. (5) Even though children's comics still fill part of the racks, adults and teenagers are the main customers at comic book stores. (6) Both children and adults enjoy reading about science fiction characters, superheroes, detectives, and magicians.

(7) The readers show as much variety as the contents of the comics they read. (8) One small company asked its readers to write in, asking them what kind of work they do. (9) Replied that they are lawyers, stewardesses, teachers, sailors, engineers, janitors, students, and businesspeople, among others. (10) Readers coming from all imaginable backgrounds. (11) Another reason for the popularity of comic books among adult readers is the types of subject matter now appearing. (12) Publishers are producing comic books for purposes other than entertainment. (13) There are instructional comic books that can teach a reader anything from auto repair to economic theory.

11. Sentence 2: **Part of this trend due to the comic book companies' recent focus on gaining a larger adult audience.**

What correction should be made to this sentence?

(1) insert a comma after trend
(2) insert is after trend
(3) change companies' to companie's
(4) change companies' to company's
(5) insert a comma after focus

12. Sentences 3 and 4: **Older readers are still happy to read the comics. That they grew up with.**

Which of the following is the best way to write the underlined portion of these sentences? If you think the original is the best way, choose option (1).

(1) comics. That
(2) comics; that
(3) comics. that
(4) comics, that
(5) comics that

13. Sentence 9: **Replied that they are lawyers, stewardesses, teachers, sailors, engineers, janitors, students, and businesspeople, among others.**

Which of the following is the best way to write the underlined portion of this sentence? If you think the original is the best way, choose option (1).

(1) Replied that they are
(2) Them replied that they are
(3) Replied that they is
(4) They replied that they are
(5) They replied that they is

14. Sentence 10: **Readers coming from all imaginable backgrounds.**

What correction should be made to this sentence?

(1) change Readers to Reader's
(2) change coming to are coming
(3) insert a semicolon after coming
(4) insert a comma after coming
(5) no correction is necessary

Answers are on page 296.

Directions: Choose the best answer to each item.

Items 1 to 5 refer to the following paragraphs.

(1) "A woman's place" these days is more frequently "in uniform." (2) As a record number of women have joined the armed forces. (3) Enlistment of women increasing in all branches of the armed forces. (4) In fact, the military are now ten percent female.

(5) The military life is not new to women. (6) In spite of what some might believe. (7) Over 200 women, many of whom were pilots and nurses, were killed in World War II; eighty nurses were captured and imprisoned in camps. (8) Today, the United States has around 1.2 million female veterans of the armed services. (9) The increased number of women is a positive trend, since the new female recruits possess extremely high skills.

1. Sentences 1 and 2: **"A woman's place" these days is more frequently "in uniform." As a record number of women have joined the armed forces.**

   Which of the following is the best way to write the underlined portion of these sentences? If you think the original is the best way, choose option (1).

   (1) uniform." As a record
   (2) uniform". As a record
   (3) uniform. As a record
   (4) uniform" as a record
   (5) uniform", as a record

2. Sentence 3: **Enlistment of women increasing in all branches of the armed forces.**

   What correction should be made to this sentence?

   (1) insert a comma after Enlistment
   (2) change women to womans
   (3) insert is after women
   (4) change the spelling of increasing to increeing
   (5) no correction is necessary

3. Sentence 4: **In fact, the military are now ten percent female.**

   What correction should be made to this sentence?

   (1) remove the comma after fact
   (2) change military to militaries
   (3) change are to is
   (4) change are to were
   (5) no correction is necessary

4. Sentences 5 and 6: **The military life is not new to women. In spite of what some might believe.**

   Which of the following is the best way to write the underlined portion of these sentences? If you think the original is the best way, choose option (1).

   (1) to women. In spite
   (2) to women; In spite
   (3) to women, in spite
   (4) to womans in spite
   (5) to women; in spite

5. Sentence 9: **The increased number of women is a positive trend, since the new female recruits possess extremely high skills.**

   Which of the following is the best way to write the underlined portion of this sentence? If you think the original is the best way, choose option (1).

   (1) is a positive trend, since
   (2) is a positive trend, Since
   (3) is a positive trend. Since
   (4) is a positive trend; since
   (5) are a positive trend, since

Answers are on page 297.

Lesson 19

Run-On Sentences

A sentence is an independent clause. It has a subject and a verb, and it expresses a complete idea. A run-on sentence occurs when two or more independent clauses are strung together without the proper punctuation or linking words.

One way to avoid a run-on sentence is to separate the two independent clauses into two different sentences using a period. Other ways to avoid a run-on—but still keep the two sentences combined—are to join the two independent clauses (1) with a semicolon; (2) with a comma and a coordinating conjunction; or (3) with a semicolon, a conjunctive adverb, and a comma.

Read the following paragraph and find the run-on sentences.

(1) The story tells of a man at an auction who sneezed he wound up being the owner of a moth-eaten moose head. (2) In reality, those who attend auctions have time to change their minds they don't have to take the moose head home. (3) One problem in attending auctions, however, is getting caught up in the excitement of the sale it goes so quickly and so noisily. (4) You must decide how much you would be willing to pay ahead of time you won't be tempted to overbid and won't regret it later. (5) You should plan ahead, you might avoid finding a home for that moose head.

Rule: Correct a run-on sentence using a period.

> **Independent clause. Independent clause.**

Example: (Sentence 3) One problem in attending auctions, however, is getting caught up in the excitement of the <u>sale it</u> goes so quickly and so noisily.

Correct: One problem in attending auctions, however, is getting caught up in the excitement of the <u>sale. It</u> goes so quickly and so noisily.

Rule: Correct a run-on sentence using a semicolon.

> **Independent clause; independent clause.**

Example: (Sentence 2) In reality, those who attend auctions have time to change their <u>minds they</u> don't have to take the moose head home.

Correct: In reality, those who attend auctions have time to change their <u>minds; they</u> don't have to take the moose head home.

Rule:	Correct a run-on sentence using a comma and a coordinating conjunction.	

Independent clause	, and , but , or , nor , for , yet , so	**independent clause.**

Example: (Sentence 1) The story tells of a man at an auction who <u>sneezed he</u> wound up being the owner of a moth-eaten moose head.

Correct: The story tells of a man at an auction who <u>sneezed, and he</u> wound up being the owner of a moth-eaten moose head.

 Remember, joining two independent clauses with a comma but without a conjunction creates a comma splice. Never use a comma alone to fix a run-on sentence.

Rule: Correct a run-on sentence using a semicolon, a conjunctive adverb, and a comma.

Independent clause	; however, ; therefore, ; also, ; then, ; nevertheless, ; next, ; consequently, ; moreover,	**independent clause.**

Example: (Sentence 4) You must decide how much you would be willing to pay ahead of <u>time you</u> won't be tempted to overbid and won't regret it later.

Correct: You must decide how much you would be willing to pay ahead of <u>time; then, you</u> won't be tempted to overbid and won't regret it later.

Example: (Sentence 5) You should plan <u>ahead, you</u> might avoid finding a home for that moose head.

Correct: You should plan <u>ahead; then, you</u> might avoid finding a home for that moose head.

Items 1 to 5 refer to the following paragraph. Choose the best answer to each item.

(1) Not all on-the-job injuries involve heavy equipment some safer occupations can also cause injuries. (2) Workers who type constantly, such as data entry operators, may suffer from overstrain of muscles their fingers may literally seize up from the repetitive finger movements. (3) A few of these typists possibly have permanent nerve damage. (4) Staring for long periods at computer screens may cause severe eyestrain the studies on long-term effects continue. (5) In some offices, continuous whines or buzzes from ventilation or machines can affect workers, even though the sounds are not loud, over time, employees may experience hearing loss.

1. Sentence 1: **Not all on-the-job injuries involve heavy equipment some safer occupations can also cause injuries.**

   What correction should be made to this sentence?

   (1) insert a comma after equipment
   (2) insert a semicolon after equipment
   (3) insert and after equipment
   (4) insert however after equipment
   (5) no correction is necessary

2. Sentence 2: **Workers who type constantly, such as data entry operators, may suffer from overstrain of muscles their fingers may literally seize up from the repetitive finger movements.**

   Which of the following is the best way to write the underlined portion of this sentence? If you think the original is the best way, choose option (1).

   (1) muscles their fingers
   (2) muscles, their fingers
   (3) muscles. Their fingers
   (4) muscles. There fingers
   (5) muscles, there fingers

3. Sentence 3: **A few of these typists possibly have permanent nerve damage.**

   What correction should be made to this sentence?

   (1) change typists to Typists
   (2) change have to has
   (3) change the spelling of permanent to permenant
   (4) insert a comma after nerve
   (5) no correction is necessary

4. Sentence 4: **Staring for long periods at computer screens may cause severe eyestrain the studies on long-term effects continue.**

   What correction should be made to this sentence?

   (1) insert a semicolon after screens
   (2) insert a comma after screens
   (3) insert a semicolon after eyestrain
   (4) change effects to affects
   (5) change continue to continues

5. Sentence 5: **In some offices, continuous whines or buzzes from ventilation or machines can affect workers, even though the sounds are not loud, over time, employees may experience hearing loss.**

   What correction should be made to this sentence?

   (1) change offices to office's
   (2) insert a comma after ventilation
   (3) insert a semicolon after machines
   (4) change the comma after workers to a semicolon
   (5) no correction is necessary

(1) Americans may not consider their country backward the rest of the world does think so. (2) The United States is one of only three countries in the world where the metric system of measurement is not standard. (3) Even England, the country that gave us our way of measuring, converted to metrics a number of years ago they wanted to compete in the foreign trade markets.

(4) Our system of measurement causes our businesses great problems internationally. (5) Some companies stock two sets of products, some measured our way, others in metrics, they can sell goods here and abroad. (6) The cost of this is high some manufacturers, including the major auto companies, have converted entirely to metrics now.

6. Sentence 1: **Americans may not consider their country backward the rest of the world does think so.**

   Which of the following is the best way to write the underlined portion of this sentence? If you think the original is the best way, choose option (1).

   (1) backward the rest
   (2) backward, the rest
   (3) backward, but the rest
   (4) backward but, the rest
   (5) backward, nor the rest

7. Sentence 2: **The United States is one of only three countries in the world where the metric system of measurement is not standard.**

   What correction should be made to this sentence?

   (1) change United States to united states
   (2) insert a comma after States
   (3) insert commas after countries and world
   (4) change world to World
   (5) no correction is necessary

8. Sentence 3: **Even England, the country that gave us our way of measuring, converted to metrics a number of years ago they wanted to compete in the foreign trade markets.**

   Which of the following is the best way to write the underlined portion of this sentence? If you think the original is the best way, choose option (1).

   (1) years ago they wanted
   (2) year's ago they wanted
   (3) years ago, they wanted
   (4) years ago, however, they wanted
   (5) years ago. They wanted

9. Sentence 5: **Some companies stock two sets of products, some measured our way, others in metrics, they can sell goods here and abroad.**

   Which of the following is the best way to write the underlined portion of this sentence? If you think the original is the best way, choose option (1).

   (1) in metrics, they can
   (2) in metrics they can
   (3) in metrics but, they can
   (4) in metrics, then, they can
   (5) in metrics, so they can

10. Sentence 6: **The cost of this is high some manufacturers, including the major auto companies, have converted entirely to metrics now.**

    Which of the following is the best way to write the underlined portion of this sentence? If you think the original is the best way, choose option (1).

    (1) high some manufacturers,
    (2) high some manufacturers
    (3) high, some manufacturers,
    (4) high some manufacturers;
    (5) high; therefore, some manufacturers,

Items 11 to 15 refer to the following paragraphs.

(1) During the Vietnam War, many of the sailors and soldiers wore personally decorated jackets. (2) They were known as "Pleiku" or "tour" jackets. (3) Soldiers or sailors would decorate them colorfully, they would be sewn with designs like maps, dragons, and flags. (4) Later, the owners added patches and written sayings that showed where, when, and with whom the soldiers or sailors were stationed. (5) The jackets became completely personalized each individual's was different.

(6) The first to wear the tour jackets were sailors. (7) The Navy issued them a working jacket it was the only Navy clothing they could change the appearance of. (8) Decorating jackets began with sailors it became common among the soldiers later.

11. Sentences 1 and 2: **During the Vietnam War, many of the sailors and soldiers wore personally decorated jackets. They were known as "Pleiku" or "tour" jackets.**

Which of the following is the best way to write the underlined portion of these sentences? If you think the original is the best way, choose option (1).

(1) jackets. They
(2) jackets, they
(3) jackets; however, they
(4) jacket they
(5) jackets; They

12. Sentence 3: **Soldiers or sailors would decorate them colorfully, they would be sewn with designs like maps, dragons, and flags.**

Which of the following is the best way to write the underlined portion of this sentence? If you think the original is the best way, choose option (1).

(1) colorfully, they would be
(2) colorfully, they would been
(3) colorfully and, they would be
(4) colorfully they would be
(5) colorfully; they would be

13. Sentence 5: **The jackets became completely personalized each individual's was different.**

Which of the following is the best way to write the underlined portion of this sentence? If you think the original is the best way, choose option (1).

(1) personalized each individual's
(2) personalized each individuals
(3) personalized; each individual's
(4) personalized; each individuals
(5) personalized; because each individual's

14. Sentence 7: **The Navy issued them a working jacket it was the only Navy clothing they could change the appearance of.**

Which of the following is the best way to write the underlined portion of this sentence? If you think the original is the best way, choose option (1).

(1) jacket it was
(2) jacket, it was
(3) jacket. It being
(4) jacket, and it was
(5) jacket and, it was

15. Sentence 8: **Decorating jackets began with sailors it became common among the soldiers later.**

Which of the following is the best way to write the underlined portion of this sentence? If you think the original is the best way, choose option (1).

(1) with sailors it became
(2) with sailors but, it became
(3) with sailors; It became
(4) with sailors, however, it became
(5) with sailors; however, it became

Answers are on page 298.

Unit 3: Sentence Structure

Directions: Choose the best answer to each item.

Items 1 to 5 refer to the following paragraphs.

(1) The next time that you're feeling blue or stressed, go ahead and cry about it. (2) This is the advice of scientists who study crying. (3) Crying being nature's way of helping the body cope with stress.

(4) The tears all may come from the same place studies have shown that the tears aren't all the same. (5) For example, when we watch a wedding or a sad movie, we cry tears that have a high protein level. (6) Smoke in the eyes makes us cry a different kind of tears these protective tears contain less protein. (7) No one knows yet why this happens; nevertheless, researchers agree it must be healthy.

1. Sentence 1: **The next time that you're feeling blue or stressed, go ahead and cry about it.**

    What corrections should be made to this sentence?

    (1) insert a comma after time
    (2) insert a comma after or
    (3) replace the comma after stressed with a semicolon
    (4) replace stressed, go with stressed. Go
    (5) no correction is necessary

2. Sentence 3: **Crying being nature's way of helping the body cope with stress.**

    What corrections should be made to this sentence?

    (1) change Crying to To cry
    (2) change being to be
    (3) change being to is
    (4) change nature's to natures'
    (5) change nature's to natures

3. Sentence 4: **The tears all may come from the same place studies have shown that the tears aren't all the same.**

    Which of the following is the best way to write the underlined portion of this sentence? If you think the original is the best way, choose option (1).

    (1) same place studies have
    (2) same place, studies have
    (3) same place and, studies have
    (4) same place, but studies have
    (5) same place; studies has

4. Sentence 6: **Smoke in the eyes makes us cry a different kind of tears these protective tears contain less protein.**

    Which of the following is the best way to write the underlined portion of this sentence? If you think the original is the best way, choose option (1).

    (1) tears these protective tears
    (2) tears. these protective tears
    (3) tears, these protective tears
    (4) tear, these protective tears
    (5) tears; these protective tears

5. Sentence 7: **No one knows yet why this happens; nevertheless, researchers agree it must be healthy.**

    Which of the following is the best way to write the underlined portion of this sentence? If you think the original is the best way, choose option (1).

    (1) happens; nevertheless,
    (2) happens; nevertheless
    (3) happens, nevertheless,
    (4) happens nevertheless
    (5) happens. nevertheless,

Answers are on page 299.

Combining Sentences

One way you can connect two sentences is with a semicolon. When you use a semicolon, you are implying that the ideas in the two sentences are closely related, but without clearly showing what the relationship is.

Another way to connect two sentences is to use a **conjunctive adverb.** A conjunctive adverb connects two sentences and shows a certain kind of relationship between the two ideas. When you connect two sentences with a conjunctive adverb, you use a semicolon before the adverb and a comma following it.

Coordinating conjunctions can also show the relationship between the ideas in two sentences. Use a comma with a coordinating conjunction when combining sentences this way. Always be sure to use a conjunctive adverb or coordinating conjunction that conveys the appropriate connection between the independent clauses.

Read the paragraph and consider how these sentences can be combined.

  (1) Jack is a stage director. (2) He wanted to start a community theater group. (3) He did not have enough money to start a theater. (4) His friends wanted to loan him the money. (5) Jack went to a bank for a loan. (6) The loan officer of the bank was a reasonable woman. (7) She granted the loan to Jack. (8) Jack found some good playwrights, actors, and designers. (9) Their company is working hard. (10) Their first play is an exceptionally funny comedy. (11) It is sure to be a hit.

Here are some rules of sentence combining and examples of how to show relationships between sentences when you combine them.

Rule: Combine sentences using a semicolon.
Example: (Sentences 1 and 2) Jack is a stage director. He wanted to start a community theater group.
Combine: Jack is a stage director; he wanted to start a community theater group.

 When combining two sentences, read both sentences and look for the relationship between their ideas. Then choose the punctuation and/or connecting words that best express that relationship.

Rule:	Combine sentences using a semicolon, a conjunctive adverb, and a comma.
Hint:	Choose the correct conjunctive adverb to show the relationship between the two ideas being combined.

Relationship	Conjunctive adverb
connects two ideas	also, furthermore, moreover, besides
contrasts two ideas	however, still, nevertheless, instead, nonetheless
compares two ideas	similarly, likewise
shows a result	therefore, thus, consequently
shows time passing	next, then, meanwhile, finally, subsequently

Example:	(Sentences 4 and 5) His friends wanted to loan him the money. Jack went to a bank for a loan.
Combine:	His friends wanted to loan him the money; instead, Jack went to a bank for a loan. (This shows a *contrast*.)
Example:	(Sentences 6 and 7) The loan officer of the bank was a reasonable woman. She granted the loan to Jack.
Combine:	The loan officer of the bank was a reasonable woman; therefore, she granted the loan to Jack. (This shows a *result*.)

Rule:	Combine sentences using a comma and a coordinating conjunction.
Hint:	Choose the correct coordinating conjunction to show the relationship between the two ideas being combined.

Relationship	Coordinating conjunction
connects two ideas	and
contrasts two ideas	but, yet
shows a cause	for
negates a possibility	nor
shows another possibility	or
shows a result	so

Example:	(Sentences 8 and 9) Jack found some good playwrights, actors, and designers. Their company is working hard.
Combine:	Jack found some good playwrights, actors, and designers, and their company is working hard. (This *connects* the two ideas.)
Example:	(Sentences 10 and 11) Their first play is an exceptionally funny comedy. It is sure to be a hit.
Combine:	Their first play is an exceptionally funny comedy, so it is sure to be a hit. (This shows a *result*.)

Items 1 to 5 refer to the following paragraph. Choose the best answer to each item.

(1) Pushcart Supermarket does not sell my favorite kind of cold cut. (2) The supermarket down the block does. (3) This store has a deli department. (4) It has many kinds of cold cuts. (5) Their selection includes turkey, ham, and roast beef. (6) There are others, too. (7) The clerk at the deli counter made me a sandwich. (8) The sandwich was larger than I'd asked for. (9) The sandwich was huge, but I ate it anyway. (10) It was twice as much food as I normally eat. (11) I felt sick.

1. Sentences 1 and 2: **Pushcart Supermarket does not sell my favorite kind of cold cut. The supermarket down the block does.**

    The most effective combination of sentences 1 and 2 would include which of the following groups of words?

    (1) cold cut, but the supermarket
    (2) cold cut, so the supermarket
    (3) cold cut; likewise, the supermarket
    (4) cold cut, however, the supermarket
    (5) cold cut, the supermarket

2. Sentences 3 and 4: **This store has a deli department. It has many kinds of cold cuts.**

    The most effective combination of sentences 3 and 4 would include which of the following groups of words?

    (1) department, but it
    (2) department, it
    (3) department; meanwhile, it
    (4) department, so it
    (5) department, but, it

3. Sentences 5 and 6: **Their selection includes turkey, ham, and roast beef. There are others, too.**

    The most effective combination of sentences 5 and 6 would include which of the following groups of words?

    (1) beef; finally, there are
    (2) beef, nor are there
    (3) beef; therefore, there are
    (4) beef, and there are
    (5) beef; there being

4. Sentences 7 and 8: **The clerk at the deli counter made me a sandwich. The sandwich was larger than I'd asked for.**

    The most effective combination of sentences 7 and 8 would include which of the following groups of words?

    (1) sandwich; consequently, the
    (2) sandwich, the sandwich
    (3) sandwich; however, the
    (4) sandwich; besides, the
    (5) sandwich, or the

5. Sentences 10 and 11: **It was twice as much food as I normally eat. I felt sick.**

    The most effective combination of sentences 10 and 11 would include which of the following groups of words?

    (1) normally eat; subsequently, I
    (2) normally eat; nevertheless, I
    (3) normally eat; still, I
    (4) normally eat, or I
    (5) normally eat, I felt

Items 6 to 10 refer to the following paragraph.

(1) The saying goes that the only sure things in life are death and taxes. (2) Most people would surely agree. (3) When April 15 comes, taxpayers take note and this is the deadline for federal taxes. (4) The tax forms take time to complete. (5) Many taxpayers tend to wait until the last minute. (6) Now the Internal Revenue Service has introduced electronic filing; therefore, some taxpayers can receive their refunds in less than two weeks. (7) The majority still prefer to use the mail. (8) Their refunds may take more time to arrive. (9) The Internal Revenue Service would like more people to take advantage of electronic filing. (10) Electronic returns are easier to process.

6. Sentences 1 and 2: **The saying goes that the only sure things in life are death and taxes. Most people would surely agree.**

   The most effective combination of sentences 1 and 2 would include which of the following groups of words?

   (1) taxes, and most
   (2) taxes, but most
   (3) taxes, most
   (4) taxes; then, most
   (5) taxes or most

7. Sentence 3: **When April 15 comes, taxpayers take note and this is the deadline for federal taxes.**

   Which of the following is the best way to write the underlined portion of this sentence? If you think the original is the best way, choose option (1).

   (1) take note and this
   (2) taking note; this
   (3) take note, this
   (4) take note, and this
   (5) take note, for this

8. Sentences 4 and 5: **The tax forms take time to complete. Many taxpayers tend to wait until the last minute.**

   The most effective combination of sentences 4 and 5 would include which of the following groups of words?

   (1) complete, but many
   (2) complete; finally, many
   (3) complete; many waiting
   (4) complete; likewise, many
   (5) complete, many

9. Sentences 7 and 8: **The majority still prefer to use the mail. Their refunds may take more time to arrive.**

   The most effective combination of sentences 7 and 8 would include which of the following groups of words?

   (1) mail, their
   (2) mail, so their
   (3) mail, but they're
   (4) mail; there
   (5) mail, consequently, their

10. Sentences 9 and 10: **The Internal Revenue Service would like more people to take advantage of electronic filing. Electronic returns are easier to process.**

    The most effective combination of sentences 9 and 10 would include which of the following groups of words?

    (1) filing, electronic
    (2) filing, or electronic
    (3) filing; consequently, electronic
    (4) filing; subsequently, electronic
    (5) filing, for electronic

Items 11 to 15 refer to the following paragraphs.

(1) The moon's pull on Earth affects tides at sea. (2) Studies suggest that it may affect people as well, for people often act differently under a full moon. (3) Violent crimes tend to rise, but accidents occur more often. (4) Some people even claim they feel more inventive, so other people claim they feel worse than usual.

(5) You might have some beliefs about the full moon. (6) Do you wait for the moon before cutting your hair? (7) Do you wait for the moon before clipping your fingernails? (8) Some people feel they must do this. (9) They might not want to admit it in public.

11. Sentence 2: **Studies suggest that it may affect people as <u>well, for</u> people often act differently under a full moon.**

Which of the following is the best way to write the underlined portion of this sentence? If you think the original is the best way, choose option (1).

(1) well, for
(2) well. for
(3) well; for
(4) well, yet
(5) well; however,

12. Sentence 3: **Violent crimes tend to <u>rise, but accidents</u> occur more often.**

Which of the following is the best way to write the underlined portion of this sentence? If you think the original is the best way, choose option (1).

(1) rise, but accidents
(2) rise, and accidents
(3) rise, therefore, accidents
(4) rise, nor do accidents
(5) rise, accidents

13. Sentence 4: **Some people even claim they feel more <u>inventive, so other</u> people claim they feel worse than usual.**

Which of the following is the best way to write the underlined portion of this sentence? If you think the original is the best way, choose option (1).

(1) inventive, so other
(2) inventive, other
(3) inventive, but other
(4) inventive, however, other
(5) inventive; yet other

14. Sentences 6 and 7: **Do you wait for the moon before cutting your hair? Do you wait for the moon before clipping your fingernails?**

The most effective combination of sentences 6 and 7 would include which of the following groups of words?

(1) hair? and do you
(2) hair, but do you
(3) hair? or do you
(4) hair; or do you
(5) hair, or do you

15. Sentences 8 and 9: **Some people feel they must do this. They might not want to admit it in public.**

The most effective combination of sentences 8 and 9 would include which of the following groups of words?

(1) this, for they
(2) this, meanwhile, they
(3) this, they
(4) this, yet they
(5) this; and they not wanting

Items 16 to 20 refer to the following paragraph.

(1) Sometimes, if anything can go wrong, it will. (2) You sit down at your electric typewriter. (3) It won't work; likewise, you must get it repaired. (4) After it's fixed, you begin to type. (5) Immediately you make a mistake. (6) You have no correction fluid. (7) You have no correction tape. (8) You begin a new sheet. (9) A storm begins outside. (10) The power goes out, or you are back where you started.

16. Sentence 3: **It won't work; likewise, you must get it repaired.**

    Which of the following is the best way to write the underlined portion of this sentence? If you think the original is the best way, choose option (1).

    (1) work; likewise, you
    (2) work, but you
    (3) work, so you
    (4) work, you
    (5) work, therefore, you

17. Sentences 4 and 5: **After it's fixed, you begin to type. Immediately you make a mistake.**

    The most effective combination of sentences 4 and 5 would include which of the following groups of words?

    (1) type; besides, immediately you make
    (2) type, immediately you make
    (3) type, or immediately you make
    (4) type; immediately making
    (5) type; then, immediately you make

18. Sentences 6 and 7: **You have no correction fluid. You have no correction tape.**

    The most effective combination of sentences 6 and 7 would include which of the following groups of words?

    (1) fluid, and you have no
    (2) fluid, but you have not
    (3) fluid; thus, you have no
    (4) fluid, you have no
    (5) fluid, so you have no

19. Sentences 8 and 9: **You begin a new sheet. A storm begins outside.**

    The most effective combination of sentences 8 and 9 would include which of the following groups of words?

    (1) sheet; nevertheless, a
    (2) sheet; meanwhile, a
    (3) sheet, so a
    (4) sheet, a
    (5) sheet, yet a

20. Sentence 10: **The power goes out, or you are back where you started.**

    Which of the following is the best way to write the underlined portion of this sentence? If you think the original is the best way, choose option (1).

    (1) out, or you
    (2) out, yet you
    (3) out, for you
    (4) out, and you
    (5) out, but you

Answers are on page 299.

Directions: Choose the best answer to each item.

Items 1 to 11 refer to the following paragraphs.

(1) One popular misconception about libraries are that they're too difficult to find things in. (2) Some people look only for fiction to read, for they don't realize there are other books available. (3) Libraries hold an enormos amount of information books. (4) These books are kept together in reference sections. (5) Filled with books meant to be used to find facts.

(6) Many libraries employ reference librarians, to. (7) They are trained to find any information you could need. (8) First you have to ask for this librarian. (9) Tell him or her what you want to know. (10) This librarian will find it. (11) Do you want to control crabgrass? (12) Do you want to write a résumé? (13) A reference librarian can help. (14) You have to ask. (15) You might not have time to go in, you can telephone in your question. (16) A question is neither too silly or too weird for a reference librarian. (17) Libraries have more to offer than just books; indeed, many offer classes, movies, and other special programs. (18) Some libraries provide typewriters and computers for the use of their patrons. (19) Who don't have other access to these devices. (20) Libraries provide so many different services. (21) They must be viewed as one of our greatest public resources. (22) If you haven't been there recently, visit your local library today.

1. Sentence 1: **One popular misconception about libraries are that they're too difficult to find things in.**

   What correction should be made to this sentence?

   (1) change the spelling of libraries to libaries
   (2) change libraries to library's
   (3) replace are with is
   (4) change they're to there
   (5) change too to to

2. Sentence 3: **Libraries hold an enormos amount of information books.**

   What correction should be made to this sentence?

   (1) change Libraries to libraries
   (2) replace hold with holds
   (3) change the spelling of enormos to enormous
   (4) change the spelling of amounts to amownts
   (5) insert a comma after information

3. Sentences 4 and 5: **These books are kept together in reference sections. Filled with books meant to be used to find facts.**

   Which of the following is the best way to write the underlined portion of this sentence? If you think the original is the best way, choose option (1).

   (1) sections. Filled with
   (2) sections; filled with
   (3) sections. Fill with
   (4) sections, filled with
   (5) sections. Being filled with

4. Sentence 6: **Many libraries employ reference librarians, to.**

   What correction should be made to this sentence?

   (1) change the spelling of libraries to libaries
   (2) change libraries to library's
   (3) change employ to are employed
   (4) change to to too
   (5) no correction is necessary

5. Sentences 8 and 9: **First you have to ask for this librarian. Tell him or her what you want to know.**

The most effective combination of sentences 8 and 9 would include which of the following groups of words?

(1) librarian, tell
(2) librarian, than tell
(3) librarian; then, tell
(4) librarian, but tell
(5) librarian, or tell

6. Sentences 11 and 12: **Do you want to control crabgrass? Do you want to write a résumé?**

The most effective combination of sentences 11 and 12 would include which of the following groups of words?

(1) crabgrass? but do you
(2) crabgrass? or do you
(3) crabgrass, but do you
(4) crabgrass, or do you
(5) crabgrass, so do you

7. Sentences 13 and 14: **A reference librarian can help. You have to ask.**

The most effective combination of sentences 13 and 14 would include which of the following groups of words?

(1) can help; however, you
(2) can help, however, you
(3) can help, you
(4) can help, for you
(5) can help; besides, you

8. Sentence 15: **You might not have time to go in, you can telephone in your question.**

What correction should be made to this sentence?

(1) remove the comma after in
(2) insert because after in
(3) insert but after in
(4) change the comma to a period
(5) no correction is necessary

9. Sentence 17: **Libraries have more to offer than just books; indeed, many offer classes, movies, and other special programs.**

What correction should be made to this sentence?

(1) change the semicolon to a comma
(2) remove the semicolon after books
(3) remove the comma after indeed
(4) remove the comma after movies
(5) no correction is necessary

10. Sentences 18 and 19: **Some libraries provide typewriters and computers for the use of their patrons. Who don't have other access to these devices.**

Which of the following is the best way to write the underlined portion of these sentences? If you think the original is the best way, choose option (1).

(1) patrons. Who don't
(2) patrons. Whom don't
(3) patrons; who don't
(4) patrons who don't
(5) patrons whom don't

11. Sentences 20 and 21: **Libraries provide so many different services. They must be viewed as one of our greatest public resources.**

The most effective combination of sentences 21 and 22 would include which of the following groups of words?

(1) services, they
(2) services, thus, they
(3) services; similarly, they
(4) services; consequently, they
(5) services they

Answers are on page 301.

Lesson 21
Parallel Structure

Parallel structure is a way to express equal and related ideas and phrases in a sentence.

When a sentence contains items in a series, each item must grammatically match the others. This is called a parallel structure. Maintaining parallelism is important to the clear expression of ideas.

Read the short paragraphs below and on page 183. Look for series of words or phrases and find the item that is not parallel.

(1) We love our pets because they live with us, knowing us well, but love us anyway. (2) We need them to charm, to entertain, and they comfort us. (3) Enough to eat, daily exercise, and a safe home are all they ask of us.

Look for items in a series separated by commas and the conjunctions *and, but, or,* or *nor.* Make sure that each item represents the same part of speech.

Rule: Use parallel adjectives and nouns in a series.
Example: (Sentence 3) Enough to eat, daily exercise, and a safe home are all they ask of us.
Correct: Enough food, daily exercise, and a safe home are all they ask of us.

Not Parallel	**Parallel**
Enough to eat (adjective-infinitive)	Enough food (adjective-noun)
daily exercise (adjective-noun)	daily exercise (adjective-noun)
safe home (adjective-noun)	safe home (adjective-noun)

Rule: Use parallel verb forms in a series.
Example: (Sentence 2) We need them to charm, to entertain, and they comfort us.
Correct: We need them to charm, to entertain, and to comfort us.

Not Parallel	**Parallel**
to charm (infinitive)	to charm (infinitive)
to entertain (infinitive)	to entertain (infinitive)
they comfort (noun-verb)	to comfort (infinitive)

Rule: Use parallel verbs in a series.
Example: (Sentence 1) We love our pets because they live with us, knowing us well, but love us anyway.
Correct: We love our pets because they live with us, know us well, but love us anyway.

Not Parallel	Parallel

because they live with us
    (present plural verb)
	because they <u>live</u> with us
	    (present plural verb)

(because they) <u>knowing</u> us
    (present participle)
	(because they) <u>know</u> us
	    (present plural verb)

(because they) love us
    (present plural verb)
	(because they) <u>love</u> us
	    (present plural verb)

(1) A renter must look sensibly, carefully, and with caution at new apartments. (2) The renter who wanting quiet, needs space, and likes value should take time to look carefully. (3) Look in the rooms, looking at the view, but most of all at the lease.

Rule:	Use parallel adverbs in a series.
Example:	(Sentence 1) A renter must look sensibly, carefully, and with caution at new apartments.
Correct:	A renter must look sensibly, carefully, and cautiously at new apartments.

Not Parallel	Parallel
sensibly (adverb)	sensibly (adverb)
carefully (adverb)	carefully (adverb)
<u>with caution</u> (prepositional phrase)	cautiously (adverb)

Rule:	Use parallel prepositional phrases in a series.
Example:	(Sentence 3) Look in the rooms, looking at the view, but most of all at the lease.
Correct:	Look in the rooms, at the view, but most of all at the lease.

Not Parallel	Parallel

Look in the rooms
   (verb–prepositional phrase)
	Look in the rooms
	   (verb–prepositional phrase)

<u>looking</u> at the view
   (participle–prepositional phrase)
	(Look) at the view
	   (verb–prepositional phrase)

(Look) at the lease
   (verb–prepositional phrase)
	(Look) at the lease
	   (verb–prepositional phrase)

Rule:	Use parallel verbs and nouns in a series.
Example:	(Sentence 2) The renter who wanting quiet, needs space, and likes value should take time to look carefully.
Correct:	The renter who wants quiet, needs space, and likes value should take time to look carefully.

Not Parallel	Parallel
<u>wanting</u> quiet (present participle–noun)	wants quiet (verb–noun)
needs space (verb–noun)	needs space (verb–noun)
likes value (verb–noun)	likes value (verb–noun)

Items 1 to 5 refer to the following paragraph. Choose the best answer to each item.

(1) Before you chase, swat, or have sprayed that cockroach, consider that "critter." (2) According to scientists, cockroaches have been scurrying, crawled, and flying about the earth far longer than humans have. (3) Roaches can live anywhere hot or cold, in cities, on farms, and jungles. (4) Cockroaches will always be with us. (5) They have been able to escape from, to adapt to, and survived everything from chemicals to nuclear radiation. (6) However, a speedy shoe, a newspaper, or swinging your hand can still handle this bug despite its proud past.

1. Sentence 1: **Before you chase, swat, or have sprayed that cockroach, consider that "critter."**

   What correction should be made to this sentence?

   (1) change you to we
   (2) change chase to chased
   (3) change chase to chases
   (4) remove have
   (5) change have sprayed to spray

2. Sentence 2: **According to scientists, cockroaches have been scurrying, crawled, and flying about the earth far longer than humans have.**

   What correction should be made to this sentence?

   (1) change scientists to scientist's
   (2) remove been
   (3) change crawled to crawl
   (4) change crawled to crawling
   (5) insert a comma after flying

3. Sentence 3: **Roaches can live anywhere hot or cold, in cities, on farms, and jungles.**

   What correction should be made to this sentence?

   (1) change live to lives
   (2) insert the before cities
   (3) change on farms to farming
   (4) insert a comma after and
   (5) insert in before jungles

4. Sentence 5: **They have been able to escape from, to adapt to, and survived everything from chemicals to nuclear radiation.**

   What correction should be made to this sentence?

   (1) change have to has
   (2) remove the to after adapt
   (3) insert have after and
   (4) insert to after and survived
   (5) change survived to to survive

5. Sentence 6: **However, a speedy shoe, a newspaper, or swinging your hand can still handle this bug despite its proud past.**

   Which of the following is the best way to write the underlined portion of this sentence? If you think the original is the best way, choose option (1).

   (1) a speedy shoe, a newspaper, or swinging your hand
   (2) a speedy shoe, a newspaper or swinging your hand
   (3) a speedy shoe, swatting with newspaper, or swinging your hand
   (4) a speedy shoe, swatting with newspaper, or a hand
   (5) a speedy shoe, a newspaper, or a hand

Items 6 to 10 refer to the following paragraph.

(1) Having good intentions, a lot of experience, and carrying a good résumé are not enough for a job interview. (2) If you walk in wearing jeans, a sweatshirt, and with sneakers on, you won't impress anyone. (3) Plan ahead to have a good appearance. (4) Wear clothes that are businesslike, conservatively, and attractive. (5) When you arrive late, you're smoking, and you have your groceries, you don't create a good impression either. (6) Behave normally, act rationally, and being responsible, and you will do well. (7) If you are confident, serious and pleasant, you stand every chance of getting the job. (8) Even if you aren't hired at the very first interview, the experience of preparing for it will probably improve your chances at the next one.

6. Sentence 1: **Having good intentions, a lot of experience, and carrying a good résumé are not enough for a job interview.**

   What correction should be made to this sentence?

   (1) change Having to To have
   (2) change Having to have
   (3) insert having before a lot
   (4) replace a lot with alot
   (5) insert a comma after résumé

7. Sentence 2: **If you walk in wearing jeans, a sweatshirt, and with sneakers on, you won't impress anyone.**

   Which of the following is the best way to write the underlined portion of this sentence? If you think the original is the best way, choose option (1).

   (1) and with sneakers on,
   (2) and wearing sneakers,
   (3) with sneakers,
   (4) and sneakers,
   (5) and sneakers on,

8. Sentence 4: **Wear clothes that are businesslike, conservatively, and attractive.**

   What correction should be make to this sentence?

   (1) change Wear to Wearing
   (2) change clothes to cloths
   (3) replace businesslike with business
   (4) change conservatively to conservative
   (5) change attractive to attractively

9. Sentence 6: **Behave normally, act rationally, and being responsible, and you will do well.**

   What corrections should be make to this sentence?

   (1) change Behave to Behaving
   (2) change normally to normal
   (3) change act to acting
   (4) change being to be
   (5) change responsible to responsibly

10. Sentence 7: **If you are confident, serious and pleasant, you stand every chance of getting the job.**

    What correction should be made to this sentence?

    (1) change confident to confidently
    (2) insert a comma after serious
    (3) replace pleasant with a pleasant person
    (4) change the spelling of getting to geting
    (5) no correction is necessary

> **tip** Be sure you don't combine different parts of speech in a series. Check that you have used all nouns, all verbs, all adjectives, or all adverbs.

Items 11 to 15 refer to the following paragraph.

(1) Either you hate it or you like it or you ignore the music playing as you shop, work, or wait for appointments. (2) The soft, familiarity, yet anonymous music plays in the background of our lives. (3) The goal of the music is to affect our behavior in stores, at work, and while waiting in stressful situations. (4) Studies have shown that music can calm us, to lower our heart rate, and reduce our blood pressure. (5) Offices that use this music report less absenteeism, better performing on the job, and less turnover of employees. (6) Stores want this music to slow down customers, to make them shop longer, and to make them decide to buy more. (7) If you detest this background hum, there are few ways to escape it; however, you can try singing to yourself, wearing earplugs, or leaving the building.

11. Sentence 2: **The soft, familiarity, yet anonymous music plays in the background of our lives.**

    What correction should be made to this sentence?

    (1) change familiarity to familiar
    (2) insert a comma after yet
    (3) change plays to to play
    (4) change plays to playing
    (5) change lives to lives'

12. Sentence 3: **The goal of the music is to affect our behavior in stores, at work, and while waiting in stressful situations.**

    What correction should be made to this sentence?

    (1) change goal to goals
    (2) insert a comma after music
    (3) change affect to effect
    (4) change to affect to affecting
    (5) remove while waiting

13. Sentence 4: **Studies have shown that music can calm us, to lower our heart rate, and reduce our blood pressure.**

    What correction should be made to this sentence?

    (1) insert a comma after shown
    (2) remove to before lower
    (3) change to lower to lowering
    (4) insert a comma after and
    (5) insert to before reduce

14. Sentence 5: **Offices that use this music report less absenteeism, better performing on the job, and less turnover of employees.**

    What correction should be made to this sentence?

    (1) insert a comma after offices
    (2) insert a comma after music
    (3) change report to reports
    (4) change performing to performance
    (5) change employees to employee's

15. Sentence 7: **If you detest this background hum, there are few ways to escape it; however, you can try singing to yourself, wearing earplugs, or leaving the building.**

    What correction should be made to this sentence?

    (1) remove the comma after hum
    (2) change the semicolon after it to a comma
    (3) replace wearing earplugs with earplugs
    (4) change leaving to leave
    (5) no correction is necessary

Answers are on page 302.

Unit 3: Sentence Structure

Directions: Choose the best <u>answer</u> to each item.

Items 1 to 5 refer to the following paragraph.

(1) The lowly blanket is a symbol of security, just ask a parent. (2) Children sleep under them, carry them around, and play with them. (3) Since most children have a favorite blanket. (4) Parents must be careful. (5) If that blanket is taken away or lost or simply to be misplaced, then everyone may end up regretting it. (6) As we get older, taller, and wiser, we still secretly love our blankets. (7) We may drape them on chairs, on walls, on beds, or on ourselves our blankets are always nearby. (8) Many adults fondly remember the feelings of security, warmth, and being happy that their childhood blankets provided.

1. Sentence 1: **The lowly blanket is a symbol of <u>security, just</u> ask a parent.**

   Which of the following is the best way to write the underlined portion of this sentence? If you think the original is the best way, choose option (1).

   (1) security, just
   (2) security; therefore, just
   (3) security; just
   (4) security just
   (5) security, and just

2. Sentences 3 and 4: **Since most children have a favorite <u>blanket. Parents</u> must be careful.**

   Which of the following is the best way to write the underlined portion of these sentences? If you think the original is the best way, choose option (1).

   (1) blanket. Parents
   (2) blanket; parents
   (3) blanket, and parents
   (4) blanket, parents
   (5) blanket, but parents

3. Sentence 5: **If that blanket is taken away or lost or simply to be misplaced, then everyone may end up regretting it.**

   What correction should be made to this sentence?

   (1) change <u>is</u> to <u>are</u>
   (2) insert a comma after <u>away</u>
   (3) remove <u>simply</u>
   (4) remove the <u>to</u> after <u>simply</u>
   (5) remove <u>to be</u>

4. Sentence 7: **We may drape them on chairs, on walls, on beds, or on <u>ourselves our blankets</u> are always nearby.**

   Which of the following is the best way to write the underlined portion of this sentence? If you think the original is the best way, choose option (1).

   (1) ourselves our blankets
   (2) ourselfs our blankets
   (3) ourselfs, but our blankets
   (4) ourselves, but our blankets
   (5) ourselves, our blankets

5. Sentence 8: **Many adults fondly remember the feelings of security, warmth, and being happy that their childhood blankets provided.**

   What correction should be made to this sentence?

   (1) change <u>fondly</u> to <u>fond</u>
   (2) change <u>security</u> to <u>secure</u>
   (3) change <u>being happy</u> to <u>happiness</u>
   (4) change <u>warmth</u> to <u>warming</u>
   (5) no correction is necessary

Answers are on page 303.

Lesson 22

Subordination

An independent clause contains a subject and predicate, which includes the verb. It contains the main idea and can stand alone as a sentence. However, if you want to add more details about the independent clause, you can use subordinate clauses.

Subordinate clauses add either essential or nonessential information to the main idea of a sentence. They are dependent on the main sentence and cannot stand alone. Two kinds of subordinate clauses are (1) adverb clauses beginning with a subordinating conjunction and (2) adjective clauses beginning with a relative pronoun.

Adverb clauses begin with subordinating conjunctions. These conjunctions set up a specific kind of relationship between the main ideas in the independent and the subordinate clauses.

Here is a list of some subordinating conjunctions and the relationships that they show.

Time	Reason/Cause	Concession	Location
after	as	although	where
before	because	even though	wherever
once	since	though	
since			
until	**Condition**	**Result/Effect**	**Choice**
when	if	in order that	rather than
whenever	even if	so	than
while	provided that	so that	whether
	unless	that	

Adjective clauses begin with relative pronouns, such as *who, that,* and *which.* Remember that *who* and *whom* always refer to people (or animals with names, such as Lassie). *That* and *which* always refer to things and animals, not people. Adjective clauses can act as appositives. Use commas to set off an adjective clause when it appears inside a sentence unless the information is essential to the sentence. Place a comma before a nonessential adjective clause that follows an independent clause.

 Remember to use a comma after a subordinate clause if that clause comes at the beginning of the sentence.

Read the paragraph below and then look at the examples.

(1) Computer graphics has become the newest expert witness in some jury trials. (2) They can use pictures or drawings alone. (3) Some lawyers are introducing computer simulations. (4) Computer images show jurors reconstructions of accidents. (5) The images are watched on a screen. (6) Juries can picture events better. (7) They can see a moving image. (8) A lawyer may improve his or her argument. (9) A lawyer may use the simulations to do this. (10) Computers may enter more courtrooms in the future. (11) Their cost is still steep.

Rule:	Use a subordinating conjunction to show a relationship between two clauses.
Example:	(Sentences 2 and 3) They can use pictures or drawings alone. Some lawyers are introducing computer simulations.
Combine:	<u>Rather than use pictures or drawings alone</u>, some lawyers are introducing computer simulations. (Relationship: choice. Type of clause: introductory.)
Example:	(Sentences 6 and 7) Juries can picture events better. They can see a moving image.
Combine:	Juries can picture events better <u>because they can see a moving image</u>. (Relationship: cause. Type of clause: essential.)
Example:	(Sentences 10 and 11) Computers may enter more courtrooms in the future. Their cost is still steep.
Combine:	Computers may enter more courtrooms in the future, <u>although their cost is still steep</u>. (Relationship: concession. Type: nonessential.)
Rule:	Use a relative pronoun to begin a subordinate clause.
Example:	(Sentences 8 and 9) A lawyer may improve his or her argument. A lawyer may use the simulations to do this.
Combine:	A lawyer <u>who uses the simulations</u> may improve his or her argument. (Relationship: describes a person. Type: essential.)
Example:	(Sentences 4 and 5) Computer images show jurors reconstructions of accidents. The images are watched on a screen.
Combine:	Computer images, <u>which are watched on a screen</u>, show jurors reconstructions of accidents. (Relationship: describes a thing. Type: nonessential.)

Items 1 to 8 refer to the following paragraph. Choose the best answer to each item.

(1) Supermarkets encourage us to buy on impulse. (2) When we enter we generally move in the direction the store chooses, down the "power" aisle. (3) This aisle is crowded with sale items, whether nonsale items may be casually displayed as well. (4) Displays that are placed midaisle will slow us down. (5) The more costly merchandise is placed at eye level when shoppers look first.

(6) The shopper which reaches the milk products in the rear of the store without picking up other items is rare. (7) We cannot leave though we pay for our purchases. (8) We stand in the checkout line. (9) We'll see more impulse buys. (10) Magazines, candy, and other small items are placed at the register. (11) You, that may have wanted only a box of crackers, will probably walk out with more than you wanted. (12) We can avoid impulse buying. (13) We understand why we do it.

1. Sentence 2: **When we enter we generally move in the direction the store chooses, down the "power" aisle.**

What correction should be made to this sentence?

(1) insert a comma after enter
(2) change move to moving
(3) change the spelling of generally to genrally
(4) change chooses to chosen
(5) no correction is necessary

2. Sentence 3: **This aisle is crowded with sale items, whether nonsale items may be casually displayed as well.**

Which of the following is the best way to write the underlined portion of this sentence? If you think the original is the best way, choose option (1).

(1) whether
(2) so that
(3) unless
(4) because
(5) although

3. Sentence 5: **The more costly merchandise is placed at eye level when shoppers look first.**

Which of the following is the best way to write the underlined portion of this sentence? If you think the original is the best way, choose option (1).

(1) when
(2) where
(3) until
(4) once
(5) which

4. Sentence 6: **The shopper which reaches the milk products in the rear of the store without picking up other items is rare.**

What correction would be made to this sentence?

(1) insert a comma after shopper
(2) replace which with who
(3) replace reaches with reach
(4) change items to item
(5) change is to are

5. Sentence 7: **We cannot leave though we pay for our purchases.**

   What correction should be made to this sentence?

   (1) insert a comma after <u>leave</u>
   (2) insert a semicolon after <u>leave</u>
   (3) replace <u>though</u> with <u>when</u>
   (4) replace <u>though</u> with <u>until</u>
   (5) replace <u>though</u> with <u>because</u>

6. Sentences 8 and 9: **We stand in the checkout line. We'll see more impulse buys.**

   The most effective combination of sentences 8 and 9 would include which of the following words?

   (1) where
   (2) because
   (3) in order to
   (4) rather than
   (5) unless

7. Sentence 11: **You, that may have wanted only a box of crackers, will probably walk out with more than you wanted.**

   What correction should be made to this sentence?

   (1) remove the comma after <u>You</u>
   (2) replace <u>that</u> with <u>who</u>
   (3) remove the comma after <u>crackers</u>
   (4) change <u>walk</u> to <u>walks</u>
   (5) change <u>than</u> to <u>then</u>

8. Sentences 12 and 13: **We can avoid impulse buying. We understand why we do it.**

   The most effective combination of sentences 12 and 13 would include which of the following words?

   (1) so
   (2) but
   (3) before
   (4) if
   (5) although

Items 9 to 11 refer to the following paragraph.

(1) You will see athletes in excellent condition at any professional soccer match. (2) Few sports are as physically demanding as soccer. (3) Even if the game is played outdoors, soccer players must endure extreme heat, high humidity, and heavy rain. (4) There are no time-outs in soccer. (5) Players have little chance to rest during each 45-minute half. (6) If a player leaves the game for any reason, he cannot return.

9. Sentences 1 and 2: **You will see athletes in excellent condition at any professional soccer match. Few sports are as physically demanding as soccer.**

   The most effective combination of sentences 1 and 2 would include which of the following groups of words?

   (1) Because you will see athletes in excellent condition
   (2) Although you will see athletes in excellent condition
   (3) Unless you see athletes in excellent condition
   (4) Because few sports are as physically demanding
   (5) Although few sports are as physically demanding

10. Sentence 3: **Even if the game is played outdoors, soccer players must endure extreme heat, high humidity, and heavy rain.**

    What correction should be made to this sentence?

    (1) replace <u>Even if</u> with <u>Since</u>
    (2) remove the comma after <u>outdoors</u>
    (3) replace the comma after <u>outdoors</u> with a semicolon
    (4) remove the comma after <u>humidity</u>
    (5) no correction is necessary

11. Sentences 4 and 5: **There are no time-outs in soccer. Players have little chance to rest during each 45-minute half.**

The most effective combination of sentences 4 and 5 would include which of the following words?

(1) so
(2) but
(3) wherever
(4) once
(5) rather than

Items 12 to 15 refer to the following paragraph.

(1) In some European countries, the state runs day-care centers for children. (2) In America, parents, who work, are on their own. (3) Many find themselves late or absent, because of child-care problems. (4) In order to eliminate this work loss some employers are providing child care. (5) For example, one factory in Indiana runs a three-shift, on-site day-care center. (6) Fathers and mothers bring their children to work with them. (7) They don't leave them with a sitter. (8) Absenteeism and tardiness have been greatly reduced by this program, which makes both employer and employee happy. (9) Employees who don't have to worry about child care tend to be far more productive than those who do.

12. Sentence 2: **In America, parents, who work, are on their own.**

Which of the following is the best way to write the underlined portion of this sentence? If you think the original is the best way, choose option (1).

(1) parents, who work,
(2) parents who work
(3) parents, which work,
(4) parents which work
(5) parents, that work,

13. Sentence 3: **Many find themselves late or absent, because of child-care problems.**

Which of the following is the best way to write the underlined portion of this sentence? If you think the original is the best way, choose option (1).

(1) absent, because
(2) absent because
(3) absent, once
(4) absent; because
(5) absent. Because

14. Sentence 4: **In order to eliminate this work loss some employers are providing child care.**

What correction should be made to this sentence?

(1) replace In order to with Even though
(2) insert a comma after eliminate
(3) insert a semicolon after loss
(4) insert a comma after loss
(5) no correction is necessary

15. Sentences 6 and 7: **Fathers and mothers bring their children to work with them. They don't leave them with a sitter.**

The most effective combination of sentences 6 and 7 would include which of the following words?

(1) but
(2) before
(3) rather than
(4) whether
(5) even if

Directions: Choose the best answer to each item.

Items 1 to 5 refer to the following paragraph.

(1) Although not frequently, acid rain occurs naturally. (2) Volcanoes spew fumes into the atmosphere. (3) The acid rain currently falling on new england and Canada, however, is not natural. (4) Cars burning oil products and coal-burning factories are loading the atmosphere with chemicals. (5) These later become acids when they mix with rainwater. (6) The acid burns the leaves of trees. (7) They need to absorb sunlight. (8) It also fills lakes and streams and kills fish and wildlife.

1. Sentences 1 and 2: **Although not frequently, acid rain occurs naturally. Volcanoes spew fumes into the atmosphere.**

   The most effective combination of sentences 1 and 2 would include which of the following words?

   (1) although
   (2) whether
   (3) before
   (4) when
   (5) unless

2. Sentence 3: **The acid rain currently falling on new england and Canada, however, is not natural.**

   What correction should be made to this sentence?

   (1) change falling to fell
   (2) change england to England
   (3) change new england to New England
   (4) replace the comma after Canada with a semicolon
   (5) change is to are

3. Sentence 4: **Cars burning oil products and coal-burning factories are loading the atmosphere with chemicals.**

   Which of the following is the best way to write the underlined portion of this sentence? If you think the original is the best way, choose option (1).

   (1) coal-burning factories are
   (2) factories burning coal are
   (3) factories burning coal, are
   (4) coal-burning factories be
   (5) factories that burn coal are

4. Sentence 5: **These later become acids when they mix with rainwater.**

   What correction should be made to this sentence?

   (1) change These to This
   (2) insert commas after These and later
   (3) insert a comma after acids
   (4) change mix to mixed
   (5) no correction is necessary

5. Sentences 6 and 7: **The acid burns the leaves of trees. They need to absorb sunlight.**

   The most effective combination of sentences 6 and 7 would include which of the following words?

   (1) which
   (2) who
   (3) so
   (4) because
   (5) after

Answers are on page 305.

Lesson 23

Misplaced Modifiers

A modifier is a word or phrase that describes another word or phrase. Adjectives, which describe nouns, and adverbs, which describe verbs, are both modifiers. Entire phrases can also be used as modifiers.

When modifiers are put in the wrong place in a sentence, they can confuse or change the sentence's meaning. These are called **misplaced modifiers.** Misplaced modifiers may seem to refer to two different words or phrases at once, or they may appear to be describing the wrong word or phrase. **Dangling modifiers** are a special kind of misplaced modifier. These occur when a sentence lacks the appropriate subject for the modifying phrase.

Because we always interpret sentences when we read them, misplaced modifiers can be hard to spot. We may read what the sentence means to say, rather than what is does say. In other words, we may mentally "correct" the sentence and understand the intended meaning; however, the sentence actually says something else, according to its structure.

Read this paragraph and find the misplaced modifiers.

(1) For our vacation, we decided finally to go canoeing on the river. (2) We began our trip by renting a canoe with high spirits. (3) Our canoe was old and wooden, which was the only choice. (4) Looking down at the river, the water was muddy and brown. (5) The oars blistered our hands when we paddled painfully. (6) Then the canoe, paddling down the river, overturned.

Now look at the following examples of how to correct misplaced modifiers.

Rule:	Avoid wrong placement of words or phrases.
Example:	(Sentence 5) The oars blistered our hands when we paddled painfully. Does <u>painfully</u> modify <u>paddled</u> or <u>blistered</u>?
Correct:	The oars painfully blistered our hands when we paddled.
Example:	(Sentence 2) We began our trip by renting a canoe with high spirits. Does <u>with high spirits</u> modify <u>canoe</u> or <u>began</u>?
Correct:	With high spirits, we began our trip by renting a canoe.

Rule:	Avoid unclear placement of words or phrases.
Example:	(Sentence 3) Our canoe was old and wooden, which was the only choice.
	Does the phrase <u>which was the only choice</u> modify <u>canoe</u> or <u>wooden</u>?
Correct:	Our canoe, which was the only choice, was old and <u>wooden</u>.
Example:	(Sentence 1) For our vacation, we decided finally to go canoeing on the river.
	Does <u>finally</u> modify <u>decided</u> or <u>to go canoeing</u>?
Correct:	For our vacation, we finally decided to go canoeing on the river.
Note:	Avoid *split infinitives,* such as <u>to finally go</u>; an adverb should not interrupt a *to + verb* phrase.

Rule:	Avoid dangling modifiers.
Example:	(Sentence 4) Looking down at the river, the water was muddy and brown.
	As written, the introductory phrase modifies <u>water</u>, the subject of the sentence. Was the water looking down? Who is the subject of the phrase?
Correct:	When we looked down at the river, the water was muddy and brown.
Example:	(Sentence 6) Then the canoe, paddling down the river, overturned.
	As written, the phrase <u>paddling down the river</u> modifies <u>canoe</u>. Was the canoe paddling? Who is the subject?
Correct:	Then while we were paddling down the river, the canoe overturned.
Hint:	Creating a subordinate clause can usually fix a dangling modifier.

 Avoid misplaced modifiers by placing modifiers as close as possible to the word or words they modify.

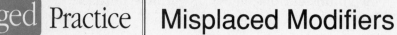

Items 1 to 12 refer to the following paragraph. Choose the best answer to each item.

(1) For some states, recycling has become a priority. (2) Landfills are all around our country at capacity. (3) Not realizing that they are not biodegradable, parents throw out billions of disposable diapers. (4) Under the soil, sanitation workers bury all these diapers. (5) Residents are required to separate their trash in certain states. (6) In containers, each household must separate bottles, cans, and paper. (7) When left at the curb, residents help the recycling effort. (8) Melted down, factories create new glass and aluminum products from cans and bottles. (9) Industries are forming to help replace biodegradable items with a promising future. (10) These factories create new jobs for workers with bottles and cans. (11) Many companies in the recycling industry has found creative new uses for used products. (12) One innovative shoe manufacturer out of worn-out tires is making the soles of its athletic shoes. (13) Publishing companies are trying to gradually increase the amount of recycled paper they use in their products.

1. Sentence 2: **Landfills are all around our country at capacity.**

   What correction should be made to this sentence?

   (1) insert a comma after Landfills
   (2) change are to is
   (3) move capacity before Landfills
   (4) move at capacity after are
   (5) no correction is necessary

2. Sentence 3: **Not realizing that they are not biodegradable, parents throw out billions of disposable diapers.**

   What correction should be made to this sentence?

   (1) change the spelling of realizing to realising
   (2) replace they with diapers
   (3) replace throw with through
   (4) replace the comma with a semicolon
   (5) no correction is necessary

3. Sentence 4: **Under the soil, sanitation workers bury all these diapers.**

   What correction should be made to this sentence?

   (1) move under the soil after diapers
   (2) remove the comma
   (3) change workers to worker
   (4) change the spelling of bury to bery
   (5) no correction is necessary

4. Sentence 5: **Residents are required to separate their trash in certain states.**

   What correction should be made to this sentence?

   (1) change the spelling of separate to seperate
   (2) change their to there
   (3) move in certain states after Residents
   (4) move in certain states after separate
   (5) change the spelling of certain to certen

5. Sentence 6: **In containers, each household must separate bottles, cans, and paper.**

What correction should be made to this sentence?

(1) move in containers after household
(2) move in containers after separate
(3) change containers to containers'
(4) change the spelling of separate to seperate
(5) move separate before each

6. Sentence 7: **When left at the curb, residents help the recycling effort.**

What correction should be made to this sentence?

(1) move when left at the curb after effort
(2) move when left at the curb after Residents
(3) insert these are after When
(4) move at the curb after residents
(5) no correction is necessary

7. Sentence 8: **Melted down, factories create new glass and aluminum products from cans and bottles.**

What correction should be made to this sentence?

(1) move melted down after from
(2) change the spelling of factories to facteries
(3) change create to creates
(4) move from cans and bottles after down
(5) no correction is necessary

8. Sentence 9: **Industries are forming to help replace biodegradable items with a promising future.**

What correction should be made to this sentence?

(1) remove are
(2) change replace to replacing
(3) move with a promising future after help
(4) move with a promising future after Industries
(5) no correction is necessary

9. Sentence 10: **These factories create new jobs for workers with bottles and cans.**

What correction should be made to this sentence?

(1) change the spelling of factories to facteries
(2) insert which before create
(3) change create to creates
(4) change create to creating
(5) move With bottles and cans before these

10. Sentence 11: **Many companies in the recycling industry has found creative new uses for used products.**

What correction should be made to this sentence?

(1) move creative after recycling
(2) move in the recycling industry after products
(3) insert a comma after industry
(4) change has to have
(5) no correction is necessary

11. Sentence 12: **One innovative shoe manufacturer out of worn-out tires is making the soles of its athletic shoes.**

    What correction should be made to this sentence?

    (1) change is to are
    (2) move out of worn-out tires after shoes
    (3) move innovative after shoes
    (4) replace its with it's
    (5) no correction is necessary

12. Sentence 13: **Publishing companies are trying to gradually increase the amount of recycled paper they use in their products.**

    What correction should be made to this sentence?

    (1) move gradually after increase
    (2) move in their products before they
    (3) change they to them
    (4) change their to they're
    (5) no correction is necessary

Items 13 to 16 refer to the following paragraph.

   (1) It's difficult to locate anything in someone else's kitchen. (2) When looking for coffee, bananas turn up. (3) Opening a door, pots and pans all fall out. (4) Nothing that is ready to eat, however, can be located in the kitchen. (5) Trying to find anything edible in a friend's kitchen is a nightmare. (6) A trip to the refrigerator searching for food usually results in nothing being found. (7) There may be some leftovers hiding in back, but finding food in the kitchen of a friend that is fresh is nearly impossible.

13. Sentence 2: **When looking for coffee, bananas turn up.**

    What correction should be made to this sentence?

    (1) move when looking for coffee after up
    (2) insert your after When
    (3) insert you're after When
    (4) move for coffee after up
    (5) change bananas to banana's

14. Sentence 3: **Opening a door, pots and pans all fall out.**

    What correction should be made to this sentence?

    (1) move opening a door after pans
    (2) move opening a door after out
    (3) insert When you're before opening
    (4) insert When you before opening
    (5) change fall to falls

15. Sentence 6: **A trip to the refrigerator searching for food usually results in nothing being found.**

    What correction should be made to this sentence?

    (1) move Searching for food before a trip
    (2) change searching for to in search of
    (3) remove searching
    (4) insert a comma after food
    (5) no correction is necessary

16. Sentence 7: **There may be some leftovers hiding in back, but finding food in the kitchen of a friend that is fresh is nearly impossible.**

    What correction should be made to this sentence?

    (1) change the spelling of hiding to hideing
    (2) move that is fresh after food
    (3) replace the comma with a semicolon
    (4) replace but with although
    (5) no correction is necessary

Answers are on page 305.

Unit 3: Sentence Structure

Directions: Choose the best answer to each item.

Items 1 to 5 refer to the following paragraph.

(1) Buyers should take care when buying a used car from a dealer with low mileage. (2) Someone else may have set back the odometer it shows the mileage. (3) Also, wear on the foot pedals informing you of a heavily driven car. (4) Most states have, however, "lemon laws" to protect consumers. (5) Oily spots under a car or excessive oil on the engine may indicate further problems as well. (6) When looking to buy, a car can't be too carefully examined. (7) Having the car whom you trust inspected by a mechanic is one way to avoid making a bad purchase. (8) If the dealer won't allow you to do this, there may be something seriously wrong with the car.

1. Sentence 1: **Buyers should take care when buying a used car from a dealer with low mileage.**

   What correction should be made to this sentence?

   (1) change care to caring
   (2) insert a comma after care
   (3) move with low mileage after car
   (4) change a dealer to dealers
   (5) no correction is necessary

2. Sentence 2: **Someone else may have set back the odometer it shows the mileage.**

   Which of the following is the best way to write the underlined portion of this sentence? If you think the original is the best way, choose option (1).

   (1) odometer it shows
   (2) odometer which shows
   (3) odometer, which shows
   (4) odometer, it shows
   (5) odometer, who shows

3. Sentence 3: **Also, wear on the foot pedals informing you of a heavily driven car.**

   What correction should be made to this sentence?

   (1) remove the comma after also
   (2) move on the foot pedals after you
   (3) insert a comma after pedals
   (4) replace informing with informs
   (5) replace informing with to inform

4. Sentence 6: **When looking to buy, a car can't be too carefully examined.**

   What correction should be made to this sentence?

   (1) insert your after When
   (2) insert you're after When
   (3) remove the comma after buy
   (4) change can't to cant
   (5) change too to to

5. Sentence 7: **Having the car whom you trust inspected by a mechanic is one way to avoid making a bad purchase.**

   What correction should be made to this sentence?

   (1) move whom you trust after mechanic
   (2) change whom to who
   (3) move making a bad purchase after mechanic
   (4) change bad to badly
   (5) no correction is necessary

Answers are on page 307.

Shift of Focus

Sentences may be grammatically correct yet confusingly written. To write clear, easy-to-understand sentences, avoid shifts of focus and construction. These shifts, within a sentence or paragraph, may include: changes in verb tense, changes in person, or number, pronoun-antecedent disagreement, and non-parallel construction. Correcting these errors may require rewriting part or all of a sentence.

The sentences in the following paragraph contain shifts in number, shifts in verb tense, and other unclear constructions. Read the sentences and consider how they could be corrected or improved.

(1) When I am sitting by myself on the bus, you never know who is going to sit down next to me. (2) Yesterday a fireman named George sat down and wouldn't stop talking. (3) He told me about a special device firefighters use for opening locked doors. (4) They are very useful when a building is on fire. (5) On Wednesday, a woman from my office sat down next to me and acts like she had never seen me before. (6) If she behaves this rudely again, I become very upset. (7) Since she wasn't speaking to me, I stared at the poster behind the driver. (8) The poster explained that buying bus tickets in advance is more efficient than when you buy them from the bus driver. (9) I ride the bus every day, and the tickets are usually bought by me in advance.

Pronoun Shifts

Rule: Avoid shifts in pronoun person or number.
Example: (Sentence 1) When I am sitting by myself on the bus, you never know who is going to sit down next to me.
Correct: When I am sitting by myself on the bus, I never know who is going to sit down next to me.

In the first sentence, there is a shift from the first person pronoun I to the second person pronoun you.

Example: (Sentences 3 and 4) He told me about a special device firefighters use for opening locked doors. They are very useful when a building is on fire.
Correct: He told me about a special device firefighters use for opening locked doors. It is very useful when a building is on fire.

In the two original sentences, there is a shift from the singular device to the plural pronoun They. This makes it unclear whether the antecedent of They is the device or the firefighters.

Shifts in Verb Tense

Rule:	Avoid shifts in verb tense within a sentence or paragraph.
Example:	(Sentence 5) On Wednesday, a woman from my office sat down next to me and acts like she had never seen me before.
Correct:	On Wednesday, a woman from my office sat down next to me and acted like she had never seen me before.

In the original sentence, the verb tense shifts from the past tense <u>sat</u> to the present tense <u>acts</u>.

Rule:	In complex sentences, use verb tenses that are consistent with each other and the time frame in which the action occurs.
Example:	(Sentence 6) If she behaves this rudely again, I become very upset.
Correct:	If she behaves this rudely again, I will become very upset.

In the first sentence, both verbs, <u>behave</u> and <u>become</u>, are in the present tense. Since the action in the independent clause will occur *after* the action in the dependent clause, the verb <u>become</u> should be changed to the future tense <u>will become</u>.

Unclear Constructions

Rule:	Make sentences consistent by using parallel construction.
Example:	(Sentence 8) The poster explained that buying bus tickets in advance is more efficient than when you buy them from the bus driver.
Correct:	The poster explained that buying bus tickets in advance is more efficient than buying them from the bus driver.

In the first sentence the two actions being compared are expressed in a nonparallel manner. The first action is expressed by a participle phrase; the second action is expressed by a dependent clause that includes the pronoun <u>you</u> and the present-tense verb <u>buy</u>. In the second sentence the parallel actions are expressed in parallel construction; both actions are expressed by participle phrases.

Rule:	To correct shifts of subject in a compound sentence, rewrite the sentence as a simple sentence with compound parts.
Example:	(Sentence 9) I ride the bus every day, and the tickets are usually bought by me in advance.
Correct:	I ride the bus every day and usually buy the tickets in advance.

The first sentence is a compound sentence with <u>I</u> functioning as the subject of the first clause and <u>me</u> as object of the preposition <u>by</u> in the second clause. The second sentence is a simple sentence with a compound verb.

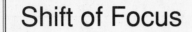

Items 1 to 5 refer to the following paragraph. Choose the best answer to each item.

(1) Becky was pleased at the results of her job search; however, her success had created a new problem for her. (2) She couldn't decide whether to accept the local school position or working in a Chicago library. (3) The job in Chicago offered an excellent salary, but she is worried about leaving home. (4) After spending several evenings debating the situation with herself, she decided to telephone Karen, an old friend who had lived in several different states. (5) "When you move to a new city, people always make new friends," advised her friend. (6) After considering Karen's advice, she decided to speak with her family members and seeing what they thought. (7) "If you move away, I never see you," said her mother. (8) "However, I won't object if you believe that the Chicago position would truly be a better situation for you."

1. Sentence 2: **She couldn't decide whether to accept the local school position or working in a Chicago library.**

   What correction should be made to this sentence?

   (1) change couldn't to could'nt
   (2) change whether to weather
   (3) change working to works
   (4) change working to to work
   (5) no correction is necessary

2. Sentence 3: **The job in Chicago offered an excellent salary, but she is worried about leaving home.**

   What correction should be made to this sentence?

   (1) change offered to offer
   (2) remove the comma after salary
   (3) change is to are
   (4) change is to was
   (5) no correction is necessary

3. Sentence 5: **"When you move to a new city, people always make new friends," advised her friend.**

   Which of the following is the best way to write the underlined portion of this sentence? If you think the original is the best way, choose option (1).

   (1) "When you move to a new city, people
   (2) "When you move to a new city, you
   (3) "When you move to a new city, they
   (4) When you move to a new city, people
   (5) "When you move to a new city people

4. Sentence 6: **After considering Karen's advice, she decided to speak with her family members and seeing what they thought.**

   What correction should be made to this sentence?

   (1) change Karen's to Karens'
   (2) change she to he
   (3) change seeing to see
   (4) change they to she
   (5) no correction is necessary

5. Sentence 7: **"If you move away, I never see you," said her mother.**

   What correction should be made to this sentence?

   (1) change the comma after away to a semicolon
   (2) insert will before never
   (3) change see to saw
   (4) change said to says
   (5) no correction is necessary

Items 6 to 10 refer to the following paragraph.

(1) Caterers are primarily known for providing the food and beverages served at large parties, company dinners, and where they get married. (2) Some caterers, however, focus their business on delivering meal service to the people who make movies and television programs. (3) A feature-length film can has a crew of two hundred people and take months to produce. (4) Every day a crew member is on the set, you will be fed by a production caterer. (5) Caterers use huge mobile kitchens to cook meals wherever a production was being filmed. (6) If the crew is filming an action sequence on a mountainside, the caterers will follow in their mobile kitchen.

6. Sentence 1: **Caterers are primarily known for providing the food and beverages served at large parties, company dinners, and where they get married.**

   What correction should be made to this sentence?

   (1) change the spelling of providing to provideing
   (2) change they to we
   (3) change they to you
   (4) replace where they get married with weddings
   (5) no correction is necessary

7. Sentence 2: **Some caterers, however, focus their business on delivering meal service to the people who make movies and television programs.**

   What correction should be made to this sentence?

   (1) remove the comma after caterers
   (2) change focus to focused
   (3) change their to your
   (4) change who to whom
   (5) no correction is necessary

8. Sentence 3: **A feature-length film can has a crew of two hundred people and take months to produce.**

   Which of the following is the best way to write the underlined portion of this sentence? If you think the original is the best way, choose option (1).

   (1) has a crew of two hundred people and take months to produce.
   (2) have a crew of two hundred people and take months to produce.
   (3) have a crew of two hundred people and took months to produce.
   (4) has a crew of two hundred people and months can be taken to produce it.
   (5) have a crew of two hundred people and taking months to produce.

9. Sentence 4: **Every day a crew member is on the set, you will be fed by a production caterer.**

   What correction should be made to this sentence?

   (1) remove the comma after set
   (2) change the comma after set to a semicolon
   (3) change you to he or she
   (4) change you to we
   (5) no correction is necessary

10. Sentence 5: **Caterers use huge mobile kitchens to cook meals wherever a production was being filmed.**

    What correction should be made to this sentence?

    (1) change use to uses
    (2) change use to using
    (3) change was to is
    (4) change was to were
    (5) no correction is necessary

Answers are on page 307.

Directions: Choose the best answer to each item.

Items 1 to 5 refer to the following paragraph.

(1) Every day, thousands of international travelers arrive at U.S. airports. (2) When you arrive at customs, their bags may be inspected by customs officials who are searching for prohibited goods. (3) They may open arriving passengers' luggage or simply asking people a few questions about the contents. (4) This inspector come from several government agencies, including the United States Department of Agriculture. (5) The USDA is responsible for making sure that no contaminated plant, vegetables, or animal products are carried into the country. (6) The agency's officers intercept about two million illegal products a year; we confiscate them at airports and postal facilities. (7) Imported fruits, vegetables, plants, and meat products are dangerous to American agriculture if they contain unwanted pests, such as fruit flies or parasites.

1. Sentence 2: **When you arrive at customs, their bags may be inspected by customs officials who are searching for prohibited goods.**

   What correction should be made to this sentence?

   (1) change you to they
   (2) remove the comma after customs
   (3) change their to our
   (4) change are to was
   (5) no correction is necessary

tip Avoid a pronoun shift by finding the antecedent for each pronoun you use. Ask yourself: What is its number? What is its gender? What is its person? Then choose a pronoun that agrees with the antecedent in number, gender, and person.

2. Sentence 3: **They may open arriving passengers' luggage or simply asking people a few questions about the contents.**

   What correction should be made to this sentence?

   (1) change arriving to arriveing
   (2) change passengers' to passengers
   (3) change asking to ask
   (4) change people to us
   (5) no correction is necessary

3. Sentence 4: **This inspector come from several government agencies, including the United States Department of Agriculture.**

   What correction should be made to this sentence?

   (1) change This inspector to These inspectors
   (2) change come to have come
   (3) change agencies to agency
   (4) change Agriculture to agriculture
   (5) no correction is necessary

4. Sentence 5: **The USDA is responsible for making sure no contaminated plant, vegetables, or animal products are carried into the country.**

   What correction should be made to this sentence?

   (1) change is to was
   (2) change making to makeing
   (3) change plant to plants
   (4) change are to is
   (5) no correction is necessary

5. Sentence 6: **The agency's officers intercept about two million illegal products a year; we confiscate them at airports and postal facilities.**

What correction should be made to this sentence?

(1) change intercept to was intercepting
(2) change the semicolon to a comma
(3) change we to they
(4) change them to they
(5) no correction is necessary

Items 6 to 10 refer to the following paragraph.

(1) Americans love to travel. (2) Trips to their national parks and monuments are particularly treasured by them. (3) Popular destinations include Yellowstone, Sequoia, and traveling to the Grand Canyon. (4) Visitors should be careful, when exploring some of the more rugged scenic areas. (5) You arrive unprepared for extreme heat, high elevation, and strenuous activity. (6) Hikers who become lost, injure themselves, or stranded are rescued and evacuated by park rangers. (7) Although help is available if visitors run into trouble, it's better if they avoid it by being careful while on the trail. (8) Remember, a safe vacation is a happy vacation.

6. Sentences 1 and 2: **Americans love to travel. Trips to their national parks and monuments are particularly treasured by them.**

The most effective combination of sentences 1 and 2 would include which of the following groups of words?

(1) Americans love to travel, and they treasure
(2) Americans love to travel, and we treasure
(3) Americans love to travel; trips to their
(4) Americans love to travel; trips to our
(5) Americans love to travel because trips to

7. Sentence 3: **Popular destinations include Yellowstone, Sequoia, and traveling to the Grand Canyon.**

What correction should be made to this sentence?

(1) change include to including
(2) insert visiting before Yellowstone
(3) change traveling to travelling
(4) remove traveling to
(5) no correction is necessary

8. Sentence 4: **Visitors should be careful, when exploring some of the more rugged scenic areas.**

What correction should be made to this sentence?

(1) change the spelling of careful to carefull
(2) remove the comma after careful
(3) change exploring to they explored
(4) change more rugged to ruggeder
(5) no correction is necessary

9. Sentence 5: **You arrive unprepared for extreme heat, high elevation, and strenuous activity.**

What correction should be made to this sentence?

(1) replace You with Many
(2) change arrive to arrives
(3) insert doing before strenuous
(4) insert did before strenuous
(5) no correction is necessary

10. Sentence 6: **Hikers who become lost, injure themselves, or stranded are rescued and evacuated by park rangers.**

What correction should be made to this sentence?

(1) change become to will become
(2) change injure themselves to injured
(3) change themselves to theirselves
(4) change stranded to stranding
(5) no correction is necessary

Answers are on page 308.

Lesson 25

Revising Sentences

When you revise sentences, you apply everything that you have previously learned about putting together sentences. The goal in revising sentences is to make them express the proper relationships between ideas.

The most important point to remember when revising sentences is that each sentence expresses a main idea. That main idea must remain the main idea in the new sentence unless you are asked to make it a supporting idea. Also, when you revise a sentence, it must be grammatically correct in its new form. Therefore, everything that you have learned in the first two units of this book also must be used.

Knowing how to work with ideas and sentence forms is an important writing skill. This lesson will teach you to apply what you have learned about word order and meaning in a sentence.

Read this short paragraph.

(1) Halloween is celebrated by children in disguise. (2) Children are dressed as different characters. (3) They go in costumes to other houses. (4) Children knock on doors. (5) Children ask for candy from the resident.

Now you have to put your knowledge of sentence order and clarity to use. Each of the examples below illustrates one kind of sentence change.

Rule:	When changing the word order in a sentence, be careful to note clarity and logic.
Example:	(Sentence 1) Halloween is celebrated by children in disguise.
Goal:	Begin sentence 1 with: <u>Children in disguise</u>
Correct:	Children in disguise celebrate Halloween.
Hint:	Notice that not every word in the original sentence is used in the revised sentence. In order to form a clear, logical sentence, the verb must change to agree with <u>Children</u> and <u>by</u> must be dropped since it is no longer needed.

Rule:	When combining sentences, identify the most important idea and change the sentences accordingly.
Example:	(Sentences 2 and 3) Children are dressed as different characters. They go in costumes to other houses.
Goal:	Combine these two sentences by using <u>who</u>.
Correct:	Children, who are dressed as different characters, go in costumes to other houses.
Hint:	Again, one of the sentences must change in order to combine them this way. As both sentences refer to clothing, the second sentence, which carries an additional, new idea—visiting houses—should become the main clause. It carries the sentence on into the next one in the paragraph.

Rule:	When combining sentences, establish a relationship between the two ideas in the sentences.
Example:	(Sentences 4 and 5) Children knock on doors. Children ask for candy from the resident.
Goal:	Choose a subordinating conjunction to join these two sentences in a relationship.
Correct:	After children knock on doors, they ask for candy from the resident.
Hint:	As these two ideas represent one action happening after another, <u>after</u> is used to set up a time relationship when combining them into one sentence. Also, notice that the second <u>Children</u> was replaced with <u>they</u> in order to avoid repeating the same noun twice in one sentence. Again, words may be dropped or changed in order to create a clearer sentence.

Before revising a sentence, identify the main idea and the relationships between the main idea and supporting ideas. Check your revised sentence to see that you have not changed those ideas or the relationships between them.

Revising Sentences

Items 1 to 7 refer to the following paragraph. Choose the best answer to each item.

(1) Moving into a small apartment is more difficult than I imagined. (2) Moving into a small apartment requires organization. (3) I have to put away my pots and pans. (4) I have to put away all my clothes. (5) Everything is out of order. (6) I can't find anything. (7) I need a maid. (8) I need someone to help me clean everything. (9) I had thought that living in a small place would be easy. (10) Living in a small place is harder than I thought. (11) Maybe I should live in a bigger apartment. (12) A bigger apartment would give more room for my furniture. (13) But what if I don't know where to put everything? (14) Maybe I should stay with my small apartment. (15) Maybe I should get rid of many of my things. (16) My new apartment is confusing my entire life.

1. Sentences 1 and 2: **Moving into a small apartment is more difficult than I imagined. Moving into a small apartment requires organization.**

   The most effective combination of sentences 1 and 2 would include which of the following groups of words?

   (1) but it requires
   (2) imagined moving
   (3) and requires
   (4) imagined into
   (5) and a small

2. Sentences 3 and 4: **I have to put away my pots and pans. I have to put away all my clothes.**

   The most effective combination of sentences 3 and 4 would include which of the following groups of words?

   (1) pans I have
   (2) my pots and pans and my clothes
   (3) pans and away
   (4) pots, pans, clothes
   (5) pots, pans, and put all

3. Sentences 5 and 6: **Everything is out of order. I can't find anything.**

   The most effective combination of sentences 5 and 6 would include which of the following groups of words?

   (1) out of order, I can't
   (2) anything because
   (3) Being out of order,
   (4) out of order, but I
   (5) can't find nothing because

4. Sentences 7 and 8: **I need a maid. I need someone to help me clean everything.**

   The most effective combination of sentences 7 and 8 would include which of the following groups of words?

   (1) maid who will
   (2) a maid I
   (3) maid, I need
   (4) maid which will
   (5) A maid needs

5. Sentences 9 and 10: **I had thought that living in a small place would be easy. Living in a small place is harder than I thought.**

   The most effective combination of sentences 9 and 10 would include which of the following groups of words?

   (1) but it
   (2) therefore, it
   (3) and it
   (4) so
   (5) because

6. Sentences 11 and 12: **Maybe I should live in a bigger apartment. A bigger apartment would give me more room for my furniture.**

   The most effective combination of sentences 11 and 12 would include which of the following groups of words?

   (1) apartment that would
   (2) apartment, it would
   (3) apartment; giving me
   (4) apartment who would
   (5) apartment, and it

7. Sentences 14 and 15: **Maybe I should stay with my small apartment. Maybe I should get rid of many of my things.**

   The most effective combination of sentences 14 and 15 would include which of the following words?

   (1) so
   (2) or
   (3) yet
   (4) for
   (5) therefore

Items 8 to 10 refer to the following paragraph.

   (1) Advances in automotive technology have increased the safety of car drivers and passengers. (2) Many new cars come equipped with dual air bags, antilock brakes, and side impact protection. (3) Some worry, however, that new car owners may feel so safe in their cars that they will drive less carefully. (4) Drivers can become overconfident. (5) As a result, they may take unnecessary chances behind the wheel. (6) The safety devices in the new cars are impressive; however, they can be neutralized by poor driving on the part of their owners.

8. Sentence 1: **Advances in automotive technology have increased the safety of car drivers and passengers.**

   If you rewrote sentence 1 beginning with

   The safety of car drivers and passengers

   the next word(s) should be

   (1) has been increased by
   (2) have been increased by
   (3) increased
   (4) is increasing the
   (5) are

9. Sentence 3: **Some worry, however, that new car owners may feel so safe in their cars that they will drive less carefully.**

   If you rewrote sentence 3 beginning with

   Some worry, however, that new car owners will drive less carefully

   the next word(s) should be

   (1) , or
   (2) in order that
   (3) , and
   (4) , but
   (5) because

10. Sentences 4 and 5: **Drivers can become overconfident. As a result, they may take unnecessary chances behind the wheel.**

    The most effective combination of sentences 4 and 5 would include which of the following groups of words?

    (1) Because drivers take unnecessary chances
    (2) Although drivers take unnecessary chances
    (3) Drivers may take unnecessary chances because
    (4) Drivers become overconfident because
    (5) Although drivers may take unnecessary chances

Answers are on page 310.

Directions: Choose the best answer to each item.

Items 1 to 6 refer to the following paragraph.

(1) Fast cars, fast money, and fast food all seems to be part of the American way of life. (2) Eating on the go, fast food is our first food of choice these days. (3) You can get anything to eat in your car, including tacos, chicken, or hamburgers. (4) Families no longer bother to pack lunches for outings in the car. (5) A fast-food restaurant will be wherever they're going. (6) Nor do families have to seek out restaurants with patient employees. (7) Their children need never leave the car. (8) Do modern children grow up thinking that food comes in a car in a bag? (9) Children fed from bags seem the norm these days. (10) Adults might do well to consider this trend. (11) Being that children eat so much of this type of food.

1. Sentence 1: **Fast cars, fast money, and fast food all seems to be part of the American way of life.**

   What correction should be made to this sentence?

   (1) insert a comma after food
   (2) change seems to seem
   (3) change be to being
   (4) change American to american
   (5) no correction is necessary

2. Sentence 2: **Eating on the go, fast food is our first food of choice these days.**

   Which of the following is the best way to write the underlined portion of this sentence? If you think the original is the best way, choose option (1).

   (1) Eating on the go, fast food
   (2) Eat on the go, fast food
   (3) Eating on the going, fast food
   (4) Eaten on the go, fast food
   (5) We are eating on the go, fast food

3. Sentences 4 and 5: **Families no longer bother to pack lunches for outings in the car. A fast-food restaurant will be wherever they're going.**

   The most effective combination of sentences 4 and 5 would include which of the following groups of words?

   (1) car, so a
   (2) car, because a
   (3) car because a
   (4) car, but a
   (5) car unless a

4. Sentences 6 and 7: **Nor do families have to seek out restaurants with patient employees. Their children need never leave the car.**

   The most effective combination of sentences 6 and 7 would include which of the following words?

   (1) for
   (2) yet
   (3) but
   (4) so
   (5) or

5. Sentence 8: **Do modern children grow up thinking that food comes in a car in a bag?**

   What correction should be made to this sentence?

   (1) change children to childrens
   (2) change grow to grown
   (3) change thinking to think
   (4) move in a bag after comes
   (5) no correction is necessary

6. Sentences 10 and 11: **Adults might do well to consider this <u>trend. Being that</u> children eat so much of this type of food.**

   Which of the following is the best way to write the underlined portion of these sentences? If you think that the original is the best way, choose option (1).

   (1) trend. Being that
   (2) trend; being that
   (3) trend, since children
   (4) trend, children
   (5) trend, eating so

Items 7 to 11 refer to the following paragraph.

   (1) We love seasonal change because we never notice the exact moment when it occurs. (2) The changes are so gradual. (3) They're so dramatic. (4) They always surprise us. (5) We know that they're coming. (6) The sun shines the most during the summer. (7) It's the warmest season of the year. (8) In the summertime, the grass is green and tall. (9) Warm breezes blow. (10) The air feels still. (11) Children can play outside, so they enjoy life more.

7. Sentence 1: **We love seasonal change because we never notice the exact moment when it occurs.**

   What correction should be made to this sentence?

   (1) replace <u>We</u> with <u>Everyone</u>
   (2) insert a comma after <u>change</u>
   (3) replace <u>it</u> with <u>they</u>
   (4) replace <u>because</u> with <u>so that</u>
   (5) no correction is necessary

8. Sentences 2 and 3: **The changes are so gradual. They're so dramatic.**

   The most effective combination of sentences 2 and 3 would include which of the following words?

   (1) because
   (2) yet
   (3) or
   (4) so
   (5) until

9. Sentences 4 and 5: **They always surprise us. We know that they're coming.**

   The most effective combination of sentences 4 and 5 would include which of the following words?

   (1) so
   (2) even though
   (3) or
   (4) when
   (5) and

10. Sentences 9 and 10: **Warm breezes blow. The air feels still.**

    The most effective combination of sentences 9 and 10 would include which of the following words?

    (1) and
    (2) yet
    (3) so
    (4) for
    (5) because

11. Sentence 11: **Children can play outside, so they enjoy life more.**

    If you rewrote sentence 11 beginning with

    <u>Children enjoy life more</u>

    the next word(s) should be

    (1) so they
    (2) until they
    (3) because they
    (4) outside
    (5) playing

Answers are on page 311.

Lesson 25

211

Directions: Choose the <u>best answer</u> to each item.

Items 1 to 6 refer to the following paragraph.

(1) The drive-in movie was perhaps the ultimate expression of the American love of cars. (2) In the heyday of the drive-in, families would packing snacks and blankets, pile into the car, and head for a movie under the stars. (3) The car of choice, of course, being the station wagon with the fold-down back gate. (4) Some families brought the entire makings of a picnic, the barbecue grill, charcoal, cooler, and lawn chairs all were packed in with the kids. (5) Not even pesky mosquitoes, teenagers, or scratchy speakers dimmed the drive-in's appeal. (6) The only things, in fact, that now lure families away are smaller cars and larger, air-conditioned indoor theaters. (7) Dying away, moviegoers seldom attend open-air cinemas. (8) Most of these hold more nostalgic memories then customers these days.

1. Sentence 2: **In the heyday of the drive-in, families would packing snacks and blankets, pile into the car, and head for a movie under the stars.**

   What correction should be made to this sentence?

   (1) remove the comma after <u>drive-in</u>
   (2) insert <u>would</u> before <u>packing</u>
   (3) change <u>packing</u> to <u>pack</u>
   (4) change <u>head</u> to <u>heading</u>
   (5) no correction is necessary

2. Sentence 3: **The car of choice, of course, being the station wagon with the fold-down back gate.**

   What correction should be made to this sentence?

   (1) move <u>of choice</u> after <u>gate</u>
   (2) remove the comma after <u>choice</u>
   (3) remove the comma after <u>course</u>
   (4) replace <u>being</u> with <u>was</u>
   (5) replace <u>being</u> with <u>be</u>

3. Sentence 4: **Some families brought the entire makings of <u>a picnic, the</u> barbecue grill, charcoal, cooler, and lawn chairs all were packed in with the kids.**

   Which of the following is the best way to write the underlined portion of this sentence? If you think the original is the best way, choose option (1).

   (1) a picnic, the
   (2) a picnic the
   (3) a picnic; the
   (4) a picnic, but the
   (5) a picnic; also, the

4. Sentence 5: **Not even pesky mosquitoes, teenagers, or scratchy speakers dimmed the drive-in's appeal.**

   What correction should be made to this sentence?

   (1) insert a comma after even
   (2) insert rowdy before teenagers
   (3) change speakers to speaker's
   (4) insert a comma after speakers
   (5) change drive-in's to drive-ins

5. Sentence 7: **Dying away, movie-goers seldom attend open-air cinemas.**

   What correction should be made to this sentence?

   (1) move dying away after moviegoers
   (2) remove the comma after away
   (3) insert As they're before dying
   (4) insert As there before dying
   (5) insert As drive-ins are before dying

6. Sentence 8: **Most of these hold more nostalgic memories then customers these days.**

   What correction should be made to this sentence?

   (1) insert a comma after these
   (2) change hold to holds
   (3) replace then with than
   (4) change customers to customer's
   (5) no correction is necessary

Items 7 to 10 refer to the following paragraph.

   (1) A gardener's desires no longer constrained by the limits of the weather. (2) In an outdoor garden, some plants cannot withstand heavy rain or frost. (3) They are easily raised in the controlled environment of a greenhouse. (4) A gardener should consider several factors before beginning construction expense is one primary concern. (5) Any prospective greenhouse owner must anticipate large fuel bills; heating a greenhouse can be very expensive.

7. Sentence 1: **A gardener's desires no longer constrained by the limits of the weather.**

   What correction should be made to this sentence?

   (1) change gardener's to gardeners
   (2) insert are after desires
   (3) insert is after desires
   (4) insert were after desires
   (5) no correction is necessary

8. Sentences 2 and 3: **In an outdoor garden, some plants cannot withstand heavy rain or frost. They are easily raised in the controlled environment of a greenhouse.**

   The most effective combination of sentences 4 and 5 would include which of the following groups of words?

   (1) rain or frost; however,
   (2) rain or frost; similarly,
   (3) rain or frost because
   (4) rain or frost, they
   (5) rain or frost they

9. Sentence 4: **A gardener should consider several factors before beginning construction expense is one primary concern.**

   What correction should be made to this sentence?

   (1) insert a comma after factors
   (2) insert a comma after construction
   (3) insert a semicolon after construction
   (4) change is to are
   (5) no correction is necessary

10. Sentence 5: **Any prospective greenhouse owner must anticipate large fuel bills; heating a greenhouse can be very expensive.**

If you rewrote sentence 6 beginning with

The cost of heating a greenhouse can be very expensive,

the next word should be

(1) so
(2) because
(3) or
(4) although
(5) meanwhile

Items 11 to 14 refer to the following paragraph.

(1) The small town is back in style with new suburban planners and architects. (2) A typical suburb usually has winding streets, ranch-style homes, and big yards these new planners are using straight streets, farm-style homes, and small yards instead. (3) The homes have front porches. (4) They are set close to neighbors' homes. (5) All the new homes are within walking distance of a central square. (6) It contains a small grocery store and other shops. (7) The main goal is to bring community spirit to the suburbs planners believe that homeowners who live closer together will talk and interact more with one another.

11. Sentence 2: **A typical suburb usually has winding streets, ranch-style homes, and big yards these new planners are using straight streets, farm-style homes, and small yards instead.**

Which of the following is the best way to write the underlined portion of this sentence? If you think the original is the best way, choose option (1).

(1) yards these new
(2) yards, these new
(3) yards; these new
(4) yards, or these new
(5) yards unless these new

12. Sentences 3 and 4: **The homes have front porches. They are set close to neighbors' homes.**

The most effective combination of sentences 3 and 4 would include which of the following groups of words?

(1) porches, they
(2) porches they
(3) porches, yet they
(4) porches, so they
(5) porches, and they

13. Sentences 5 and 6: **All the new homes are within walking distance of a central square. It contains a small grocery store and other shops.**

The most effective combination of sentences 5 and 6 would include which of the following groups of words?

(1) square contains
(2) square who contains
(3) square, which contains
(4) square; however, it contains
(5) square it contains

14. Sentence 7: **The main goal is to bring community spirit to the suburbs planners believe that homeowners who live closer together will talk and interact more with one another.**

Which of the following is the best way to write the underlined portion of this sentence? If you think the original is the best way, choose option (1).

(1) suburbs planners
(2) suburbs, planners
(3) suburbs. planners
(4) suburbs. Planners
(5) suburbs but planners

Items 15 to 20 refer to the following paragraph.

(1) The planet Mars, one of Earth's nearest neighbors, has always captured the imagination of scientists and writers. (2) Historically, the question asked was whether or not life existed on that planet by both groups. (3) When looking through a telescope lens, Mars appears to have waterways or canals crossing its surface. (4) Observers wondered for many years about possible life on that planet because of the apparent waterways. (5) Such writers as Edgar Rice Burroughs imagined a planet of exotic races, sharp swords, and strange creatures. (6) Another writer, H. G. Wells, to describe a Martian invasion of Earth as "The War of the Worlds." (7) Even later, Ray Bradbury told stories of deserted palaces and deserts that were empty. (8) Some people had had high expectations for the unmanned space flight to Mars. (9) They were disappointed when it found no signs of life. (10) However, scientists' fascination with Mars still continues.

15. Sentence 2: **Historically, the question asked was whether or not life existed on that planet by both groups.**

    What correction should be made to this sentence?

    (1) remove the comma after Historically
    (2) change the spelling of whether to wether
    (3) insert a comma after whether
    (4) move by both groups after asked
    (5) move on that planet after asked

tip Don't try to express too many ideas in one sentence. Often two shorter sentences are clearer than one long sentence.

16. Sentence 3: **When looking through a telescope lens, Mars appears to have waterways or canals crossing its surface.**

    What correction should be made to this sentence?

    (1) replace When with Whenever
    (2) replace looking with one looks
    (3) change appears to appear
    (4) change the spelling of appears to appeers
    (5) change its to it's

17. Sentence 4: **Observers wondered for many years about possible life on that planet because of the apparent waterways.**

    If you rewrote sentence 4 beginning with

    Because of the apparent waterways,

    the next word would be

    (1) observers
    (2) wondering
    (3) for
    (4) about
    (5) possible

18. Sentence 6: **Another writer, H. G. Wells, to describe a Martian invasion of Earth as "The War of the Worlds."**

    What correction should be made to this sentence?

    (1) remove the comma after writer
    (2) remove the comma after Wells
    (3) remove to
    (4) change to describe to describing
    (5) change to describe to described

19. Sentence 7: **Even later, Ray Bradbury told stories of deserted palaces <u>and deserts that were empty</u>.**

    Which of the following is the best way to write the underlined portion of this sentence? If you think the original is the best way, choose option (1).

    (1) and deserts that were empty
    (2) and deserts that was empty
    (3) and deserts who were empty
    (4) and empty deserts
    (5) and deserts being empty

20. Sentences 8 and 9: **Some people had had high expectations for the unmanned space flight <u>to Mars. They were</u> disappointed when it found no signs of life.**

    The most effective combination of sentences 8 and 9 would include which of the following groups of words?

    (1) to Mars, they were
    (2) to Mars, unless they were
    (3) to Mars, because they were
    (4) to Mars, so they were
    (5) to Mars; meanwhile, they were

<u>Items 21 to 24</u> refer to the following paragraph.

(1) Badgers are the great individualists of the animal world. (2) Their fierce appearance, sharp teeth, and finger-length claws can support the badger's claim to privacy. (3) Living alone in burrows that they dig, badgers each have their own territories. (4) They dislike other animals so much. (5) Badgers don't even associate with other badgers. (6) These relatives of the weasel will challenge anything that moves, in fact. (7) The badger's loose hide enables it to turn around when caught. (8) It rakes opponents with its claws. (9) Rattlesnakes, dogs, and other animals have been stood up to by badgers that were angry. (10) Since the loser in a badger fight gets eaten, many animals are happy to give badgers plenty of space.

21. Sentence 2: **Their fierce appearance, sharp teeth, and finger-length claws can support the badger's claim to privacy.**

    What correction should be made to this sentence?

    (1) change Their to They're
    (2) change the spelling of appearance to appearence
    (3) change the spelling of length to legnth
    (4) change badger's to badgers
    (5) no correction is necessary

22. Sentences 4 and 5: **They dislike other animals so much. Badgers don't even associate with other badgers.**

    The most effective combination of sentences 4 and 5 would include which of the following groups of words?

    (1) so much because badgers
    (2) Even though they dislike
    (3) Because they dislike
    (4) so much, but badgers
    (5) so much since badgers

23. Sentences 7 and 8: **The badger's loose hide enables it to turn around when caught. It rakes opponents with its claws.**

    The most effective combination of sentences 7 and 8 would include which of the following groups of words?

    (1) caught it rakes
    (2) caught, it rakes
    (3) caught, yet it rakes
    (4) caught; then, it rakes
    (5) caught, nor rakes

24. Sentence 9: **Rattlesnakes, dogs, and other animals have been stood up to by badgers that were angry.**

    If you rewrote sentence 9 beginning with

    Angry badgers

    the next words should be

    (1) have been stood up to
    (2) stood up to
    (3) have stood up to
    (4) been stood up to
    (5) were stood up to

Items 25 to 28 refer to the following paragraph.

   (1) Cat owners are divided on the issue of whether to declaw their beloved animals. (2) On the one hand, cat owners without claws feel bad about the idea of leaving their animals. (3) Cats need their claws for climbing trees, fighting with other cats, and to catch prey. (4) On the other hand, cats can cause great damage. (5) They use the walls, furniture, and other household items as scratching posts. (6) Some cat owners are parents. (7) They worry that the cats may injure their children. (8) Many veterinarians insist that declawing is not an inhumane practice, provided that the declawed cat remains indoors. (9) Others maintain that declawing should be performed only in extreme situations. (10) Cats that are allowed to roam outside should not be declawed. (11) They will be vulnerable to attack from other animals. (12) A consultation with a veterinarian is suggested for cat owners who are struggling with this difficult issue.

25. Sentence 2: **On the one hand, cat owners without claws feel bad about the idea of leaving their animals.**

    What correction should be made to this sentence?

    (1) remove the comma after hand
    (2) move without claws after hand
    (3) move without claws after animals
    (4) change bad to badly
    (5) no correction is necessary

26. Sentence 3: **Cats need their claws for climbing trees, fighting with other cats, and to catch prey.**

    What correction should be made to this sentence?

    (1) change need to needs
    (2) change climbing trees to climb trees
    (3) change fighting with other cats to fights
    (4) change to catch prey to catching prey
    (5) no correction is necessary

27. Sentences 4 and 5: **On the other hand, cats can cause great damage. They use the walls, furniture, and other household items as scratching posts.**

    The most effective combination of sentences 4 and 5 would include which of the following groups of words?

    (1) great damage unless
    (2) great damage so
    (3) great damage before
    (4) great damage, or
    (5) great damage if

28. Sentences 6 and 7: **Some cat owners are parents. They worry that the cats may injure their children.**

    The most effective combination of sentences 6 and 7 would include which of the following groups of words?

    (1) Cat owners who are parents worry
    (2) Cat owners, who are parents,
    (3) Cat owners who are worried
    (4) Cat owners are worried
    (5) Cat owner's parents worry that

Answers are on page 312.

Performance Analysis
Unit 3 Cumulative Review: Sentence Structure

Name: _____ **Class:** _____ **Date:** _____

Use the Answer Key on pages 312–314 to check your answers to the Unit 3 Cumulative Review: Sentence Structure. Then use the chart to figure out the skill areas in which you need additional review. Circle on the chart the numbers of the test items you answered correctly. Then go back and review the lessons for the skill areas that are difficult for you. For additional review, see the *Steck-Vaughn GED Writing Skills Exercise Book,* Unit 3: Sentence Structure.

Skill	Question	Lesson for Review
Sentence Fragments	2 7 18	18
Run-on Sentences	3 9 11 14	19
Combining Sentences	8 12 20 23 28	20
Parallel Structure	1 4 19 21	21
Subordination	6 13 22 27	22
Misplaced Modifiers	5 15 16 25	23
Shift of Focus	26	24
Revising Sentences	10 17 24	25

Posttest

WRITING SKILLS

Directions

The Writing Skills Posttest is intended to measure your ability to use clear and effective English. It is a test of English as it should be written, not as it might be spoken.

This test consists of paragraphs with numbered sentences. Some of the sentences contain errors in sentence structure, usage, or mechanics (spelling, punctuation, and capitalization). After reading the numbered sentences, answer the multiple choice questions that follow. Some questions refer to sentences that are correct as written. The best answer for these questions is the one that leaves the sentence as originally written. The best answer for some questions is the one that produces a sentence that is consistent with the verb tense and point of view used throughout the paragraph.

You should spend no more than 75 minutes answering the 55 questions on this test. Work carefully, but do not spend too much time on any one question. Do not skip any items. Make a reasonable guess when you are not sure of an answer. You will not be penalized for incorrect answers.

When time is up, mark the last item you finished. This will tell you whether you can finish the real GED Test in the time allowed. Then complete the test.

Record your answers to the questions on a copy of the answer sheet on page 332. Be sure that all required information is properly recorded on the answer sheet.

To record your answers, mark the numbered space on the answer sheet that corresponds to the answer you choose for each question on the test.

Example:

Sentence 1: **We were all honored to meet governor Phillips.**

What correction should be made to this sentence?

(1) insert a comma after <u>honored</u>
(2) change the spelling of <u>honored</u> to <u>honered</u>
(3) change <u>governor</u> to <u>Governor</u>
(4) replace <u>were</u> with <u>was</u>
(5) no correction is necessary   ① ② ● ④ ⑤

In this example, the word <u>governor</u> should be capitalized; therefore, answer space 3 would be marked on the answer sheet.

When you finish the test, use the Correlation Chart on page 234 to determine whether you are ready to take the real GED Test, and, if not, which skill areas need additional review.

Do not rest the point of your pencil on the answer sheet while you are considering your answer. Make no stray or unnecessary marks. If you change an answer, erase your first mark completely. Mark only one answer space for each question; multiple answers will be scored as incorrect. Do not fold or crease your answer sheet.

Adapted with permission of the American Council on Education.

Directions: Choose the best answer to each item.

Items 1 to 4 refer to the following paragraph.

(1) The number of families with two working parents have increased greatly over the past 15 years. (2) This increase has brought many changes to the family and place of working. (3) Today, working parents are willing to accept a job at lower wages if it allow for increased time at home with their children. (4) Some parents may choose not to accept a job promotion if they means more time at work and less time with their families. (5) Others may take only those jobs that are near home or child care.

1. Sentence 1: **The number of families with two working parents have increased greatly over the past 15 years.**

   What correction should be made to this sentence?

   (1) insert a comma after families
   (2) change parents to parent
   (3) insert a comma after parents
   (4) change have to has
   (5) no correction is necessary

2. Sentence 2: **This increase has brought many changes to the family and place of working.**

   Which of the following is the best way to write the underlined portion of this sentence? If you think the original is the best way, choose option (1).

   (1) family and place of working
   (2) family, and working place
   (3) family and working places
   (4) families and to the workplace
   (5) family and to the workplace

3. Sentence 3: **Today, working parents are willing to accept a job at lower wages if it allow for increased time at home with their children.**

   Which of the following is the best way to write the underlined portion of this sentence? If you think the original is the best way, choose option (1).

   (1) if it allow
   (2) if it allows
   (3) if they allows
   (4) if they allow
   (5) if it allowance

4. Sentence 4: **Some parents may choose not to accept a job promotion if they means more time at work and less time with their families.**

   What correction should be made to this sentence?

   (1) change parents to parent's
   (2) insert a comma after promotion
   (3) replace they with it
   (4) change means to mean
   (5) change their to they're

Items 5 to 13 refer to the following paragraphs.

(1) Sucessful job hunting requires careful preparation. (2) First, you need to list the kinds of jobs you would like. (3) Then you need to determine what skills, training, and the required experience for these jobs. (4) One of the best ways to determine these requirements is to ask people which are now doing those jobs.

(5) Next, you need to list your qualifications and see if they match any of the jobs we have selected. (6) If not, you need to think again about what jobs you want. (7) For example, you probably cannot start as manager of a restaurant. (8) You may be able to start in one of the many other jobs in a restaurant and work your way up.

(9) When you select a job that you want, which matches your qualifications, you needed to go for an interview. (10) You need to look and act your best at the interview. (11) Try to learn about it before you go for an interview. (12) Stress your qualifications for the job, your knowledge of the job, and be interested in it.

5. Sentence 1: **Sucessful job hunting requires careful preparation.**

   What correction should be made to this sentence?

   (1) change the spelling of Sucessful to Successful
   (2) insert a comma after hunting
   (3) change requires to require
   (4) change the spelling of preparation to preperation
   (5) no correction is necessary

6. Sentence 2: **First, you need to list the kinds of jobs you would like.**

   What correction should be made to this sentence?

   (1) change need to needed
   (2) change jobs to job
   (3) replace you would with we would
   (4) change would like to would have liked
   (5) no correction is necessary

7. Sentence 3: **Then you need to determine what skills, training, and the required experience for these jobs.**

   Which of the following is the best way to write the underlined portion of this sentence? If you think the original is the best way, choose option (1).

   (1) training, and the required experience
   (2) training, and experience are required
   (3) training, and experience is required
   (4) training, and experience was required
   (5) training; and experience are required

8. Sentence 4: **One of the best ways to determine these requirements is to ask people <u>which are</u> now doing those jobs.**

Which of the following is the best way to write the underlined portion of this sentence? If you think the original is the best way, choose option (1).

(1) which are
(2) who are
(3) whom are
(4) which, are
(5) who, are

9. Sentence 5: **Next, you need to list your qualifications and see if they match any of the jobs we have selected.**

What correction should be made to this sentence?

(1) remove the comma after <u>Next</u>
(2) insert a comma after <u>see</u>
(3) change <u>we have</u> to <u>you has</u>
(4) change <u>we have</u> to <u>you have</u>
(5) no correction is necessary

10. Sentences 7 and 8: **For example, you probably cannot start as a manager of a restaurant. You may be able to start in one of the many other jobs in a restaurant and work your way up.**

The most effective combination of sentences 7 and 8 would include which of the following groups of words?

(1) restaurant and you
(2) restaurant but you
(3) restaurant; but, you
(4) restaurant; because you
(5) restaurant; however, you

11. Sentence 9: **When you select a job that you want, which matches your qualifications, you needed to go for an interview.**

What correction should be made to this sentence?

(1) change <u>you want</u> to <u>you will want</u>
(2) replace <u>which</u> with <u>who</u>
(3) remove the comma after <u>qualifications</u>
(4) change <u>needed</u> to <u>need</u>
(5) no correction is necessary

12. Sentence 11: **Try to <u>learn about it</u> before you go for an interview.**

Which of the following is the best way to write the underlined portion of this sentence? If you think the original is the best way, choose option (1).

(1) learn about it
(2) learn about that
(3) learn about the business and the job
(4) learn about this
(5) learn about which

13. Sentence 12: **Stress your qualifications for the job, your knowledge of the job, and <u>be interested in it.</u>**

Which of the following is the best way to write the underlined portion of this sentence? If you think the original is the best way, choose option (1).

(1) be interested in it
(2) whether you are interested
(3) tell them you are interested in the job
(4) you're interest in the job
(5) your interest in the job

Items 14 to 21 refer to the following paragraphs.

(1) The U.S. Postal Service has come a long way since its founding by ben franklin in the late 1700s. (2) Back then it took days to travel across the 13 colonies by horseback. (3) Later came the Pony Express, carrying the mail from the midwest to california. (4) Next came the railroads, trucks, and finally came the speedy airplanes. (5) The post office says that mail within the 50 states can usually be delivered within three to five days airmail to most European countries takes five to six days.

(6) The cost of first class mail has rose dramatically since Colonial days. (7) One ounce of first class mail cost less than 5 cents to mail in 1800. (8) By 1995 the cost was up to 32 cents, it appears that the cost will continue to rise.

(9) Many people are upset by the rapidly increasing cost of postage. (10) However, the U.S. Postal Service despite its faults do the finest job in the world of fast, accurate delivery of mail. (11) The relative cost in terms of dollars are less now than in 1800.

14. Sentence 1: **The U.S. Postal Service has come a long way since its founding by ben franklin in the late 1700s.**

What correction should be made to this sentence?

(1) change Postal Service to postal service
(2) change Service to service
(3) change ben franklin to Ben franklin
(4) change ben franklin to Ben Franklin
(5) no correction is necessary

15. Sentence 3: **Later came the Pony Express, carrying the mail from the midwest to california.**

What correction should be made to this sentence?

(1) change came to come
(2) change midwest to Midwest
(3) change california to California
(4) change midwest to california to Midwest to California
(5) no correction is necessary

16. Sentence 4: **Next came the railroads, trucks, and finally came the speedy airplanes.**

Which of the following is the best way to write the underlined portion of this sentence? If you think the original is the best way, choose option (1).

(1) finally came the speedy airplanes
(2) finally came the airplanes
(3) finally the speedy airplanes
(4) finally, the airplanes
(5) finally came the super speedy airplanes

17. Sentence 5: **The post office says that mail within the 50 states can usually be delivered within three to five days airmail to most European countries takes five to six days.**

Which of the following is the best way to write the underlined portion of this sentence? If you think the original is the best way, choose option (1).

(1) days airmail
(2) days, airmail
(3) days; and airmail
(4) days; airmail
(5) days; but airmail

18. Sentence 6: **The cost of first class mail has rose dramatically since Colonial days.**

    What correction should be made to this sentence?

    (1) change first class to First Class
    (2) change has to have
    (3) change rose to risen
    (4) change Colonial to colonial
    (5) change days to Days

19. Sentence 8: **By 1995 the cost was up to 32 cents, it appears that the cost will continue to rise.**

    Which of the following is the best way to write the underlined portion of this sentence? If you think the original is the best way, choose option (1).

    (1) cents, it appears
    (2) cents it appears
    (3) cents, and it appears
    (4) cents; and it appears
    (5) cents because it appears

20. Sentence 10: **However, the U.S. Postal Service despite its faults do the finest job in the world of fast, accurate delivery of mail.**

    Which of the following is the best way to write the underlined portion of this sentence? If you think the original is the best way, choose option (1).

    (1) Service despite its faults do
    (2) Service, despite its faults, do
    (3) Service, despite its faults, does
    (4) Service; despite its faults, does
    (5) Service, despite its faults; does

21. Sentence 11: **The relative cost in terms of dollars are less now than in 1800.**

    What correction should be made to this sentence?

    (1) insert a comma after cost
    (2) change dollars to dollar
    (3) change are to is
    (4) insert a comma after dollars
    (5) no correction is necessary

Items 22 to 29 refer to the following paragraphs.

(1) Gun control is an intensive controversial issue. (2) Those against gun control laws argue that the United States constitution protects a civilian's right to bear arms. (3) Those in favor of gun control support passing laws to regulate or has prohibited the sale of certain weapons.

(4) One bill who would regulate gun sales requires a seven-day waiting period before a gun could be issued. (5) This wait would serve as a "Cooling off" period for those who would purchase a gun in the heat of anger. (6) They also would allow time for the person's background to be checked.

(7) Those against gun control laws claim that a seven-day wait is too long and unnecessary. (8) They argue that the number of gun sales, prevented by background investigations, is small. (9) They also point out that anyone intent on buying a gun could do so through illegal means. (10) In fact, a study by the Justice Department says that five out of six criminals do not get his or her weapons from legitimate gun dealers.

22. Sentence 1: **Gun control is an intensive controversial issue.**

What correction should be made to this sentence?

(1) change Gun control to Gun Control
(2) change is to are
(3) change intensive to intensely
(4) change issue to issues
(5) no correction is necessary

23. Sentence 2: **Those against gun control laws argue that the United States constitution protects a civilian's right to bear arms.**

What correction should be made to this sentence?

(1) change States to State's
(2) change constitution to Constitution
(3) insert a comma after constitution
(4) change protects to have been protected
(5) no correction is necessary

24. Sentence 3: **Those in favor of gun control support passing laws to regulate or has prohibited the sale of certain weapons.**

Which of the following is the best way to write the underlined portion of this sentence? If you think the original is the best way, choose option (1).

(1) or has prohibited
(2) or prohibiting
(3) or have prohibits
(4) or to be prohibiting
(5) or to prohibit

25. Sentence 4: **One bill who would regulate gun sales requires a seven-day waiting period before a gun could be issued.**

What correction should be made to this sentence?

(1) change bill to Bill
(2) change who to that
(3) change regulate to regulated
(4) insert a comma after sales
(5) insert a semicolon after period

26. Sentence 5: **This wait would serve as a "Cooling off" period for those who would purchase a gun in the heat of anger.**

Which of the following is the best way to write the underlined portion of this sentence? If you think the original is the best way, choose option (1).

(1) as a "Cooling off" period
(2) as a, "Cooling off," period
(3) as a "cooling off" period
(4) as a "Cooling Off" period
(5) as a, "cooling off," period

27. Sentence 6: **They also would allow time for the person's background to be checked.**

What correction should be made to this sentence?

(1) change They to It
(2) change They to He
(3) change allow to allows
(4) change person's to persons
(5) change person's to persons'

28. Sentence 8: **They argue that the number of gun sales, prevented by background investigations, is small.**

Which of the following is the best way to write the underlined portion of this sentence? If you think the original is the best way, choose option (1).

(1) sales, prevented by background investigations,
(2) sales, prevented by background investigations
(3) sales prevented by background investigations
(4) sales prevention by background investigations
(5) sales; prevented by background investigations

29. Sentence 10: **In fact, a study by the Justice Department says that five out of six criminals do not get his or her weapons from legitimate gun dealers.**

Which of the following is the best way to write the underlined portion of this sentence? If you think the original is the best way, choose option (1).

(1) his or her
(2) he or she
(3) them
(4) our
(5) their

Items 30 to 37 refer to the following paragraphs.

(1) The Berlin Wall was built in 1961, and a shadow of despair was cast over the whole world. (2) It was the ultimate symbol of persecution separating the stark, harsh dictatorship of the Communist East from the booming economy of the democratic West.

(3) Virtually countless hundreds of people risked death to cross over, under, and through the wall. (4) Many of these people lose their lives seeking the freedom that we Americans take for granted.

(5) The harder the Communist countries tried to stop the flow of people to the West, the harder they tried to succeed. (6) We have never known what it is like to live under a harsh dictatorship with secret police looking over your shoulder, with constant shortages of food and other consumer goods, and in crowded living conditions.

(7) The sudden, dramatic shift in political conditions throughout the Communist East in 1989 that resulted in the destruction of the Berlin Wall had gave birth to hope. (8) Perhaps we were beginning an era of world cooperation, and understanding that would rise above politics and communism. (9) Maybe those who gave their lives escaping from persecution did not die in vain. (10) The free world celebrated as the Berlin Wall came tumbling down.

30. Sentence 1: **The Berlin Wall was built in 1961, and a shadow of despair was cast over the whole world.**

If you rewrote sentence 1 beginning with

A shadow of despair was cast over the whole world

the next word should be

(1) when
(2) but
(3) for
(4) therefore
(5) and

31. Sentence 3: **Virtually countless hundreds of people risked death to cross over, under, and through the wall.**

Which of the following is the best way to write the underlined portion of this sentence? If you think the original is the best way, choose option (1).

(1) Virtually countless hundreds
(2) Virtually hundreds
(3) Countless hundreds
(4) Hundreds
(5) Countless, virtually, hundreds

32. Sentence 4: **Many of these people lose their lives seeking the freedom that we Americans take for granted.**

Which of the following is the best way to write the underlined portion of this sentence? If you think the original is the best way, choose option (1).

(1) lose
(2) loose
(3) lost
(4) loses
(5) will have lost

33. Sentence 5: **The harder the Communist countries tried to stop the flow of people to the West, the harder they tried to succeed.**

What correction should be made to this sentence?

(1) change they to these
(2) change they to it
(3) change they to the people
(4) change the spelling of succeed to suceed
(5) no correction is necessary

34. Sentence 6: **We have never known what it is like to live under a harsh dictatorship with secret police looking over your shoulder, with constant shortages of food and other consumer goods, and in crowded living conditions.**

What correction should be made to this sentence?

(1) change known to knowed
(2) change your shoulder to their shoulder
(3) change your shoulder to our shoulders
(4) change your shoulder to his shoulder
(5) no correction is necessary

35. Sentence 7: **The sudden, dramatic shift in political conditions throughout the Communist East in 1989 that resulted in the destruction of the Berlin Wall had gave birth to hope.**

What correction should be made to this sentence?

(1) change East to east
(2) insert a comma after East
(3) change resulted to will result
(4) change Berlin Wall to berlin wall
(5) change had gave to gave

36. Sentence 8: **Perhaps we were beginning an era of world cooperation, and understanding that would rise above politics and communism.**

Which of the following is the best way to write the underlined portion of this sentence? If you think the original is the best way, choose option (1).

(1) cooperation, and understanding
(2) cooperation; and understanding
(3) cooperation and understanding
(4) cooperation; and, understanding
(5) cooperation and; understanding

37. Sentence 10: **The free world celebrated as the Berlin Wall came tumbling down.**

If you rewrote sentence 10 beginning with

As the Berlin Wall came tumbling down,

the next words should be

(1) but the free world
(2) the free world
(3) because the free world
(4) consequently the free world
(5) and the free world

Items 38 to 44 refer to the following paragraphs.

(1) The medical profession continues to stress the effects of cholesterol and fat in the diet as they relate to heart disease. (2) Experts do not agree on the level at which cholesterol becomes a risk factor. (3) Ten years ago there wasn't concern unless a cholesterol level reached 300. (4) Since then experts say that increased risk of heart disease begins at a cholesterol level of 180.

(5) Studies show that about 70 percent of people can reduce their cholesterol 15 to 25 percent by eating less food that is high in fat and cholesterol. (6) According to Dr. John LaRosa chairman of the American Heart Association's task force on cholesterol issues keeping your cholesterol level low improves your chances of a long, healthy life. (7) The American public are encouraged to read labels and to choose products with low amounts of fat and cholesterol.

(8) Today, doctors recommends replacing whole-milk products with those made with low-fat or skim milk. (9) Eating lean meat and increasing your intake of fiber oat bran and beans help reduce cholesterol levels in the bloodstream. (10) Exercising keeps you fit and seems to help clear cholesterol from the arteries. (11) Evidence is strong that what you eat can affect your cholesterol level and therefore your risk of heart disease.

38. Sentences 3 and 4: **Ten years ago there wasn't concern unless a cholesterol level reached 300. Since then experts say that increased risk of heart disease begins at a cholesterol level of 180.**

The most effective combination of sentences 3 and 4 would include which of the following groups of words?

(1) reached 300; consequently, since then
(2) reached 300; maybe since then,
(3) reached 300, then since then,
(4) reached 300; however, since then
(5) reached 300; because since then,

39. Sentence 5: **Studies show that about 70 percent of people can reduce their cholesterol 15 to 25 percent by eating less food that is high in fat and cholesterol.**

What correction should be made to this sentence?

(1) change show to showing
(2) insert a comma after people
(3) change their to they're
(4) insert a comma after fat
(5) no correction is necessary

40. Sentence 6: **According to Dr. John LaRosa chairman of the American Heart Association's task force on cholesterol issues keeping your cholesterol level low improves your chances of a long, healthy life.**

Which of the following is the best way to write the underlined portion of this sentence? If you think the original is the best way, choose option (1).

(1) LaRosa chairman of the American Heart Association's task force on cholesterol issues keeping
(2) LaRosa, chairman of the American Heart Association's task force on cholesterol issues keeping
(3) LaRosa, chairman of the American Heart Association's task force on cholesterol issues, keeping
(4) LaRosa, chairman of the American Heart Association's task force, on cholesterol issues keeping
(5) LaRosa, chairman of the American Heart Association's task force on cholesterol issues; keeping

41. Sentence 7: **The American public are encouraged to read labels and to choose products with low amounts of fat and cholesterol.**

What correction should be made to this sentence?

(1) change American to american
(2) change are to is
(3) insert a comma after labels
(4) change to choose to have chosen
(5) no correction is necessary

42. Sentence 8: **Today, doctors recommends replacing whole-milk products with those made with low-fat or skim milk.**

Which of the following is the best way to write the underlined portion of this sentence? If you think the original is the best way, choose option (1).

(1) Today, doctors recommends
(2) Today, doctors' recommends
(3) Today, doctor's recommend
(4) Today, doctors recommend
(5) Today, Doctors recommend

43. Sentence 9: **Eating lean meat and increasing your intake of fiber oat bran and beans help reduce cholesterol levels in the bloodstream.**

Which of the following is the best way to write the underlined portion of this sentence? If you think the original is the best way, choose option (1).

(1) fiber oat bran and beans
(2) fiber, oat bran, and beans
(3) fiber, oat bran; and beans
(4) fiber oat bran, and beans
(5) fiber, oat bran and, beans

44. Sentence 10: **Exercising keeps you fit and seems to help clear cholesterol from the arteries.**

What correction should be made to this sentence?

(1) change the spelling of Exercising to Exersizing
(2) replace Exercising with Since exercising
(3) change you to your
(4) insert a comma after fit
(5) no correction is necessary

Items 45 to 50 refer to the following paragraphs.

(1) Controlling pesticides has become a serious problem. (2) The resistance of bugs to pesticides has caused a demand for stronger and stronger pesticides. (3) This we now know have resulted in the carry-over of pesticides into the food chain.

(4) Pesticides can cause serious illnesses in adults and children, they can cause birth defects in babies. (5) The solution to this problem involves many different efforts. (6) One approach is to breed insects that are sterile so it cannot reproduce and will gradually die out. (7) Another approach is to breed natural enemies for a selected bug that will not cause harm themselves.

(8) Its also possible to breed plants that are resistant to or can even repel certain bugs. (9) Still another approach is to develop pesticides that are effective but not harmful to humans.

(10) All the solutions require a long time and a lot of research and development money. (11) Unfortunately, developing a new, stronger pesticide is quicker and cheaper than the safer alternatives.

45. Sentence 2: **The resistance of bugs to pesticides has caused a demand for stronger and stronger pesticides.**

What correction should be made to this sentence?

(1) change the spelling of resistance to resistence
(2) change has to have
(3) change has caused to causes
(4) change stronger and stronger to strong and strong
(5) no correction is necessary

46. Sentence 3: **This we now know have resulted in the carry-over of pesticides into the food chain.**

Which of the following is the best way to write the underlined portion of this sentence? If you think the original is the best way, choose option (1).

(1) This we now know have
(2) This, we now know, have
(3) This, we now know, has
(4) This, we now know has
(5) This we now know, have

47. Sentence 4: **Pesticides can cause serious illnesses in adults and children, they can cause birth defects in babies.**

What correction should be made to this sentence?

(1) change children to childs
(2) change children, they to children, and they
(3) change children, they to children; and they
(4) change babies to babys'
(5) no correction is necessary

48. Sentence 6: **One approach is to breed insects that are sterile so it cannot reproduce and will gradually die out.**

    Which of the following is the best way to write the underlined portion of this sentence? If you think the original is the best way, choose option (1).

    (1) that are sterile so it
    (2) who are sterile so it
    (3) that are sterile so they
    (4) who are sterile so they
    (5) whom are sterile so they

49. Sentence 8: **Its also possible to breed plants that are resistant to or can even repel certain bugs.**

    What correction should be made to this sentence?

    (1) change Its to It's
    (2) change Its to Its'
    (3) replace that with who
    (4) change the spelling of resistant to resistent
    (5) no correction is necessary

50. Sentence 11: **Unfortunately, developing a new, stronger pesticide is quicker and cheaper than the safer alternatives.**

    What correction should be made to this sentence?

    (1) remove the comma after Unfortunately
    (2) remove the comma after new
    (3) change is to are
    (4) replace than with then
    (5) no correction is necessary

Items 51 to 55 refer to the following paragraph.

(1) Legalized gambling is a controversial. (2) Contradictory and sometimes emotional subject. (3) Betting on horse races at state-run betting parlors are legal but private betting through a bookie is not. (4) There is some charitable organizations that have "casino nights" with roulette, blackjack, and craps. (5) These games are illegal in all states except nevada, when run by private individuals. (6) Poker, a card game is popular, but a high-stakes game in your home could be illegal.

51. Sentences 1 and 2: **Legalized gambling is a controversial. Contradictory and sometimes emotional subject.**

The most effective combination of sentences 1 and 2 would include which of the following groups of words?

(1) controversial; contradictory and
(2) controversial, contradictory, and
(3) controversial, and contradictory and
(4) controversial, as a result of a contradictory and
(5) controversial; as a result of a contradictory and

52. Sentence 3: **Betting on horse races at state-run betting parlors are legal but private betting through a bookie is not.**

Which of the following is the best way to write the underlined portion of this sentence? If you think the original is the best way, choose option (1).

(1) parlors are legal but private
(2) parlors are legal, but private
(3) parlors are legal; but private
(4) parlors is legal but private
(5) parlors is legal, but private

53. Sentence 4: **There is some charitable organizations that have "casino nights" with roulette, blackjack, and craps.**

What correction should be made to this sentence?

(1) change There is to There were
(2) change There is to There are
(3) change There is to They are
(4) change charitable to Charitable
(5) no correction is necessary

54. Sentence 5: **These games are illegal in all states except nevada, when run by private individuals.**

What correction should be made to this sentence?

(1) change states to States
(2) replace except with accept
(3) change nevada, to Nevada
(4) change nevada, to Nevada,
(5) no correction is necessary

55. Sentence 6: **Poker, a card game is popular, but a high-stakes game in your home could be illegal.**

What correction should be made to this sentence?

(1) remove the comma after Poker
(2) change is to was
(3) insert a comma after card game
(4) insert a comma after home
(5) no correction is necessary

Answers are on page 314.

≣Posttest Correlation Chart: Writing Skills

Name: _____ **Class:** _____ **Date:** _____

This chart can help you determine your strengths and weaknesses on the content and skill areas of the Writing Skills GED Test. Use the Answer Key on pages 314–319 to check your answers to the test. Then circle on the chart the numbers of the test items you answered correctly. Put the total number correct for each content area and skill area in each row and column. If you answered fewer than 55 questions correctly, look at the total items correct in each column and row and decide which areas are difficult for you. Use the page references to study those areas. Use a copy of the Study Record Sheet on page 31 to guide your studying.

Content/ Item Type	Sentence Correction	Sentence Revision	Rewrite/ Combine	Total Correct	Page Ref.
Mechanics *(Pages 32–99)*					
Capitalization	14, 15, 23, 54			_____ out of 4	34–39
Commas	39, 50, 55	19, 28, 36, 40, 43		_____ out of 8	44–59
Semicolons		17		_____ out of 1	60–65
Apostrophes and Quotation Marks	49	26		_____ out of 2	66–73
Spelling	5, 44			_____ out of 2	74–99
Usage *(Pages 100–159)*					
Subject-Verb Agreement	1, 21, 41, 53	20, 42, 46, 52		_____ out of 8	108–113
Verb Tenses and Irregular Verbs	6, 11, 18, 35	32		_____ out of 5	114–127
Personal Pronouns	9, 25, 34	3, 8		_____ out of 5	128–135
Pronouns and Antecedents	4, 27, 33	12, 29, 48		_____ out of 6	136–141
Indefinite Pronouns					142–147
Adjectives and Adverbs	22, 45			_____ out of 2	148–153
Sentence Structure *(Pages 160–218)*					
Sentence Fragments			51	_____ out of 1	162–167
Run-on Sentences			10	_____ out of 1	168–173
Combining Sentences	47		38	_____ out of 2	174–181
Parallel Structure		2, 7, 13, 16, 24		_____ out of 5	182–187
Subordination			30, 37	_____ out of 2	188–193
Misplaced Modifiers					194–199
Shift of Focus					200–205
Revising Sentences		31		_____ out of 1	206–211

© 1996 Steck-Vaughn Company. *GED Writing Skills.* Permission granted to reproduce for classroom use.

For additional help, see the Steck-Vaughn GED Writing Skills Exercise Book.

Simulated GED Test

WRITING SKILLS

Directions

The Writing Skills Simulated Test is intended to measure your ability to use clear and effective English. It is a test of English as it should be written, not as it might be spoken.

This test consists of paragraphs with numbered sentences. Some of the sentences contain errors in sentence structure, usage, or mechanics (spelling, punctuation, and capitalization). After reading the numbered sentences, answer the multiple-choice questions that follow. Some questions refer to sentences that are correct as written. The best answer for these questions is the one that leaves the sentence as originally written. The best answer for some questions is the one that produces a sentence that is consistent with the verb tense and point of view used throughout the paragraph.

You should spend no more than 75 minutes answering the 55 questions on this test. Work carefully, but do not spend too much time on any one question. Do not skip any items. Make a reasonable guess when you are not sure of an answer. You will not be penalized for incorrect answers.

When time is up, mark the last item you finished. This will tell you whether you can finish the real GED Test in the time allowed. Then complete the test.

Record your answers to the questions on a copy of the answer sheet on page 332. Be sure that all required information is properly recorded on the answer sheet.

To record your answers, mark the numbered space on the answer sheet that corresponds to the answer you choose for each question on the test.

Example:

Sentence 1: **We were all honored to meet governor Phillips.**

What correction should be made to this sentence?

(1) insert a comma after honored
(2) change the spelling of honored to honered
(3) change governor to Governor
(4) replace were with was
(5) no correction is necessary   ① ② ● ④ ⑤

In this example, the word governor should be capitalized; therefore, answer space 3 would be marked on the answer sheet.

When you finish the test, use the Correlation Chart on page 250 to determine whether you are ready to take the real GED Test, and, if not, which skill areas need additional review.

Do not rest the point of your pencil on the answer sheet while you are considering your answer. Make no stray or unnecessary marks. If you change an answer, erase your first mark completely. Mark only one answer space for each question; multiple answers will be scored as incorrect. Do not fold or crease your answer sheet.

Adapted with permission of the American Council on Education.

Directions: Choose the best answer to each item.

Items 1 to 8 refer to the following paragraphs.

(1) Organ transplants are becoming more and more common. (2) In the past kidney transplants were about the only common organ transplants. (3) Today, we hear of heart, lung, liver, and eye transplants, in addition to kidney transplants. (4) Sources of organs for transplants are people which are killed in accidents or who die of illnesses that do not affect the organ being used.

(5) A big problem with organ transplants is that it often tries to reject the organ. (6) It sometimes requires the use of strong drugs to prevent this rejection. (7) As better transplant methods and better antirejection drugs are developed, transplants will become more common and more successful. (8) Some concerns, are heard, that organ transplants are too common now. (9) There is also concern about people selling their organs.

(10) Someday the transplanting of most body organs may become common and routine. (11) More and more people are making advance arrangements to donate its organs when they die, so that someone else can live.

1. Sentence 2: **In the past kidney transplants were about the only common organ transplants.**

What correction should be made to this sentence?

(1) replace past with passed
(2) insert a semicolon after past
(3) insert a comma after past
(4) change were to was
(5) no correction is necessary

2. Sentence 3: **Today, we hear of heart, lung, liver, and eye transplants, in addition to kidney transplants.**

What correction should be made to this sentence?

(1) replace hear with here
(2) replace eye with I
(3) remove the comma after eye transplants
(4) change addition to edition
(5) no correction is necessary

3. Sentence 4: **Sources of organs for transplants are people which are killed in accidents or who die of illnesses that do not affect the organ being used.**

Which of the following is the best way to write the underlined portion of this sentence? If you think the original is the best way, choose option (1).

(1) people which are
(2) people which is
(3) people who are
(4) people who is
(5) people who were

4. Sentence 5: **A big problem with organ transplants is that it often tries to reject the organ.**

   Which of the following is the best way to write the underlined portion of this sentence? If you think the original is the best way, choose option (1).

   (1) is that it
   (2) are that it
   (3) is that the body receiving the transplant
   (4) are that the body receiving the transplant
   (5) is because the body receiving the transplant

5. Sentence 6: **It sometimes requires the use of strong drugs to prevent this rejection.**

   If you rewrote sentence 6 beginning with

   The use of strong drugs

   the next words should be

   (1) is sometimes required
   (2) are sometimes required
   (3) were sometimes required
   (4) is, in any case, required
   (5) are, in any case, required

6. Sentence 8: **Some concerns, are heard, that organ transplants are too common now.**

   Which of the following is the best way to write the underlined portion of this sentence? If you think the original is the best way, choose option (1).

   (1) concerns, are heard, that
   (2) concerns are heard, that
   (3) concerns, are heard that
   (4) concerns are heard that
   (5) concerns are, heard that

7. Sentence 9: **There is also concern about people selling their organs.**

   What correction should be made to this sentence?

   (1) change selling to having sold
   (2) replace their with they're
   (3) change their to his
   (4) change their to its
   (5) no correction is necessary

8. Sentence 11: **More and more people are making advance arrangements to donate its organs when they die, so that someone else can live.**

   What correction should be made to this sentence?

   (1) change its to they're
   (2) change its to their
   (3) insert a comma after organs
   (4) change they to we
   (5) no correction is necessary

Items 9 to 16 refer to the following paragraphs.

(1) We have come a long way from the first room-size vacuum tube computers to todays purse-size laptop computers. (2) We will probably have intelligent computers like Hal in the movie 2001 when the year 2001 arrives.

(3) There is computers in every part of our lives. (4) They are in our cars, supermarkets and discount stores have them, and on the desks of at least some employees in even the smallest businesses. (5) Computers are in the space shuttle and satellites. (6) They are in the thermostat on your furnace and in the burglar alarm systems of offices. (7) Computers can be very small and simple or very large and complex.

(8) The one problem with computers is that, at least so far, they are very dumb. (9) Computers are only as smart as the person entering the information.

(10) The main benifit of computers is that they process extremely complicated data very, very fast. (11) However, they process wrong data just as fast as correct data, which results in errors. (12) Skillful, accurate keyboarding and data entry is critical to successful computer operations.

9. Sentence 1: **We have come a long way from the first room-size vacuum tube computers to todays purse-size laptop computers.**

What correction should be made to this sentence?

(1) insert a comma after way
(2) change the spelling of vacuum to vaccum
(3) change todays to todays'
(4) change todays to today's
(5) no correction is necessary

10. Sentence 2: **We will probably have intelligent computers like Hal in the movie 2001 when the year 2001 arrives.**

If you rewrote sentence 2 beginning with

When the year 2001

the next words should be

(1) arrives, we
(2) arrives; we
(3) arrives; because, we
(4) arrives; as a result, we
(5) arrives, but we

11. Sentence 3: **There is computers in every part of our lives.**

What correction should be made to this sentence?

(1) change There is to There was
(2) change There is to There are
(3) replace our with their
(4) change our to ours
(5) no correction is necessary

12. Sentence 4: **They are in our cars, supermarkets and discount stores have them, and on the desks of at least some employees in even the smallest businesses.**

Which of the following is the best way to write the underlined portion of this sentence? If you think the original is the best way, choose option (1).

(1) supermarkets and discount stores have them,
(2) our supermarkets and discount stores have them,
(3) our supermarkets and discount stores,
(4) at the supermarkets and discount stores,
(5) on the supermarkets and discount stores,

13. Sentences 5 and 6: **Computers are in the space shuttle and satellites. They are in the thermostat on your furnace and in the burglar alarm systems of offices.**

Which of the following is the best way to write the underlined portion of this sentence? If you think the original is the best way, choose option (1).

(1) satellites. They
(2) satellites; and they
(3) satellites and they
(4) satellites, they
(5) satellites they

14. Sentence 8: **The one problem with computers is that, at least so far, they are very dumb.**

Which of the following is the best way to write the underlined portion of this sentence? If you think the original is the best way, choose option (1).

(1) is that, at least so far, they
(2) are, that at least so far, they
(3) are that at least so far they
(4) is that at least so far they
(5) are that, at least so far; they

15. Sentence 10: **The main benifit of computers is that they process extremely complicated data very, very fast.**

What correction should be made to this sentence?

(1) change the spelling of benifit to benefit
(2) change is to are
(3) replace they with it
(4) replace extremely with extreme
(5) no correction is necessary

16. Sentence 12: **Skillful, accurate keyboarding and data entry is critical to successful computer operations.**

What correction should be made to this sentence?

(1) change is to are
(2) change is to has been
(3) change the spelling of successful to successfull
(4) replace to with too
(5) no correction is necessary

Items 17 to 24 refer to the following paragraphs.

(1) In spite of our freedom of speech in the united states, there are many forms of censorship. (2) Common forms we are familiar with is the censorship of profanity on live radio and television and similar censorship in newspapers. (3) We also see it in the ratings on movies, videotapes, and magazines.

(4) Controversial types of censorship occur in schools when school administrators try to censor student newspapers or when parents or other groups try to censor sex education courses, certain library books, or even textbooks. (5) A famous case of censorship occurred long ago in Tennessee. (6) A teacher named John Scopes, against state law, taught the theory of evolution as proposed by Charles Darwin. (7) Scopes is arrested and tried in a trial that was known as the Scopes Monkey Trial.

(8) Censorship is very severe in nondemocratic countries where the government dictates what the people can see hear and say with penalties as severe as death for breaking the law. (9) You tend to take our right to free speech and all that goes with it for granted. (10) We need to be aware that censorship takes many forms and we should constantly be alert to threats to our free speech.

17. Sentence 1: **In spite of our freedom of speech in the united states, there are many forms of censorship.**

What corrections should be made to this sentence?

(1) change freedom of speech to Freedom of Speech
(2) insert a comma after freedom
(3) change united states to United States
(4) remove the comma after states
(5) no correction is necessary

18. Sentence 2: **Common forms we are familiar with is the censorship of profanity on live radio and television and similar censorship in newspapers.**

What correction should be made to this sentence?

(1) change we are to we is
(2) change we are to we our
(3) change with is to with our
(4) change with is to with are
(5) no correction is necessary

19. Sentence 3: **We also see it in the ratings on movies, videotapes, and magazines.**

Which of the following is the best way to write the underlined portion of this sentence? If you think the original is the best way, choose option (1).

(1) movies, videotapes, and magazines
(2) Movies, videotapes, and Magazines
(3) Movies, Videotapes, and magazines
(4) Movies, Videotapes, and Magazines
(5) movies, Videotapes, and Magazines

20. Sentences 5 and 6: **A famous case of censorship occurred long ago in Tennessee. A teacher named John Scopes, against state law, taught the theory of evolution as proposed by Charles Darwin.**

The most effective combination of sentences 5 and 6 would include which words?

(1) when
(2) but
(3) if
(4) and
(5) while

21. Sentence 7: **Scopes is arrested and tried in a trial that was known as the Scopes Monkey Trial.**

What correction should be made to this sentence?

(1) change Scopes to Scopes'
(2) change is to will be
(3) change is to was
(4) replace that with who
(5) no correction is necessary

22. Sentence 8: **Censorship is very severe in nondemocratic countries where the government dictates what the people can see hear and say with penalties as severe as death for breaking the law.**

What correction should be made to this sentence?

(1) replace Censorship is with Censorship are
(2) change the spelling of government to goverment
(3) replace what with that
(4) change see hear and say to see, hear, and say
(5) no correction is necessary

23. Sentence 9: **You tend to take our right to free speech and all that goes with it for granted.**

What correction should be made to this sentence?

(1) change You tend to We tend
(2) replace to with too
(3) change right to write
(4) replace for with fore
(5) no correction is necessary

24. Sentence 10: **We need to be aware that censorship takes many forms and we should constantly be alert to threats to our free speech.**

Which of the following is the best way to write the underlined portion of this sentence? If you think the original is the best way, choose option (1).

(1) forms and we
(2) forms; and we
(3) forms; and, we
(4) forms, and, we
(5) forms, and we

Items 25 to 32 refer to the following paragraphs.

(1) The social security system was back in the beginning originally created to supplement retirement income. (2) The social security act of 1935 never intended for social security to be the only source of retirement income. (3) When enacted it did not provide for our widows, orphans, and those whom have disabilities.

(4) The system grew over the years; and the costs jumped sharply due to added benefits and inflation. (5) Also, since people now live longer due to improved health care. (6) The number of people receiving benefits has grown faster than the number of people paying into social security. (7) This caused the system to run out of money, required major changes, and increased taxes on those people which were working to support those who were retired.

(8) The social security system is now sound again. (9) In fact, it has large surpluses, which the government is using to fund other programs, temporarily. (10) This practice could lead to more problems in the future.

(11) We have to keep in mind that everything has a cost. (12) If we want the government to provide for us in our old age, we will have to pay for it in our youth.

25. Sentence 1: **The social security system was back in the beginning originally created to supplement retirement income.**

What correction should be made to this sentence?

(1) remove the word <u>back</u>
(2) remove the phrase <u>in the beginning</u>
(3) remove the phrase <u>back in the beginning</u>
(4) remove the word <u>originally</u>
(5) no correction is necessary

26. Sentence 2: **The social security act of 1935 never intended for social security to be the only source of retirement income.**

What correction should be made to this sentence?

(1) change <u>social security act</u> to <u>Social security act</u>
(2) change <u>social security act</u> to <u>Social Security Act</u>
(3) change the spelling of <u>intended</u> to <u>entended</u>
(4) change <u>retirement income</u> to <u>Retirement Income</u>
(5) no correction is necessary

27. Sentence 3: **When enacted it did not provide for our widows, orphans, and those whom have disabilities.**

Which of the following is the best way to write the underlined portion of this sentence? If you think the original is the best way, choose option (1).

(1) those whom have disabilities
(2) those who have disabilities
(3) those which have disabilities
(4) those whom are disabled
(5) disabilities

28. Sentence 4: **The system grew over the years; and the costs jumped sharply due to added benefits and inflation.**

   Which of the following is the best way to write the underlined portion of this sentence? If you think the original is the best way, choose option (1).

   (1) years; and the
   (2) year's; and the
   (3) years, and the
   (4) years; and, the
   (5) year's, and the

29. Sentences 5 and 6: **Also, since people now live longer due to improved health care. The number of people receiving benefits has grown faster than the number of people paying into social security.**

   Which of the following is the best way to write the underlined portion of this sentence? If you think the original is the best way, choose option (1).

   (1) health care. The number
   (2) health care, the number
   (3) health care; the number
   (4) health care, while the number
   (5) Health Care, the number

30. Sentence 7: **This caused the system to run out of money, required major changes, and increased taxes on those people which were working to support those who were retired.**

   What correction should be made to this sentence?

   (1) change money to Money
   (2) change taxes to Taxes
   (3) change which to who
   (4) change which to whom
   (5) no correction is necessary

31. Sentence 9: **In fact, it has large surpluses, which the government is using to fund other programs, temporarily.**

   What correction should be made to this sentence?

   (1) remove the comma after fact
   (2) change the spelling of which to witch
   (3) change the spelling of government to goverment
   (4) change using to used
   (5) move temporarily between the words using and to

32. Sentence 12: **If we want the government to provide for us in our old age, we will have to pay for it in our youth.**

   If you rewrite sentence 12 beginning with

   We will have to pay in our

   the next words should be

   (1) youth, if we want
   (2) youth if we want
   (3) youth; if, we want
   (4) youth if, we want
   (5) youth; if we want

Items 33 to 36 refer to the following paragraphs.

(1) The Academy Awards, or Oscars, are awarded each year by the academy of Motion Picture Arts and Sciences. (2) These are the oldest and best known awards in the entertainment industry. (3) Oscars are awarded for best picture, best director, best actor, best actress, and best supporting actress as well as several other categories.

(4) What does an Oscar look like? (5) It is a gold-plated bronze statue that is about 10 inches high and weighs about 7 pounds.

(6) The Academy Awards ceremony has become a popular TV show each Spring. (7) It is a showcase of personalities and talent in the entertainment industry. (8) The Oscars are sought after and valued highly by every actor and actress, and they are a real prize. (9) Any film that wins one or more Oscars is just about guaranteed a good box office income.

33. Sentence 1: **The Academy Awards, or Oscars, are awarded each year by the academy of Motion Picture Arts and Sciences.**

What correction should be made to this sentence?

(1) change academy to Academy
(2) change Oscars to oscars
(3) change Arts and Sciences to arts and sciences
(4) change the spelling of Sciences to Sceinces
(5) no correction is necessary

34. Sentences 4 and 5: **What does an Oscar look like? It is a gold-plated bronze statue that is about 10 inches high and weighs about 7 pounds.**

The most effective combination of sentences 4 and 5 would include which of the following groups of words?

(1) An Oscar looks like it is a gold-plated
(2) An Oscar looks like a gold-plated
(3) An Oscar is a gold-plated
(4) It is a gold-plated
(5) An Oscar is like a gold-plated

35. Sentence 6: **The Academy Awards ceremony has become a popular TV show each Spring.**

What correction should be made to this sentence?

(1) change Academy Awards to academy awards
(2) change the spelling of become to becume
(3) replace has with have
(4) change Spring to spring
(5) no correction is necessary

36. Sentence 8: **The Oscars are sought after and valued highly by every actor and actress, and they are a real prize.**

Which of the following is the best way to write the underlined portion of this sentence? If you think the original is the best way, choose option (1).

(1) actress, and they are
(2) actress; and they are
(3) actress, and the Oscars are
(4) actress, and they is
(5) actress; and, they are

Items 37 to 40 refer to the following paragraphs.

(1) The supermarket scanner, a device that reads the prices on groceries at the checkout and records them, is a fairly new application of computer technology. (2) The technical name for these devices are "optical character readers." (3) The scanner is the input part of a computer system. (4) It is often connected to a computer voice who names the item being scanned.

(5) The scanner shines a light on the bar code on an item and reads the code. (6) The bar code is the small box or block with the rows of vertical lines on the package with different widths and spacing. (7) This code identifies what the item is and what it costs. (8) To change the price on an item, someone enters the code for the item in the computer and changes the price.

37. Sentence 1: **The supermarket scanner, a device that reads the prices on groceries at the checkout and records them, is a fairly new application of computer technology.**

    What correction should be made to this sentence?

    (1) remove the comma after scanner
    (2) change scanner to Scanner
    (3) remove the comma after them
    (4) change them, is to them; is
    (5) no correction is necessary

38. Sentence 2: **The technical name for these devices are "optical character readers."**

    Which of the following is the best way to write the underlined portion of this sentence? If you think the original is the best way, choose option (1).

    (1) these devices are
    (2) which these devices are
    (3) these devices will be
    (4) these devices is
    (5) these devices were

39. Sentence 4: **It is often connected to a computer voice who names the item being scanned.**

    What correction should be made to this sentence?

    (1) replace It with They
    (2) change is to was
    (3) change is to are
    (4) replace who with that
    (5) no correction is necessary

40. Sentence 6: **The bar code is the small box or block with the rows of vertical lines on the package with different widths and spacing.**

    What correction should be made to this sentence?

    (1) replace bar code with Bar Code
    (2) change is to were
    (3) change is to are
    (4) move on the package after spacing
    (5) no correction is necessary

Items 41 to 48 refer to the following paragraphs.

(1) Alfred Nobel a Swedish chemist invented dynamite. (2) When he died, he left $9 million to a fund to award prizes to outstanding persons each year in the areas of world peace chemistry physics literature and medicine. (3) Nobel felt bad about creating something so destructive as dynamite, he started this fund to compensate for his guilt.

(4) The prizes, which began in 1901, are awarded by various organizations in Sweden. (5) The peace prize is awarded by a committee of five elected by the norwegian parliament. (6) A sixth prize in economics was established in 1969 by the Swedish Central Bank.

(7) The prizes are awarded each year on december 10, the anniversary of Alfred Nobel's death. (8) The Nobel prize consists of a large sum of cash and a medal. (9) The cash for each category are an equal share of the income from the original $9 million.

41. Sentence 1: **Alfred Nobel a Swedish chemist invented dynamite.**

Which of the following is the best way to write the underlined portion of this sentence? If you think the original is the best way, choose option (1).

(1) Nobel a Swedish chemist invented
(2) Nobel, a Swedish chemist invented
(3) Nobel a Swedish chemist, invented
(4) Nobel, a Swedish chemist, invented
(5) Nobel, a swedish chemist, invented

42. Sentence 2: **When he died, he left $9 million to a fund to award prizes to outstanding persons each year in the areas of world peace chemistry physics literature and medicine.**

Which of the following is the best way to write the underlined portion of this sentence? If you think the original is the best way, choose option (1).

(1) world peace chemistry physics literature and
(2) world peace chemistry, physics literature and
(3) world peace, chemistry, physics, literature, and
(4) world peace, chemistry, physics literature and
(5) world peace chemistry, physics, literature, and

43. Sentence 3: **Nobel felt bad about creating something so destructive as dynamite, he started this fund to compensate for his guilt.**

    What correction should be made to this sentence?

    (1) remove the comma after dynamite
    (2) change dynamite, he to dynamite; he
    (3) change started to starts
    (4) change fund to Fund
    (5) no correction is necessary

44. Sentence 4: **The prizes, which began in 1901, are awarded by various organizations in Sweden.**

    What correction should be made to this sentence?

    (1) remove the comma after prizes
    (2) change began to begun
    (3) remove the comma after 1901
    (4) replace Sweden with sweden
    (5) no correction is necessary

45. Sentence 5: **The peace prize is awarded by a committee of five elected by the norwegian parliament.**

    What correction should be made to this sentence?

    (1) change peace to piece
    (2) change committee to Committee
    (3) insert a comma after elected
    (4) change norwegian to Norwegian
    (5) no correction is necessary

46. Sentence 6: **A sixth prize in economics was established in 1969 by the Swedish Central Bank.**

    If you rewrote sentence 6 beginning with

    In 1969 the Swedish Central Bank

    the next words should be

    (1) established
    (2) was established
    (3) will establish
    (4) establishing
    (5) will have been established

47. Sentence 7: **The prizes are awarded each year on december 10, the anniversary of Alfred Nobel's death.**

    Which of the following is the best way to write the underlined portion of this sentence? If you think the original is the best way, choose option (1).

    (1) year on december 10, the
    (2) year, on december 10, the
    (3) year on December 10, the
    (4) year, on December 10, the
    (5) year on, December 10, the

48. Sentence 9: **The cash for each category are an equal share of the income from the original $9 million.**

    What correction should be made to this sentence?

    (1) change the spelling of category to catagory
    (2) insert a comma after category
    (3) change are to is
    (4) change share to shares
    (5) change share to sharing

(1) We hear alot of talk about acid rain. (2) Acid rain is caused by sulfur in the smoke from electric power plants, that burn high-sulfur coal. (3) The sulfur fumes mix with moisture in the air and turn into sulfuric acid, which can be carried hundreds of miles before it falls back to the ground as acid rain.

(4) Most of the acid rain comes from power plants in the midwest, and most of the damage occurs in the Northeast and Canada. (5) Acid rain poisons rivers and lakes and kills trees. (6) It also attacks the stone in old, historic buildings.

(7) The power plants could stop using high-sulfur coal and switch to cleaner coal oil gas or nuclear energy. (8) Any of these would result in higher costs, which would be passed on to electricity users. (9) Other solutions would be to clean it before burning or to clean the smoke after burning. (10) A solution to the acid rain problem must be found soon, however, it will not be without cost to everyone.

49. Sentence 1: **We hear alot of talk about acid rain.**

What correction should be made to this sentence?

(1) replace hear with here's
(2) replace hear with here
(3) replace hear with hears
(4) change the spelling of alot to a lot
(5) no correction is necessary

50. Sentence 2: **Acid rain is caused by sulfur in the smoke from electric power plants, that burn high-sulfur coal.**

Which of the following is the best way to write the underlined portion of this sentence? If you think the original is the best way, choose option (1).

(1) power plants, that burn
(2) Power Plants that burn
(3) power plants; burning
(4) power plants that burn
(5) power plants, which burn

51. Sentence 4: **Most of the acid rain comes from power plants in the midwest, and most of the damage occurs in the Northeast and Canada.**

What correction should be made to this sentence?

(1) change midwest to Midwest
(2) remove the comma after midwest
(3) change Northeast to northeast
(4) replace Canada with canada
(5) no correction is necessary

52. Sentences 5 and 6: **Acid rain poisons rivers and lakes and kills <u>trees. It</u> also attacks the stone in old, historic buildings.**

Which of the following is the best way to write the underlined portion of these sentences? If you think the original is the best way, choose option (1).

(1) trees. It
(2) trees; and it
(3) trees and it
(4) trees and, it
(5) trees; and, it

53. Sentence 7: **The power plants could stop using high-sulfur coal and switch to <u>cleaner coal oil gas or</u> nuclear energy.**

Which of the following is the best way to write the underlined portion of this sentence? If you think the original is the best way, choose option (1).

(1) cleaner coal oil gas or
(2) cleaner, coal, oil, gas, or
(3) cleaner coal, oil, gas, or
(4) cleaner coal, oil gas, or
(5) cleaner, coal oil gas or

54. Sentence 9: **Other solutions would be to clean it before burning or to clean the smoke after burning.**

What correction should be made to this sentence?

(1) insert a comma after <u>solutions</u>
(2) insert a comma after <u>be</u>
(3) replace it with <u>the coal</u>
(4) replace it with <u>its</u>
(5) no correction is necessary

55. Sentence 10: **A solution to the acid rain problem must be found <u>soon, however, it will not</u> be without cost to everyone.**

Which of the following is the best way to write the underlined portion of this sentence? If you think the original is the best way, choose option (1).

(1) soon, however, it will not
(2) sooner; however it will not
(3) soon; however, it will not
(4) soon because it will not
(5) soon; however it will not

Answers are on page 319.

Simulated Test Correlation Chart: Writing Skills

Name: _____   **Class:** _____   **Date:** _____

This chart can help you determine your strengths and weaknesses on the content and skill areas of the Writing Skills GED Test. Use the Answer Key on pages 319–323 to check your answers to the test. Then circle on the chart the numbers of the test items you answered correctly. Put the total number correct for each content area and skill area in each row and column. If you answered fewer than 55 questions correctly, look at the total items correct in each column and row and decide which areas are difficult for you. Use the page references to study those areas. Use a copy of the Study Record Sheet on page 31 to guide your studying.

Content/ Item Type	Sentence Correction	Sentence Revision	Rewrite/ Combine	Total Correct	Page Ref.
Mechanics *(Pages 32–99)*					
Capitalization	17, 26, 33, 35 45, 51	19, 47		_____ out of 8	34–39
Commas	1, 22, 37, 44	6, 28, 41, 42, 50, 53	32	_____ out of 11	44–59
Semicolons		55		_____ out of 1	60–65
Apostrophes and Quotation Marks	9			_____ out of 1	66–73
Spelling	2, 15, 49			_____ out of 3	74–99
Usage *(Pages 100–159)*					
Subject-Verb Agreement	11, 16, 18, 48	14, 38	5	_____ out of 7	108–113
Verb Tenses and Irregular Verbs	21, 7		46	_____ out of 3	114–127
Personal Pronouns	3, 23, 27, 30, 39			_____ out of 5	128–135
Pronouns and Antecedents	8, 54	4, 36		_____ out of 4	136–141
Indefinite Pronouns					142–147
Adjectives and Adverbs					148–153
Sentence Structure *(Pages 160–218)*					
Sentence Fragments		29	10	_____ out of 2	162–167
Run-on Sentences	43	13, 24, 52		_____ out of 4	168–173
Combining Sentences			34	_____ out of 1	174–181
Parallel Structure		12		_____ out of 1	182–187
Subordination			20	_____ out of 1	188–193
Misplaced Modifiers	31, 40			_____ out of 2	194–199
Shift of Focus					200–205
Revising Sentences	25			_____ out of 1	206–211

For additional help, see the Steck-Vaughn GED Writing Skills Exercise Book.

Answers and Explanations

Answers and Explanations

PRETEST

(Pages 14–29)

PRETEST

1. **(4) doctor, and** (Mechanics/Capitalization and punctuation) Doctor is not attached to a specific name here and should not be capitalized, as in options (1), (3), and (5). Also, the conjunction and joins two independent clauses of the compound sentence and should have a comma in front of it, not a semicolon, so options (2) and (3) are incorrect.

2. **(5) no correction is necessary** (Mechanics/Spelling—homonyms) Yous is not a word, so option (1) is incorrect. Option (2) is incorrect because heard is the past-tense form of the verb and the passage is written in the present tense. Option (3) confuses hear, which means "to gain information through the ear," with its homonym. In option (4), there is no reason to capitalize siren.

3. **(2) remove the comma after speedometer** (Mechanics/Punctuation—overuse of commas) Because this is not a compound sentence, the comma is not needed after speedometer. In option (1), your is a possessive pronoun and should not be changed to the contraction you're. Two parts of a verb phrase, are and going, should not be separated by a comma, so option (3) is incorrect. In option (4), the singular verb is is incorrect.

4. **(3) rearview mirror, you** (Sentence structure/Fragment; Mechanics/Punctuation—commas after introductory elements) By combining sentences (6) and (7), a complete sentence (one dependent and one independent clause) is created. When the dependent clause comes first, a comma is needed after the dependent clause, so option (5) is wrong. When you look in the rearview mirror is a fragment, so option (1) is incorrect. Option (2) incorrectly uses a semicolon after the dependent clause.

5. **(4) insert a semicolon after faster** (Sentence structure/Run-on sentence) When two sentences (two independent clauses) are combined into one sentence without a coordinating conjunction, a semicolon must be used. A comma is used with a conjunction, so option (3) is incorrect. Option (5) would leave the run-on sentence uncorrected and create a fragment.

6. **(5) they slow down and stare** (Usage/Pronoun reference—agreement with antecedent and subject-verb agreement) A plural pronoun is needed to agree with the antecedent people, which is plural, so they is correct as in option (5). Everyone and everybody are singular, so options (1) and (2) are incorrect. Because they is plural, it requires the plural verbs slow and stare; options (3) and (4) are incorrect because slows and stares are singular.

7. **(3) change says, "may to says, "May** (Mechanics/Capitalization) The first word of a sentence in quotation marks is capitalized, so May should be capitalized. There is no reason for the changes in options (1), (2), (4), and (5).

8. **(4) gas, car repairs, food,** (Mechanics/Punctuation—commas between items in series) Items in series should be separated by commas. Options (1), (2), (3), and (5) do not correctly use commas to separate each item.

9. **(5) no correction is necessary** (Mechanics/Capitalization; Usage/Verb tense and subject-verb agreement) The passage is written in present tense and Daydreaming is singular, so the verb is is correct, making options (2) and (3) incorrect. In options (1) and (4), Daydreaming and popular are capitalized correctly.

10. **(3) change contains to contain** (Usage/Subject-verb agreement and verb tense) This sentence has a plural subject and requires the plural verb contain. The passage is in the present tense, so option (4) is incorrect. There is no reason for the changes in options (1) and (2).

11. **(2) if you control it and do not** (Usage/Verb tense; Mechanics/ Punctuation and capitalization) Control is present tense, which is consistent with the rest of the sentence and paragraph. Options (3) and (5) add unnecessary punctuation, and Do Not is incorrectly capitalized in option (4).

12. **(4) mood when you're** (Mechanics/Contractions) You're is a contraction meaning "you are." No ownership is expressed, so the possessive pronoun your is not correct, as in options (1) and (5). A comma is not needed

because the dependent clause is restrictive, so option (2) is incorrect.

13. **(2) change will begin to begin** (Usage/Verb tense) Verb tense should be consistent in the same sentence. Need and do get are present tense. The verb will begin is future tense and should be changed to present tense begin, so options (1) and (4) are incorrect. Option (3) is incorrect because the possessive pronoun your is needed, not the contraction you're.

14. **(3) job, such as pushing a lawn mower** (Usage/Verb tense—verb forms) Only option (3) correctly joins the dependent clause to the independent clause. The verb doing in sentence 6 is present tense; the verb pushed in sentence (7) is past tense. The two verbs should be parallel in form—doing and pushing. Options (1), (2), (4), and (5) are incorrect because the verb push, though present tense, is not parallel to the verb doing.

15. **(2) daydreaming while you are** (Sentence structure/Fragment and improper subordination) Sentence 9 is a fragment, so option (1) is incorrect. The sentences should be joined to clarify the relationship between the two thoughts. Because sentence 9 becomes a dependent clause, semicolons should not be used to connect it to the independent clause. Therefore, options (3) and (5) are incorrect. Option (4) is incorrect because the possessive pronoun your cannot replace you are.

16. **(3) change when you drive a car to driving a car** (Sentence structure/ Parallelism) This sentence contains a listing in which all items should be parallel. To create parallel structure, the verb in the third item of the list should also end in -ing. None of the other options results in a parallel structure.

17. **(3) Yes, anyone** (Mechanics/Punctuation— commas after introductory elements and capitalization) The word Yes is an introductory element that is not part of the main idea. It should be followed by a comma, not a semicolon as in option (5). There is no reason to capitalize anyone, as in options (2) and (4).

18. **(3) and tightening the screws in the door** (Sentence structure/Parallelism) This sentence contains three items in series. The verbs in the first two items end in -ing, so the last item should begin with tightening for

parallel structure. None of the other options results in a series with parallel structure.

19. **(3) add a comma after *Tricks*** (Mechanics/Punctuation—appositives) The title of the reference guide is an appositive that explains which reference guide. Nonrestrictive appositives should be set off by commas. Removing the comma in option (1) would be incorrect because the appositive is not restrictive. There is no reason for the changes in options (2) and (4).

20. **(2) change is to are** (Usage/Subject-verb agreement) Preparations is plural, so the verb are is correct, as in option (2). Option (1) is incorrect because a comma is not necessary. Options (3) and (4) incorrectly change the verb to past tense.

21. **(2) messy, you will** (Sentence structure/Improper coordination and subordination) In the rewritten sentence, the word because, a subordinate conjunction, is used to connect ideas of unequal rank. When the subordinate idea comes first in the sentence, it must be followed by a comma. Semicolons are not used to join clauses of unequal rank, so options (1) and (3) are wrong. Option (4) creates a run-on. In option (5), a comma after you incorrectly separates a subject and verb.

22. **(1) change There is to There are** (Usage/Subject-verb agreement—expletive) The expletive there is not the subject of the sentence; paints is the subject. Therefore, the plural verb are is required. In options (2), (3), and (4), there is no reason to capitalize oil-base, latex, or paints.

23. **(3) remove the comma after and** (Mechanics/Punctuation—overuse of commas) The comma after and would separate subject and verb, since the conjunction and is joining two subjects. This is an inverted sentence, in which the verb comes before the subject. There is no reason for the changes in options (1), (2), and (4).

24. **(3) one is born a handy person; the** (Sentence structure/Comma splice and run-on sentence; Usage/Verb tense) Two independent clauses must be joined either with a coordinating conjunction and a comma or with a semicolon. Therefore, options (1), (2), and (5) are incorrect. The paragraphs are written in present tense. For consistency, the past-tense

was born should be changed to present-tense is born, so option (4) is incorrect.

25. **(3) disease; it** (Sentence structure/Comma splice; Mechanics/Punctuation—semicolons) Option (3) is correct because two complete ideas need to be joined either with a semicolon alone or with a comma and a coordinating conjunction. Option (1) is a comma splice. Options (2), (4), and (5) all incorrectly join the two independent clauses.

26. **(3) replace some people get emotional with emotion** (Sentence structure/Parallelism) Option (3) is correct because three items in a series should all be of parallel structure. The first two items, hysteria and ignorance, are nouns. The last item should be changed to a noun, emotion. Option (5) is incorrect because the last item is not a noun. Option (1) is incorrect because the verb must be singular to agree with the singular subject a lot. In option (2) ignorance is spelled correctly. In option (4) the noun ignorance is parallel to the other nouns in the series; ignorant is an adjective.

27. **(1) and** (Sentence structure/Improper coordination and subordination) Option (1) is correct because the connecting word and shows the relationship between the two complete ideas. Options (2), (3), (4) and (5) are incorrect because they change the relationship between the two ideas expressed in the original sentence.

28. **(1) change We to You** (Usage/Pronoun reference—pronoun shift) Option (1) is correct because the rest of the paragraph uses the pronoun you. For consistency, this sentence should use the same pronoun. Options (2) and (3) are incorrect because the rest of the paragraphs uses you. Option (4) is incorrect because get is the correct present-tense verb.

29. **(2) infected; you** (Mechanics/Punctuation; Sentence structure/Improper coordination and subordination) Option (2) is correct because two sentences can be joined either with a semicolon alone or with a comma and a coordinating conjunction. In option (1), the sentences are incorrectly joined by a semicolon and and. Option (3) creates a run-on sentence. Option (4) is incorrect because it uses a comma without a coordinating conjunction. Option (5) is wrong because there is no cause-and-effect relationship between the two sentences, as suggested by because.

30. **(4) your** (Mechanics/Possessives and contractions) Option (4) is correct because the possessive pronoun your is needed in this sentence. Option (1) is incorrect because the word you're is a contraction meaning "you are." Option (2) is incorrect because the possessive pronoun your does not require an apostrophe. Their and my, in options (3) and (5), are pronouns that are inconsistent with those used in the rest of the paragraph.

31. **(5) no correction is necessary** (Mechanics/Punctuation and spelling) In option (1), removing the comma after mask would be incorrect; a comma is needed to separate items in series. The adverbial clause when giving medical attention to . . . does not need a comma or a semicolon because it's second in the sentence, so options (2) and (3) are incorrect. Option (4) is incorrect because needles is spelled correctly.

32. **(3) change it's to its** (Mechanics/Contractions) Option 3 is correct because the possessive pronoun its is needed, rather than it's, the contraction of it is. In option (1), symptoms is spelled correctly. In option (2), removing the comma after AIDS would create a run-on sentence. A comma is needed to separate the two clauses. Option (4) is incorrect because there is spelled correctly.

33. **(4) public that the use of marijuana should be legalized.** (Usage/Pronoun reference—ambiguous reference) They could refer to either experts or public, so options (1) and (3) are wrong. Option (4) avoids the ambiguous reference and correctly keeps the quotation indirect. Options (2) and (5) are incorrect because the first word of a complete quotation should be capitalized, and a comma is used to set off a direct quotation.

34. **(2) change which to who** (Usage/Pronoun reference—wrong relative pronoun) The relative pronoun which refers to animals, places, or things—not to people. Who and whom refer to people. Option (2) is correct because who is the subject of the verb want; who is a subject pronoun. Option (1) is incorrect because Peoples is not a word. Option (3) is incorrect because whom is an object pronoun. Option (4) is incorrect because comparison is spelled correctly.

35. **(3) motive, and it** (Sentence structure/Run-on sentence) The original sentence is a run-on, a compound sentence with no conjunction.

Option (3) correctly joins the sentences with a comma and the coordinating conjunction and. Options (1), (2), and (5) do not correct the run-on. Option (4) is incorrect because a semicolon is not used with the coordinating conjunction but.

36. **(3) change whom to who** (Usage/Pronoun reference—wrong relative pronoun) The relative pronoun who in option (3) is correct because it is the subject of the verb were. The relative pronoun which is not used to refer to people, so option (2) is incorrect. Option (1) is incorrect because encourage is spelled correctly. Option (4) is incorrect because the plural verb were is needed.

37. **(5) no correction is necessary** (Mechanics/Punctuation, capitalization, and spelling) A semicolon is used to join sentences without a coordinating conjunction. In option (1), answer is spelled correctly. In option (2), removing the semicolon would result in a run-on. In options (3) and (4), education is spelled correctly and should not be capitalized.

38. **(3) change affects to affect** (Usage/Subject-verb agreement) Drugs is plural and requires the plural verb affect. There is no reason for the changes in options (1), (2), and (4).

39. **(1) change j. gutenberg to J. Gutenberg** (Mechanics/Capitalization) J. Gutenberg is a person's name and should be capitalized. There is no reason for the changes in options (2), (3), and (4).

40. **(5) page and days,** (Sentence structure/Fragment) The phrase days, weeks, or months is a modifier of the verb took and should not be separated from the verb by punctuation. Therefore, options (1), (2), (3), and (4) are incorrect.

41. **(3) replace are with were** (Usage/Verb tense—word clues to tense in paragraphs) The previous sentences are written in the past tense. For consistency and clarity, this sentence should also be written in past tense, using were. There is no reason for the changes in options (1), (2), and (4).

42. **(4) We even hear** (Usage/Pronoun reference—pronoun shift; Mechanics/Spelling—homonyms) The rest of the paragraph is written with the pronoun we; changing to you, or to they as in options (1), (2), and (5), is a pronoun shift. Hear means "to

gain information through the ear"; here refers to a location, making option (3) incorrect.

43. **(4) move quickly and easily after to be made** (Sentence structure/ Misplaced modifier) The type has not been set quickly and easily; the printed page is made quickly and easily. The modifier quickly and easily should be placed as close as possible to the phrase to be made. Therefore, options (1) and (2) are incorrect. There is no reason for the change in option (3).

44. **(3) information spread** (Sentence structure/Parallelism; Usage/Pronoun reference—vague reference) There is no antecedent for the pronoun it, so options (1) and (2) are wrong. The pronoun should be replaced with a noun, such as information. The three items in series should be of parallel structure; the last two, people and civilization, start with a noun, so the first one should also start with a noun, information. Option (4) incorrectly places a comma between the subject and verb. Option (5) incorrectly shifts to future tense.

45. **(3) young, the** (Sentence structure/ Fragment; Mechanics/Punctuation—commas after introductory elements) Sentence 2 is a fragment. When a fragment (dependent clause) is joined to a sentence (independent clause), a comma is required after the dependent clause; therefore, option (5) is incorrect. In options (2) and (4), however and because express relationships that are not meant in the sentence.

46. **(2) change There is to There are** (Usage/Subject-verb agreement—expletive) The subject of the sentence is kinds. Kinds is plural, so the plural verb are is correct. Their is a possessive pronoun, but no possession is shown here; therefore, option (1) is incorrect. Option (3) is incorrect because There's is a contraction of There is.

47. **(2) change increase to increases** (Usage/Subject-verb agreement) The subject of the sentence is insurance, which is singular, so the singular verb increases is required. There is no reason for the changes in options (1), (3), and (4).

48. **(4) remove the comma after permanent** (Mechanics/Punctuation—overuse of commas) A comma is not necessary before the conjunction and; the rest of the sentence is not

an independent clause. There is no reason for the changes in options (1), (2), (3), and (5).

49. **(1) itself** (Usage/Reflexive pronouns) The reflexive pronoun itself is one word, not two as in option (2). Options (3) and (4) are incorrect because there is no such word as theirself or themself. Option (5) is incorrect because whole life is singular and themselves is plural.

50. **(1) retire, whole life** (Mechanics/ Punctuation—commas after introductory elements and capitalization) When you retire is a dependent clause that needs to be set off by a comma, not a semicolon, when it comes at the beginning of a sentence; therefore, options (2), (3), and (5) are wrong. There is no reason to capitalize whole life, as in option (4).

51. **(3) change the spelling of accomodate to accommodate** (Mechanics/Spelling) Option (3) shows the correct spelling of accommodate. Option (2) shows an incorrect spelling. There is no reason for the changes in options (1) and (4).

52. **(5) today than in** (Sentence structure/ Clarity) Than is used to compare today with the past; then is used in reference to time, so options (1) and (4) are wrong. A comma is not needed, as in option (2), because the dependent clause is restrictive. Option (3) eliminates the comparison that is meant.

53. **(1) change There is to There are** (Usage/Subject-verb agreement) The subject of the sentence is people, which is plural, so the plural verb are is needed. There is no reason for the changes in options (2), (3), and (4).

54. **(4) However, we** (Mechanics/ Capitalization and punctuation; Sentence structure/Clarity) The phrase on account of this simply makes the sentence wordy and should be eliminated. Therefore, options (1) and (2) are wrong. A comma is needed after the introductory element however, so option (3) is incorrect. There is no reason to capitalize we, as in option (5).

55. **(2) change nation, is to nation, are** (Usage/Subject-verb agreement; Mechanics/ Punctuation) The subject we is plural and requires the plural verb are. Option (1) is incorrect because the word nation is part of the phrase as a nation, which should be set off

by commas. There is no reason for the changes in options (3) and (4).

UNIT 1: MECHANICS
Lesson 1

All items in this section are related to rules of mechanics.

GED Practice: Using Capitalization (Pages 36–38)
1. **(2) Percy Drive, Indianapolis, Indiana** (Capitalization) Option (2) is correct because Percy Drive is the specific name of a street. Indianapolis is capitalized because it is the name of a city. Indiana is the name of a state and should be capitalized. Options (1), (3), and (4) do not include all the necessary corrections.

2. **(4) Wednesday, Mr. Larry Garwood** (Capitalization) Option (4) is correct because Wednesday is the name of a day and should be capitalized. Mr. is a title and should be capitalized. Larry Garwood is a specific person's name and should be capitalized. Options (1), (2), and (3) do not include all the necessary corrections.

3. **(2) Garwood, We, Memorial Day** (Capitalization) Option (2) is correct because Mr. Garwood is the specific name of a person and should be capitalized. We is the first word of a sentence and should be capitalized. Memorial Day is a specific holiday and each word should be capitalized. Summer is the name of a season and should not be capitalized. Options (1), (3), and (4) do not include all the necessary corrections.

4. **(1) Fourth, July, Saturday, holiday** (Capitalization) Option (1) is correct because Fourth of July is the name of a specific holiday, but only the important words Fourth and July need to be capitalized. Saturday is a day of the week and should be capitalized. There is no reason to capitalize holiday. Options (2), (3), and (4) do not include all the necessary corrections.

5. **(4) change middle East to Middle East** (Capitalization) Option (4) is correct because Middle East is a specific area of the world, so both words should be capitalized. Options (1) and (3) are incorrect because titles attached to specific names are properly capitalized. Option (2) is incorrect because Kissinger should be capitalized; it is the name of a specific person.

6. **(2) replace Vice President ford with Vice President Ford** (Capitalization) Option (2) is correct because a person's name, Ford, is a proper noun and should be capitalized. For the same reason, option (4) is incorrect. Option (1) is incorrect because there is no reason to capitalize the common noun presidency here. Option (3) is incorrect because Vice is part of the title and should be capitalized.

7. **(2) change Fall to fall** (Capitalization) Option (2) is correct because seasons of the year are not capitalized. Option (1) is incorrect because Election Day is a national holiday and should be capitalized. Option (3) is incorrect because Americans, the name of a specific nationality, should be capitalized. Option (4) is incorrect because polls should not be capitalized here.

8. **(4) change south to South** (Capitalization) Option (4) is correct because South needs to be capitalized; it refers here to a specific region of the country, not a direction. In option (3), there is no reason to capitalize the word the. In options (1) and (2), Bill and Clinton are proper names and must be capitalized.

9. **(2) change State to state** (Capitalization) Option (2) is correct because since state is not the name of a specific region, it does not need to be capitalized. Option (1) is incorrect because there is no need to capitalize the common noun nation. Option (3) is incorrect because California is the name of a specific place and should be capitalized. Option (4) is incorrect because presidents is not a proper noun and should not be capitalized.

10. **(1) change John f. Kennedy to John F. Kennedy** (Capitalization) Option (1) is correct because all parts of a specific person's name should be capitalized. Option (2) is incorrect because the name of a religion should be capitalized. Option (3) is incorrect because there is no reason to capitalize elected. Option (4) is incorrect because there is no reason to capitalize the before United States; it is not part of the name of the country.

11. **(4) change let to Let** (Capitalization) Option (4) is correct because the first word of a quotation should be capitalized. Option (1) is incorrect because there is no reason to capitalize the common noun inauguration. Option (2) is incorrect because January is the name of a month and should be capitalized. Option (3) is incorrect because President is

attached to a specific name and should be capitalized.

12. **(1) change Attorney General to attorney general** (Capitalization) Option (2) is correct because the title attorney general is not attached to a specific name and should not be capitalized. Options (2) and (3) are incorrect because Federal Bureau of Investigation is the name of a specific organization and all important words in the name must be capitalized. Option (4) is incorrect because there is no reason to capitalize the words organized crime.

13. **(5) no correction is necessary** (Capitalization) Options (1) and (2) are incorrect because there is no need to capitalize the common nouns assassination and holiday. Option (3) is incorrect because Birthday in this sentence is part of the name of a specific holiday and should be capitalized. Option (4) is incorrect because birthday is not part of the name of a holiday in this sentence.

GED Mini-Test: Lesson 1 (Page 39)

1. **(4) change west to West** (Capitalization) Option (4) is correct because in this sentence West refers to a specific region of the country and should be capitalized. Options (1) and (2) are incorrect because the last names of families are proper nouns and should be capitalized. Option (3) is incorrect because there is no reason to capitalize families.

2. **(4) change Spring to spring** (Capitalization) Option (4) is correct because seasons of the year should not be capitalized. Option (1) is incorrect because specific family names are capitalized. Option (2) is incorrect because Winnebago is the brand name of a recreational vehicle and should be capitalized. Option (3) is incorrect because Grand Canyon is the name of a specific place and should be capitalized.

3. **(1) change their to Their** (Capitalization) Option (1) is correct because a sentence begins with a capital letter. Option (2) is incorrect because the names of months are capitalized. Option (3) and (4) are incorrect because there is no reason to capitalize trip or mishaps.

4. **(4) change Doctor to doctor** (Capitalization) Option (4) is correct because Doctor is not attached to a specific name here and should not be capitalized. Option (1) is incorrect because there is no reason to

capitalize <u>daughter</u>. Options (2) and (3) are incorrect because <u>Susan</u> and <u>Colorado</u>, specific names of a person and a place, need to be capitalized.

5. **(5) no correction is necessary** (Capitalization) Options (1) and (2) are incorrect because <u>Texas</u> and <u>Rosa Valdez</u> are specific names of a place and a person and should be capitalized. Options (3) and (4) are incorrect because there is no reason to capitalize <u>mother</u> or <u>camping store</u>.

Lesson 2

All items in this section are related to rules of mechanics.

GED Practice: Using End Punctuation (Page 41)

1. **(3) no correction is necessary** (Punctuation/End punctuation) Option (3) is correct because this is a statement that expresses a complete thought; it does not ask a question or require emphasis, so it should end with a period.

2. **(1) change the question mark to a period** (Punctuation/End punctuation) Option (1) is correct because this is a statement that expresses a complete thought; it does not ask a question or require emphasis, so it should end with a period.

3. **(1) change the question mark to a period** (Punctuation/End punctuation) Option (1) is correct because this is a statement that expresses a complete thought; it does not ask a question or require emphasis, so it should end with a period.

4. **(2) change the exclamation mark to a question mark** (Punctuation/End punctuation) Option (2) is correct because this sentence asks a question that requires an answer.

5. **(2) change the period to an exclamation mark** (Punctuation/End punctuation) Option (2) is correct because this sentence expresses a strong feeling or emotion; therefore, it should end with an exclamation mark.

6. **(1) change the question mark to a period** (Punctuation/End punctuation) Option (1) is correct because this is a statement that expresses a complete thought; it does not ask a question or require emphasis, so it should end with a period.

GED Mini-Test: Lesson 2 (Pages 42–43)

1. **(2) change the exclamation mark to a question mark** (End punctuation) Option (2) is correct because the sentence asks a direct question.

2. **(3) no correction is necessary** (End punctuation) Option (3) is correct because the sentence expresses a strong feeling, so the exclamation mark is the correct end punctuation.

3. **(1) change the question mark to a period** (End punctuation) Option (1) is correct because this is a statement that expresses a complete thought; it does not ask a question or require emphasis, so it should end with a period. Option (2) is incorrect because <u>you</u> is not a proper noun and does not require capitalization.

4. **(2) change <u>Health Professionals</u> to <u>health professionals</u>** (Capitalization) Option (2) is correct because occupations that are not part of a specific person's title do not need to be capitalized. Option (1) is incorrect because the sentence does not ask a question.

5. **(1) change the period to an exclamation mark** (End punctuation) Option (1) is correct because the sentence expresses a strong feeling of urgency, so an exclamation mark is required. Option (2) is incorrect because the sentence does not ask a question.

6. **(5) no correction is necessary** (End punctuation/Capitalization) Options (1) and (2) are incorrect because the statement expresses a complete thought; it does not ask a question or require emphasis, so it should end with a period. Option (3) is incorrect because there is no reason to capitalize <u>wife</u>. Option (4) is incorrect because <u>Sabrina</u> is a proper noun, which requires capitalization.

7. **(1) change the question mark to a period** (End punctuation) Option (1) is correct because the statement expresses a complete thought; it does not ask a question, so it should end with a period. Option (2) is incorrect because the sentence does not require emphasis. Option (3) is incorrect because there is no reason to capitalize <u>first</u>. Option (4) is incorrect because the names of months should be capitalized.

8. **(1) change the exclamation mark to a period** (End punctuation) Option (1) is correct

Answers and Explanations

because the statement expresses a complete thought; it does not require emphasis, so it should end with a period. Option (2) is incorrect because the sentence does not ask a question. Options (3) and (4) are incorrect because there is no reason to capitalize either weekend or birthday.

9. **(2) change morris to Morris**
(Capitalization) Option (2) is correct because the specific names of places are always capitalized. Option (1) is incorrect because the sentence does not express emphasis so it should end with a period. Option (3) is incorrect because Hotel is part of the specific name of a place and must be capitalized. Option (4) is incorrect because Buffalo is the name of a city and must be capitalized.

10. **(1) change the question mark to an exclamation mark** (End punctuation) Option (1) is correct because the statement expresses a strong feeling. Therefore, Option (2) is incorrect. Option (3) is incorrect because a sentence begins with a capital letter. Option (4) is incorrect because quotation marks are always used in pairs.

Lesson 3

All items in this section are related to rules of mechanics.

GED Practice: Using Commas (Page 45)
1. **(3) insert a comma after Friday**
(Punctuation/Commas between items in series) Option (3) is correct because Friday is the first item in the list of days. Option (1) is incorrect because a prepositional phrase should not be separated from the rest of the sentence. There is no reason for the comma in option (2). Option (4) is incorrect because commas are needed between items in series.

2. **(1) insert a comma after Sandwiches**
(Punctuation/Commas between items in series) Option (1) is correct because Sandwiches is one of the items in the list and should be set off with a comma. Options (2) and (3) are incorrect because each item in series should be separated by a comma. Option (4) is incorrect because it would separate the subject from the verb.

3. **(4) insert commas after both cheese and beef** (Punctuation/Commas between items in series) Option (4) is correct because the items ham and cheese, roast beef, and tuna salad

should be separated with commas; they are items in series that make up a compound subject. Option (1) is incorrect because the phrase ham and cheese describes one sandwich and should not be divided by a comma. Options (2) and (3) are incorrect because all items in the series must be correctly separated by commas.

4. **(4) remove the comma after drinks**
(Punctuation/Commas between items in series) Option (4) is correct; because this sentence has only two items in a list, a comma is not needed. Option (1) is incorrect because it would separate a verb from its direct object. Option (2) is incorrect because the subject manager should not be separated from the verb expects. Option (3) is incorrect because a prepositional phrase should not be separated from the rest of the sentence by a comma.

5. **(5) no correction is necessary**
(Punctuation/Commas between items in a series) Option (1) is incorrect because a comma is not used to separate two items in a series. Option (2) is incorrect because a comma should not be placed after the conjunction and. Options (3) and (4) are incorrect because the sentence expresses strong emotion.

GED Practice: Using Commas (Pages 48–49)
1. **(3) remove the comma after and**
(Punctuation/Commas between items in series) Option (3) is correct because a comma should not be placed after the conjunction and; it goes only before the conjunction. Option (1) is incorrect because the subject people should not be separated from the verb are. Option (2) is incorrect because afraid is the first item in the list and should be followed by a comma. Option (4) is incorrect because the prepositional phrase in their homes should not be set off with a comma.

2. **(5) no correction is necessary**
(Punctuation/Appositives, overuse of commas, and commas between items in series) Options (1) and (2) are incorrect because the phrase a gas from uranium in the soil further explains Radon; therefore, the phrase is an appositive and should be set off by commas. Option (3) is incorrect because the prepositional phrase through cracks should not be set off by a comma. Option (4) is incorrect because basements is an item in series and should be followed by a comma.

3. **(1) insert a comma after <u>Whellan</u>**
(Punctuation/Appositives) Option (1) is correct because the phrase <u>a government official</u> further explains who <u>Floyd Whellan</u> is; therefore, the phrase is an appositive and should be set off by commas. Option (2) is incorrect because the comma is needed both after the appositive and before the direct quote. Option (3) is incorrect because a prepositional phrase should not be set off by a comma. Option (4) is incorrect because a comma should not separate two items that are joined by the conjunction <u>and</u>.

4. **(2) insert a comma after <u>gas</u>**
(Punctuation/Appositives) Option (2) is correct because the phrase <u>a radioactive gas</u> further explains <u>radon</u>; therefore, the phrase is an appositive and should be set off by commas. Option (1) is incorrect because the appositive should be set off by a comma from the noun that it describes. Option (3) is incorrect because a comma is not needed before the conjunction <u>or</u> when it joins only two items. There is no reason for the change in option (4).

5. **(5) no correction is necessary**
(Punctuation) Option (1) is incorrect because these are not anyone's exact words. Option (2) is incorrect because this is not a series of three items; <u>radon gas</u> is one item. Option (3) is incorrect because a comma is not needed to separate two items in a series. Option (4) is incorrect because <u>radon</u> is a common noun and should not be capitalized.

6. **(1) insert a comma after <u>Yes</u>**
(Punctuation/Commas after introductory elements) Option (1) is correct because <u>Yes</u> is an introductory element that should be set off by a comma. Options (2) and (4) are incorrect because a prepositional phrase should not be set off by a comma. Option (3) is incorrect because <u>people</u> is not a proper noun and so should not be capitalized.

7. **(2) insert a comma after <u>said</u>**
(Punctuation/Commas with direct quotations) Option (2) is correct because a comma is needed before a direct quotation. Option (1) is incorrect because the subject <u>manager</u> should not be separated from the verb <u>said</u> by a comma. Option (3) is incorrect because the first word of a quotation starts with a capital letter. Option (4) is incorrect because a single adjective should not be separated from the noun it is describing.

8. **(5) no correction is necessary**
(Capitalization; Punctuation/Commas with direct quotations and commas after introductory elements) Option (1) is incorrect because <u>receptionist</u> is a common noun and should not be capitalized. Option (2) is incorrect because direct quotations are separated from the rest of the sentence by a comma. Option (3) is incorrect because a comma is needed after a person's name in direct address. Option (4) is incorrect because <u>Ellen</u> is a proper noun and should be capitalized.

9. **(4) insert a comma after <u>Tuesday</u>**
(Punctuation/Commas separating dates) Option (4) is correct because a comma is needed to separate the day of the week from the name of the month. Option (1) is incorrect because the subject <u>receptionist</u> should not be separated from the verb <u>asked</u>. Option (2) is incorrect because the sentence does not ask a question. Option (3) is incorrect because the name of the month should not be separated from the numeric day.

10. **(3) remove the comma after <u>Sunday</u>**
(Punctuation/Commas between items in a series) Option (3) is correct because a comma is not needed when there are only two items in a series. Option (1) is incorrect because a comma is needed after a long introductory phrase. Option (2) is incorrect because the subject <u>Ellen</u> should not be separated from the verb <u>was</u>. Option (4) is incorrect because the names of days of the week must be capitalized.

GED Practice: Using Commas (Pages 51–52)

1. **(2) insert a comma after <u>television</u>**
(Punctuation/Commas after introductory elements) Option (2) is correct because the sentence begins with the dependent clause <u>If our nation did away with television</u>, which should be set off with a comma. Options (1) and (3) are incorrect because <u>nation</u> and <u>television</u> are common nouns and should not be capitalized. Option (4) is incorrect because the subject should not be separated from the verb by a comma.

2. **(4) remove the comma after <u>more</u>**
(Punctuation/Commas with dependent clauses) Option (4) is correct because the dependent clause comes after the independent clause, so it should not be set off by a comma. Option (1) is incorrect because <u>young</u> is the

first word of the sentence and should be capitalized. Options (2) and (3) are incorrect because the parenthetical expression no doubt should be set off with commas.

3. **(2) insert a comma after evening** (Punctuation/Commas between independent clauses) Option (2) is correct because the coordinating conjunction but joins two independent clauses and should have a comma before it. Option (1) is incorrect because the comma would separate the subject reading from the verb is. Option (3) is incorrect because evening is a common noun and should not be capitalized. Option (4) is incorrect because the comma goes before, not after, the conjunction but.

4. **(5) no correction is necessary** (Capitalization; Punctuation/Commas between items in a series, and commas in complex sentences) Options (1) and (2) are incorrect because items in a series must be separated by commas. Option (3) is incorrect because the comma is needed to separate the dependent clause. Option (4) is incorrect because sports, movies, and videos are not proper nouns and do not need to be capitalized.

5. **(3) insert a comma after Washington** (Punctuation/Commas between cities, districts, and states) Option (3) is correct because a comma is needed to separate the name of a town from a state or country. Options (1) and (2) are incorrect because the parenthetical expression for example must be set off by commas. Option (4) is incorrect because Washington, D.C. is an appositive and should be set off by commas.

6. **(4) remove the comma after overall** (Punctuation/Commas between items in series) Option (4) is correct because overall job performance is one term, which should not be broken by punctuation. Options (1) and (2) are incorrect because there is no reason to use a comma after realize or habits. Option (3) is incorrect because commas are needed to separate items in series.

7. **(2) insert a comma after nutritionist** (Punctuation/Appositives) Option (2) is correct because nutritionist is part of the descriptive phrase (appositive) that describes the noun Ruth Lahiff and should be set off by commas. Option (1) is incorrect because the comma sets off the appositive. Option (3) is incorrect because there is no reason to use a comma

after decided. Option (4) is incorrect because the comma would divide the verb to find.

8. **(3) insert a comma after employees** Punctuation/Commas after introductory elements) Option (3) is correct because a comma is needed to set off an introductory clause that cannot stand alone. Option (1) is incorrect because there is no reason for a comma after data. Option (2) is incorrect because 500 county employees is one item and should not be broken by punctuation. Option (4) is incorrect because a comma is needed before a direct quotation.

9. **(2) insert a comma after added** (Punctuation/Commas with direct quotations) Option (2) is correct because a direct quotation should be set off from the rest of the sentence by a comma. Therefore, Option (1) is incorrect. Options (3) and (4) are incorrect because commas are needed to separate all three items in the series.

10. **(4) insert a comma after coffee** (Punctuation/Commas with direct quotations) Option (4) is correct because a direct quotation should be set off from the rest of the sentence by a comma. Option (1) is incorrect because a comma is needed after an introductory phrase. Option (2) is incorrect because the comma would separate the dependent clause in the direct quotation. Option (3) is incorrect because a comma is needed between burgers and fries in the series.

GED Mini-Test: Lesson 3 (Pages 53–54)

1. **(3) change Department of Health to department of health** (Capitalization) Option (3) is correct because department of health is capitalized only when it names the health department of a specific state. Option (1) is incorrect because state is a common noun and should not be capitalized. Option (2) is incorrect because the subject state should not be separated from the verb has. Option (4) is incorrect because the nonessential phrase which deals with issues of public health and safety should be set off with a comma.

2. **(2) insert a comma after informative** (Punctuation/Commas) Option (2) is correct because a comma is needed to separate the adjectives informative and up-to-date, which both modify report. Option (1) is incorrect because Department of Health should be capitalized when it names the health

department of a specific state. Option (3) is incorrect because <u>killer bees</u> is a compound word treated as a <u>single noun</u>; there is no reason to separate <u>dangerous</u> from <u>killer</u>. Option (4) is incorrect because a comma is needed after <u>bees</u> to set off the nonessential phrase that <u>further</u> describes the bees.

3. **(4) change the comma after <u>given</u> to a period** (Punctuation/End punctuation) Option (4) is correct because a comma is not end punctuation; the sentence needs a period. Option (1) is incorrect because <u>health departments</u> is a common noun and should not be capitalized. Option (2) is incorrect because a comma would separate the subject and verb. Option (3) is incorrect because commas are needed between each of the items in series.

4. **(4) insert a comma after <u>bleeding</u>** (Punctuation/Commas after introductory elements) Option (4) is correct because the sentence starts with a long dependent clause that should be set off by a comma. Option (1) is incorrect because the names of diseases are not capitalized. Options (2) and (3) are incorrect because <u>rash</u> and <u>fever</u> are items in series and should be separated by commas.

5. **(3) insert a comma after <u>homes</u>** (Punctuation/Commas in complex sentences) Option (3) is correct because a comma is needed to separate the introductory dependent clause from the independent clause. Option (1) is incorrect because <u>while</u> should not be separated from the clause. Option (2) is incorrect because the sentence does not ask a question. Option (4) is incorrect because it would separate the subject <u>many</u> from the verb.

6. **(2) insert a comma after <u>example</u>** (Punctuation/Commas and parenthetical expressions) Option (2) is correct because <u>for example</u> adds nothing to the meaning of the sentence; parenthetical expressions need to be set off by commas. Because <u>for example</u> needs to be set off by commas, option (1) is incorrect. Option (3) is incorrect because the comma after <u>own</u> correctly separates the introductory dependent clause from the independent clause. Option (4) is incorrect because <u>plumber</u> is not a proper noun and does not need be capitalized.

7. **(1) insert a comma after <u>However</u>** (Punctuation/Commas and introductory elements) Option (1) is correct because

<u>However</u> is an introductory word that needs to be set off by a comma. Option (2) is incorrect because <u>landlord</u> is not a proper noun and does not need be capitalized. Option (3) is incorrect because the comma after <u>apartment</u> correctly separates the dependent clause from the independent clause that follows it. Option (4) is incorrect because items in a series should be separated by commas.

8. **(3) replace the period with a question mark** (End punctuation) Option (3) is correct because the sentence asks a question. Option (1) is incorrect because the coordinating conjunction <u>but</u> joins two independent clauses and should have a comma before it. Option (2) is incorrect because there is no reason for a comma after <u>but</u>. Option (4) is incorrect because two items joined by a conjunction do not need to be separated by a comma.

9. **(3) remove the comma after <u>yearly</u>** (Punctuation/Commas and items in a series) Option (3) is correct because the two adjectives <u>yearly</u> and <u>property</u> should not be separated by a comma; <u>and</u> cannot be used between them without changing the meaning. Option (1) is incorrect because <u>Although</u> should not be set off from the clause it introduces. Option (2) is incorrect because the comma after <u>rent</u> correctly separates the introductory dependent clause from the independent clause. Option (4) is incorrect because there is no reason to set off <u>dollars</u> from <u>a month</u>.

Lesson 4

All items in this section are related to rules of mechanics.

GED Practice: Avoiding Unnecessary Commas (Pages 56–57)

1. **(2) remove the comma after <u>rainfall</u>** (Punctuation/Unnecessary commas) Option (2) is correct because a comma should not separate the subject <u>rainfall</u> from the verb <u>has increased</u>. Option (1) is incorrect because the sentence does not express strong feeling. Option (3) is incorrect because a comma should not separate the adjective <u>recent</u> from the noun that it modifies. Option (4) is incorrect because <u>Canyon</u> is part of a specific place name and must be capitalized.

2. **(3) remove the comma after <u>winds</u>** (Punctuation/Unnecessary commas) Option (3) is correct because a comma is not needed after

the last item in a series. Options (1) and (2) are incorrect because commas are needed after the first two items in a series. Option (4) is incorrect because commas are not needed between only two items.

3. **(3) remove the commas after houses and Canyon** (Punctuation/Unnecessary commas) Option (3) is correct because which were built near the bottom of Arbor Canyon is an essential phrase. Options (1) and (2) are incorrect because both commas must be removed so the essential phrase which were built near the bottom of Arbor Canyon is not set off by commas. Option (4) is incorrect because Arbor Canyon is a specific place name and should be capitalized.

4. **(5) no correction is necessary** (End Punctuation; Punctuation/Unnecessary commas; Capitalization) Option (1) is incorrect; the comma is necessary because but connects the two independent clauses. Option (2) is incorrect because experts is not a proper noun. Option (3) is incorrect because a comma should not separate the subject experts from the verb think. Option (4) is incorrect because the sentence does not ask a question.

5. **(1) change avenue to Avenue** (Capitalization) Option (1) is correct because Avenue is part of a street name and needs to be capitalized. Option (2) is incorrect because the comma correctly sets off the long introductory phrase. Option (3) is incorrect because a comma is not needed between only two items. Option (4) is incorrect because there is no reason for a comma after me.

6. **(3) remove the comma after technicians** (Punctuation/Unnecessary commas) Option (3) is correct because a comma is not needed after the last item in a series. Options (1) and (2) are incorrect because a comma is needed after the second item, doctors. Option (4) is incorrect because who worked at Canetti Hospital is an essential phrase that should not be set off by commas.

7. **(1) remove the comma after extension** (Punctuation/Unnecessary commas) Option (1) is correct because the comma incorrectly separates the subject extension from the verb has. Options (2) and (3) are incorrect because commas must be used to set off items in a series. Option (4) is incorrect because public parking is not a proper noun.

8. **(1) insert a comma after started** (Punctuation/Commas in complex sentences) Option (1) is correct because a comma is needed to separate the introductory dependent clause. Options (2) and (3) are incorrect because a comma after the subject people would incorrectly separate it from the verb began. Option (4) is incorrect because the sentence does not express strong feeling.

9. **(3) remove the comma after two** (Punctuation/Unnecessary commas) Option (3) is correct because a comma is not needed to separate only two items. Options (1) and (2) are incorrect because the parenthetical expression for example should be set off by commas. Option (4) is incorrect because there is no reason for a comma after three.

GED Mini-Test: Lesson 4 (Pages 58–59)

1. **(5) no correction is necessary** (Punctuation/Commas and introductory elements; Unnecessary commas; Capitalization) Option (1) is incorrect because people is not a proper noun. Option (2) is incorrect because a comma is needed after the introductory phrase; the sentence would be unclear without it. Option (3) is incorrect because a comma would separate the subject from the verb. Option (4) is incorrect because a comma is not needed to separate only two items.

2. **(3) insert a comma after editors** (Punctuation/Commas and items in a series) Option (3) is correct because a comma is needed to separate items in a series. Option (1) is incorrect because For example is a parenthetical expression that should be set off by a comma. Option (2) is incorrect because a comma is needed after items in a series. Option (4) is incorrect because a comma is not needed after the last item in a series.

3. **(2) insert a comma after machine** (Punctuation/Commas and introductory elements) Option (2) is correct because With the help of a computer or fax machine is a long introductory phrase that should be set off by a comma. Options (1) and (3) are incorrect because there should be no comma following computer; a comma is not needed to separate only two items. Option (4) is incorrect because the sentence does not ask a question.

4. **(3) remove the comma after home** (Punctuation/Unnecessary commas) Option (3)

is correct because the comma after <u>home</u> incorrectly separates the subject from the verb. Option (1) is incorrect because the comma correctly sets off the parenthetical expression <u>On the one hand</u>. Option (2) is incorrect because <u>who work at home</u> is an essential phrase. Option (4) is incorrect because the two adjectives <u>reliable</u> and <u>affordable</u> describe the same noun. They should be separated by a comma since <u>and</u> can be placed between them without changing the meaning of the sentence.

5. **(5) no correction is necessary** (Punctuation/Unnecessary commas; Commas and interrupting phrases) Options (1), (2), and (3) are incorrect because <u>especially jazz</u> is a nonessential phrase that should be preceded and followed by commas. Option (4) is incorrect because there is no reason to separate the adverb <u>reasonably</u> from the adjective <u>loud</u>.

6. **(3) remove the comma after instruments** (Punctuation/Unnecessary commas) Option (3) is correct because a comma is not needed after the last item in a series. Options (1) and (2) are incorrect because commas must be used to separate items in a series. Option (4) is incorrect because <u>at a higher volume</u> is an essential phrase.

7. **(4) remove the comma after stereo** (Punctuation/Unnecessary commas) Option (4) is correct because <u>without using headphones</u> is an essential phrase. Option (1) is incorrect because <u>mother</u> is not a proper noun. Options (2) and (3) are incorrect because <u>however</u> is a parenthetical expression and needs to be set off by commas.

8. **(4) remove the comma after peace** (Punctuation/Unnecessary commas) Option (4) is correct because a comma is not needed to separate only two items. Option (1) is incorrect because the subject <u>she</u> should not be separated from the verb <u>makes</u> by a comma. Option (2) is incorrect because a comma would incorrectly separate the dependent clause that comes at the end of the sentence. Option (3) is incorrect because the subject <u>music</u> should not be separated from the verb <u>disturbs</u> by a comma.

9. **(2) insert a comma after playing** (Punctuation/Commas in compound sentences) Option (2) is correct because a comma is needed to join the two parts of the compound

sentence connected by <u>but</u>. Option (1) is incorrect because <u>with music playing</u> is an essential phrase; it should not be set off by commas. Option (3) is incorrect because a comma is not needed to separate only two items. Option (4) is incorrect because <u>with headphones on</u> is an essential phrase.

Lesson 5

All items in this section are related to rules of mechanics.

GED Practice: Using Semicolons (Pages 61–63)

1. **(3) and helpless; they** (Punctuation/Semicolon) Option (3) is correct because a semicolon is used to join two independent clauses that could stand alone and are not joined by a linking word. Options (1) and (2) are incorrect because the two independent clauses must be joined with either a semicolon or a comma and a coordinating conjunction. Option (4) is wrong because a semicolon is not normally used with the conjunction <u>and</u>. Option (5) is wrong because the linking word <u>however</u> requires a semicolon before it and a comma after it.

2. **(5) baby; however, your** (Punctuation/Semicolon) Option (5) is correct because the two clauses are joined by the linking word <u>however</u>. A semicolon is needed before the linking word, and a comma is needed after the linking word. Options (1), (2), (3), and (4) use semicolons and commas incorrectly.

3. **(1) baby, and you** (Punctuation/Commas and semicolons between independent clauses) Option (1) is correct because the two clauses that could stand alone are joined by a comma and the conjunction <u>and</u>. A comma is needed before <u>and</u>, so options (2) and (5) are incorrect. Semicolons are not normally used with <u>and</u>, so options (3) and (4) are wrong.

4. **(1) baby; and it** (Punctuation/Commas and semicolons between independent clauses) Normally a semicolon would not be needed with the conjunction <u>and</u>; however, other commas are used in the first independent clause, so a semicolon should be used before the conjunction. Punctuation is not needed after <u>and</u>, so options (3), (4), and (5) are incorrect. Option (2) would create a run-on sentence.

5. **(2) insert a comma after therefore** (Punctuation/Semicolon) A semicolon joins two

UNIT 1

independent clauses joined by the linking word <u>therefore</u>; a comma is required after the linking word. Option (1) is incorrect because a comma alone cannot join two independent clauses. Option (3) is incorrect because the comma is necessary to separate items in a series. Option (4) is incorrect because the last item in a series does not require a comma.

6. **(2) insert a comma after <u>job</u>** (Punctuation/ Commas between independent clauses) Option (2) is correct because it correctly links two independent clauses with a connecting word; a comma after <u>job</u> is all that is needed. Option (1) is incorrect because a prepositional phrase should not be set off with commas. Options (3) and (4) are incorrect because there is no need for a semicolon.

7. **(3) insert a semicolon after <u>up</u>** (Punctuation/Semicolon and overuse of commas) Option (3) is correct because a semicolon should be used with a connecting word to join two independent clauses when one clause contains commas. Option (1) is incorrect because the comma after <u>You</u> is needed to separate items in a series. Option (2) is incorrect because the comma would separate the subject from the verb. Option (4) is incorrect because a semicolon is not used between an independent and a dependent clause.

8. **(5) no correction is necessary** (Punctuation/Commas and semicolons between independent clauses and overuse of commas) Option (5) is correct because this sentence consists of two independent clauses that are correctly joined with a semicolon. Option (1) is incorrect because the dependent clause <u>when a person works too hard</u> is essential to the sentence and should not be separated by a comma. There is no reason for the commas in option (2). Option (3) would create a comma splice, and option (4) would create a run-on sentence.

9. **(2) change the comma after <u>job</u> to a semicolon** (Punctuation/Semicolon) Option (2) is correct because a semicolon after <u>job</u> is needed to join two independent clauses with the linking word <u>therefore</u>. Option (1) is incorrect because putting commas after <u>person</u> and <u>boring</u> would incorrectly set off information that is necessary to the sentence. Option (3) is incorrect because there is no reason to use two semicolons. Option (4) is

incorrect because a subject and a verb should not be separated with a comma.

10. **(4) insert a semicolon after <u>well</u>** (Punctuation/Semicolon) Option (4) is correct because this run-on sentence is corrected by putting a semicolon between the two independent clauses. Options (1) and (2) are incorrect because the phrase <u>who enjoy their jobs</u> is essential to the sentence and should not be set off with commas. Option (3) is wrong because it would create a comma splice.

11. **(5) no correction is necessary** (Punctuation/Overuse of commas) The long phrase after <u>Many</u> is essential to the sentence and should not be set off with commas. Although the sentence is long, it does not contain two clauses that can stand alone and needs no additional punctuation. Options (2) and (4) incorrectly separate the subject and verb. There is no reason to insert commas as in option (3).

12. **(4) change the period to a question mark** (End punctuation) Option (4) is correct because the sentence asks a question. Option (1) is incorrect because <u>increase your job satisfaction</u> is one of three items in a series and needs to be set off by a comma . Options (2) and (3) are incorrect because items in a series are separated by commas, not semicolons.

13. **(3) change the comma after <u>problem</u> to a semicolon** (Punctuation/ Semicolon) Option (3) is correct because a semicolon is necessary to join two independent clauses. Options (1) and (4) are incorrect because <u>First</u> is an introductory word and needs to be set off by a comma. Option (2) is incorrect because the comma should be replaced by a semicolon, not removed.

14. **(3) areas, you** (Punctuation/Commas in complex sentences) Option (3) is correct because a comma is necessary to separate the introductory dependent clause from the independent clause. Options (1), (2), and (4) are incorrect because an introductory dependent clause should be separated from an independent clause by a comma, not a semicolon. Option (5) is incorrect because a comma is needed between the clauses.

15. **(3) responsibilities; indeed, a new** (Punctuation/Semicolon) Option (3) is correct because the proper punctuation for <u>indeed</u>, a linking word joining two independent clauses,

is a semicolon before, a comma following. Options (1), (2), and (5) are incorrect because there is no semicolon before <u>indeed</u>. Option (4) is incorrect because there is no comma following <u>indeed</u>.

GED Mini-Test: Lesson 5 (Pages 64–65)

1. **(3) considered a sport; but** (Punctuation/Commas and semicolons between independent clauses) Option (3) is correct because the sentence contains two independent clauses and one clause contains commas. Option (1) is incorrect because a semicolon is necessary before the conjunction <u>but</u>. Options (2), (4), and (5) are incorrect because a period is end punctuation rather than internal punctuation.

2. **(1) at 2:00 A.M.; he was** (Punctuation/Commas and semicolons between independent clauses and overuse of commas) Option (1) is correct because the sentence has two independent clauses that are correctly joined by a semicolon. Options (2) and (3) are incorrect because they add unnecessary commas. Option (4) is incorrect because it creates a comma splice. Option (5) is incorrect because it creates a run-on sentence.

3. **(5) McGarrity's arrest was** (Punctuation/Overuse of commas) Option (5) is correct because the sentence needs no punctuation except the period at the end. Options (1), (2), (3), and (4) incorrectly include unnecessary punctuation.

4. **(5) no correction is necessary** (Capitalization/Punctuation/Commas after introductory elements, overuse of commas, and end punctuation) Option (1) is incorrect because <u>Game Commissioner</u> is a title directly preceding a person's name and should be capitalized. Option (2) is incorrect because a comma is needed after an introductory phrase. Option (3) is incorrect because a comma should not be used before a prepositional phrase. In option (4), a period is correct because this is a statement, not a question.

5. **(2) insert a comma after year** (Punctuation/Commas in compound sentences) Option (2) is correct because a comma separates two independent clauses when they are joined by <u>and</u>. Option (1) is incorrect because there is no reason to set off <u>next year</u> from the rest of the sentence. Option (3) is incorrect because a semicolon is not used before <u>and</u>. Option (4) is

incorrect because these are not two complete sentences.

6. **(3) replace the comma after <u>later</u> with a semicolon** (Punctuation/Semicolon) Option (3) is correct because the sentence is a comma splice; a semicolon is needed to join the two independent clauses. Option (1) is incorrect because the phrase that follows <u>people</u> is necessary to the sentence and should not be set off with commas. Option (2) is incorrect because it would create a run-on sentence. Option (4) is incorrect because it would separate a subject and verb with a comma.

7. **(1) remove the comma after <u>schools</u>** (Punctuation/Overuse of commas) Option (1) is correct because the subject <u>schools</u> should not be separated from the verb <u>are geared</u>. Option (2) is incorrect because a prepositional phrase should not be set off with a comma. Option (3) is incorrect because it would cause a comma splice. Option (4) is incorrect because it would create a run-on sentence.

8. **(5) no correction is necessary** (Capitalization/Punctuation/Semicolon and overuse of commas) Option (5) is correct because two independent clauses are correctly linked by a semicolon. Options (1), (2), and (4) are incorrect because there is no need for any additional capitalization or punctuation in the sentence. Option (3) is incorrect because it would create a comma splice.

9. **(1) change <u>Fall</u> to <u>fall</u>** (Capitalization) Option (1) is correct because seasons of the year are not capitalized. Option (2) is incorrect because <u>community college</u> is not a specific name. Option (3) is incorrect because a prepositional phrase should not be separated with commas. Option (4) is incorrect because a comma is not necessary if a dependent clause follows an independent clause.

10. **(2) important; however, people need** (Punctuation/Semicolon) The proper punctuation for <u>however</u>, a linking word joining two independent clauses, is a semicolon before, a comma following. Options (1) and (5) are incorrect because there is no semicolon before <u>however</u>. Option (3) is incorrect because there should be a comma after <u>however</u>. Option (4) is incorrect because a comma should not separate the subject <u>people</u> from the verb <u>need</u>.

Answers and Explanations

Lesson 6

All items in this section are related to rules of mechanics.

GED Practice: Using Apostrophes (Page 67)

1. **(2) replace dont with don't** (Punctuation/ Apostrophe) Option (2) is correct because don't, meaning "do not," should have an apostrophe in place of the missing letter. Options (1), (3), and (4) do not show correct contractions.

2. **(5) no correction is necessary** (Punctuation/Apostrophe) Option (1) is incorrect because Helens' is a plural possessive and the singular possessive is needed. Option (2) is incorrect because Helens is plural, not possessive. Options (3) and (4) are incorrect because the plural animals and cats are correct; possessives aren't necessary.

3. **(2) change womens to women's** (Punctuation/Apostrophe) Option (2) is correct because the possessive of a plural noun that does not end in -s is formed by adding 's. Option (1) is incorrect because women is already plural without adding s. There is no reason for the changes in options (3) and (4).

4. **(4) change owner's to owners** (Punctuation/Apostrophe) Option (4) is correct because owners should not show possession. Boys is a plural noun ending in -s, so the possessive is formed by adding an apostrophe after the s. Option (1) is incorrect because possession is meant; the club belongs to the boys. Option (2) is incorrect because the word club implies that more than one boy is meant. Option (3) is incorrect because the possessive isn't necessary.

5. **(3) change it's to its** (Punctuation/ Apostrophe) Option (3) is correct because the possessive pronoun its does not need an apostrophe; therefore, option (2) is incorrect. Option (1) is incorrect because take's is not a proper contraction. Option (4) is incorrect because the possessive isn't necessary.

6. **(3) replace its with it's** (Punctuation/ Apostrophe) Option (3) is correct because its is a possessive pronoun; a contraction is needed here. It's means "it is." Option (1) is incorrect because I'd is a contraction meaning "I would," not "I had," here. The sentence needs the verb is, so option (2) is incorrect. Option (4) is incorrect because our is a possessive pronoun that does not use an apostrophe.

7. **(2) change Ill to I'll** (Punctuation/ Apostrophe) Option (2) is correct because an apostrophe replaces wi in I will. Option (1) is incorrect because a comma follows an introductory word in a sentence. Option (3) is incorrect because the apostrophe is in the wrong place. Option (4) is incorrect because the sentence does not ask a question.

GED Practice: Using Quotation Marks (Pages 69–71)

1. **(4) remove both quotation marks** (Punctuation/Quotation marks) Option (4) is correct because quotation marks are used around exact quotations or special words; hot is not special in this sentence. Option (1) is incorrect because the possessive isn't necessary; the plural employees is correct. Options (2) and (3) are incorrect because the apostrophe replaces the second i in it is.

2. **(4) insert a quotation mark after statement,** (Punctuation/Quotation marks) Option (4) is correct because quotation marks are used in pairs, and the final quotation mark should come after the comma that sets off the direct quotation. Option (1) is incorrect because the exact words said should be in quotation marks. Option (2) is incorrect because I'm is a contraction meaning "I am." Option (3) is incorrect because a comma is needed to set off the direct quotation from the rest of the sentence.

3. **(4) remove both quotation marks** (Punctuation/Quotation marks) Option (4) is correct because quotation marks are used only for someone's exact words. Options (1), (2), and (3) are incorrect because no quotation marks are needed for an indirect quotation.

4. **(3) replace beeper"? with beeper?"** (Punctuation/Quotation marks) Option (2) is correct because end punctuation that is part of the direct quotation goes before the last quotation mark. Options (1) and (4) are incorrect because this sentence contains a direct quotation, which should be set off with a pair of quotation marks. Option (2) is incorrect because the contraction don't, meaning "do not," requires an apostrophe in place of the missing letter.

5. **(5) no correction is necessary** (Punctuation/Quotation marks and apostrophe) Option (5) is correct because quotation marks are used to set off an

unusual term or an exact phrase used by a specific person. Therefore, options (1), (2), and (3) are incorrect. Option (4) is incorrect because the possessive isn't necessary.

6. **(2) insert a quotation mark before man's** (Punctuation/Quotation marks) Option (2) is correct because the phrase to be quoted is "man's best friend." Option (1) is incorrect because the possessive isn't necessary. Option (3) is incorrect because man is a singular noun; the correct possessive is formed by adding 's. Option (4) is incorrect because a period is end punctuation.

7. **(2) insert a comma after said** (Punctuation/Quotation marks) Option (2) is correct because a comma is needed after said to set off the quoted sentence. Option (1) is incorrect because the commas after Grover and spokesman set off an appositive. Option (3) is incorrect because there is no reason for the comma after the verb is. Option (4) is incorrect because cats is correct; only the plural form of the word is needed here.

8. **(4) insert a quotation mark after companions,** (Punctuation/Quotation marks) Option (4) is correct because companions, ends the direct quotation that begins with Dogs; quotation marks are used in pairs. Option (1) is incorrect because this sentence contains a direct quote. Option (2) is incorrect because the possessive isn't necessary. Option (3) is incorrect because children is a plural word not ending in -s; the possessive is formed by adding 's.

9. **(1) insert a quotation mark before When** (Punctuation/Quotation marks) Option (1) is correct because the complete quotation begins with the first word in the sentence, so a quotation mark should be inserted before When. Option (2) is incorrect because it's is a contraction meaning "it is," which is the subject and verb of the main clause. Option (3) is incorrect because a direct quotation should be set off from the rest of the sentence by a comma. Option (4) is incorrect because Grover's tells whose sister it is, so an apostrophe is needed.

10. **(3) change the comma after pets to a semicolon** (Punctuation/Semicolon) Option (3) is correct because pets marks the end of the first of two independent clauses; since other commas are used in the second clause, a semicolon is needed. There is no reason for a

comma after which as in option (1). Option (2) is incorrect because only the plural pets is needed here. Option (4) is incorrect because ownership is shown and the possessive form is needed.

11. **(4) change cats' to cats** (Punctuation/Quotation marks) Option (4) is correct because the plural form of the word cats, not the possessive, is all that is needed. Option (1) is incorrect because 's is added to the singular noun cemetery to show possession. Option (2) is incorrect because no possession is shown. Option (3) is incorrect because two independent clauses are joined by a semicolon, not a comma, when no conjunction is used.

12. **(3) remove both quotation marks** (Punctuation/Quotation marks) Option (3) is correct because why . . . pets is not a direct quotation. Options (1) and (4) are incorrect because no possession is shown. Option (2) is incorrect because to explain is the correct infinitive form of the verb.

13. **(4) insert a comma after Marcus** (Punctuation/Appositives) Option (4) is correct because a comma is needed to set off the appositive pet owner. Option (1) is incorrect because no possession is shown. Option (2) is incorrect because dogs is part of a direct quotation, and quotation marks come in pairs. Option (3) is incorrect because appositives are set off by commas, not semicolons.

14. **(2) change Dog's to Dogs** (Punctuation/Apostrophe) Option (2) is correct because no possession is shown. Option (1) is incorrect because no possession is shown; dogs' is a plural possessive. Option (3) is incorrect because the subject of the sentence Dogs should not be separated from the verb need by a comma. Option (4) is incorrect because items in a series need to be separated by commas.

15. **(3) insert a quotation mark before Even** (Punctuation/Quotation marks) Option (3) is correct because quotation marks are used in pairs and Even is the beginning of a direct quotation. Option (1) is incorrect because Helen is singular and 's is the correct singular possessive ending. Option (2) is incorrect because the commas are needed to set off the appositive Helen's roommate. Option (4) is incorrect because a comma, not a semicolon, is used to set off an introductory dependent clause.

16. **(3) change owners to owner's**
(Punctuation/Apostrophe) Option (3) is correct
because owners should have the singular
possessive ending 's. Option (1) is incorrect
because the conjunction but that joins two
independent clauses should be preceded by a
comma. Option (2) is incorrect because owners
is singular, as indicated by the article a, and
should not have the plural possessive ending
s'. Option (4) is incorrect because no
possession is shown.

GED Mini-Test: Lesson 6 (Pages 72–73)

1. **(1) change your's to yours**
(Punctuation/Apostrophe) Option (1) is correct
because yours is a possessive pronoun that
does not need an apostrophe to show
possession. Options (2) and (3) are incorrect
because the introductory dependent clause
should be set off with a comma, not a
semicolon. Option (4) is incorrect because the
possessive of a singular noun, Bob, is formed
by adding 's.

2. **(3) insert a quotation mark before and**
(Punctuation/Quotation marks) Option (3) is
correct because the quoting of Bob's exact
words begins again after says Bob; quotation
marks are used in pairs. Options (1) and (4)
are incorrect because in a contraction the
apostrophe should be placed where the
missing letters would go. Option (2) is
incorrect because before ends the first part of
the quotation; quotation marks are used in
pairs.

3. **(4) insert a comma after enthusiasm**
(Punctuation/Commas between items in
series) Option (4) is correct because items in
series should be separated by commas;
therefore, option (3) is incorrect. Options (1)
and (2) are incorrect because no possession is
shown in the sentence other than his.

4. **(3) remove the quotation mark after easy**
(Punctuation/Quotation marks) Option (3) is
correct because even though this looks like a
direct quote, it is not. The possible source of
the quote, the lucky ones who've been there, is
too vague to be quoted directly. Option (1) is
incorrect because this is not a direct quote and
needs no quotation marks. Option (2) is
incorrect because in a contraction the
apostrophe takes the place of missing letters.
Option (4) is incorrect because no possession is
shown.

5. **(4) change shows to shows'** (Punctuation/
Apostrophe) Option (4) is correct because
shows is possessive and needs an apostrophe;
add an apostrophe to a plural noun that ends
in -s to form the possessive. Options (1) and
(2) are incorrect because no possession is
meant. Option (3) is incorrect because a
semicolon is needed to join two independent
clauses when no conjunction is used.

6. **(5) no correction is necessary**
(Punctuation/Apostrophe; Commas and items
in a series) Options (1) and (2) are incorrect
because no possession is shown. Option (3) is
incorrect because the possessive pronoun their
does not need an apostrophe. Option (4) is
incorrect because two items joined by a
conjunction do not need to be separated by a
comma.

7. **(2) change nerves' to nerves** (Punctuation/
Apostrophe) Option (2) is correct because no
possession is shown. Option (1) is incorrect
because Everyone's requires an apostrophe to
show possession. Option (3) is incorrect
because Everyone's . . . edge is a direct
quotation. Option (4) is incorrect because no
possession is shown.

8. **(5) no correction is necessary**
(Punctuation/Commas after introductory
elements; Possessives; Contractions) Option
(1) is incorrect because a comma is necessary
to set off the introductory element However.
Options (2) and (3) are incorrect because no
possession is shown. Option (4) is incorrect
because contractions require an apostrophe in
place of the missing letters.

9. **(4) insert a quotation mark before it**
(Punctuation/Quotation marks) Option (4) is
correct because quotation marks are used in
pairs around the words that are quoted.
Option (1) is incorrect because a comma is
needed after an introductory word. Option (2)
is incorrect because a comma is needed to
separate a direct quotation from the rest of
the sentence. Option (3) is incorrect because
the comma should go before the quotation
mark.

10. **(5) no correction is necessary**
(Punctuation/Apostrophe and quotation
marks; Capitalization; Possessives) Option (1)
is incorrect because no possession is shown in
the sentence besides his. In option (2), Bob
must be capitalized because it is a proper
noun and the first word in the sentence.

Option (3) is incorrect because <u>his</u> is a possessive pronoun that does not use an apostrophe. Option (4) is incorrect because quotation marks are not needed around <u>game-show</u>.

11. **(1) remove both quotation marks** (Punctuation/Apostrophe and quotation marks) Option (1) is correct because this is not a direct quotation. Option (2) is incorrect because the apostrophe replaces the <u>o</u> in the contraction of <u>does not</u>. Option (3) is incorrect because a comma is not needed. Option (4) is incorrect because these are not Bob's exact words.

Lesson 7

All items in this section are related to rules of mechanics.

GED Practice: Basic Spelling Rules and Contractions (Pages 76–77)

1. **(4) change the spelling of goeing to going** (Spelling) Option (4) is correct because you don't add an <u>e</u> when you add the suffix <u>-ing</u>. Option (1) is incorrect because seasons are not capitalized. Options (2) and (3) are incorrect because the singular subject <u>strain</u> takes the singular verb <u>is</u>.

2. **(1) change Its to It's** (Contractions) Option (1) is correct because <u>It's</u> is a contraction of <u>It is</u>. Option (2) is incorrect because a semicolon separates independent clauses. Option (3) is incorrect because you don't double the last consonant when it is preceded by a consonant. Option (4) is incorrect because <u>then</u> means "at a certain time."

3. **(1) change the spelling of noticable to noticeable** (Spelling) Option (1) is correct because the final <u>e</u> is kept when adding the suffix <u>-able</u> to <u>notice</u>. Option (2) is incorrect because the plural <u>victims</u> should not be a possessive. Options (3) and (4) are incorrect because <u>including</u> and <u>coughing</u> are spelled correctly.

4. **(1) change Theyr'e to They're** (Contractions) Option (1) is correct because the apostrophe replaces the <u>a</u> in <u>they are</u>. Options (2) and (3) are incorrect because <u>experiencing</u> is spelled correctly. Option (4) is incorrect because a comma is needed after each item in a series.

5. **(3) change the spelling of unecessary to unnecessary** (Spelling) Option (3) is correct because the spelling of <u>necessary</u> does not

change when the prefix <u>un-</u> is added. Option (1) is incorrect because the last consonant is not doubled when the first syllable of a word is stressed, as in <u>VIsit</u>. Option (2) is incorrect because a semicolon separates independent clauses. Option (4) is incorrect because people's professions are not capitalized.

6. **(2) change Yo'ud to You'd** (Contractions) Option (2) is correct because an apostrophe should replace the letters <u>woul</u> when forming the contraction of <u>you would</u>. Option (1) is incorrect because an apostrophe is needed when forming a contraction. Options (3) and (4) are incorrect because <u>off</u> and <u>variety</u> are spelled correctly.

7. **(1) change Youll to You'll** (Contractions) Option (1) is correct because an apostrophe is needed to replace the letters <u>wi</u> when forming the contraction <u>you will</u>. Option (2) is incorrect because <u>making</u> is spelled correctly. Option (3) is incorrect because <u>steps</u> is plural, not possessive, and so does not need an apostrophe. Option (4) is incorrect because there is no reason to capitalize <u>week</u>.

8. **(2) change geting to getting** (Spelling) Option (2) is correct because the <u>t</u> is doubled when the suffix <u>-ing</u> is added to <u>get</u>. Option (1) is incorrect because <u>judgment</u> is spelled correctly. Option (3) is incorrect because <u>shot</u> is the correct singular noun; the plural <u>shots</u> would not agree with the singular article <u>a</u>. Option (4) is incorrect because the names of months are capitalized.

9. **(5) no correction is necessary** (Spelling and contractions) Options (1) and (2) are incorrect because an apostrophe is needed to replace the second <u>o</u> in the contraction of <u>Do not</u>. Option (3) is incorrect because the <u>e</u> is not dropped when adding the suffix <u>-less</u> to the word <u>use</u>. Option (4) is incorrect because the semicolon separates two independent clauses.

10. **(5) no correction is necessary** (Spelling and contractions) Options (1) and (2) are incorrect because <u>especially</u> and <u>dangerous</u> are spelled correctly. Option (3) is incorrect because the plural of <u>child</u> is <u>children</u>. Option (4) is incorrect because <u>senior citizens</u> is not a proper noun.

11. **(1) change the spelling of encourageing to encouraging** (Spelling) Option (1) is correct because the <u>e</u> is dropped when adding a suffix that starts with a vowel. Option (2) is

incorrect because grandparents is not a proper noun. Options (3) and (4) are incorrect because elderly and neighbors are spelled correctly.

12. **(3) change the spelling of healthyer to healthier** (Spelling) Option (1) is incorrect because the y in hurry is not changed to an i when the suffix -ing is added. Option (2) is incorrect because means is not possessive. Option (4) is incorrect because season is not a proper noun.

GED Mini-Test: Lesson 7 (Pages 78–79)

1. **(4) change the spelling of missplacing to misplacing** (Spelling) Option (4) is correct because the spelling of placing does not change when the prefix mis- is added. Option (1) is incorrect because neighbor is part of an appositive phrase and must be set off by commas. Options (2) and (3) are incorrect because neighbor and noticed are spelled correctly.

2. **(3) change the spelling of worryed to worried** (Spelling) Option (3) is correct because the y in worry is changed to an i when the suffix -ed is added. Option (1) is incorrect because friend is spelled correctly. Option (2) is incorrect because the last consonant, t, should not be doubled when the suffix -ing is added to wait. Option (4) is incorrect because the apostrophe replaces the letters wi in we will.

3. **(2) change the spelling of locateing to locating** (Spelling) Option (2) is correct because the final e is dropped when adding the suffix -ing to locate. Option (1) is incorrect because days of the week are capitalized. Option (3) is incorrect because the last consonant, t, should be doubled when the suffix -ing is added to sit. Option (4) is incorrect because a semicolon is necessary to join two independent clauses.

4. **(3) change were'nt to weren't** (Contractions) Option (3) is correct because the apostrophe replaces the letter o in were not. Options (1) and (4) are incorrect because the final e's are dropped when adding the suffix -ing to become and frustrate. Option (2) is incorrect because i comes before e in unbelievable.

5. **(2) change the spelling of foriegn to foreign** (Spelling) Option (2) is correct because foreign is an exception to the i before e rule. Option (1) is incorrect because the subject should not be separated from the verb by a comma. Option (3) is incorrect because

the semicolon is necessary between two independent clauses. Option (4) is incorrect because the e is not dropped when adding the suffix -ly to prohibitive.

6. **(5) no correction is necessary** (Punctuation/Apostrophe, Commas in complex sentences; Spelling; Contractions) Option (1) is incorrect because the apostrophe replaces the second letter o in does not. Option (2) is incorrect because a comma is necessary after the introductory dependent clause. Option (3) is incorrect because the last consonant, d, should not be doubled when the suffix -ing is added to avoid. Option (4) is incorrect because the e is not dropped when adding the suffix -ous to outrage.

7. **(3) remove the commas after tourist and courier** (Punctuation/Commas and essential phrases) Option (3) is correct because the phrase flying . . . courier is essential to the meaning of the sentence. Option (1) is incorrect because tourist is not a proper noun. Option (2) is incorrect because y is not changed to i when the suffix -ing is added. Option (4) is incorrect because the last consonant, t, should be doubled when the suffix -ed is added to permit.

8. **(2) change the spelling of companys to companies** (Spelling) Option (2) is correct because the y changes to an i, and es is added to make company plural. Option (1) is incorrect because there is no reason for a comma after companies. Option (3) is incorrect because possession is shown. Option (4) is incorrect because the last consonant, p, should be doubled when the suffix -ing is added to ship.

9. **(1) change Theres to There's** (Contractions) Option (1) is correct because the apostrophe replaces the letter i in there is. Option (2) is incorrect for the same reason. Option (3) is incorrect because people should not be separated from the essential phrase who . . . arrangements. Option (4) is incorrect because the e is not dropped when adding the suffix -ment to arrange.

Lesson 8

All items in this section are related to rules of mechanics.

GED Practice: Correct Spelling (Pages 84–86)

1. **(3) change carefuly to carefully** (Spelling) Option (3) is correct because there are two l's in carefully.

2. **(3) change nieghbors to neighbors**
(Spelling) Option (3) is correct; neighbors
follows the rule of i before e except when
sounded as a.

3. **(1) change befour to before** (Spelling)
Option (1) is correct; before is not spelled like
the number four.

4. **(2) change unecessary to unnecessary**
(Spelling) Option (2) is correct because
unnecessary needs two n's.

5. **(5) no correction is necessary.** (Spelling)
Option (5) is correct because all words in this
sentence are spelled correctly.

6. **(3) change couragous to courageous**
(Spelling) Option (3) is correct because the e in
courage should be retained when a suffix is
added.

7. **(3) change unnacceptable to
unacceptable** (Spelling) Option (3) is correct
because there is no reason to double the n
when adding the prefix un- to acceptable.

8. **(5) no correction is necessary** (Spelling)
Option (5) is correct because all words in this
sentence are spelled correctly.

9. **(4) change personel to personnel**
(Spelling) Option (4) is correct because
personnel is spelled with two n's.

10. **(3) change consceintious to conscientious**
(Spelling) Option (3) is correct; conscientious
is an exception to the i before e except after c
rule.

11. **(3) change appropreate to appropriate**
(Spelling) Option (3) is correct; the -iate
ending is the commonly misspelled part of the
word appropriate.

12. **(3) change oportunity to opportunity**
(Spelling) Option (3) is correct; the commonly
misspelled part of opportunity is the double p.

13. **(2) change anual to annual** (Spelling)
Option (2) is correct because there are two n's
in annual.

14. **(1) change suceeded to succeeded**
(Spelling) Option (1) is correct because
succeeded is spelled with two c's.

15. **(4) change finanshal to financial** (Spelling)
Option (4) is correct; the -cial ending is a
commonly misspelled part of the word
financial.

16. **(2) change forhead to forehead** (Spelling)
Option (2) is correct; the introductory fore- is a
commonly misspelled part of the word
forehead.

17. **(5) no correction is necessary** (Spelling)
Option (5) is correct because all words in this
sentence are spelled correctly.

Lesson 9

All items in this section are related to rules of
mechanics.

GED Practice: Possessives and Homonyms (Pages 89–90)

1. **(5) no correction is necessary** (Spelling/
Homonyms) Option (1) is incorrect because
two, the number, is the correct word in this
sentence. Option (2) is incorrect because sons,
meaning "male children," is the correct word
in this sentence. Option (3) is incorrect
because to is part of the infinitive form of the
verb to go. Option (4) is incorrect because
week, meaning "seven days," is the correct
word in this sentence.

2. **(3) change there to their** (Spelling/
Homonyms; Possessives) Option (3) is correct
because the sons own the swim trunks, so the
possessive pronoun their is needed. Option (1)
is incorrect because 's is added after a singular
noun to show possession. Option (2) is
incorrect because to is part of the infinitive
form of the verb to bring. Option (4) is
incorrect because the preposition for is the
correct word in the sentence.

3. **(1) change whether to weather** (Spelling/
Homonyms) Option (1) is correct because
weather, meaning "the climate," is the correct
word in the sentence. Option (2) is incorrect
because to is part of the infinitive form of the
verb to be. Option (3) is incorrect because
might, meaning "possible," is the correct word
in the sentence. Option (4) is incorrect because
too, meaning "also," is the correct word in the
sentence.

4. **(4) change four to for** (Spelling/Homonyms)
Option (4) is correct because the preposition
for is the correct word in this sentence. Option
(1) is incorrect because weather, referring to

the climate, is correct in this sentence. Option (2) is incorrect because the possessive isn't necessary. Option (3) is incorrect because whole, meaning "entire," is correct in this sentence.

5. **(2) change boy's to boys'** (Spelling/Homonyms; Possessives) Option (2) is correct because there are two boys so the plural possessive boys' is needed. Option (1) is incorrect because the verb would is the correct word in this sentence. Option (3) is incorrect because the possessive isn't necessary. Option (4) is incorrect because great, meaning "very good," is the correct word in this sentence.

6. **(1) replace hear with here** (Spelling/Homonyms) Option (1) is correct because here, meaning "at this place," is the correct word for this sentence; hear refers to listening. Option (2) is incorrect because the number four is spelled correctly. Option (3) is incorrect because the possessive pronoun his does not have an apostrophe. Option (4) is incorrect because way, meaning "direction," is correctly used.

7. **(1) replace passed with past** (Spelling/Homonyms) Option (1) is correct because past, meaning "time before," is correct in this sentence. Option (2) is incorrect because a comma is needed to set off the long introductory phrase. Option (3) is incorrect because made is a verb meaning "created something" and is correct in this sentence. Option (4) is incorrect because great means "large in size."

8. **(4) replace feet with feat** (Spelling/Homonyms) Option (4) is correct because feat, meaning "accomplishment," is the correct word in this sentence. Option (1) is incorrect because a semicolon is not used when two independent clauses are joined by a conjunction. Option (2) is incorrect because publisher is not a proper noun. Option (3) is incorrect because for is used correctly as a preposition in this sentence.

9. **(2) replace know with no** (Spelling/Homonyms) Option (2) is correct because know means "to have knowledge of"; no means "very little or none." Option (1) is incorrect because knows is correctly used in the sentence. Option (3) is incorrect because one refers to a number or to a person in general; it is correctly used in the sentence. Option (4) is incorrect because will is a helping verb used

with be; it is correct in the original sentence; we'll is a contraction meaning "we will."

10. **(3) replace board with bored** (Spelling/Homonyms) Option (3) is correct because bored, meaning "not interested," is the correct word in this sentence. Option (1) is incorrect because Mr. Patterson's should have the singular possessive ending 's. Option (2) is incorrect because plain, meaning "simple," is the correct word in this sentence. Option (4) is incorrect because the comma correctly sets off the introductory dependent clause.

GED Mini-Test: Lesson 9 (Pages 91–93)

1. **(3) replace sense with since** (Spelling/Homonyms) Option (3) is correct because since means "because" in this sentence; sense means "to become aware of or understand something." Option (1) is incorrect because weather refers to the climate. Option (2) is incorrect because in a contraction the apostrophe is placed where the letter is missing. Option (4) is incorrect because one is a pronoun that refers to choice.

2. **(3) change you're to your** (Spelling/Homonyms) Option (3) is correct because a possessive word, your, is needed in this sentence; you're is a contraction meaning "you are." Option (1) is incorrect because the contraction you'll requires an apostrophe. Option (2) is incorrect because right means "correct" in this sentence. Option (4) is incorrect because the possessive pronoun its does not require an apostrophe; it's is a contraction meaning "it is."

3. **(4) replace they're with their** (Spelling/Homonyms; Possessives) Option (4) is correct because their is a possessive pronoun; they're is a contraction meaning "they are." Option (2) is incorrect because made, meaning "to have done something," is correctly used. Option (3) is incorrect because there refers to a place. Option (1) is incorrect because the possessive isn't necessary.

4. **(3) replace who's with whose** (Spelling/Homonyms; Possessives) Option (3) is correct because the possessive pronoun whose does not use an apostrophe; who's is a contraction meaning "who is." Option (1) is incorrect because the possessive pronoun Your is needed in the sentence. Option (2) is incorrect because the helping verb be is correctly used. Option (4) is incorrect because union's (like

UNIT 1

management's) is a noun that shows possession and needs an apostrophe.

5. **(1) replace witch with which** (Spelling/ Homonyms) Option (1) is correct because which, meaning "the one that," is the correct word in this sentence. Option (2) is incorrect because effects, meaning "results," is the correct word in this sentence. Option (3) is incorrect because effects should be plural not possessive. Option (4) is incorrect because the possessive pronoun is needed to show whose decisions.

6. **(3) replace the comma after it with a semicolon** (Punctuation/Semicolon) Option (3) is correct because this sentence is made up of two independent clauses that should be separated by a semicolon, not a comma, since no coordinate conjunction is used between the clauses. Option (1) is incorrect because seems means "appears" and is correct. Options (2) and (4) are incorrect because the contractions don't and hadn't each require an apostrophe in place of the missing letter.

7. **(1) change threw to through** (Spelling/ Homonyms) Option (1) is correct because through is a preposition meaning "by means of"; threw means "tossed." Option (2) is incorrect because the second part of the sentence is not a clause that could stand alone; commas are needed to set off the interrupting expression however. Options (3) and (4) are incorrect because for and no are correct.

8. **(4) change there to their** (Spelling/ Homonyms; Possessives) Option (4) is correct because their is a possessive pronoun; there indicates a place. Options (1) and (3) are incorrect because cards and department stores are not proper nouns and should not be capitalized. Option (2) is incorrect because a semicolon is not used with a coordinate conjunction unless there are other commas in the sentence.

9. **(1) remove the comma after Anyone** (Punctuation/Overuse of commas) Option (1) is correct because there is no reason to set off Anyone with a comma; it is the subject of the verb knows. Option (2) is incorrect because the contraction who's means "who has"; whose is a possessive pronoun. Option (3) is incorrect because the phrase who's ever lost a credit card is necessary to the meaning of the sentence and should not be set off with

commas. Option (4) is incorrect because the phrase about how to . . . is essential to the meaning of information and should not be set off by a comma.

10. **(3) replace mite with might** (Spelling/ Homonyms) Option (3) is correct. Mite means "a small amount"; the sentence requires might, a helping verb for be, to go with who, the subject of the dependent clause. Options (1), (2), and (4) are incorrect because the words are used correctly in the original sentence.

11. **(5) no correction is necessary** (Spelling/ Homonyms; Possessives; Capitalization) Option (1) is incorrect because your is a possessive pronoun and is used correctly in the sentence. Option (2) is incorrect because there is no reason for a semicolon after should. Option (3) is incorrect because store and company are common nouns and should not be capitalized. Option (4) is incorrect because the possessive pronoun whose is correct here, not the contraction who's.

12. **(2) replace principle with principal** (Spelling/Homonyms) Option (2) is correct because principal, meaning "main," is the correct word in this sentence. Option (1) is incorrect because one, the number, is the correct word in this sentence. Option (3) is incorrect because the possessive isn't necessary. Option (4) is incorrect because having is correctly spelled.

13. **(4) replace some with sum** (Spelling/ Homonyms) Option (4) is correct because sum, meaning "amount," is the correct word in this sentence. Option (1) is incorrect because friends is spelled correctly. Option (2) is incorrect because new, meaning "latest," is the correct word in this sentence. Option (3) is incorrect because the possessive pronoun whose is the correct word in this sentence.

14. **(2) replace maid with made** (Spelling/ Homonyms) Option (2) is correct because made, meaning "created or done," is the correct word in this sentence. Option (1) is incorrect because a comma is required after an introductory dependent clause. Options (3) and (4) are incorrect because the possessive pronoun their is the correct word in this sentence.

15. **(2) replace brake with break** (Spelling/ Homonyms) Option (2) is correct because

break, meaning "to interrupt," is the correct word in this sentence. Option (1) is incorrect because the contraction it's is the correct word in this sentence. Option (3) is incorrect because purchasing is spelled correctly. Option (4) is incorrect because to is the correct word in this sentence.

16. **(5) no correction is necessary** (Spelling/ Homonyms) Option (1) is incorrect because the verb would is the correct word in this sentence. Option (2) is incorrect because the apostrophe replaces the o in the contraction of did not. Option (3) is incorrect because the pronoun their is the correct word in this sentence. Option (4) is incorrect because the past tense of pay is paid.

GED Cumulative Review
Unit 1: Mechanics (Pages 94–98)

1. **(2) views of their employees** (Spelling; Punctuation/Overuse of commas; Possessives) Option (2) is correct because the correct spelling is views, following the i before e rule. Option (3) is incorrect because there is no reason to set off the prepositional phrase of their employees with a comma. Option (4) is incorrect because the possessive pronoun their is needed. Option (5) is incorrect because the possessive isn't necessary.

2. **(1) communicate with management is** (Spelling; Punctuation/Semicolon and overuse of commas) Option (1) is correct because all words are spelled correctly and there is no need for any punctuation in this sentence. Option (2) is incorrect because comunicate is a misspelling. Options (3) and (5) are incorrect because the phrase through an employee . . . is essential to the meaning of the sentence and should not be set off with a comma or semicolon. Option (4) is incorrect because the comma would separate the subject way from the verb is.

3. **(4) change the question mark to a period** (Punctuation/End punctuation) Option (4) is correct because this is a statement and does not require an answer. Options (1) and (3) are incorrect because surveys and experts should be plural, not possessive. Option (2) is incorrect because usually is spelled correctly.

4. **(3) change Company to company** (Capitalization) Option (3) is correct because company is not part of a proper name and should not be capitalized. Option (1) is incorrect because the possessive pronoun

Their is correct in the sentence. Option (2) is incorrect because the possessive isn't necessary. Option (4) is incorrect because confidentiality is a common noun and should not be capitalized.

5. **(1) insert commas after questions and salary** (Punctuation/Commas; Semicolons; Spelling) Option (1) is correct because a nonessential phrase is set off from a sentence with commas. Option (2) is incorrect because receive is spelled correctly. Option (3) is incorrect because a semicolon separates independent clauses. Option (4) is incorrect because the contraction they're is the correct word in this sentence.

6. **(4) surveys. Then** (Punctuation/End punctuation; Capitalization) Option (4) is correct because two ideas that can stand alone should not be linked by a comma. Of the revision options given, starting a new sentence is the best alternative. (A semicolon would also be correct here, but it is not one of the answer choices.) Options (2) and (5) are incorrect because the sentence neither expresses an idea of strong emotion nor asks a question. Option (3) is incorrect because a sentence must start with a capital letter.

7. **(1) change the semicolon to a comma** (Punctuation/Commas after introductory elements) Option (1) is correct because a comma is used after an introductory phrase. Option (2) is incorrect because the possessive isn't necessary. Option (3) is incorrect because to is used with the infinitive verb form; too means "also." Option (4) is incorrect because recommend is spelled correctly.

8. **(4) but as one worker stated, "I liked** (Punctuation/Quotation marks, commas with quotation marks, and overuse of commas) Option (4) is correct because quotation marks are needed at the beginning of an exact quotation. All other punctuation is correct. Option (2) is incorrect because a direct quotation is set off by a comma. Option (3) is incorrect because it includes within the quotation marks the words that identify the speaker. There is no reason for the comma after but in option (5).

9. **(3) insert a semicolon after workable** (Punctuation/Semicolon) Option (3) is correct because a semicolon is used to join two independent clauses without a conjunction. Option (1) is incorrect because the possessive

pronoun their is correct. Option (2) is incorrect because employees is meant in the plural and the plural possessive is formed by the apostrophe following the s. Option (4) is incorrect because the possessive isn't necessary.

10. **(1) improved, along** (Punctuation/Commas, semicolons, end punctuation) Option (1) is correct because a comma separates a nonessential dependent and an independent clause. Option (2) is incorrect because it removes the comma. Option (3) is incorrect because a semicolon separates two independent clauses. Options (4) and (5) create fragments; also, in option (4), a sentence must start with a capital letter.

11. **(5) no correction is necessary** (Capitalization; Punctuation/ Semicolon, quotation marks, and apostrophe) Option (1) is incorrect because there is no reason to capitalize written. Option (2) is incorrect because there is no reason to put a semicolon after written. Option (3) is incorrect because special terms, such as displaced homemakers, are often put in quotes, and quotation marks are used in pairs. Option (4) is incorrect because the possessive isn't necessary.

12. **(3) change And to and** (Capitalization) Option (3) is correct because such words as and, in, of, on, and for are not capitalized unless they are the first or last word of the title. Option (1) is incorrect because to is used as a preposition in this sentence; too means "also." Option (2) is incorrect because the comma after publication is needed to set off the title, as an appositive, from the rest of the sentence. Option (4) is incorrect because punctuation should go before the quotation mark.

13. **(3) insert a comma after Livingood** (Punctuation/Appositives) Option (3) is correct because a comma is used to set off a nonessential descriptive phrase (appositive) from the rest of the sentence. Option (1) is incorrect because a quotation mark is needed before Depression, which begins the doctor's exact words. Option (2) is incorrect because the preposition to is correct in this sentence. Option (4) is incorrect because a prepositional phrase should not be separated from the rest of the sentence by a comma.

14. **(1) insert a quotation mark after But,** (Punctuation/Quotation marks) Option (1) is

correct because quotation marks should set off the exact words quoted; the quotation mark comes after the punctuation (comma) that follows the words quoted. Option (2) is incorrect because we is part of the direct quotation and quotation marks are used in pairs. Option (3) is incorrect because the correct spelling is beginning. Option (4) is incorrect because the possessive pronoun its is correct here.

15. **(3) insert a comma after problem** (Punctuation/Appositives) The phrase a growing problem is an appositive and should be set off by commas from the rest of the sentence; therefore, option (3) is correct and option (2) is incorrect. Option (1) is incorrect because Teenage is the first word in the sentence and needs to be capitalized. Option (4) is incorrect because the correct spelling is increasing.

16. **(5) no correction is necessary** (Punctuation/Quotation marks and overuse of commas; Spelling/Homonyms; Capitalization) Option (1) is incorrect because quotation marks are needed to set off the exact words of the quotation. Option (2) is incorrect because the possessive pronoun your is correct, not the contraction you're. Option (3) is incorrect because there is no reason to capitalize someone. Option (4) is incorrect because there is no reason to set off the prepositional phrase during this time with a comma.

17. **(2) insert a quotation mark after problem,** (Punctuation/Quotation marks) Option (2) is correct because the words of a direct quotation must be enclosed in quotation marks. Option (1) is incorrect because there is no reason to capitalize biggest. Option (3) is incorrect because a period is correct here to separate two thoughts that can stand alone. Option (4) is incorrect because the contraction what's, which means "what is," is correct here.

18. **(4) change Solution to solution** (Capitalization) Option (4) is correct because the common noun solution should not be capitalized. Options (1) and (2) are incorrect because commas are needed to separate items in a list. Option (3) is incorrect because counseling is spelled correctly.

19. **(1) remove the commas after People and depression** (Punctuation/Commas and essential phrases) Option (1) is correct because an essential phrase should not be set

off by commas. Option (2) is incorrect because semicolons are used to join independent clauses. Option (3) is incorrect because great, meaning "very good," is the correct word in this sentence. Option (4) is incorrect because knowledge is spelled correctly.

20. **(4) replace who's with whose** (Spelling/ Homonyms) Option (4) is correct because the possessive pronoun whose is the correct word in this sentence. Option (1) is incorrect because Unfortunately is spelled correctly. Option (2) is incorrect because the possessive isn't necessary. Option (3) is incorrect because Americans is a proper noun and must be capitalized.

21. **(2) better; indeed, the** (Punctuation/ Semicolon) Option (2) is correct because both a semicolon and a comma are necessary to join two independent clauses joined by the linking word indeed. Options (1), (3), (4), and (5) are incorrect because the semicolon is missing. Options (3), (4), and (5) are also missing the comma after indeed.

22. **(5) no correction is necessary** (Punctuation/Commas between items in series; Capitalization; Spelling) Option (1) is incorrect because the comma is needed here to separate items in a list. Option (2) is incorrect because there is no reason to capitalize learning. Options (3) and (4) are incorrect because communicate and getting are spelled correctly in the original sentence.

23. **(2) insert a comma after reporter** (Punctuation/Appositives) The descriptive phrase television reporter is an appositive that should be set off by commas; therefore, option (2) is correct and option (1) is incorrect. Option (3) is incorrect because White House is the name of a specific building and is capitalized. Option (4) is incorrect because national is not a proper noun and should not be capitalized.

24. **(3) insert a semicolon after none** (Punctuation/Semicolon) Option (3) is correct because a semicolon is used to join two independent clauses without a conjunction. Option (1) is incorrect because the names of languages, such as English, are always capitalized. Options (2) and (4) are incorrect because almost and neighborhood are spelled correctly in the original sentence.

25. **(2) change week's to weeks** (Punctuation/ Apostrophe) Option (2) is correct because the plural weeks, not the possessive week's should be used here. Option (1) is incorrect because the commas are needed after when and kindergarten to set off a nonessential phrase. Option (3) is incorrect because kindergarten is correctly spelled. Option (4) is incorrect because boy's correctly shows possession.

UNIT 2: USAGE
Lesson 10

All items in this section are related to rules of usage.

GED Practice: Parts of Speech (Page 105)

1. **(5) Do athletes deserve to** (Parts of speech/ Verbs) Option (5) is correct because the subject athletes should follow the verb Do. The end punctuation indicates that the sentence is a question, and the question is clearer with the subject following the verb. Option (1) is incorrect because the sentence is not clearly a question with athletes preceding the verb. Option (2) is incorrect because to is the correct word in an infinitive, not two. Option (3) is incorrect because the possessive isn't necessary. Option (4) is incorrect because the subject athletes should not be separated from the verb do deserve by a comma.

2. **(3) insert commas after workers and models** (Parts of speech/Nouns) Option (3) is correct because the appositive phrase real role models should be set off by commas. Option (1) is incorrect because safety is a common noun. Option (2) is incorrect because commas must be added before and after the appositive phrase. Option (4) is incorrect because the last consonant r should not be doubled when adding the suffix -ly.

3. **(3) Firefighters, police officers, ambulance drivers, and nurses are more** (Parts of speech/Verbs) Option (3) is correct because every sentence requires a verb; here are is added. Options (1) and (2) are incorrect because there is no verb. Option (4) is incorrect because there is an unnecessary comma after nurses. Option (5) is incorrect because police officers, ambulance drivers, and nurses are common nouns; no capitalization is necessary.

4. **(3) replace the second a baseball player with he** (Parts of speech/ Pronouns) Option (3) is correct because replacing a baseball player with the pronoun he eliminates

UNIT 2

unnecessary repetition. Option (1) is incorrect because the apostrophe replaces the o in the contraction doesn't. Option (2) is incorrect because the subject baseball player should not be separated from the verb doesn't save by a comma. Option (4) is incorrect because home run is a common noun; no capitalization is necessary.

5. **(1) There should be a limit** (Parts of speech/Verbs) Options (2) and (3) are incorrect because there is the correct word in this sentence. Options (4) and (5) are incorrect because the subject limit should follow the verb should be in a sentence beginning with There.

GED Mini-Test: Lesson 10 (Pages 106–107)

1. **(3) insert is after Sahara** (Parts of speech) Option (3) is correct because every sentence must have a verb. Option (1) is incorrect because strong emotion is not expressed; an exclamation mark is unnecessary. Option (2) is incorrect because Sahara is a specific place name; it must be capitalized. Option (4) is incorrect because a semicolon is only used to join independent clauses.

2. **(3) move enormous after This** (Parts of speech) Option (3) is correct enormous is an adjective modifying the subject desert; modifiers should be placed near the words they modify. Option (1) is incorrect because a comma would separate the subject from the verb. Option (2) is incorrect North and West Africa are specific place names; they must be capitalized. Option (4) is incorrect because the possessive isn't necessary.

3. **(2) insert the desert before inspires** (Parts of speech) Option (2) is correct because every sentence must have a subject. Option (1) is incorrect because the preposition for is the correct word in this sentence, not four, the number. Option (3) is incorrect because a comma is necessary to set off the introductory prepositional phrase; people is the object of a preposition, not the subject of the sentence. Option (4) is incorrect because the sentence does not ask a question.

4. **(3) replace the second the temperature with it** (Parts of speech) Option (3) is correct because a pronoun should replace the noun already named to avoid repetition. Option (1) is incorrect because an independent clause requires a verb, in this case is. Option (2) is incorrect because a semicolon is used to join

two independent clauses. Option (4) is incorrect because in the shade is an essential phrase and should not be set off by a comma.

5. **(4) change plants' to plants** (Punctuation/Apostrophe) Option (4) is correct because the possessive isn't necessary. Option (1) is incorrect because great, meaning "huge," is the correct word in this sentence. Option (2) is incorrect because surprised is part of the complete verb; every sentence must have a verb. Option (3) is incorrect because variety is correctly spelled.

6. **(1) move are after There** (Parts of speech) Option (1) is correct because the verb precedes the subject in sentences beginning with There. Option (2) is incorrect because are is part of the complete verb; every sentence must have a verb. Option (3) is incorrect because decide is spelled correctly. Option (4) is incorrect because which, the relative pronoun, is the correct word in this sentence.

7. **(5) no correction is necessary** (Parts of speech; Punctuation/Apostrophe; Homonyms; Spelling; Commas in complex sentences) Option (1) is incorrect because the comma is required to separate the introductory dependent clause. Option (2) is incorrect because the e is dropped when adding the suffix -ing to the verb choose. Option (3) is incorrect because there is the correct word in this sentence, not the contraction they're. Option (4) is incorrect because the possessive isn't necessary.

8. **(2) move sell after companies** (Parts of speech) Option (2) is correct because the verb should follow the subject in most sentences. Option (1) is incorrect because the comma correctly sets off the introductory element. Option (3) is incorrect because the number two is the correct word in this sentence. Option (4) is incorrect because the possessive isn't necessary.

9. **(2) insert a comma after term life** (Parts of speech) Option (2) is correct because the individual nouns forming a compound subject of three or more nouns must be separated by commas. Option (1) is incorrect because a comma is necessary after the first noun in the series. Option (3) is incorrect because every sentence needs a verb. Option (4) is incorrect because offer is spelled correctly.

10. **(1) insert is after insurance** (Parts of speech) Option (1) is correct because every sentence must have a verb. Option (2) is incorrect because semicolons are used between independent clauses. Option (3) is incorrect because the possessive pronoun its is the correct word in this sentence. Option (4) is incorrect because the possessive is necessary.

11. **(1) move can after How** (Parts of speech) Option (1) is correct because when the verb in a question consists of two or more words, part of the verb appears before the subject, and the other part appears after it. Option (2) is incorrect because both parts of the verb would come before the subject. Option (3) is incorrect because the pronoun them correctly stands in for an already named noun. Option (4) is incorrect because no strong emotion is shown.

Lesson 11

All items in this section are related to rules of usage.

GED Practice: Subject-Verb Agreement
(Pages 110–112)

1. **(2) change hope to hopes** (Subject-verb agreement) Option (2) is correct because the subject Vince requires the singular verb form hopes. Option (1) is incorrect because the possessive isn't necessary. Option (3) is incorrect because sign is not the main verb that must agree with the subject in this sentence. Option (4) is incorrect because baseball is a common noun and should not be capitalized.

2. **(5) no correction is necessary** (Usage/Subject-verb agreement; Mechanics/Capitalization) Option (5) is correct because the plural verb form have offered agrees with the plural subject Firebirds. Option (1) is incorrect because the subject should be plural. Option (2) is incorrect because Firebirds requires a plural verb form. Option (3) is incorrect because the action part of the verb does not need to change, only the helping verb. Option (4) is incorrect because spring is the name of a season and should not be capitalized.

3. **(1) change are to is** (Subject-verb agreement) Option (1) is correct because the subject of the sentence, opportunity, requires the third-person singular verb form is. Options (2) and (3) are not singular forms of the verb be. Option (4) is incorrect because the word opportunity is spelled correctly.

4. **(3) change plays to play** (Subject-verb agreement) Option (3) is correct because the compound subject requires the plural verb form play. Option (1) is incorrect because the word two, a number, is used correctly. Option (2) is incorrect because the phrase Raul and Al, an appositive, must be set off by two commas. Option (4) is incorrect because sandlot is a common noun and should not be capitalized.

5. **(5) no correction is necessary** (Subject-verb agreement/Capitalization) Option (1) is incorrect because proper nouns are capitalized. Option (2) is incorrect because neither and nor go together. Option (3) is incorrect because the verb have agrees with friends. Option (4) is incorrect because the possessive isn't necessary.

6. **(4) change are to is** (Subject-verb agreement) Option (4) is correct because team is one group acting as a whole unit; therefore, a singular verb form is required. Option (1) is incorrect because team is a common noun and should not be capitalized. Option (2) is incorrect because the possessive isn't necessary. Option (3) is incorrect because were is not a singular verb form.

7. **(1) change are to is** (Subject-verb agreement) Option (1) is correct because a singular verb form is needed to agree with the singular subject someone. Options (2) and (3) are incorrect because were and be are not singular verb forms. Option (4) is incorrect because the action verb does not need to change to make the subject and verb agree; the word bounds has a meaning different from what is meant.

8. **(1) change want to wants** (Subject-verb agreement) Option (1) is correct because the verb wants matches the singular subject Anna. Option (2) is incorrect because verbs do not show possession. Option (3) is incorrect because a prepositional phrase should not be separated from the rest of the sentence by a comma. Option (4) is incorrect because movie is a common noun and should not be capitalized.

9. **(2) change has to have** (Subject-verb agreement) Option (2) is correct because the verb have matches the plural subject Hahns. Option (1) is incorrect because the possessive isn't necessary. Options (3) and (4) are incorrect because the words <u>against</u> and <u>fourth</u> are spelled correctly.

10. **(3) change <u>is</u> to <u>are</u>** (Subject-verb agreement) Option (3) is correct because the third-person plural verb <u>are</u> matches the plural noun <u>things</u>. Options (1) and (2) are incorrect because <u>They're</u>, a contraction meaning "they are," and <u>Their</u>, a possessive pronoun, would not make sense in the sentence. Option (4) is incorrect because <u>be</u> is not a plural verb form.

11. **(4) change <u>do</u> to <u>does</u>** (Subject-verb agreement) Option (4) is correct because the verb <u>does</u> agrees with the singular subject <u>Jim</u>. Options (1) and (3) are incorrect because the phrase <u>Anna's husband</u> should be set off by commas. Option (2) is incorrect because <u>husband</u> is a common noun and should not be capitalized.

12. **(5) no correction is necessary** (Subject-verb agreement/Parts of speech/Commas) Option (1) is incorrect because <u>prefers</u> agrees with <u>He</u>. Option (2) is incorrect because there is no such verb form as <u>to goes</u>. Option (3) is incorrect because you must use <u>to</u> plus the present form of the verb to form the infinitive. Option (4) is incorrect because there is no reason to add a comma.

13. **(2) change the spelling of <u>pursuades</u> to <u>persuades</u>** (Subject-verb agreement/Spelling/End punctuation) Option (2) is correct because <u>persuades</u> is the correct spelling. Therefore Options (1) and (3) are incorrect. Option (4) is incorrect because the sentence doesn't show strong feeling.

14. **(1) change the first <u>go</u> to <u>goes</u>** (Subject-verb agreement/Commas) Option (1) is correct because the singular verb <u>goes</u> agrees with <u>Anna</u>. Option (2) is incorrect because an introductory dependent clause and an independent clause are separated by a comma. Option (3) is incorrect because a semicolon separates two independent clauses. Option (4) is incorrect because the future tense requires the simple form of the verb.

15. **(4) change <u>are</u> to <u>is</u>** (Subject-verb agreement) <u>Are</u> agrees with the singular subject <u>Ms. Boles</u>. Option (1) is incorrect because a pair of commas is needed to set off the appositive the warehouse <u>manager</u>. In option (2), <u>Boles</u> must be capitalized because it is a proper noun. Option (3) is incorrect

because <u>manager</u> is a common noun and should not be capitalized.

16. **(4) change <u>is</u> to <u>are</u>** (Subject-verb agreement) <u>Are</u> agrees with the compound subject, <u>Veterans Day holiday</u> and <u>Thanksgiving holiday</u>. Option (1) is incorrect because <u>decides</u> agrees with <u>she</u>. Option (2) is incorrect because <u>Day</u> must be capitalized as part of the name of the holiday. Option (3) is incorrect because <u>holiday</u> is a common noun and should not be capitalized.

17. **(2) change <u>disagree</u> to <u>disagrees</u>** (Subject-verb agreement) The word <u>union</u> is one group acting together; therefore, the singular verb form <u>disagrees</u> is correct. Option (2) is incorrect because <u>union</u> is a common noun and should not be capitalized. In option (3) the essential clause <u>to cancel . . .</u> should not be separated from the rest of the sentence. Option (4) is incorrect because only one holiday is referred to in this sentence.

18. **(1) change <u>points</u> to <u>point</u>** (Subject-verb agreement) Option (1) is correct because <u>point</u> agrees with the compound plural subject <u>Ms. Cervantes and Mr. Murray</u>. Option (2) is incorrect because a comma should not be used to separate the essential clause <u>that the company . . .</u> from the rest of the sentence. Option (3) is incorrect because the verb <u>has</u> agrees with the singular subject <u>company</u>. Option (4) is incorrect because the possessive isn't necessary.

19. **(3) change <u>is</u> to <u>are</u>** (Subject-verb agreement) Option (3) is correct because <u>are</u> agrees with the nearest subject, <u>workers</u>, which is plural. Option (1) is an incorrect spelling. Option (2) is incorrect because <u>workers</u> is a common noun and should not be capitalized. Option (4) is incorrect because <u>was</u> is a singular verb form.

GED Mini-Test: Lesson 11 (Page 113)

1. **(2) change <u>is</u> to <u>are</u>** (Subject-verb agreement) Option (2) is correct because <u>are</u> agrees with the compound subject <u>Levi and his partners</u>. Option (1) is incorrect because <u>partners</u> is a common noun and should not be capitalized. Option (3) is incorrect because <u>advertise</u> is spelled correctly. Option (4) is incorrect because the possessive pronoun <u>their</u> is correct.

2. **(1) change <u>feels</u> to <u>feel</u>** (Subject-verb agreement) Option (1) is correct because <u>feel</u>

agrees with the compound subject Evie and John. Option (2) is incorrect because the dependent clause should not be separated from the rest of the sentence by a comma. Option (3) is incorrect because money is a common noun and should not be capitalized. Option (4) is incorrect because there is no reason to set off the prepositional phrase into billboard publicity with a comma.

3. **(2) change believes to believe** (Subject-verb agreement) Option (2) is correct because believe agrees with the compound subject Corey and Levi. Option (1) is incorrect because the first word in a sentence must be capitalized. Option (3) is incorrect because the essential clause beginning with that should not be set off with a comma. Option (4) is incorrect because the plural verb are does not agree with the singular subject of the dependent clause, combination.

4. **(3) change wants to want** (Subject-verb agreement) Option (3) is correct because the plural verb want agrees with the nearest subject, partners. Option (1) is incorrect because nor must be paired with neither. Option (2) is incorrect because no possession is shown. Option (4) is incorrect because the homonym waist would not make sense in the sentence.

5. **(5) no correction is necessary** (Punctuation/Semicolon; Subject-verb agreement; Spelling) Option (1) is incorrect because the plural verb have agrees with the plural subject several. Option (2) is incorrect because interviewed is spelled correctly. Option (3) is incorrect because the semicolon correctly separates two independent clauses. Option (4) is incorrect because the verb is agrees with the singular subject Levi.

Lesson 12

All items in this section are related to rules of usage.

GED Practice: Irregular Verbs (Pages 116–118)

1. **(3) change shaked to shaken** (Irregular verbs) Option (3) is correct because the past participle is needed with the helping verb was. Option (1) is incorrect because were is a plural form and would not agree with the singular subject. Options (2) and (4) are not correct past participle forms of shake.

2. **(2) change swear to sworn** (Irregular verbs) Option (2) is correct because sworn is the past

participle form of swear, which is needed with the helping verb have. Options (1) and (3) are incorrect past participle forms. Option (4) is incorrect because appointment is singular and the singular verb was is needed.

3. **(3) change wrote to written** (Irregular verbs) Option (3) is correct because written is the past participle form of the verb write, which is needed with the helping verb had. Options (1) and (2) are not correct past participle forms. Option (4) is incorrect because address is spelled correctly.

4. **(5) no correction is necessary** (Usage/ Irregular verbs; Mechanics/Capitalization) Option (5) is correct because went is the correct past form of the verb go. Options (1), (2), and (3) are not correct past forms. Option (4) is incorrect because building is a common noun and should not be capitalized.

5. **(4) change sawed to saw** (Irregular verbs) Option (4) is correct because saw is the correct past form of the verb see. Option (1) is incorrect because their is a possessive pronoun and no possession is shown. Options (2) and (3) are incorrect because they are not past forms.

6. **(1) change drived to drove** (Irregular verbs) Option (1) is correct because drove is the past form of the verb drive. Options (2) and (3) are not correct past forms. Option (4) is incorrect because there is no reason to use a comma to separate the prepositional phrase from the rest of the sentence.

7. **(1) change knowed to knew** (Subject-verb agreement) Option (1) is correct because knew is the correct past form of the verb know. Option (2) is incorrect because known needs a helping verb. Option (3) is incorrect because the preposition for, not the number four, is correct. Option (4) is incorrect because spring is the name of a season and should not be capitalized.

8. **(2) change eaten to ate** (Irregular verbs) Option (2) is correct because ate is the correct past form of the verb eat. Options (1), (3), and (4) are incorrect because they are not past forms of eat.

9. **(2) change weared to wore** (Irregular verbs) Option (2) is correct because wore is the correct past form of the verb wear. Options (1) and (3) are incorrect because they are not

correct past forms. Option (4) is incorrect because jogging is a common noun and should not be capitalized.

10. **(2) change drive to drove** (Irregular verbs) Option (2) is correct because drove is the correct past form of drive. Options (1) and (3) are incorrect because they are not correct past forms. Option (4) is incorrect because drive is not the past participle form of drive and is not used with a helping verb.

11. **(4) change run to ran** (Irregular verbs) Option (4) is correct because ran is the correct past form of run. Option (1) is incorrect because the possessive pronoun their is not needed. Option (2) is incorrect because they're, meaning "they are," would not make sense. Option (3) is incorrect because runned is not the past form of run.

12. **(3) change swum to swam** (Irregular verbs) Option (3) is correct because swam is the correct past form of swim. Options (1) and (2) are not past forms of swim. Option (4) is incorrect because swum cannot express a condition or be used reflexively.

13. **(5) no correction is necessary** (Irregular verbs) Option (1) is incorrect because the past tense is needed. Option (2) is incorrect because rided is not a past form of ride. Option (3) is incorrect because ridden requires a helping verb. Option (4) is incorrect because had ridden is the past perfect form of the verb, and the past tense is needed.

14. **(2) change knew to known** (Irregular verbs) Option (2) is correct because known is the correct past participle form of the verb know; the past participle form is required because of the helping verb had. Options (1), (3), and (4) are not past participle forms.

15. **(2) change gave to given** (Irregular verbs) Option (2) is correct because given is the correct past participle form of the verb give. Option (1) is incorrect because gaved is not a past participle form. Option (3) is incorrect because birthday is a common noun and should not be capitalized. Option (4) is incorrect because were does not agree with the singular subject plant.

16. **(1) change grew to grown** (Irregular verbs) Option (1) is correct because grown is the correct past participle form of the verb grow. Options (2) and (3) are incorrect because they

are not past participles. Option (4) is incorrect because passed, meaning "to go by," would not make sense in the sentence.

17. **(3) change blown to blew** (Irregular verbs) Option (3) is correct because blew is the correct past form of the verb blow. Option (1) is incorrect because occasion is spelled correctly. Option (2) is incorrect because blowed is not the past form of blow. Option (4) is incorrect because the past form blew is not used with a helping verb.

18. **(1) change shook to shaken** (Irregular verbs) Option (1) is correct because shaken is the correct past participle form of the verb shake which is needed with the helping verb had. Option (2) is incorrect because shaked is not a past participle. Options (3) and (4) are incorrect because its is the correct possessive form.

19. **(5) no correction is necessary** (Irregular verbs) Option (1) is incorrect because the past tense is needed. Option (2) is incorrect because heared is not the correct past tense of hear. Option (3) is incorrect because the plural verb like agrees with the plural plants. Option (4) is incorrect because the present tense is needed in the relative clause.

20. **(2) change begun to began** (Irregular verbs) Option (2) is correct because began is the correct past form of the verb begin. Option (1) is incorrect because beginned is not a form of begin. Option (3) is incorrect because sanging is not a form of the verb sing. Option (4) is incorrect because the possessive pronoun his does not need an apostrophe.

GED Mini-Test: Lesson 12 (Page 119)

1. **(3) change know to known** (Irregular verbs) Option (3) is correct because known is the correct past participle form of the verb know. Options (1) and (2) are incorrect because neither has nor had can work with know as a past participle; additionally has can be used only with a singular subject. Option (4) is incorrect because knew is the past form, not the past participle.

2. **(4) change began to begun** (Irregular verbs) Option (4) is correct because begun is the past participle form and is used with the helping verb has. Option (1) is incorrect because were does not agree with a singular subject. Options (2) and (3) are incorrect because neither is the past participle form.

UNIT 2

3. **(1) insert have before grown** (Irregular verbs) Option (1) is correct because have grown is the correct past participle form of the verb grow. Options (2) and (4) are incorrect because neither is the past form of the verb grow. Option (3) is incorrect because the singular verb grows does not agree in number with customers.

4. **(3) take out have** (Irregular verbs) Option (3) is correct because choose is the correct present-tense form and does not need a helping verb. Option (1) is incorrect because are does not agree with the singular subject problem. Option (2) is incorrect because choosed is not the correct past form of choose. Option (4) is incorrect because look does not agree with the singular subject produce.

5. **(1) change drove to driven** (Irregular verbs) Option (1) is correct because driven is the correct past-participle form of the verb drive. Option (2) is incorrect because the past-participle form driven is needed, not the present-tense drive. Option (3) is incorrect because the semicolon correctly separates two independent clauses. Option (4) is incorrect because there is no reason to divide the prepositional phrase at organic groceries and farmer's markets.

Lesson 13

All items in this section are related to rules of usage.

GED Practice: Verb Tenses (Pages 124–125)

1. **(3) change begun to began** (Verb tenses) Option (3) is correct because began is past tense; the action in the sentence happened in the past. Options (1), (2), and (4) are not past tense verb forms.

2. **(3) change drived to drive** (Verb tenses) Option (3) is correct because the future tense is formed by adding will to the present form, drive. Options (1) and (2) are incorrect because shall drived is not a correct future tense form. There is no reason for the comma in option (4).

3. **(4) change have to has** (Verb tenses) Option (4) is correct because has is used to form the present perfect tense when the subject is singular. Option (1) is incorrect because Ms. is a title attached to a proper name and should be capitalized. Option (2) is incorrect because the subject and verb should not be separated by a comma. Option (3) is incorrect because

was earned could be used only if the action happened to the subject; in this case, the subject Ms. Hauser is doing the action.

4. **(3) change being to been** (Verb tenses) Option (3) is correct because been is the correct past participle for the verb be. The past participle is needed because the verb is in past perfect tense. Option (1) is incorrect because a comma is needed to set off an introductory element. Option (2) is incorrect because has been is present perfect tense and the action is clearly in the past. Option (4) is incorrect because license is spelled correctly.

5. **(2) change maked to made** (Irregular verbs) Option (2) is correct because made is the correct past participle form of the verb make. Option (1) is incorrect because the helping verb was is correctly used with the past participle. Option (3) is incorrect because it is not the past participle form of make. Careful is spelled correctly, so option (4) is incorrect.

6. **(5) has trained** (Verb tenses) Option (5) is correct because present perfect tense is needed. This action has occurred in the past and will continue to happen. Options (1), (2), (3), and (4) are not present perfect tense verbs.

7. **(2) replace will train with trained** (Verb tenses) Option (2) is correct because trained is the correct past form of the verb train; the word recently suggests the action has already happened. Option (1) is incorrect because train is not past tense. Option (3) is incorrect because trane is not a correct spelling. Option (4) is incorrect because the word male is used correctly.

8. **(4) said** (Verb tenses) Option (4) is correct because past tense is needed; the word touched is a clue that this action took place in the past. Options (1), (2), (3), and (5) are incorrect because none is a correct past-tense form of the verb say.

9. **(4) shifted** (Verb tenses) The action described took place in the past; therefore, option (4) is correct because shifted is the correct past tense form. Options (1), (2), (3), and (5) are incorrect because none is a correct past tense form.

10. **(1) remove has** (Verb tenses) The verb learned is a clue that past tense is needed; the helping verb has makes the tense present perfect. Therefore, option (1) is correct because

heard is the correct past form of the verb hear. Option (2) is incorrect because the original word is used correctly. Options (3) and (4) are incorrect because neither expresses past tense; also, option (4) can agree only with a plural subject.

11. **(3) change learned to taught** (Verb tenses) Option (3) is correct because taught is a past participle and it means "to give knowledge." Options (1) and (2) are incorrect because changing the tense will not correct the problem of wrong verb usage. Option (4) is incorrect because teaching is not the past participle form.

GED Mini-Test: Lesson 13 (Pages 126–127)

1. **(3) has been forgetting** (Verb tenses) Option (3) is correct because a present perfect tense is needed. Options (1), (4), and (5) are incorrect because none is a correct verb form. Option (2) is incorrect because the word recently indicates the action is past or continuing into the present, not future.

2. **(3) change was to were** (Verb tenses) Option (3) is correct because were is correct when a wish is being expressed; therefore, options (2) and (4) are incorrect. Option (1) is incorrect because wish does not agree with the singular subject she.

3. **(1) change decide to decides** (Subject-verb agreement) Option (1) is correct because decides agrees with the singular subject Ms. Barlow. Option (2) is incorrect because it is an incorrect verb form. Option (3) is incorrect because have does not agree with the subject Ms. Barlow. Option (4) is incorrect because system is singular and requires the singular verb is.

4. **(4) change was needed to needs** (Verb tenses) Option (4) is correct because present tense is necessary. Option (1) is incorrect because written needs a helping verb. Option (2) is incorrect because wrote is not the past participle form. Option (3) is incorrect because the plural verb were does not agree with the singular subject she.

5. **(1) proceeds** (Usage/Verb tenses and subject-verb agreement; Mechanics/Spelling) Option (1) is correct because proceeds is spelled correctly, is the correct verb tense, and agrees with the singular subject she. Option (2) is incorrect because it is the wrong verb tense. Option (3) is incorrect because proceeds is

spelled correctly. Option (4) is incorrect because future perfect tense changes the meaning of the sentence. In option (5), proceed does not agree with the singular subject she.

6. **(2) change will have used to will use** (Verb tenses) Option (2) is correct because future tense is necessary; the action use will occur next month. Option (1) is incorrect because feeled is not the past tense form of feel. Option (3) is incorrect because possession is not shown. Option (4) is incorrect because too, meaning "also," is used correctly.

7. **(5) no correction is necessary** (Verb tenses) Option (1) is incorrect because the present perfect progressive form requires the helping verb form has been. Option (2) is incorrect because worked cannot be used with has been. Option (3) is incorrect because bookstore is not a proper noun. Option (4) is incorrect because one, meaning the number, is the correct word in the sentence.

8. **(3) remove have** (Verb tenses) Option (3) is correct because will receive is a future tense verb and this future action will occur after the action from the first present perfect verb. Option (1) is incorrect because completion of the probation period is not a past event. Option (2) is incorrect because it changes the meaning of the sentence. Option (4) is incorrect because have receive is not a correct verb form.

9. **(4) change helped to helping** (Verb tenses) Option (4) is correct because this is an action that is ongoing, so the -ing ending is needed. Option (1) is incorrect because a comma should not separate the subject and the verb. Option (2) is incorrect because were does not agree with the singular subject part. Option (3) is incorrect because it is not a correct verb form.

10. **(3) change are to is** (Subject-verb agreement) Option (3) is correct because is agrees with the singular subject he. Option (1) is incorrect because it does not result in a correct verb form. Option (2) is incorrect because were does not agree with the singular subject. Option (4) is incorrect because the present form is needed in an infinitive.

11. **(2) change taught to teach** (Verb tenses) Option (2) is correct because future tense is constructed using the present form of the verb. Option (1) is incorrect because learn

Answers and Explanations

means "to receive instruction"; the manager is giving, not receiving, the instruction. Option (3) is incorrect because teached is not a form of the verb teach. Option (4) is incorrect because microfilm is not a proper name and should not be capitalized.

Lesson 14

All items in this section are related to rules of usage.

**GED Practice: Personal Pronouns
(Pages 131–133)**

1. **(2) change I to me** (Personal pronouns) Option (2) is correct because an object pronoun is needed as a direct object of the verb hit. Option (1) is incorrect because mine is used only when it stands alone. Option (3) is incorrect because the pronoun is not both the doer and receiver of the action, nor is it used for emphasis. Option (4) is incorrect because us is an object pronoun and should not be used as a subject.

2. **(4) change their's to theirs** (Personal pronouns) Option (4) is correct because an apostrophe is not used in the possessive pronoun theirs. Option (1) is incorrect because his does not need an apostrophe. Option (2) is incorrect because was does not agree with the plural compound subject. Option (3) is incorrect because their is used only before a noun.

3. **(3) change I to me** (Personal pronouns) Option (3) is correct because my wife or I is a direct object, which requires an object pronoun, me. Options (1) and (2) are incorrect because itself is correctly used as an intensive pronoun; it gives emphasis to accident. Option (4) is incorrect because myself is not an object pronoun.

4. **(3) change her to herself** (Personal pronouns) Option (3) is correct because a reflexive pronoun is needed; the subject my wife did the action and received the action. Option (1) is incorrect because mine should be used only when it stands alone. Options (2) and (4) are incorrect because neither is a reflexive pronoun, no possession should be shown, and her's is not a correct pronoun form.

5. **(4) replace theirselves with themselves** (Personal pronouns) Option (4) is correct because theirselves is not a word and is always incorrect; the proper reflexive pronoun

is themselves. Option (1) is incorrect because the apostrophe replaces the o in did not. Option (2) is incorrect because possessive personal pronouns never contain apostrophes. Option (3) is incorrect because a comma is the correct punctuation before a conjunction that joins two independent clauses.

6. **(3) change ours to our** (Personal pronouns) Option (3) is correct because ours should be used only when it stands alone. Option (1) is incorrect because meeted is not a correct past form. Option (2) is incorrect because this sentence requires a past-tense verb. Option (4) is incorrect because the writer shares in the possession being expressed; therefore, our is needed.

7. **(3) change Us to We** (Personal pronouns) Option (3) is correct because we is a subject pronoun. Options (1) and (2) are incorrect because them and him are object pronouns. Option (4) is incorrect because the action is happening in the present; therefore, the past participle is not needed.

8. **(4) change there to their** (Personal pronouns) Their is needed to show possession. Option (1) is incorrect because a future-tense verb does not use the past participle part of the verb. Option (2) is incorrect because parents is a common noun and should not be capitalized. Option (3) is incorrect because they're, meaning "they are," would not make sense.

9. **(4) change yourself to you** (Personal pronouns) Option (4) is correct because you is a subject pronoun; yourself is not. Option (1) is incorrect because an object pronoun is needed. Options (2) and (3) are incorrect because neither is a subject pronoun.

10. **(1) change us to our** (Personal pronouns) Option (1) is correct because a possessive pronoun is needed. Options (2) and (3) are incorrect because neither is a possessive pronoun. Option (4) is incorrect because experience is spelled correctly.

11. **(3) replace them with they** (Personal pronouns) Option (3) is correct because the subject pronoun they is needed; a comparison using as is being made with the subject We. Option (1) is incorrect because Us is an object pronoun; the subject pronoun We is required here. Option (2) is incorrect because the e should be dropped when adding the suffix -ing

to hope. Option (4) is incorrect because their is a possessive pronoun, and the subject pronoun they is required.

12. **(2) change I to me** (Personal pronouns) Option (2) is correct because an object pronoun is needed for a direct object of the verb informed. Option (1) is incorrect because we is not an object pronoun. Options (3) and (4) are incorrect because a present-tense verb is needed in the clause that three fourths . . .

13. **(1) change concern to concerns** (Subject-verb agreement/Personal pronouns/Verb tenses/Spelling) Option (1) is correct because the singular verb concerns agrees with the singular subject It. Option (2) is incorrect because the object pronoun me is needed in this sentence. Option (3) is incorrect because the verb is agrees with the noun statistic. Option (4) is incorrect because so, meaning "very," is the correct word in this sentence.

14. **(2) change me to I** (Personal pronouns) Option (2) is correct because a subject pronoun is needed. Option (1) is incorrect because us is not a subject pronoun. Option (3) is incorrect because a comma should not separate the subject and the verb. Option (4) is incorrect because the singular verb drives does not agree with the compound subject.

15. **(3) change Us to We** (Personal pronouns) Option (3) is correct because a subject pronoun is needed. Options (1) and (2) are incorrect because neither is a subject pronoun. Option (4) is incorrect because takes is a singular verb and does not agree with the plural subject.

16. **(5) no correction is necessary** (Subject-verb agreement/Spelling/Capitalization) Option (1) is incorrect because the singular verb has offered agrees with the singular subject. Option (2) is incorrect because the final r in offer is not doubled when the suffix -ed is added. Option (3) is incorrect because anyone, meaning "any person," is correct. Option (4) is incorrect because the name of a city is capitalized.

17. **(1) change you're to your** (Personal pronouns) Option (1) is correct because a possessive pronoun is needed before name. The contraction you're, which means "you are," does not make sense in the sentence; therefore, option (2) is incorrect. Option (3) is incorrect because you are is the subject and

verb of the if clause. Option (4) is incorrect because ride is used as a noun in this sentence, not as a verb.

GED Mini-Test: Lesson 14 (Pages 134–135)

1. **(5) no correction is necessary** (Subject-verb agreement and verb tenses; Mechanics/Punctuation—overuse of commas) Option (1) is incorrect because lives does not agree with the plural subject we. Options (2) and (3) are incorrect because neither results in a correct verb form. Option (4) is incorrect because there is no reason to separate the prepositional phrase from the rest of the sentence with a comma.

2. **(2) change its to it** (Personal pronouns) Option (2) is correct because its is a possessive pronoun; a subject pronoun is needed. Option (1) is incorrect because they does not agree with the singular verb has. Option (3) is incorrect because them is not a subject pronoun. Option (4) is incorrect because the helping verb is needed to create the present perfect tense.

3. **(2) change ours to our** (Personal pronouns) Option (2) is correct because ours should be used only when the possessive stands alone. Option (1) is incorrect because surrounds does not agree with the plural subject billboards. Option (3) is incorrect because the possessive isn't necessary. Option (4) is incorrect because the contraction they're, meaning "they are," would not make sense in the sentence.

4. **(4) change them to they** (Personal pronouns) Option (4) is correct because a subject pronoun is necessary. Option (1) is incorrect because ours should be used only when the possessive stands alone. Option (2) is incorrect because are is not a possessive pronoun. Option (3) is incorrect because theirselves is not a word.

5. **(3) change me to I** (Personal pronouns) Option (3) is correct because a subject pronoun is needed in the compound subject. Options (1) and (2) are incorrect because neither is a subject pronoun. Option (4) is incorrect because committee is spelled correctly.

6. **(5) no correction is necessary** (Personal pronouns) Option (1) is incorrect because your is not a subject pronoun. Options (2), (3), and (4) are incorrect because we, they, and I are not object pronouns.

Answers and Explanations

7. **(1) change Us to We** (Personal pronouns/Subject-verb agreement/Verb tenses/Spelling) Option (1) is correct because a subject pronoun is needed. Option (2) is incorrect because the plural verb are agrees with the plural subject. Option (3) is incorrect because the present progressive form requires the present participle. Option (4) is incorrect because altogether, meaning "completely" or "totally," is the correct word in this sentence.

8. **(3) change hers to her** (Personal pronouns) Option (3) is correct because hers is used only when it stands alone. Options (1) and (2) are incorrect because neither is a correct verb-tense form. Option (4) is incorrect because herself is not a possessive pronoun.

9. **(2) change herself to her** (Personal pronouns) Option (2) is correct because her is an object of the verb help. The course is the doer of the action, not Joyce, so a reflexive pronoun is incorrect. Option (1) is incorrect because a subject pronoun is needed. Option (3) is incorrect because the word understand is a clue that a present-tense form is needed. Option (4) is incorrect because it results in an incorrect verb form.

10. **(5) no correction is necessary** (Personal pronouns, irregular verbs, and verb tenses) Option (1) is incorrect because a subject pronoun is needed. Option (2) is incorrect because learned, meaning "received instruction," is the correct verb; also, teached is not the correct past form of the verb teach. Option (3) is incorrect because the sentence requires a present-tense verb. Option (4) is incorrect because adult is singular and requires the singular verb form reads.

11. **(2) change herself to she** (Personal pronouns) Option (2) is correct because a subject pronoun is needed in the compound subject. Option (1) is incorrect because her is not a subject pronoun. Options (3) and (4) are incorrect because the possessive pronoun their is correct.

12. **(3) change too to two** (Spelling/Personal pronouns/Commas) Option (3) is correct because two, the number, is the correct word in this sentence. Option (1) is incorrect because the subject pronoun they is correct. Option (2) is incorrect because there is no reason to add a comma. Option (4) is incorrect because hours, a unit of time is the correct word in this sentence.

Lesson 15

All items in this section are related to rules of usage.

GED Practice: Pronouns and Antecedents (Pages 138–139)

1. **(2) change its to my** (Pronouns and antecedents/Commas) Option (2) is correct because the pronoun my agrees in person and number with the antecedent I. Option (1) is incorrect because a subject pronoun, not a possessive pronoun, is correct. Option (3) is incorrect because mine is used only when it stands alone. Option (4) is incorrect because a comma separates two independent clauses joined by but.

2. **(4) change her to their** (Pronouns and antecedents) Option (4) is correct because their agrees in number with the plural subject Taylors. Option (1) is incorrect because Taylors is a proper noun and should be capitalized. Option (2) is incorrect because is does not agree with the plural subject. Option (3) is incorrect because the past participle made does not make sense in the sentence.

3. **(3) change their to her** (Pronouns and antecedents) Option (3) is correct because her agrees with the singular compound subject Either Rita or Virginia; it also agrees in gender with the subject. Option (1) is incorrect because nor should not be paired with either. Option (2) is incorrect because offered is the correct verb tense. Option (4) is incorrect because his does not agree in gender with the subject.

4. **(3) said his wife** (Pronouns and antecedents) Option (3) is correct because his agrees in number and gender with the antecedent Fred Curtis. Option (2) is incorrect because say does not agree in number with the subject, nor is it the correct tense for this sentence. Option (4) is incorrect because her does not agree in gender with the antecedent subject. Option (5) is incorrect because wife is a common noun and should not be capitalized.

5. **(4) change her to his or her** (Pronouns and antecedents) Option (4) is correct because the antecedent is singular and the gender is not specified. Option (1) is incorrect because the plural people agrees with neither Each nor her. Option (2) is incorrect because brought, a past-tense verb, is not used with should. Option (3) is incorrect because their is a plural pronoun, which does not agree with the singular antecedent Each person.

6. **(4) change his to their** (Pronouns and antecedents) Option (4) is correct because *their* agrees in number with the plural antecedent *Wellstons*. Options (1) and (2) are incorrect because the subject pronoun *I* is required: *me* is an object pronoun. Option (3) is incorrect because the singular pronoun *her* disagrees with its plural antecedent *Wellstons*.

7. **(4) change their to his or her** (Pronouns and antecedents) Option (4) is correct because the gender of the antecedent is unclear; an *employee* may be male or female. Option (1) is incorrect because the subject pronoun *I* is correctly used. Option (2) is incorrect because *compliment* meaning "congratulate," is used correctly; *complement*, means "something that completes." Option (3) is incorrect because *they're* is a contraction for "they are," which does not make sense in this sentence.

8. **(3) change his to their** (Pronouns and antecedents) Option (3) is correct because *their* agrees with the plural antecedent *plumbers*. Option (1) is incorrect because *plumbers* is the subject and possession is not meant. Option (2) is incorrect because *has* does not agree with the plural subject. Option (4) is incorrect because *his or her*, a singular compound pronoun, does not agree with the plural antecedent.

9. **(2) change their to his** (Pronouns and antecedents) Option (2) is correct because *his* agrees in number with the singular antecedent *Mr. Tim Bickel*. Option (1) is incorrect because *ours* should be used only when it stands alone. Option (3) is incorrect because *her* does not agree in gender with the antecedent. Option (4) is incorrect because a possessive, not a plural, is needed.

10. **(1) change her to their** (Pronouns and antecedents) Option (1) is correct because *their* agrees in number with the plural compound antecedent *Fran, Dora, and Carol*. Options (2) and (3) are incorrect because both are singular pronouns. Option (4) is incorrect because *has* does not agree with the plural subject.

11. **(1) change his to its** (Pronouns and antecedents) Option (1) is correct because the antecedent *company* requires a pronoun of neuter gender. Option (2) is incorrect because *it's*, meaning "it is," is not a possessive pronoun. Option (3) is incorrect because *their*

does not agree in number with *company*. Option (4) is incorrect because the apostrophe is needed to show possession.

12. **(5) no correction is necessary** (Pronouns and antecedents/Personal pronouns/Possessives/Spelling) Option (1) is incorrect because the possessive isn't necessary. Option (2) is incorrect because *they* is the subject of the independent clause. Option (3) is incorrect because the independent clause is in the future, not the past tense. Option (4) is incorrect because *theirselves* is not a word; the proper reflexive pronoun is *themselves*.

GED Mini-Test: Lesson 15 (Pages 140–141)

1. **(3) change Me and Joan to Joan and I** (Personal pronouns) Option (3) is correct because the subject pronoun *I* is needed and should come last in the compound subject. Options (1) and (2) are incorrect because neither makes both corrections. Option (4) is incorrect because *Tuesday's* is possessive and needs an apostrophe.

2. **(5) no correction is necessary** (Pronoun and antecedents) Option (1) is incorrect because *We* is a subject pronoun. Option (2) is incorrect because *our* is the correct possessive form. *Our's* is not a word. Option (3) is incorrect because *view* is spelled correctly. Option (4) is incorrect because it agrees with its singular antecedent *fire drill* in sentence 1.

3. **(2) change his to their** (Pronouns and antecedents) Option (2) is correct because *their* agrees in number with the plural antecedent *employees*. Option (1) is incorrect because *second* does not need to be capitalized since it is not part of a proper name. Option (3) is incorrect because *his or her* is singular and does not agree with the plural antecedent *employees*. Option (4) is incorrect because the past-tense form *rang* is not used with *did*.

4. **(3) change they to it** (Pronouns and antecedents) Option (3) is correct because *it* agrees with the singular antecedent *door*. Option (1) is incorrect because *myself* should not be used as a subject. Option (2) is incorrect because the preposition *through* is used correctly; *threw* is the past-tense of the verb *throw*. Option (4) is incorrect because *them* does not agree with the singular subject *it*. Option (5) is incorrect because the pronoun and antecedent do not agree.

Answers and Explanations

5. **(2) his** (Pronouns and antecedents) Option (2) is correct because <u>his</u> agrees in gender with the antecedent <u>Jason</u>. Option (1) is incorrect because <u>her</u> does not agree in gender with Jason. Option (3) is incorrect because <u>him</u> is an object pronoun, not a possessive form. Option (4) is incorrect because <u>their</u> does not agree in number with <u>Jason</u>. Option (5) is incorrect because <u>hers</u> does not agree in gender with <u>Jason</u>.

6. **(4) change their to his** (Pronouns and antecedents) Option (4) is correct because with a compound antecedent joined by <u>neither/nor</u>, the pronoun should agree with the nearer antecedent. <u>His</u> agrees with the singular antecedent, <u>Howard</u>. Options (1) and (2) are incorrect because <u>either/or</u> and <u>neither/nor</u> are the correct forms. Option (3) is incorrect because the sentence is in the past tense and <u>got</u> is the correct past-tense form.

7. **(3) change his to their** (Pronouns and antecedents) Option (3) is correct because the antecedent is plural, <u>the plant manager and the foreman</u>. Option (1) is incorrect because the apostrophe replaces the <u>o</u> in the contraction of <u>did not</u>. Option (2) is incorrect because <u>were</u> does not agree in number with its subject <u>exit</u>. Option (4) is incorrect because the singular <u>his or her</u> disagrees with the plural antecedent.

8. **(3) change her to she** (Personal pronouns) Option (3) is correct because the subject pronoun <u>she</u> is needed to go with the verb <u>needs</u>. Option (1) is incorrect because <u>have</u> does not agree in number with the singular subject <u>Jenny</u>. Option (2) is incorrect because <u>his or her</u> is not a subject pronoun. Option (4) is incorrect because <u>need</u> does not agree in number with the subject <u>she</u>.

9. **(3) change their to his or her** (Pronouns and antecedents) Option (3) is correct because the antecedent <u>he or she</u> agrees with the singular pronoun <u>Everyone</u>. Option (1) is incorrect because <u>knowledge</u> is spelled correctly. Option (2) is incorrect because <u>our</u> is a first-person pronoun, and a third-person pronoun is needed to agree with <u>Everyone</u>. Option (4) is incorrect because <u>procedures</u> is spelled correctly.

10. **(4) change he to she** (Pronouns and antecedents) Option (4) is correct because <u>she</u> agrees in gender with the antecedent <u>Joan</u>. Option (1) is incorrect because <u>let's</u>, a

contraction for "let us," requires an apostrophe. Option (2) is incorrect because <u>her</u> is a possessive pronoun, not a subject pronoun. Option (3) is incorrect because <u>him</u> is neither a subject nor a feminine gender pronoun.

11. **(4) change our to his or her** (Pronouns and antecedents) Option (4) is correct because the plural <u>our</u> must be changed to the singular <u>his or her</u> to agree in number with the singular antecedent <u>each employee</u>. Option (1) is incorrect because <u>There's</u> is the correct contraction of <u>There is</u>. Option (2) is incorrect because a comma is not needed. Option (3) is incorrect because <u>their</u> is a plural pronoun and <u>our</u> must be replaced by a singular pronoun.

12. **(3) change Us to We** (Pronouns) Option (3) is correct because <u>We</u> is a subject pronoun and agrees with the rest of the paragraph. Option (1) is incorrect since the singular verb <u>is</u> agrees with the subject <u>fire safety</u>. Option (2) is incorrect because the verb <u>taken</u> needs to be followed by the adverb <u>seriously</u>, not the adjective <u>serious</u>. Option (4) is incorrect since <u>must</u> cannot be followed by any form of the verb but <u>realize</u>.

Lesson 16

All items in this section are related to rules of usage.

GED Practice: Indefinite Pronouns
(Pages 145–146)

1. **(3) to wear his or her uniform** (Indefinite pronouns) Option (3) is correct because the indefinite pronoun and antecedent <u>everybody</u> requires a singular pronoun; <u>his or her</u> is the best choice because the gender is unclear. Options (2) and (4) are incorrect because <u>theirs</u> and <u>hers</u> are used only when they stand alone. Option (5) is incorrect because <u>its</u> does not agree in gender with its antecedent <u>everybody</u>.

2. **(3) change their gloves to his glove** (Indefinite pronouns) Option (3) is correct because a singular pronoun is needed to agree with the singular antecedent <u>Neither</u>. Option (1) is incorrect because <u>his</u> agrees in number with <u>Neither</u>. Option (2) is incorrect because <u>her</u> does not agree in gender. Option (4) is incorrect because a possessive pronoun is needed.

3. **(5) no correction is necessary**
(Usage/Indefinite pronouns and irregular verbs; Mechanics/Spelling—homonyms) Option (5) is correct because Who is correctly used as a subject. Options (1) and (2) are incorrect because neither Whom nor Whose can function as the subject of the verb left. Option (3) is incorrect because leaved is not a correct verb form. Option (4) is incorrect because here, meaning "a place," is used correctly.

4. **(2) change Whoever to Whomever**
(Indefinite pronouns) Option (2) is correct because Whomever is the object of the preposition to: this gum belongs to whomever. Option (1) is incorrect because Whosever is not a pronoun. Option (3) is incorrect because an object pronoun is needed. Option (4) is incorrect because the singular noun gum requires a singular verb, belongs.

5. **(4) replace nobody with anybody**
(Indefinite pronouns) Option (4) is correct because nobody and didn't create a double negative. Replacing nobody with anybody eliminates the double negative. Options (1) and (2) are incorrect because the plural possessive their is the correct word in this sentence. Option (3) is incorrect because them is the object of the preposition for; they is a subject pronoun.

6. **(4) change their to his or her** (Indefinite pronouns) Option (4) is correct because his or her agrees with the singular antecedent everyone. Options (1) and (2) are incorrect because advises and exercises are spelled correctly. Option (3) is incorrect because him is an object pronoun, not a possessive pronoun.

7. **(4) change her to his or her** (Indefinite pronouns) Option (4) is correct because the singular pronoun antecedent anyone does not have a clear gender. Option (1) is incorrect because medical is not part of a proper name and should not be capitalized. Option (2) is incorrect because the object pronoun whom cannot be used as a subject. Option (3) is incorrect because want does not agree with the singular subject anyone.

8. **(3) change her to his or her** (Indefinite pronouns) Option (3) is correct because everybody is singular but does not have a clear gender. Option (1) is incorrect because chose is the past form and is not used with

should. Option (2) is incorrect because the plural pronoun their does not agree with the singular antecedent everybody. Option (4) is incorrect because hers is a possessive pronoun that must stand alone.

9. **(4) change theirselves to themselves**
(Indefinite pronouns) Option (4) is correct because the plural themselves agrees with the plural antecedent most; theirselves is not a word. Options (1) and (2) are incorrect because a singular verb will not agree with the plural subject most. Option (3) is incorrect because himself is not plural and does not agree with the plural antecedent most.

10. **(2) change neither to either** (Indefinite pronouns) Option (2) is correct because a negative has already been used in the sentence, the word nothing; the word either has the same basic meaning as neither, but without the negative. Option (1) is incorrect because sees does not agree with the first-person singular subject. Options (3) and (4) are incorrect because both result in double negatives in the sentence.

11. **(2) replace are with is** (Indefinite pronouns) Option (2) is correct because the singular pronoun much requires the singular verb is. Option (1) is incorrect because Too, meaning "very," is the correct word in this sentence. Option (3) is incorrect because Too . . . chosen is an exact quote and needs to be preceded and followed by quotation marks. Option (4) is incorrect because the abbreviation for the title "Doctor" should be capitalized.

GED Mini-Test: Lesson 16 (Page 147)
1. **(4) change their to his or her** (Indefinite pronouns) Option (4) is correct because the antecedent Anyone is singular with unclear gender. Option (1) is incorrect because the plural verb like does not agree with the singular subject Anyone. Option (2) is incorrect because the plural verb are does not agree with the singular subject Anyone. Option (3) is incorrect because the antecedent Anyone has an unclear gender.

2. **(3) change his to their** (Indefinite pronouns) Option (3) is correct because the plural possessive pronoun their agrees with the plural antecedent and subject several. Option (1) is incorrect because the singular verb has does not agree with the plural subject. Option (2) is incorrect because his or her is singular

and does not agree with the plural subject. Option (4) is incorrect because theirs is a possessive pronoun that it used only when it stands alone.

3. **(3) change his or her to their** (Indefinite pronouns) Option (3) is correct because a plural pronoun is needed to agree with the plural antecedent few; his or her is singular. Option (1) is incorrect because has does not agree with the plural subject few. Option (2) is incorrect because the present perfect tense is formed with the verb's past participle, not the present form of the verb. Option (4) is incorrect because theirselves is not a word.

4. **(2) change whom to who** (Indefinite pronouns) Option (2) is correct because the pronoun who is needed as the subject of the clause. Option (1) is incorrect because the commas are needed to set off a nonessential clause. Option (3) is incorrect because whose shows possession, which is not necessary in this sentence. Option (4) is incorrect because are does not agree with the singular subject Karla.

5. **(4) change her to his or her** (Indefinite pronouns) Option (4) is correct because a singular pronoun is needed to agree with the antecedent someone, but the gender is unclear. Option (1) is incorrect because we requires the plural verb form need. Option (2) is incorrect because hers is used only when it stands alone and is specifically feminine gender. Option (3) is incorrect because their is plural and does not agree with the antecedent someone.

6. **(1) change Whomever to Whoever** (Indefinite pronouns) Option (1) is correct because Whoever is used as a subject. Option (2) is incorrect because Whosever is not a correct pronoun form. Options (3) and (4) are incorrect because neither plural verb form can agree with the singular subject.

Lesson 17

All items in this section are related to rules of usage.

GED Practice: Adjectives and Adverbs
(Pages 150–151)

1. **(4) change compactly to compact** (Adjectives and adverbs) Option (4) is correct because an adjective is needed to describe the stroller; compactly is an adverb. Options (1) and (2) are incorrect because both are plural verb forms that do not agree with the singular

subject. Option (3) is incorrect because no comparison is made in this sentence; also, compacter is an incorrect comparative form.

2. **(4) change quick to quickly** (Adjectives and adverbs) Option (4) is correct because an adverb is needed to describe how the cloth fades. The word quick is an adjective; quickly is an adverb. Option (1) is incorrect because the present-tense is is consistent with the verb tense used throughout the paragraph. Option (2) is incorrect because easily is correctly used as an adverb; it tells how washable. Option (3) is incorrect because they does not agree with the singular antecedent padding.

3. **(3) change good to well** (Adjectives and adverbs) Option (3) is correct because an adverb is needed to tell how the hood held up; well is an adverb. Options (1) and (2) are incorrect because no comparison is made in this sentence. Option (4) is incorrect because goodest is not a correct adverb form.

4. **(3) change lightest to lighter** (Adjectives and adverbs) Option (3) is correct because two things are compared. Option (1) is incorrect because make does not agree with the singular subject carriage. Options (2) and (4) are incorrect because more is not needed when an ending is added to a word to show comparison.

5. **(2) replace a better with the best** (Adjectives and adverbs) Option (2) is correct because more than two things are compared. Option (1) is incorrect because got is the past form which is not used with will. Options (3) and (4) are incorrect because neither is a correct comparative or superlative form; gooder is not a word.

6. **(4) replace less with few** (Adjectives and adverbs) Option (4) is correct because few is used with a quantity that can be counted, like companies. Option (1) is incorrect because the superlative most should not be used with adjectives ending in -est. Option (2) is incorrect because the possessive isn't necessary. Option (3) is incorrect because a semicolon connects two independent clauses.

7. **(3) change more to most** (Adjectives and adverbs) Option (3) is correct because the superlative form is needed to compare more than two techniques. Option (1) is incorrect because memory is a common noun and should not be capitalized. Option (2) is incorrect

because <u>techniques</u> must be plural. Option (4) is incorrect because <u>best</u> is not the superlative form of <u>more</u>.

8. **(4) change <u>simpler</u> to <u>simple</u>** (Adjectives and adverbs) Option (4) is correct because no comparison is being made. Option (1) is incorrect because a singular verb is needed to agree with <u>idea</u>. Options (2) and (3) are incorrect because the superlative and comparative forms are not needed.

9. **(2) change <u>best</u> to <u>most</u>** (Adjectives and adverbs) This sentence requires the superlative adverb form of <u>helpful</u>. Option (2) gives the correct superlative form: <u>most helpful</u>. Options (1), (3), and (4) all give incorrect forms; <u>helpfuller</u>, in option (4), is not a word.

10. **(2) really good idea** (Adjectives and adverbs) <u>Good</u> is an adjective, which requires an adverb modifier, <u>really</u>; therefore, option (2) is correct. <u>Good</u> correctly modifies the noun <u>idea</u>, so options (3) and (4) are incorrect. Option (5) modifies <u>real</u> but does not correct the problem.

11. **(1) change <u>most</u> to <u>more</u>** (Adjectives and adverbs) Option (1) is correct because the comparative adjective is needed. What is being compared is not two or more different times, but <u>more</u> and <u>fewer</u>, which is implied. Option (2) is incorrect because <u>more effective</u> is the correct comparative form; <u>effectiver</u> is not a word. Option (3) is incorrect because <u>effect</u> is a noun and an adjective is needed. Option (4) is incorrect because <u>it</u> is the subject of the verb <u>will be</u>; the contraction <u>it's</u>, meaning "it is," would not make sense in the sentence.

12. **(1) replace <u>easy</u> with <u>easily</u>** (Adjectives and adverbs) Option (1) is correct because the word being modified is the verb <u>retain</u>; the adverb <u>easily</u> is required. Option (2) is incorrect because the superlative <u>most</u> should not be used with adjectives ending in -est. Option (3) is incorrect because the comparative <u>more</u> should not be used with adjectives ending in -er. Option (4) is incorrect because the sentence requires the comparative <u>better</u> rather than the superlative <u>best</u>.

GED Mini-Test: Lesson 17 (Pages 152–153)

1. **(3) change <u>fewer</u> to <u>less</u>** (Adjectives and adverbs) Option (3) is correct because <u>less</u> applies to things that cannot be counted; <u>fewer</u> is used with things that can be counted. Option (1) is incorrect because <u>Americans</u> is a proper name and is always capitalized. Option (2) is incorrect because <u>is</u> does not agree with the plural subject <u>Americans</u>. Option (4) is incorrect because <u>their</u> correctly agrees with its plural antecedent <u>Americans</u>.

2. **(4) change <u>less</u> to <u>least</u>** (Adjectives and adverbs) Option (4) is correct because more than two foods are compared. Option (1) is incorrect because a lengthy introductory phrase should be set off by a comma. Option (2) is incorrect because <u>has</u> does not agree with the plural subject <u>we</u>. Option (3) is incorrect because <u>lessest</u> is not a correct superlative form.

3. **(3) change <u>the worst</u> to <u>worse</u>** (Adjectives and adverbs) Option (3) is correct because only two things are compared. Option (1) is incorrect because <u>are</u> does not agree with the singular subject. Options (2) and (4) are incorrect because <u>worser</u> and <u>badder</u> are not correct comparative forms.

4. **(4) change <u>the highest</u> to <u>higher</u>** (Adjectives and adverbs) Option (4) is correct because only two things are compared. Option (1) is incorrect because <u>seem</u> does not agree with the singular subject <u>bacon</u>. Option (2) is incorrect because a comma is necessary after an introductory dependent clause. Option (3) is incorrect because <u>more high</u> is not a correct comparative form.

5. **(5) no correction is necessary** (Adjectives and adverbs) Option (5) is correct because two items are correctly compared. Option (1) is incorrect because <u>more lower</u> is not a correct comparative form. Option (2) is incorrect because <u>lowlier</u> is the comparative form of <u>lowly</u>, meaning "humble, meek, or plain"; in this sentence, the comparative form of <u>low</u> is needed. Option (3) is incorrect because <u>low</u> does not show comparison. Option (4) is incorrect because the superlative is used only to compare more than two items.

6. **(4) change <u>most</u> to <u>more</u>** (Adjectives and adverbs) Option (4) is correct because only two things are being compared: tuna and red meat. Option (1) is incorrect because <u>were</u> does not agree with the singular subject <u>tuna</u>. Option (2) is incorrect because <u>they</u> does not agree with the singular antecedent <u>tuna</u>. Option (3) is incorrect because <u>become</u> does not agree with the singular subject.

7. **(2) change best to better** (Adjectives and adverbs) Option (2) is correct because two things are compared. Option (1) is incorrect because are does not agree with the singular subject popcorn. Option (3) is incorrect because the subject pronoun they cannot be used as the object of a preposition. Option (4) is incorrect because yourself is not an object pronoun.

8. **(4) change low to lowest** (Adjectives and adverbs) Option (4) is correct because more than two items are being compared, so the superlative form is needed. Option (1) is incorrect because four, the number, is used correctly. Option (2) is incorrect because has does not agree with the plural compound subject. Option (3) is incorrect because four things are being compared; lower is the comparative form, used for comparing just two things.

9. **(4) replace the period with a question mark** (End punctuation) Option (4) is correct because the sentence asks a question that requires an answer. Option (1) is incorrect because the superlative most should be used to form the superlative of adjectives with two or more syllables. Option (2) is incorrect because the adverb quickly correctly modifies the verb driving. Option (3) is incorrect because the possessive your is the correct word in this sentence, not the contraction you're.

10. **(2) change bad to badly** (Adjectives and adverbs) Option (2) is correct because bad is an adjective; the adverb badly is needed to modify the verb fared. Option (1) is incorrect because it is a singular pronoun; the plural they is needed to agree with the plural antecedent systems. Option (3) is incorrect because the adjective recent correctly modifies the noun test. Option (4) is incorrect because the semicolon correctly connects the two independent clauses.

11. **(1) change worse to worst** (Adjectives and adverbs) Option (1) is correct because the superlative form worst is required; a comparison is being made to all thieves, not two thieves. Option (2) is incorrect because most should not be used with the comparative form worse. Option (3) is incorrect because thief is correctly spelled. Option (4) is incorrect because seems, meaning "appears," is the correct word in this sentence.

GED Cumulative Review
Unit 2: Usage (Pages 154–158)

All items in this section are related to the rules of usage.

1. **(2) change thinks to think** (Subject-verb agreement) Option (2) is correct because the plural subject people requires the plural verb form. Option (1) is not correct because the verb thought would make this sentence past tense; the action of the paragraph is in the present tense. Option (3) is incorrect because the dependent clause beginning with that is essential and, therefore, should not be set off by a comma. Option (4) is incorrect because bank teller is used as a common noun. Option (5) is incorrect because the verb form must agree in number with the singular subject working, of the clause.

2. **(3) change more to most** (Adjectives and adverbs) Option (3) is correct because more than two things are being compared—all possible jobs. Option (1) is incorrect because the apostrophe in teller's is needed to show possession. Option (2) is incorrect because teller is singular and correctly shows possession by adding 's. Option (4) is incorrect because your is not a subject pronoun.

3. **(4) Althea has been working as a teller** (Verb tenses) Option (4) is correct because the words Since January require the verb-tense form has been working to show that the subject started working in the past and is still working as a teller. Option (1) is incorrect because worked incorrectly changes the action to past tense. Option (2) is incorrect because the verb must agree in number with the singular subject Althea. Option (3) is incorrect because the time reference Since January requires a verb form that shows time passing, not the present tense.

4. **(4) change their to her** (Pronoun antecedent agreement) Option (4) is correct because the pronoun her agrees with the antecedent pronoun she. Option (1) is incorrect because go does not agree in number with the singular pronoun subject she. Option (2) is incorrect because no comparison is being made. Option (3) is incorrect because there refers to a place; it is not a possessive pronoun. Option (5) is incorrect because them is not a possessive pronoun.

5. **(2) Althea needs a good understanding of math** (Subject-verb agreement) Option (2) is

correct because the singular subject <u>Althea</u> and the verb form <u>needs</u> agree in number. Options (1) and (4) are incorrect because the verb forms do not agree in number with the singular subject <u>Althea</u>. In option (3), <u>has need</u> is not a correct verb form.

6. **(1) even people who are rude** (Verb tenses, subject-verb agreement, and adjectives and adverbs) Option (1) is correct because the present-tense verb form <u>are</u> is needed to maintain the present tense of the passage. Option (2) is incorrect because the past perfect verb-tense form <u>had been</u> requires a point-in-time reference, <u>which</u> is not found in this sentence. Option (3) is incorrect because the singular verb <u>is</u> does not agree with the plural subject. Option (4) is incorrect because the future tense <u>will</u> does not make sense with the present tense of the sentence. Option (5) is incorrect because no comparison is being made.

7. **(3) change review to reviews** (Subject-verb agreement) Option (3) is correct because <u>reviews</u> agrees with the singular subject <u>she</u>. Option (1) is incorrect because the comma after <u>day</u> is necessary to separate the introductory phrase from the rest of the sentence. Option (2) is incorrect because the adverb <u>carefully</u> is used correctly; <u>careful</u> is an adjective. Option (4) is incorrect because <u>review</u> is the correct spelling. Option (5) is incorrect because the past perfect <u>had made</u> requires a point-in-time reference, <u>which</u> is not found in this sentence.

8. **(5) change her to she** (Personal pronouns) Option (5) is correct because <u>she</u> is the pronoun subject of the dependent clause beginning with <u>until</u>; <u>her</u> is an object pronoun. Option (1) is incorrect because <u>finds</u> agrees with the singular pronoun subject <u>she</u>. Option (2) is incorrect because the comma is needed to separate the introductory clause from the rest of the sentence. Option (3) is incorrect because the present-tense verb form <u>stays</u> maintains the present tense of the sentence. Option (4) is incorrect because <u>stays</u> agrees with the singular pronoun subject <u>she</u>.

9. **(2) change whom to who** (Indefinite pronouns) Option (2) is correct because <u>who</u> should be used as the subject of the verb <u>are</u>. Option (1) is incorrect because the comma correctly sets off the introductory dependent clause. Option (3) is incorrect because <u>who . . .</u>

<u>sixty</u> is an essential phrase. Option (4) is incorrect because <u>belief</u> is spelled correctly.

10. **(2) change more finest to finest** (Adjectives and adverbs) Option (2) is correct because the comparative <u>more</u> should not be used with an adjective ending in -est. Option (1) is incorrect because the singular verb <u>is</u> agrees with the singular subject. Option (3) is incorrect because the superlative <u>most</u> should not be used with an adjective ending in -est. Option (4) is incorrect because the possessive isn't necessary.

11. **(4) replace preceded with proceeded** (Verb tenses) Option (4) is correct because <u>proceeded</u>, meaning "continued or went ahead," is the correct word in this sentence. Option (1) is incorrect because the adverb <u>musically</u> correctly modifies the adjective <u>active</u>. Option (2) is incorrect because the possessive <u>our</u> is the correct word in this sentence. Option (3) is incorrect because the plural verb <u>have</u> doesn't agree with the singular subject.

12. **(2) change been made to have been made** (Verb tenses) Option (2) is correct because the point-in-time reference <u>since its invention in the 1800s</u> calls for the present perfect form <u>have been made</u>. Option (1) is incorrect because the modifier <u>many</u> requires a plural, <u>changes</u>. Option (3) is incorrect because <u>American</u> is the adjectival form of a proper noun and should be capitalized. Option (4) is incorrect because the clause beginning with <u>since</u> is essential and should not be set off by a comma. Option (5) is incorrect because the possessive pronoun <u>its</u> is used correctly.

13. **(3) change was to were** (Subject-verb agreement) Option (3) is correct because <u>were</u> agrees with the plural subject <u>Games</u>. Option (1) is incorrect because <u>before the 1930s</u> establishes the past tense of the sentence. Option (2) is incorrect because there is no reason to put a comma after <u>Games played</u>. Option (4) is incorrect because the time reference <u>before the 1930s</u> shows that the action took place in the past; <u>have been scheduled</u> is present perfect tense and conveys that the action is continuing.

14. **(3) A starting pitcher was expected** (Subject-verb agreement) Option (3) is correct because the singular helping verb <u>was</u> agrees with the singular subject <u>pitcher</u>. Options (1) and (2) are incorrect because the plural

Answers and Explanations

helping verbs were and have do not agree with the singular subject. Option (4) is incorrect because starting pitcher is a common noun and should not be capitalized. Option (5) is incorrect because the past perfect had been expected would require a point-in-time reference in the sentence.

15. **(3) change realize to realizes** (Indefinite pronouns) Option (3) is correct because Everyone, a singular indefinite pronoun, requires the singular form realizes. Option (1) is incorrect because who . . . country is an essential phrase. Option (2) is incorrect because the subject form who should be used in front of watches. Option (4) is incorrect because they is plural; the antecedent is the singular baseball.

16. **(2) change a growing sense is to is a growing sense** (Parts of speech) Option (2) is correct because the subject follows the verb in sentences beginning with there. Option (1) is incorrect because There is the correct word in this sentence. Option (3) is incorrect because costs is a verb in this sentence; it cannot be possessive. Option (4) is incorrect because too meaning "very" is the correct word in this sentence.

17. **(4) change he to him** (Personal pronouns) Option (4) is correct because the verb let needs an object pronoun, him. Options (1) and (2) are incorrect because has and was do not agree with the subject pronoun you; also, option (2) changes the meaning of the sentence. Option (3) is incorrect because the introductory dependent clause should be separated from the rest of the sentence with a comma. Option (5) is incorrect because play agrees with the singular subject pronoun.

18. **(1) change be to are** (Irregular verbs and subject-verb agreement) Option (1) is correct because are agrees in number with the plural subject These. Option (2) is incorrect because the verb is does not agree in number with the plural subject. Option (3) is incorrect because themselves is the correct reflexive pronoun. Option (4) is incorrect because the dependent clause introduced by when is essential. Option (5) is incorrect because the joining word or makes the subject singular; the verb starts would not agree with the singular subject.

19. **(5) change its to his or her** (Pronoun antecedent agreement) Option (5) is correct because the antecedent child may be either

masculine or feminine, but not neuter. Option (1) is incorrect because the dependent clause introduced by that is an indirect quotation, which should not be set off by a comma. Option (2) is incorrect because cartoons is a common noun and should not be capitalized. Option (3) is incorrect because increase agrees with the compound subject watching . . . and playing. Option (4) is incorrect because it's is a contraction meaning "it is."

20. **(2) change is to are** (Subject-verb agreement) Option (2) is correct because are agrees with the compound subject competition and combat. Option (1) is incorrect because say agrees with the plural subject experts. Option (3) is incorrect because was does not agree with the compound subject competition and combat. Option (4) is incorrect because society is a common noun and should not be capitalized.

21. **(3) change promotes to promote** (Subject-verb agreement) Option (3) is correct because the plural verb promote agrees with the plural subject guns. Option (1) is incorrect because a semicolon is used to join two independent clauses; In . . . years is not an independent clause. Option (2) is incorrect because whether, meaning "if," is the correct word in this sentence. Option (4) is incorrect because the plural verb have doesn't agree with the singular subject question.

22. **(2) change was to is** (Verb tenses) The answer is something that is true in the present; therefore, option (2) is correct and option (1) is incorrect. Options (3) and (4) are incorrect because there is no reason to use these punctuation marks in the sentence. Option (5) is incorrect because squirrel is a common noun and should not be capitalized.

23. **(5) no correction is necessary** (Indefinite pronouns; Mechanics/Capitalization) Option (5) is correct because the plural pronoun their agrees with the plural indefinite antecedent others. Options (1) and (2) are incorrect because his and her are singular and do not agree with others. Options (3) and (4) are incorrect because both colonies and underground are common nouns and should not be capitalized.

24. **(3) change them to their** (Personal pronouns) Option (3) is correct because the possessive pronoun their is needed; them is an object pronoun. Option (1) is incorrect because

the subject and verb should not be separated by a comma. Option (2) is incorrect because forgetting is spelled correctly. Option (4) is incorrect because buried is used as an adjective modifying nuts; bury cannot be used this way.

25. **(4) change finds to find** (Subject-verb agreement) Option (4) is correct because the plural verb form find agrees with the plural subject people. Option (1) is incorrect because Some is correctly used as an adjective. Option (2) is incorrect because people is already a plural noun without adding s. Option (3) is incorrect because two independent clauses not joined by a conjunction should be separated by a semicolon. Option (5) is incorrect because very modifies sociable.

26. **(4) replace the second squirrels with they** (Parts of speech) Option (4) is correct because the pronoun they should replace the noun squirrels to avoid repetition. Option (1) is incorrect because the singular is doesn't agree with the plural subject squirrels. Option (2) is incorrect because the adverb naturally correctly modifies the adjective aggressive; the adjective natural cannot be used to modify another adjective. Option (3) is incorrect because the semicolon is correctly used here before however followed by an independent clause.

UNIT 3: SENTENCE STRUCTURE
Lesson 18

All items in this section are related to rules of sentence structure.

GED Practice: Sentence Fragments (Pages 164–166)

1. **(4) department for cat care when he** (Fragments) Option (4) is correct because it joins the dependent clause (sentence 2) to the independent clause and eliminates the fragment. Option (2) is incorrect because a comma is used only when the dependent clause is nonessential. Option (3) is incorrect because a semicolon is not used to set off a dependent clause. In option (5), quotation marks are not needed because this is not a direct quotation.

2. **(2) system to inform** (Fragments) Option (2) is correct because it joins a fragment missing both a subject and a complete verb to an existing sentence. Option (3) results in a

fragment. Option (4) is incorrect because a comma is not used when the clause is essential information. Option (5) is incorrect because a semicolon is used only to join independent clauses.

3. **(2) insert he after the comma** (Fragments) Option (2) is correct because the subject is missing from this sentence; he is a subject pronoun. Option (1) is incorrect because the comma is needed after an introductory word. Options (3), (4), and (5) are incorrect because they do not add the needed subject to this sentence.

4. **(4) house several** (Fragments) Option (4) is correct because it joins a fragment missing both a subject and a verb to an existing sentence. Option (2) is incorrect because it does not correct the fragment; also a sentence starts with a capital letter. Option (3) is incorrect because a comma is used only when the dependent clause is nonessential. Option (5) is incorrect because a semicolon is used to join two independent clauses.

5. **(3) police, who had to check** (Fragments) Option (3) is correct because it joins the relative clause fragment beginning with who to the sentence containing its antecedent, police. The comma shows that the relative clause is nonessential. Option (2) results in a sentence fragment. Option (4) is incorrect because a semicolon is used only to join independent clauses. Option (5) is incorrect because whom cannot be used as a subject.

6. **(4) cooking, or wood** (Fragments) Option (4) is correct because it joins a nonessential dependent clause fragment to a nearby independent clause. Options (2) and (3) are incorrect because a semicolon is used only to join independent clauses. Option (5) uses an incorrect comma after, not before, the conjunction or, a connecting word.

7. **(3) ovens are changing** (Fragments) Option (3) is correct because it gives this fragment a complete verb. Options (2) and (4) do not add the necessary complete verb, and option (2) also contains an unnecessary comma. In option (5), the plural ovens does not agree with the singular verb.

8. **(2) change Less expensive to They're less expensive** (Fragments) Option (2) is correct because it gives this fragment both a subject and a verb; they're gives the subject they and

the verb are. The possessive pronoun Their, option (1), cannot be used as a subject. Option (3) confuses than with then, which shows time. In option (4), the comma is unnecessary. Option (5) is incorrect because possession is not shown.

9. **(5) cooking, which is one** (Fragments) Option (5) is correct because it joins this relative clause fragment to the sentence containing the word that it describes, speed. Option (2) is incorrect because a comma, not a semicolon, is used to join a dependent clause with an independent clause. Option (3) is incorrect because the verb is is necessary in the dependent clause. Option (4) changes the second clause into a fragment containing no subject or verb.

10. **(3) In fact, they are required** (Sentence fragments) Option (3) is correct because it eliminates the fragment by adding a subject, they. Options (1) and (5) are incorrect because the resulting sentences contain no subject. Option (2) is incorrect because the singular subject it disagrees with the plural verb are. Option (4) is incorrect because the first letter of a sentence must be capitalized.

11. **(2) insert is after trend** (Fragments) Option (2) is correct because this sentence does not have a complete verb. Options (1) and (5) are incorrect because commas are unnecessary. Options (3) and (4) incorrectly show the plural possessive form.

12. **(5) comics that** (Fragments) Option (5) is correct because it joins the relative clause fragment with the sentence containing the antecedent comics. Option (4) also does this, but it incorrectly separates essential information with a comma. Option (2) incorrectly uses a semicolon to separate an independent and dependent clause. Option (3) does not eliminate the fragment.

13. **(4) They replied that they are** (Fragments) Option (4) is correct because it adds the needed subject to make the fragment a sentence. Option (2) is incorrect because Them is an object pronoun; a subject pronoun is needed. Options (3) and (5) are incorrect because the singular form is does not agree with the plural subject they; option (3) also results in a fragment.

14. **(2) change coming to are coming** (Fragments) Option (2) is correct because are

coming is a complete verb; a form of be is needed with the present participle when the subject is doing the action. Option (1) is incorrect because Readers does not need to show possession. Options (3) and (4) are incorrect because there is no reason to separate the prepositional phrase from the rest of the sentence.

GED Mini-Test: Lesson 18 (Page 167)

1. **(4) uniform" as a record** (Fragments) Option (4) is correct because it joins the dependent clause fragment with the independent clause; no comma is needed here because the dependent clause is essential. Options (2) and (3) do not correct the fragment. Option (5) incorrectly places the comma outside the quotation mark.

2. **(3) insert is after women** (Fragments) Option (3) is correct because this fragment lacks a complete verb; increasing requires the helping verb is. Option (1) is incorrect because a comma should not separate the subject and verb. Option (2) is incorrect because women is the correct plural form of "woman." Option (4) is incorrect because increasing is spelled correctly.

3. **(3) change are to is** (Usage/Subject-verb agreement) Option (3) is correct because military is singular and needs a singular verb, is. Option (1) is incorrect because a comma is needed after the introductory phrase. Option (2) is incorrect because the military is not plural in this kind of usage. Option (4) is incorrect because were does not agree with the singular subject.

4. **(3) to women, in spite** (Fragments) Option (3) is correct because it joins the dependent clause (sentence 7) with the independent clause; the dependent clause is not essential, so a comma is needed. Options (2) and (5) incorrectly join a dependent and independent clause with a semicolon. In option (2), In should not be capitalized. Option (4) is incorrect because womans is not the correct plural form of woman.

5. **(1) is a positive trend, since** (Sentence fragments) Option (1) is correct because the comma properly joins the dependent clause to the independent clause. Option (2) is incorrect because since is neither the first word of a sentence nor a proper noun. Option (3) results in a fragment. Option (4) is incorrect because a semicolon is used only to join independent

clauses. Option (5) is incorrect because the plural verb <u>are</u> doesn't agree with the singular subject <u>number</u>.

Lesson 19

All items in this section are related to rules of sentence structure.

GED Practice: Run-On Sentences (Pages 170–172)

1. **(2) insert a semicolon after <u>equipment</u>** (Sentence structure/Run-on sentences) Option (2) is correct because it joins two independent clauses with a semicolon. Option (1) is incorrect because it is a comma splice. Option (3) is incorrect because the sentences are intended to show contrast. Option (4) is a run-on sentence.

2. **(3) muscles. Their fingers** (Sentence structure/Run-on sentences) Option (3) is correct because it uses a period to separate the independent clauses of the run-on into two sentences. Options (2) and (5) are comma splices. Option (4), like option (5), incorrectly uses the homonym <u>there</u>, rather than <u>their</u>.

3. **(5) no correction is necessary** (Mechanics/Capitalization, Usage/Subject-verb agreement, spelling, and punctuation—overuse of commas) Option (1) is incorrect because <u>typists</u> is a common noun and should not be capitalized. Option (2) is incorrect because <u>typists</u> is plural and requires the plural verb <u>have</u>. Option (3) is incorrect because <u>permanent</u> is spelled correctly. Option (4) incorrectly places a comma between an adjective and the noun it describes.

4. **(3) insert a semicolon after <u>eyestrain</u>** (Sentence structure/Run-on sentences) Option (3) is correct because it separates these two independent clauses by using a semicolon. Option (1) creates sentence fragments. Option (2) incorrectly separates the subject from the verb with a comma. Option (4) does not correct the run-on and uses the wrong homonym. Option (5) is incorrect because <u>continues</u> does not agree with the plural subject <u>studies</u>.

5. **(4) change the comma after <u>workers</u> to a semicolon** (Run-on sentences) Option (4) is correct because the semicolon corrects the run-on. Option (1) is incorrect because it does not correct the run on, and no possession is shown. Option (2) is incorrect because it does not correct the run-on, and only two items in a series do not need to be separated by a

comma. Option (3) is incorrect because it does not correct the run-on, and <u>In . . . machines</u> is not an independent clause.

6. **(3) backward, but the rest** (Sentence structure/Run-on sentences) Option (3) is correct because it corrects the run-on by using a comma and coordinating conjunction. Option (2) creates a comma splice. In option (4), the comma should be placed before the conjunction. Option (5) uses the wrong conjunction; <u>nor</u> does not fit the meaning of the sentence.

7. **(5) no correction is necessary** (Sentence structure/Capitalization) Option (1) is incorrect because the name of a country is capitalized. Option (2) is incorrect because there is no reason to separate the subject and verb with a comma. Option (3) is incorrect because <u>in the world</u> is essential information and so is not set off by commas. Option (4) is incorrect because <u>world</u> is not a proper noun.

8. **(5) years ago. They wanted** (Sentence structure/Run-on sentences) Option (5) is correct because it corrects the run-on by using a period. Option (2) does not correct the run-on and incorrectly makes <u>years</u> possessive. Option (3) creates a comma splice. Option (4) is incorrect because a semicolon is required with the conjunctive adverb <u>however</u>.

9. **(5) in metrics, so they can** (Sentence structure/Comma splice) Option (5) is correct because it corrects the comma splice by using a comma and a coordinating conjunction. Option (2) is a run-on sentence. In option (3), the comma should be inserted before the conjunction. In option (4), a semicolon is required with the conjunction <u>then</u>.

10. **(5) high; therefore, some manufacturers,** (Sentence structure/Run-on sentences) Option (5) is correct because it corrects the run-on by using a semicolon, a conjunctive adverb, and a comma. Option (2) does not correct the run-on, and removes a necessary comma. Option (3) is a comma splice. Option (4) creates fragments.

11. **(1) jackets. They** (Sentence structure/Run-on sentences/Comma splice) Option (2) is incorrect because it is a comma splice. Option (3) is incorrect because no contrast is intended. Option (4) is incorrect because it is a run-on sentence. Option (5) is incorrect because a clause after a semicolon doesn't begin with a capital letter.

Answers and Explanations

12. **(5) colorfully; they would be** (Sentence structure/Comma splice) Option (5) is correct because it corrects the comma splice by using a semicolon. Option (2) does not correct the comma splice and uses an incorrect verb. Option (3) incorrectly places a comma after the conjunction and. Option (4) is a run-on sentence.

13. **(3) personalized; each individual's** (Sentence structure/Run-on sentences) Option (3) is correct because it corrects the run-on by using a semicolon. Option (4) also uses the semicolon but lacks the possessive form of individual, as does the run-on in option (2). Option (5) is incorrect because a semicolon should be used to separate an independent and a dependent clause.

14. **(4) jacket, and it was** (Sentence structure/Run-on sentences) Option (4) is correct because it corrects the run-on by using a comma and coordinating conjunction. Option (2) is a comma splice. Option (3) creates a sentence fragment. Option (5) is incorrect because the comma should be placed before, not after, the coordinating conjunction.

15. **(5) with sailors; however, it became** (Sentence structure/Run-on sentences) Option (5) is correct because it corrects a run-on by using a semicolon, a conjunctive adverb, and a comma. Option (2) is incorrect because the comma should be placed before, not after a coordinating conjunction. Option (3) is incorrect because the word following a semicolon is not capitalized unless it is a proper name. Option (4) incorrectly uses a comma before a conjunctive adverb.

GED Mini-Test: Lesson 19 (Page 173)
1. **(5) no correction is necessary** (Sentence structure/Fragments) Options (1) and (2) are incorrect because the commas are not necessary. Options (3) and (4) create fragments because there is no verb in the first part of the sentence; are feeling belongs to the relative clause beginning with that.

2. **(3) change being to is** (Sentence structure/Fragments) Option (3) is correct because it corrects the fragment by putting in a complete verb. Option (1) results in a fragment. Option (2) is an incorrect verb form. Option (4) is incorrect because nature's is used correctly as the singular possessive term. Option (5) is incorrect because possession must be shown.

3. **(4) same place, but studies have** (Sentence structure/Run-on sentences) Option (4) is correct because it corrects the run-on by using a comma and coordinating conjunction. Option (2) is a comma splice. Option (3) incorrectly places a comma after the conjunction and. Option (5) is incorrect because the plural subject studies requires the plural verb have.

4. **(5) tears; these protective tears** (Sentence structure/Run-on sentences) Option (5) is correct because it corrects the run-on by using a semicolon. Option (2) is a capitalization error. Both options (3) and (4) make comma splices.

5. **(1) happens; nevertheless,** (Sentence structure/Comma splice/Run-on sentences) Option (1) is correct because the two independent clauses are joined by a semicolon, and the linking word nevertheless is followed by a comma. Option (2) is incorrect because a comma follows the word happens. Option (3) is a comma splice. Option (4) is incorrect because it is a run-on sentence. Option (5) is incorrect because a sentence starts with a capital letter.

Lesson 20

All items in this section are related to rules of sentence structure.

GED Practice: Combining Sentences (Pages 176–179)
1. **(1) cold cut, but the supermarket** (Sentence combining) Option (1) is correct because but shows a contrast. Option (2) incorrectly shows a cause-and-effect relationship. Option (3) incorrectly compares the two sentences. Option (4) is incorrect because a semicolon should be used before a conjunctive adverb. Option (5) is a comma splice.

2. **(4) department, so it** (Sentence combining) Option (4) is correct because it shows a result. Option (1) shows a contrast not present in the sentences. Option (2) is a comma splice. Option (3) incorrectly implies a time sequence. Option (5) contains an unnecessary comma after but.

3. **(4) beef, and there are** (Sentence combining) Option (4) is correct because it simply joins the two related sentences. Option (1) gives a wrong time indicator. Option (2) incorrectly negates a sentence that is meant to be a possibility. Option (3) shows a cause-and-

effect relationship that does not exist. Option (5) creates a fragment.

4. **(3) sandwich; however, the** (Sentence combining) Option (3) is correct because it shows the contrast made in the second sentence. Option (1) shows a consequence that is not implied. Option (2) is a comma splice. Option (4) ignores the contrast meant. Option (5) shows the two sentences as possibilities, which they are not.

5. **(1) normally eat; subsequently, I** (Combining Sentences) Option (1) is correct because subsequently shows the correct time sequence. Options (2) and (3) are incorrect because nevertheless and still imply contrasts; there is no contrast present in the sentences. Option (4) is incorrect because or incorrectly indicates another possibility. Option (5) is a comma splice.

6. **(1) taxes, and most** (Combining sentences) Option (1) is correct because it simply links the two related independent clauses using a coordinating conjunction. Option (2) is incorrect because it incorrectly shows a contrast. Option (3) is a comma splice. Option (4) shows the second idea as happening after the first, which it does not. Option (5) incorrectly shows the two sentences as possibilities; it also omits the comma before the coordinating conjunction or.

7. **(5) take note, for this** (Combining sentences) Option (5) is correct because the coordinating conjunction for shows the second idea as a cause of the first. Options (1) and (4) are incorrect because they simply link two ideas when a cause-and-effect relationship is shown. Option (2) creates a fragment of the first independent clause. Option (3) is a comma splice.

8. **(1) complete, but many** (Combining sentences) Option (1) is correct because it uses the conjunction but to show contrast. Option (2) is incorrect because it shows a time sequence not indicated in the sentences. Option (3) creates a fragment. Option (4) is incorrect because the conjunctive adverb likewise shows a comparison not meant in the sentences. Option (5) is a comma splice.

9. **(2) mail, so their** (Combining sentences) Option (2) is correct because it correctly shows a result. Option (1) is a comma splice. In option (3), the conjunction but shows a

contrast, which could be meant, but the possessive pronoun their is needed, not the contraction they're. Option (4) is incorrect because there does not show possession. Option (5) is incorrect because a semicolon is needed before a conjunctive adverb.

10. **(5) filing, for electronic** (Combining sentences) Option (5) is correct because for shows the second sentence as the cause of the first. Option (1) is a comma splice. Option (2) is incorrect because or incorrectly indicates another possibility. Option (3) is incorrect because consequently indicates that the second sentence is a result of the first. Option (4) is incorrect because subsequently implies a nonexistent time-order relationship.

11. **(1) well, for** (Combining sentences) Option (1) is correct because two independent clauses joined by for are separated by a comma. Option (2) is incorrect because a sentence begins with a capital letter. Option (3) is incorrect because independent clauses joined by for are separated by a comma. Options (4) and (5) are incorrect because no contrast is shown in the sentence.

12. **(2) rise, and accidents** (Combining sentences) Option (2) is correct because it simply links the two sentences. Option (1) shows a contrast that does not make sense here. Option (3) is incorrect because a semicolon should come before a conjunctive adverb. The use of nor in option (4) changes the meaning of the second sentence entirely. Option (5) is a comma splice.

13. **(3) inventive, but other** (Combining sentences) Option (3) is correct because it shows the contrast between inventive and worse than usual. Option (1) is incorrect because there is no cause-and-effect relationship. Option (2) is a comma splice. Option (4) is incorrect because a semicolon should be used before a conjunctive adverb. Option (5) incorrectly uses a semicolon with the coordinating conjunction yet.

14. **(5) hair, or do you** (Combining sentences) Option (5) is correct because it links two alternative possibilities. Options (1) and (3) are incorrect because a question mark is not internal punctuation. Option (2) incorrectly shows a contrast that is not present in the sentences. Option (4) is incorrect because a comma, not a semicolon, is used with the conjunction or.

15. **(4) this, yet they** (Combining sentences) Option (4) is correct because it shows the suggested contrast between people's public and private behavior. Option (1) sets up a cause-and-effect relationship that changes the meaning of the sentences. Option (2) is incorrect because a semicolon should be used before a conjunctive adverb. Option (3) is a comma splice. Option (5) creates a fragment.

16. **(3) work, so you** (Combining sentences) Option (3) is correct because it shows a cause-and-effect relationship; the condition in sentence 1 causes the need in sentence 2. Option (1) compares two ideas that cannot really be compared. Option (2) incorrectly shows a contrast. Option (4) is a comma splice. Option (5) is incorrect because a semicolon should be used before a conjunctive adverb.

17. **(5) type; then, immediately you make** (Combining sentences) Option (5) is correct because it shows one action happening after another, a time sequence. Option (1) compares two actions that cannot be compared. Option (2) is a comma splice. Option (3) incorrectly shows the sentences as alternate possibilities. Option (4) creates a fragment.

18. **(1) fluid, and you have no** (Combining sentences) Option (1) is correct because it connects two equal, related ideas. Option (2) shows a contrast that is not meant. Options (3) and (5) incorrectly show a cause-and-effect relationship. Option (4) is a comma splice.

19. **(2) sheet; meanwhile, a** (Combining sentences) Option (2) is correct because it shows the actions happening at the same time. Options (1) and (5) are incorrect because they both show a contrast that is not meant. Option (3) incorrectly shows a cause-and-effect relationship. Option (4) is a comma splice.

20. **(4) out, and you** (Combining sentences) Option (4) is correct because it links the two related ideas. Option (1) incorrectly shows the sentences as alternate possibilities. Options (2) and (5) show a contrast not supported by the ideas in the sentences. Option (3) is incorrect because it reverses the cause-and-effect relationship.

GED Mini-Test: Lesson 20 (Pages 180–181)

1. **(3) replace are with is** (Usage/Subject-verb agreement) Option (3) is correct because the subject is misconception not libraries; the singular verb is is needed. In option (1)

libraries is spelled correctly. Option (2) is incorrect because possession is not shown. Option (4) is incorrect because the contraction they're, meaning "they are," is needed in this sentence. In option (5), too, meaning "very," is correct; to is a preposition.

2. **(3) change the spelling of enormos to enormous** (Mechanics/Spelling) Option (3) is correct because enormous is the correct spelling. Option (1) is incorrect because Libraries should be capitalized; it is the first word in the sentence. Option (2) is incorrect because hold agrees in number with libraries. In option (4), amounts is spelled correctly. Option (5) incorrectly places a comma between an adjective and the noun it describes.

3. **(4) sections, filled with** (Sentence structure/Fragments) Option (4) is correct because it connects a fragment with no subject or verb to a complete sentence; a comma is used because the phrase is nonessential. Option (2) incorrectly uses a semicolon to join a dependent clause with an independent clause. Options (3) and (5) are fragments.

4. **(4) change to to too** (Mechanics/Spelling—homonyms) Option (4) is correct because too means "also." Option (1) is incorrect because libraries is spelled correctly. Option (2) is incorrect because possession is not shown. Option (3) is an incorrect verb form for this sentence.

5. **(3) librarian; then, tell** (Sentence structure/Sentence combining) Option (3) is correct because it uses a conjunctive adverb to show one action happening after another. Options (1) and (2) are comma splices. Option (2) also confuses the word than. Option (4) shows a contrast that is not meant. Option (5) incorrectly shows the sentences as alternate possibilities.

6. **(4) crabgrass, or do you** (Sentence structure/Sentence combining) Option (4) is correct because it links two possibilities. Options (1) and (2) are both examples of improper punctuation; a question mark is not internal punctuation. Option (3) shows a contrast that is not meant. Option (5) makes the second sentence the result of the first, which it is not.

7. **(1) can help; however, you** (Sentence structure/Sentence combining) Option (1) is correct because it shows the contrast implied in the sentences. Option (2) is incorrect because a semicolon should be used before a conjunctive adverb. Option (3) is a comma splice. Option (4) incorrectly shows cause. The linking word besides in option (5) does not make sense here.

8. **(3) insert but after in** (Sentence structure/Comma splice) Option (3) is correct because it corrects the comma splice and shows the contrast present in the two sentences. Option (1) is incorrect because it is a run-on sentence. Option (2) incorrectly shows a cause-and-effect relationship. Option (4) is incorrect because a sentence begins with a capital letter.

9. **(5) no correction is necessary** (Combining sentences) Options (1) and (2) are incorrect because indeed, a conjunctive adverb joining two independent clauses, should be preceded by a semicolon. Option (3) is incorrect because a conjunctive adverb joining two independent clauses should be followed by a comma. Option (4) is incorrect because movies, the second item in a series of three, should be followed by a comma.

10. **(4) patrons who don't** (Combining sentences; Fragments) Option (4) is correct because who...devices cannot stand alone and must be joined to the prior sentence; it is an essential phrase that should not be preceded by punctuation. Option (1) is a fragment. Options (2) and (5) are incorrect because the subject pronoun who is required as subject of the verb don't have. Option (3) is incorrect because semicolons are used to join independent clauses.

11. **(4) services; consequently, they** (Combining sentences) Option (4) is correct because consequently shows the proper cause-and-effect relationship. Option (1) is a comma splice. Option (2) is incorrect because the conjunctive adverb thus should be preceded by a semicolon, not a comma. Option (3) is incorrect because similarly creates an incorrect comparison between two different ideas. Option (5) is a run-on sentence.

Lesson 21

All items in this section are related to rules of sentence structure.

GED Practice: Parallel Structure (Pages 184–186)
1. **(5) change have sprayed to spray** (Parallelism) Option (5) is correct because this clause contains a series of present-tense verbs and spray is a present-tense form. Options (1), (2), (3), and (4) do not correct the parallel structure error.

2. **(4) change crawled to crawling** (Parallelism) Option (4) is correct because crawling matches the others in this -ing series. Option (1) is incorrect because no possession is shown. Option (2) removes a necessary part of the main verb phrase. Option (3) does not correct the parallel structure error. There is no reason for the comma in option (5).

3. **(5) insert in before jungles** (Parallelism) Option (5) is correct because it adds a preposition to the third item in a series of prepositional phrases. Option (1) is incorrect because lives does not agree with the plural subject roaches. Options (2) and (3) do not correct the parallel structure error. Option (4) incorrectly places a comma after the conjunction and.

4. **(5) change survived to to survive** (Parallelism) Option (5) is correct because it changes the verb survived to a third verb phrase in a series. Option (1) is incorrect because has does not agree with the plural subject They. Options (2) and (3) do not correct the parallel structure error. Option (4) is incorrect because the preposition to is not needed between the verb and its object.

5. **(5) a speedy shoe, a newspaper, or a hand** (Parallelism) Option (5) is correct because it replaces a participle-noun phrase with a noun in series of nouns. Option (1) is incorrect because it contains the participle-noun phrase swinging your hand. Option (2) doesn't correct the unparallel structure and also is missing a comma after the second item in the series. Option (3) is incorrect because with two phrases and one noun, it does not correct the unparallel structure. Option (4) is incorrect because it contains the participle-noun phrase swatting with newspaper.

6. **(3) insert having before a lot** (Parallelism) Option (3) is correct because it creates a verb phrase to match the other verb phrases in the series. Options (1) and (2) do not correct the parallel structure error. Option (4) is a misspelling of the two words a lot. Option (5) is incorrect because it separates the compound subject from the verb.

7. **(4) and sneakers,** (Parallelism) Option (4) is correct because it changes this prepositional phrase to a single noun like the other items in this series. Option (2) reintroduces wearing, which is not necessary. Option (3) is still a prepositional phrase. The preposition on, in option (5), upsets the parallel series of nouns.

8. **(4) change conservatively to conservative** (Parallelism) Option (4) is correct because it changes the adverb conservatively to an adjective to match the other adjectives in this series. Option (1) creates a fragment. In option (2), clothes is used correctly. Option (3) makes the adjective a noun and thereby unparallel. Option (5) changes an adjective to an adverb, which does not correct the unparallel structure.

9. **(4) change being to be** (Parallelism) Option (4) is correct because it changes the present participle being to the simple present verb be. The others in this series are verb-adverb combinations, but since be is a linking verb, an adjective will work in the place of an adverb. Options (1) and (3) do not correct the unparallel structure of the verbs in the series. Option (2) changes an adverb to an adjective, which incorrectly modifies the verb Behave. Option (5) changes the adjective to an adverb, which does not correct the parallel structure error.

10. **(2) insert a comma after serious** (Commas and items in a series) Option (2) is correct because a comma is necessary after serious, the second item in a series of three adjectives. Option (1) is incorrect because it would produce unparallel structure by changing an adjective to an adverb. Option (3) is incorrect because it would create unparallel structure by replacing an adjective with an adjective-noun combination. Option (4) is incorrect because the t in get is doubled when the suffix -ing is added.

11. **(1) change familiarity to familiar** (Parallelism) Option (1) is correct because it changes this adverb into an adjective so it is parallel to soft and anonymous. There is no reason for the comma in option (2). Options (3) and (4) create sentence fragments. Option (5) is incorrect because no possession is shown.

12. **(5) remove while waiting** (Parallelism) Option (5) is correct because it creates a series of parallel prepositional phrases. Option (1) is incorrect because goals does not agree with

the singular verb is. Option (2) is incorrect because a comma would separate the subject from the verb. Option (3) is wrong because affect is used correctly. Option (4) changes the meaning of the sentence.

13. **(2) remove to before lower** (Parallelism) Option (2) is correct because it gives this phrase an active verb, making it parallel with the other clauses. There is no reason for the comma in option (1). Options (3) and (5) do not correct the parallel structure error. Option (4) is incorrect because a comma is not needed after the conjunction and.

14. **(4) change performing to performance** (Parallelism) Option (4) is correct because it provides a noun to match the other nouns in the series. There is no reason for the commas in options (1) and (2). In option (3), reports does not agree with the plural subject offices. Option (5) is incorrect because no possession is shown.

15. **(5) no correction is necessary** (Parallelism; Combining sentences) Option (5) is correct because three present participles are in parallel structure. Option (1) is incorrect because the comma correctly separates the introductory dependent clause. Option (2) is incorrect because the semicolon correctly precedes the conjunctive adverb that joins two independent clauses. Option (3) is incorrect because replacing wearing earplugs with a noun alone would create unparallel structure. Option (4) is incorrect because replacing the participle leaving with the present plural verb leave would create unparallel structure.

GED Mini-Test: Lesson 21 (Page 187)

1. **(3) security; just** (Comma splice) Option (3) is correct because it connects two independent clauses with a semicolon. Option (2) incorrectly shows the second sentence as a result of the first. Option (4) is a run-on. Using the conjunction and, option (5), makes no sense.

2. **(4) blanket, parents** (Fragments) Option (4) is correct because it links a dependent clause with an independent clause. Option (2) results in a fragment. Options (3) and (5) are incorrect because a dependent clause should not be joined to an independent clause with a conjunction.

3. **(5) remove to be** (Parallelism) Option (5) is correct because it removes the infinitive to be

UNIT 3

so the last phrase matches the others in this series. Option (1) is incorrect because are does not agree with the singular subject blanket. Option (2) is incorrect; when all items in a series are joined by conjunctions, no commas are needed. Option (4) does not correct the unparallel structure.

4. **(4) ourselves, but our blankets** (Run-on sentences) Option (4) is correct because it joins two independent clauses using a coordinating conjunction. Options (2) and (3) are incorrect because ourselfs is not a word. Option (5) is a comma splice.

5. **(3) change being happy to happiness** (Parallelism) Option (3) is correct because it replaces a participle with a noun; the other two items in the series are nouns. Option (1) is incorrect because fondly is the correct adverbial form modifying the verb remember. Option (2) is incorrect because it replaces a noun with an adjective; the structure remains unparallel. Option (4) is incorrect because it adds a participle; the structure remains unparallel.

Lesson 22

All items in this section are related to rules of sentence structure.

GED Practice: Subordination (Pages 190–192)

1. **(1) insert a comma after enter** (Subordination) Option (1) is correct because an introductory subordinate clause is always followed by a comma. Option (2) is incorrect because moving is an incorrect verb form here and creates a fragment. In option (3), generally is spelled correctly. Option (4) is incorrect because chosen needs a helping verb.

2. **(5) although** (Subordination) Option (5) is correct because it best expresses the relationship between these two ideas. Options (1), (2), (3), and (4) do not make sense in the sentence.

3. **(2) where** (Subordination) Option (2) is correct because the second idea refers to a location. Options (1), (3), (4), and (5) do not make sense in the sentence.

4. **(2) replace which with who** (Subordination) Option (2) is correct because this relative pronoun clause needs a pronoun referring to people, not to things. Option (1) is incorrect because it would separate the

subject from the verb. Option (3) is incorrect because the verb reach does not agree with the singular subject shopper. There is no reason for the change in option (4). Option (5) is incorrect because is agrees with shopper.

5. **(4) replace though with until** (Subordination) Option (4) is correct because it uses a subordinating conjunction that indicates time to clarify the main meaning of the sentence. Option (1) is incorrect because the subordinate clause is essential to the meaning here. Option (2) creates a fragment. Options (3) and (5) are incorrect because neither makes sense in the sentence.

6. **(1) where** (Subordination) Option (1) is correct because it refers to location. Options (2), (3), (4), and (5) do not make sense of the sentences.

7. **(2) replace that with who** (Subordination) Option (2) is correct because it uses the relative pronoun who to refer to people. Options (1) and (3) are incorrect because the commas are both necessary to set off the nonessential clause. Option (4) is incorrect because walks does not agree with the singular subject you. Option (5) is incorrect because it confuses than and then; than is correct because a comparison is being made.

8. **(4) if** (Subordination) Option (4) is correct because if shows that a condition, if we understand, must be present before the other idea. Options (1), (2), (3), and (5) do not make sense in combining these sentences.

9. **(4) Because few sports are as physically demanding** (Subordination) Option (4) is correct because it best expresses the causal relationship between the two sentences. Option (1) is incorrect because the causal relationship is reversed. Options (2) and (5) are incorrect because there is no concession expressed. Option (3) is incorrect because there no condition expressed.

10. **(1) replace Even if with Since** (Subordination) Option (1) is correct because since expresses cause; the relationship between the two clauses is causal, not conditional. Options (2) and (3) are incorrect because. a comma is necessary following an introductory subordinate clause. Option (4) is incorrect because a comma is necessary to separate three items in a series.

11. **(1) so** (Subordination) Option (1) is correct because *so* expresses effect (the effect of no time-outs is little chance to rest). Options (2), (3), (4), and (5) are incorrect because they do not express effect. Options (2) and (5) express choice. Option (3) expresses place. Option (4) expresses time.

12. **(2) parents who work** (Subordination) Option (2) is correct because it both keeps the relative pronoun that refers to people and removes the commas incorrectly setting off this essential clause. Options (3) and (5) use both the commas and relative pronouns that refer to things. Although option (4) removes the commas, it does not use the correct relative pronoun.

13. **(2) absent because** (Subordination) Option (2) is correct because it takes away the comma setting off this essential clause. Option (3) does not make sense. Options (4) and (5) create fragments.

14. **(4) insert a comma after loss** (Subordination) Option (4) is correct because a comma is necessary after the introductory subordinate clause. Option (1) makes a concession in the wrong situation. In option (2), the comma would separate the verb and its object. Option (3) creates a fragment.

15. **(3) rather than** (Subordination) Option (3) is correct because it relates the two ideas by showing one as an untaken option. Option (1) contrasts the ideas but misses the main meaning of these two sentences. Options (2), (4), and (5) do not correctly relate the two sentences.

GED Mini-Test: Lesson 22 (Page 193)

1. **(4) when** (Sentence structure/Subordination) Option (4) is correct because it places these two ideas in a time perspective; one must happen before the other can happen. Options (1), (2), (3), and (5) are incorrect because each shows a relationship between the ideas that is more the opposite of what is meant.

2. **(3) change new england to New England** (Mechanics/Capitalization) Option (3) is correct because it capitalizes the entire proper name of a region of the United States. Option (1) changes the present participle *falling* to past tense, which does not make sense; besides, the sentence already has a main verb, *is*. Option (2) capitalizes only half of the

region's name. Option (4) creates fragments by putting a semicolon between the subject and verb in this sentence. In option (5) the verb *are* does not agree with the singular subject *rain*.

3. **(2) factories burning coal are** (Sentence structure/Parallelism) Option (2) is correct because it changes the second part of the compound subject to a form parallel with the first. Option (3) is incorrect because it would separate the compound subject from the verb. In option (4), *be* is an incorrect verb form here. Option (5) is not parallel because it uses a relative clause, not an *-ing* verb form.

4. **(5) no correction is necessary** (Pronouns/Commas/Verb tenses) Option (1) is incorrect because the plural *These* correctly refers to *chemicals*. Option (2) is incorrect because *later* is an essential part of the sentence. Option (3) is incorrect because there is no reason to add a comma. Option (4) is incorrect because the sentence is in the present tense.

5. **(1) which** (Sentence structure/Subordination) Option (1) is correct because it combines the two sentences using a relative pronoun that refers to things. Option (2) is incorrect because it uses the pronoun *that* refers to people. Options (3), (4), and (5) do not make sense in combining these sentences.

Lesson 23

All items in this section are related to rules of sentence structure.

GED Practice: Misplaced Modifiers
(Pages 196–198)

1. **(4) move at capacity after are** (Misplaced modifiers) Option (4) is correct because it moves the wrongly placed phrase next to the verb that it modifies. In option (1), the comma would separate the subject from the verb. Option (2) is incorrect because *is* does not agree with the plural subject *Landfills*. Option (3) separates the preposition *at* from its object.

2. **(2) replace they with diapers** (Misplaced modifiers) Option (2) is correct because it clarifies *they*; in the original sentence *not biodegradable* modified *parents*. Option (1) is incorrect because *realizing* is spelled correctly. Option (3) is incorrect because the verb *throw* is used correctly; *through* is a preposition. Option (4) creates a fragment.

3. **(1) move <u>under the soil</u> after <u>diapers</u>** (Misplaced modifiers) Option (1) is correct because it moves the wrongly placed modifying phrase next to the word it modifies. Option (2) removes a necessary comma after an introductory phrase. There is no reason for the change in option (3). In option (4), <u>bury</u> is spelled correctly.

4. **(3) move <u>in certain states</u> after <u>Residents</u>** (Misplaced modifiers) Option (3) is correct because it moves the wrongly placed phrase near the word it modifies. In options (1) and (5) <u>separate</u> and <u>certain</u> are spelled correctly. In option (2), the possessive pronoun <u>their</u> is used correctly. Option (4) moves the phrase to a location where it is still misplaced.

5. **(2) move <u>in containers</u> after <u>separate</u>** (Misplaced modifiers) Option (2) is correct because it moves this misplaced phrase next to the word it modifies. Option (1) moves the phrase next to the wrong word. Option (3) is incorrect because no possession is shown. In option (4), <u>separate</u> is spelled correctly. There is no reason for the change in option (5).

6. **(3) insert <u>these are</u> after <u>When</u>** (Misplaced modifiers) Option (3) is correct because it inserts a subject and a verb into the dangling modifier, transforming the phrase into a dependent clause. Options (1) and (2) are still dangling modifiers. Option (4) moves another modifying phrase into a wrong position.

7. **(1) move <u>melted down</u> after <u>from</u>** (Misplaced modifiers) Option (1) is correct because it moves this misplaced phrase next to the words it modifies. In option (2), <u>factories</u> is spelled correctly. Option (3) uses a singular verb that does not agree with the subject <u>factories</u>. Option (4) moves another phrase into an incorrect location.

8. **(4) move <u>with a promising future</u> after <u>Industries</u>** (Misplaced modifiers) Option (4) is correct because it takes this phrase with unclear reference and moves it to a definite modifying location. Option (1) is incorrect because removing part of the verb makes the sentence into a fragment. Options (2) and (3) do not correct the misplaced modifier.

9. **(5) move <u>With bottles and cans</u> before <u>these</u>** (Misplaced modifiers) Option (5) is correct because it moves this wrongly placed phrase so that it modifies <u>factories</u>. In option (1), factories is spelled correctly. Options (2)

and (4) make this sentence into a fragment. Option (3) uses a singular verb that does not agree with the plural subject.

10. **(4) change <u>has</u> to <u>have</u>** (Subject-verb agreement) Option (4) is correct the plural subject <u>companies</u> requires the plural verb <u>have</u>. Options (1) and (2) are incorrect because all the modifiers and modifying phrases are in the correct locations. Option (3) is incorrect because a comma would separate the subject from the verb.

11. **(2) move <u>out of worn-out tires</u> after <u>shoes</u>** (Misplaced modifiers) Option (2) is correct because it moves the wrongly placed phrase near the phrase it modifies. Option (1) is incorrect because the singular subject <u>manufacturer</u> requires the singular verb <u>is</u>. Option (3) is incorrect because the modifier <u>innovative</u> is already next to the noun it modifies. Option (4) is incorrect because the possessive <u>its</u> is the correct word in this sentence.

12. **(1) move <u>gradually</u> after <u>increase</u>** (Misplaced modifiers) Option (1) is correct because <u>to gradually increase</u> is a split infinitive; moving <u>gradually</u> corrects the problem. Option (2) is incorrect because it moves the phrase into the wrong location. Option (3) is incorrect because a subject pronoun is needed as subject of the verb <u>use</u>. Option (4) is incorrect because the possessive <u>their</u> is the correct word in this sentence.

13. **(3) insert <u>you're</u> after <u>When</u>** (Misplaced modifiers) Option (3) is correct because it adds a subject and verb to the dangling modifier, transforming it into a dependent clause. Option (1) still leaves a dangling modifier. Option (2) is incorrect because <u>your</u> is a possessive pronoun that does not correct the dangling modifier. Option (4) moves another modifier into an incorrect location. Option (5) is incorrect because no possession is shown.

14. **(3) insert <u>When you're</u> before <u>opening</u>** (Misplaced modifiers) Option (3) is correct because it changes this dangling modifier to a dependent clause by adding a subordinate conjunction, a subject, and a verb. Options (1) and (2) are still dangling modifiers. Option (4) is incorrect because <u>opening</u> needs a helping verb. Option (5) is incorrect because <u>falls</u> does not agree with the plural compound subject <u>pots and pans</u>.

15. (3) remove searching (Misplaced modifiers) Option (3) corrects this modification problem by dropping the -ing verb while leaving the sense of the sentence clear. In option (1), searching modifies trip, and in option (2), in search of modifies refrigerator; neither makes sense. Option (4) is incorrect because there is no reason to add a comma.

16. (2) move that is fresh after food (Misplaced modifiers) Option (2) is correct because it moves the misplaced phrase next to the noun that it modifies. Option (1) is incorrect because e is dropped when adding the suffix -ing to hide. Option (3) is incorrect because a comma is the correct punctuation before a coordinating conjunction joining a compound sentence. Option (4) is incorrect because although incorrectly indicates a relationship of concession between the two independent clauses.

GED Mini-Test: Lesson 23 (Page 199)

1. (3) move with low mileage after car (Misplaced modifiers) Option (3) is correct because it moves the misplaced phrase next to the word it modifies. Option (1) results in an incorrect verb form. Option (2) is incorrect because it separates an essential clause from the main clause with a comma. There is no reason for the change in option (4).

2. (3) odometer, which shows (Run-on sentences) Option (3) is correct because it changes the second independent clause in this run-on sentence into a nonessential relative clause. Option (2) is incorrect because it does not use a comma to set off the nonessential clause. Option (4) is a comma splice. Option (5) uses the wrong relative pronoun; who refers to people.

3. (4) replace informing with informs (Fragments) Option (4) is correct because it gives a complete verb to correct the fragment. Option (1) removes a necessary comma after an introductory word. Option (2) moves a modifier to the wrong position. The comma in option (3) is incorrect because it would separate the subject from the verb. Option (5) is still a fragment because it uses an infinitive verb phrase, not a complete verb.

4. (2) insert you're after When (Misplaced modifiers) Option (2) is correct because it adds a subject and a verb to the dangling modifier, transforming it to a dependent clause. Option (1) is incorrect because there is no reason for

the possessive pronoun your. Option (3) removes a necessary comma after an introductory phrase. Option (4) is the wrong form of a contraction. In option (5), too, meaning "overly," is used correctly.

5. (1) move whom you trust after mechanic (Misplaced modifiers) Option (1) is correct because it moves the misplaced phrase next to the noun that it modifies. Option (2) is incorrect because who is a subject pronoun; whom is necessary here as object of the verb trust. Option (3) is incorrect because it moves the phrase into the wrong location. Option (4) is incorrect because badly is an adverb; the adjective bad is required here to modify the noun purchase.

Lesson 24

All items in this section are related to rules of sentence structure.

GED Practice: Shift of Focus (Pages 202–203)

1. (4) change working to to work (Shift of focus/Parallelism) Option (4) is correct because replacing the participle working with the infinitive to work creates parallel construction. Option (1) is incorrect an apostrophe replaces the o in the contraction couldn't. Option (2) is incorrect because whether meaning "if" is the correct word in this sentence. Option (3) is incorrect because an infinitive is needed to create parallel construction, not the present tense works.

2. (4) change is to was (Shift of focus/Verb tense) Option (4) is correct because is creates an unnecessary verb tense shift; the past tense was is consistent with the rest of the paragraph. Option (1) is incorrect because the plural verb offer disagrees with the singular subject job. Option (2) is incorrect because the comma is required before the coordinating conjunction to separate the two independent clauses. Option (3) is incorrect because the plural verb are disagrees with the singular subject she.

3. (2) "When you move to a new city, you (Shift of focus/Shift of person) Option (2) is correct because the original sentence shifts from the second person you to the third person people; replacing people with you maintains consistency of person. Option (1) is incorrect because the sentence shifts from the second person you to the third person people. Option (3) is incorrect because the sentence shifts from the second person you to the third person they. Option (4) is incorrect because quotation marks come in pairs; "When you move . . . is part of an exact quote. Option (5) is incorrect because a comma is necessary after the introductory dependent clause.

4. **(3) change seeing to see** (Shift of focus/Parallelism) Option (3) is correct because replacing the participle seeing with see creates parallel construction with the verb speak. Option (1) is incorrect because the apostrophe precedes the s in a singular possessive. Option (2) is incorrect because the masculine pronoun he disagrees in gender with its antecedent Becky. Option (4) is incorrect because the pronoun she disagrees in gender and number with its antecedent family members.

5. **(2) insert will before never** (Shift of focus/Sequence of tenses) Option (2) is correct since in the first clause if implies a possible condition taking place in the future; the action in the second clause must also take place in the future. Option (1) is incorrect because semicolons are not used between a dependent clause and an independent clause. Option (3) is incorrect because the action in the second clause must take place in the future, not the past. Option (4) is incorrect because the action throughout the paragraph takes place in the past tense; the present tense says is inconsistent with that time frame.

6. **(4) replace where they get married with weddings** (Shift of focus/Parallelism) Option (4) is correct because replacing the phrase where . . . married with weddings creates parallel construction in a series of three nouns. Option (1) is incorrect because the e is dropped when adding the suffix -ing to provide. Options (2) and (3) are incorrect because the error in parallel construction is not corrected.

7. **(5) no correction is necessary** (Shift of focus/Verb tense; Pronouns; Commas and interrupters) Option (1) is incorrect because the comma correctly precedes the parenthetical expression however. Option (2) is incorrect because changing to the past tense focused is an unnecessary shift of verb tense; the rest of the paragraph is in the present tense. Option (3) is incorrect because replacing the third person their with the second person your is an unnecessary shift of person; the antecedent of the pronoun is the third person

caterers. Option (4) is incorrect because the subject pronoun who is correct as the subject of the verb make.

8. **(2) have a crew of two hundred people and take months to produce.** (Verb tense) Option (2) is correct because have is the correct verb form with can. Options (1) and (4) are incorrect because the third person has cannot be used with can. Also, Option (4) creates nonparallel structure. Option (3) is incorrect because the past tense took creates an unnecessary shift in verb tense; have is in the present tense. Option (5) is incorrect because the participle taking is not parallel in structure with have.

9. **(3) change you to he or she** (Shift of focus) Option (3) is correct because it corrects the shift in person between the third person crew member and the second person you. Option (1) is incorrect because the comma correctly sets of the introductory clause. Option (2) is incorrect because semicolons are used between independent clauses. Option (4) is incorrect because the first person plural we disagrees with the singular antecedent crew member.

10. **(3) change was to is** (Shift of focus/Verb tense) Option (3) is correct because it corrects the shift in verb tense by replacing the past tense was; the present tense is used in the first clause and the rest of the paragraph. Option (1) is incorrect because the singular verb uses disagrees with the plural subject Caterers. Option (2) is incorrect because replacing use with using turns the sentence into a fragment. Option (4) is incorrect because the plural verb were disagrees with the singular subject production.

GED Mini-Test: Lesson 24 (Pages 204–205)

1. **(1) change you to they** (Shift of focus/Shift of person) Option (1) is correct because the second person pronoun you disagrees in person with its antecedent travelers in the previous sentence; they agrees with the antecedent. Option (2) is incorrect because the comma is required after the introductory dependent clause. Option (3) is incorrect because the first person our does not agrees in person with any antecedent. Option (4) is incorrect because replacing are with was produces an unnecessary verb tense shift from present to past.

2. **(3) change asking to ask** (Shift of focus/Parallelism) Option (3) is correct

because replacing the participle asking with ask creates parallel construction with the other verb open. Option (1) is incorrect because the e is dropped when adding the suffix -ing to arrive. Option (2) is incorrect because possession is shown. Option (4) is incorrect because using the first person us creates an unnecessary shift from the third person.

3. **(1) change This inspector to These inspectors** (Shift of focus/Shift of number) Option (1) is correct because replacing the singular This inspector with the plural These inspectors maintains consistency in number with the previous sentences. Option (2) is incorrect because the plural verb have come disagrees with the singular subject inspector. Option (3) is incorrect because the modifier several requires the plural agencies. Option (4) is incorrect because Agriculture is part of the name of an organization and must be capitalized.

4. **(3) change plant to plants** (Shift of focus/Parallelism) Option (3) is correct because replacing plant with plants creates parallel construction in a series of three plural nouns. Option (1) is incorrect because the past tense was is not consistent with the present tense of the sentence. Option (2) is incorrect because the e is dropped when adding the suffix -ing to make. Option (4) is incorrect because is disagrees with the plural subject products.

5. **(3) change we to they** (Shift of focus/Shift in person) Option (3) is correct because the first person we disagrees with its third person antecedent officers. Option (1) is incorrect because the singular was intercepting disagrees in number with the plural subject officers; it also disagrees in tense with the verb in the second clause. Option (2) is incorrect because the semicolon correctly joins two independent clauses. Option (4) is incorrect because the object pronoun them is required as object of the verb confiscate.

6. **(1) Americans love to travel, and they treasure** (Shift of focus/Parallelism) Option (1) is correct because it creates parallel construction between the verbs love and treasure; the construction also avoids shift of subject between clauses. Option (2) is incorrect because it creates shift of person between the third person Americans and the first person we. Options (3) and (4) neither

create parallel construction nor avoid shift of subject. Trips is the subject of the second clause. Also, in Option (4), the first person pronoun our disagrees with the third person Americans. Option (5) is incorrect because because implies a cause-and-effect relationship not present in the original sentences.

7. **(4) remove traveling to** (Shift of focus/Parallelism) Option (4) is correct because removing the participle traveling to creates parallel construction in a series of three nouns. Option (1) is incorrect because replacing the verb include with the participle including makes the sentence into a fragment. Option (2) is incorrect because inserting the participle visiting does not create parallel construction. Option (3) is incorrect because the final consonant l is not doubled when adding the suffix -ing to travel.

8. **(2) remove the comma after careful** (Punctuation/Commas) Option (2) is correct because the comma is unnecessary when the dependent clause follows the independent clause. Option (1) is incorrect because careful is spelled correctly. Option (3) is incorrect because the past tense they explored is inconsistent with the time frame indicated by the verb in the first clause. Option (4) is incorrect because more is used to form the comparative rugged; ruggeder is not a word.

9. **(1) replace You with Many** (Shift of focus/Shift of person) Option (1) is correct because replacing You with Many corrects the disagreement in person with the antecedent visitors. Option (2) is incorrect because the third person singular verb arrives disagrees with the second person You. Options (3) and (4) are incorrect because inserting either the participle doing or the past tense verb did creates an error in parallel construction; the other items in the series are noun phrases.

10. **(2) change injure themselves to injured** (Shift of focus/Parallelism) Option (2) is correct because replacing the present tense verb injure with the past participle injured creates parallel construction in a series of past participles. Option (1) is incorrect because changing become to the future tense is inconsistent with the time relationship indicated by the present tense verb are. Option (3) is incorrect because themselves is the correct reflexive pronoun; theirselves is not a word. Option (4) is incorrect because

replacing the past participle stranded with the present participle stranding does not correct the error in parallel construction.

Lesson 25

All items in this section are related to rules of sentence structure.

GED Practice: Revising Sentences (Pages 208–209)

1. **(3) and requires** (Sentence structure/ Parallelism) Option (3) is correct because it links the second sentence to the first using a parallel verb to create a sequence; the second subject, Moving . . . , is dropped to avoid repetition. Option (1) is incorrect because it combines the two ideas by contrasting them. Option (2) creates a run-on. Option (4) eliminates the subject from the second sentence but does not link the subject of the first sentence. Option (5) is incorrect because it changes the meaning; in the original sentence 2, the subject of requires is Moving, not apartment.

2. **(2) my pots and pans and my clothes** (Sentence structure/Parallelism) Option (2) is correct because it combines the two sentences using a parallel series. Option (1) is a run-on. In options (3) and (5), the items in the series are not parallel. In option (4) the word and is missing from the series.

3. **(2) anything because** (Sentence structure/ Subordination) Option (2) is correct because it shows a cause-and-effect relationship between the two sentences by creating a subordinate clause. Option (1) is a comma splice. Option (3) creates a dangling modifier. Option (4) sets up a contrast between two ideas that is not meant. Option (5) uses the double negative can't . . . nothing.

4. **(1) maid who will** (Sentence structure/ Subordination) Option (1) is correct because it retains the main idea and creates a relative clause that describes the maid. Option (2) is a run-on. Option (3) is a comma splice. Option (4) uses the wrong relative pronoun for referring to a person. Option (5) uses the wrong subject to keep the main idea intact.

5. **(1) but it** (Sentence structure/Coordination) Option (1) is correct because it coordinates the two ideas and shows their contrast. Options (2) and (4) show the second idea as the result of the first, which it is not. Option (3) ignores

the contrast and only links the ideas. Option (5) shows an incorrect cause-and-effect relationship.

6. **(1) apartment that would** (Sentence structure/Subordination) Option (1) is correct because it combines the two sentences into a main clause with a relative subordinate clause modifying apartment. Option (2) is a comma splice. Option (3) creates a fragment. Option (4) uses the wrong relative pronoun to refer to a thing. Option (5) links the two ideas but ignores the relationship between them.

7. **(2) or** (Sentence structure/Coordination) Option (2) is correct because it presents the two ideas as alternative possibilities. Option (1) makes one idea the result of the other, which is incorrect. Option (3) contrasts the two ideas. Options (4) and (5) show an incorrect cause-and-effect relationship.

8. **(1) has been increased by** (Sentence structure/Subject-verb agreement) Option (1) is correct because it keeps the meaning of the original sentence and adjusts the verb to agree with the new singular subject safety. Options (2) and (5) are incorrect because the singular subject does not agree with the plural verbs have been and are. Options (3) and (4) are incorrect because the relationship between safety and advances is reversed.

9. **(5) because** (Sentence structure/ Subordination) Option (5) is correct because the subordinating conjunction because maintains the original relationship between the two ideas. Option (1) is incorrect because it presents the two ideas as alternate possibilities. Option (2) is incorrect because it shows an incorrect relationship of result. Option (3) is incorrect because it links the ideas without maintaining the relationship of cause. Option (4) is incorrect because but incorrectly contrasts the two ideas.

10. **(3) Drivers may take unnecessary chances because** (Sentence structure/ Subordination) Option (3) is correct because it maintains the relationship of cause and effect between the two ideas. Options (1) and (4) are incorrect because the cause and effect relationship is reversed. Options (2) and (5) are incorrect because although indicates a relationship of concession rather than cause and effect.

Answers and Explanations

1. **(2) change seems to seem** (Usage/Subject-verb agreement) Option (2) is correct because it changes the verb to agree with the plural compound subject. The comma in option (1) would separate the subject from the verb. Option (3) results in an incorrect verb form. Option (4) is incorrect because the proper adjective American should be capitalized.

2. **(4) Eaten on the go, fast food** (Sentence structure/Misplaced modifier) Option (4) is correct because it changes the dangling modifier so that it modifies fast food. Options (2) and (3) do not correct the dangling modifier. Option (5) is a comma splice.

3. **(3) car because a** (Sentence structure/Subordination) Option (3) is correct because it relates the two ideas by showing cause; the dependent clause thus formed is essential, so no comma is used. Option (1) implies a result that is not meant by the ideas in the sentences. Option (2) shows cause but separates the new essential clause with a comma. Option (4) contrasts the ideas, which is incorrect. Option (5) incorrectly shows a conditional relationship.

4. **(1) for** (Sentence structure/Coordination) Option (1) is correct because it shows cause. Options (2) and (3) show a contrast, which is not meant. Option (4) shows the second idea as a result of the first, which it is not. Option (5) presents the two ideas as alternative possibilities, which is incorrect.

5. **(4) Move in a bag after comes** (Sentence structure/Misplaced modifier) Option (4) is correct because it moves the phrase next to the word it modifies. Option (1) is an incorrect plural form. Option (2) is incorrect because the past participle grown is not used to form present tense with the helping verb do. Option (3) creates an incorrect verb form.

6. **(3) trend, since children** (Sentence structure/Subordination) Option (3) is correct because it uses a subordinating conjunction that shows reason or cause. Option (2) creates a fragment. Option (4) is a comma splice. Option (5) results in a dangling modifier.

7. **(5) no correction is necessary** (Sentence structure/Subordination; Usage/Subject-verb agreement; Pronoun-antecedent agreement) Option (1) is incorrect because the indefinite pronoun Everyone is singular; it disagrees with the plural verb love. Option (2) is incorrect because a comma is unnecessary if the information in the dependent clause is essential to the main idea. Option (3) is incorrect because they disagrees in number with its antecedent change. Option (4) is incorrect because so that implies a relationship of effect that is not present in the sentence.

8. **(2) yet** (Sentence structure/Coordination) Option (2) is correct because it contrasts the small changes with their dramatic effect. Options (1) and (4) are incorrect because they show cause-and-effect relationships not implied by the sentences. Option (3) is incorrect because the two ideas are not alternate possibilities. Option (5) is incorrect because it suggests a time sequence between ideas that is not implied by the sentences.

9. **(2) even though** (Sentence structure/Subordination) Option (2) is correct because it shows the second idea as a concession. Option (1) is incorrect because it shows the second sentence as a result, which is not implied in the original sentence. Option (3) is incorrect because the two ideas are not alternate possibilities. Option (4) is incorrect because it shows an incorrect time relationship. Option (5) is incorrect because it simply links the two ideas; a relationship of concession is required.

10. **(2) yet** (Sentence structure/Subordination; Pronoun-antecedent agreement) Option (2) is correct because yet shows the differences between the two ideas. Option (1) is incorrect because and simply joins the sentences but does not indicate the differences. Options (3), (4), and (5) are incorrect because they indicate a cause-and-effect relationship that is not implied in the original sentences.

11. **(3) because they** (Sentence structure/Subordination) Option (3) is correct because it shows cause—why children are enjoying life more in the summer. Option (1) is incorrect because so they reverses the relationship between the two ideas. Option (2) is incorrect because until they suggests an incorrect time relationship. Option (4) is incorrect because it ignores the idea of playing. Option (5) is incorrect because it ignores the idea of being outside.

UNIT 3

All items in this section are related to rules of sentence structure.

1. **(3) change <u>packing</u> to <u>pack</u>** (Sentence structure/Parallelism) The other items in this series use a present-tense verb, not a participle. Option (1) removes a necessary comma after the introductory phrase. Option (2) creates an incorrect verb form. Option (4) does not result in parallel structure.

2. **(4) replace <u>being</u> with <u>was</u>** (Sentence structure/Fragments) Option (4) gives this fragment a complete verb. Option (1) misplaces a modifier. Options (2) and (3) each take away one of the commas needed to set off the interrupting phrase. Option (5) is an incorrect verb form.

3. **(3) a picnic; the** (Sentence structure/Comma splice) Option (3) corrects the comma splice by linking these two independent clauses with a semicolon. Option (2) is a run-on. Option (4) shows a contrast that is not meant. Option (5) incorrectly shows the second idea as additional to the first.

4. **(2) insert <u>rowdy</u> before <u>teenagers</u>** (Sentence structure/Parallelism) All items in this series are nouns preceded by adjective modifiers. There is no reason for the comma in option (1). Option (3) is incorrect because the possessive isn't necessary. Option (4) separates the subject from the verb. Option (5) is incorrect because possession is meant.

5. **(5) insert <u>As drive-ins are</u> before <u>dying</u>** (Sentence structure/Misplaced modifiers) Option (5) turns the dangling modifier into a dependent clause by adding a subordinating conjunction, a subject, and a verb. Option (1) misplaces the modifier. Option (2) removes a necessary comma after the introductory phrase. Option (3) uses only a pronoun, <u>they</u>, as the subject in the subordinate clause; the pronoun antecedent would be unclear, resulting in a misplaced modifier. Option (4) does not make sense.

6. **(3) replace <u>then</u> with <u>than</u>** (Sentence structure/Subordination) Option (3) uses the correct subordinating conjunction for the comparison. Option (1) separates the subject from the verb. In option (2), <u>holds</u> does not agree with the plural subject. Option (4) is incorrect because possession is not shown.

7. **(2) insert <u>are</u> after <u>desires</u>** (Sentence structure/Fragments) Option (2) is correct because this fragment lacks a complete verb; inserting <u>are</u> corrects the fragment. Option (1) is incorrect because possession is shown. Option (3) is incorrect because the singular verb <u>is</u> disagrees with the plural subject <u>desires</u>. Option (4) is incorrect because the verb <u>were</u> is past tense; the rest of the paragraph is in the present tense.

8. **(1) rain or frost; however,** (Sentence structure/Coordination) Option (1) is correct because the conjunctive adverb <u>however</u> correctly indicates the contrast between the outdoor and greenhouse environments. Option (2) is incorrect because <u>similarly</u> incorrectly indicates that the two environments are similar. Option (3) is incorrect because <u>because</u> indicates a cause-and-effect relationship not present in the two original sentences. Option (4) is incorrect because it is a comma splice. Option (5) is incorrect because the lack of punctuation creates a run-on sentence.

9. **(3) insert a semicolon after <u>construction</u>** (Sentence structure/Run-on sentences) Option (3) is correct because it corrects the run-on by connecting the two independent clauses with a semicolon. Option (1) is incorrect because a comma after <u>factors</u> does not correct the run-on. Option (2) is incorrect because it would create a comma splice. Option (4) is incorrect because the singular verb <u>is</u> agrees with the singular subject <u>expense</u>.

10. **(1) so** (Sentence structure/Sentence revising) Option (1) is correct because <u>so</u> correctly indicates that the second idea—owner should anticipate large fuel bills—is the result of the first. Option (2) is incorrect because <u>because</u> reverses the relationship of ideas. Option (3) is incorrect because or incorrectly indicates alternate possibilities. Option (4) is incorrect because <u>although</u> indicates a relationship of concession not present in the original sentence. Option (5) is incorrect because <u>meanwhile</u> indicates a relationship of time not present in the original sentence.

11. **(3) yards; these new** (Sentence structure/Run-on sentences) Option (3) corrects this run-on with a semicolon. Option (2) is a comma splice. Option (4) incorrectly makes the second idea an alternative to the first. Option (5) incorrectly makes the first idea conditional upon the second.

12. **(5) porches, and they** (Sentence structure/Coordination) Option (5) simply links the two ideas. Option (1) is a comma splice. Option (2) is a run-on. Option (3) incorrectly contrasts the two ideas. Option (4) incorrectly establishes the second idea as a result of the first.

13. **(3) square, which contains** (Sentence structure/Subordination) Option (3) changes the second sentence into a subordinate clause using a relative pronoun. Option (1) lacks a conjunction to relate the second sentence to the first. Option (2) uses the wrong relative pronoun. Option (4) incorrectly contrasts the two ideas. Option (5) is a run-on.

14. **(4) suburbs. Planners** (Sentence structure/Run-on sentences) Option (4) is correct because it changes a run-on sentence into two sentences. Option (2) is incorrect because it is a comma splice. Option (3) is incorrect because a sentence must begin with a capital letter. Option (5) is incorrect because but shows contrast, which is not intended.

15. **(4) move by both groups after asked** (Sentence structure/Misplaced modifiers) Option (4) moves the phrase next to the word it modifies. Option (1) removes a necessary comma after an introductory word. In option (2), whether is spelled correctly. There is no reason for the comma in option (3). Option (5) misplaces a modifying phrase.

16. **(2) replace looking with one looks** (Sentence structure/Misplaced modifiers) Option (2) inserts both a subject and a verb into this dangling modifier. Option (1) still leaves a dangling modifier. In option (3), appear does not agree with the singular subject; although it ends in an s, Mars is singular. In option (4), appears is spelled correctly. Option (5) is incorrect because the possessive pronoun its is needed.

17. **(1) observers** (Sentence structure/Clarity) Option (1) keeps the main clause and main idea intact. Option (2) creates a fragment. Options (3), (4), and (5) reorder the words of the sentence awkwardly.

18. **(5) change to describe to described** (Sentence structure/Fragments) Option (5) gives this fragment a complete verb. Options (1) and (2) each remove a necessary comma. In option (3), describe does not agree with the singular subject. Option (4) is still a fragment.

19. **(4) and empty deserts** (Sentence structure/Parallelism) Option (4) gives an adjective and a noun only, matching the other item, deserted palaces, in this series. Options (1), (2), and (3) all use a relative clause and so are not parallel. Option (2) contains a subject-verb disagreement, and option (3) uses an incorrect pronoun. Option (5) does not match the series because it uses a participle.

20. **(4) to Mars, so they were** (Sentence structure/Coordination) Option (4) uses a coordinating conjunction to establish a result relationship between the two ideas. Option (1) is a comma splice. Option (2) establishes an incorrect conditional relationship. Option (3) shows a cause and effect that are nearly the opposite of the actual meaning. Option (5) shows the two attitudes as having occurred at the same time, which they did not.

21. **(5) no correction is necessary** (Parallel Structure/Usage/Personal pronouns; Mechanics/Spelling and punctuation—apostrophe) Option (1) is incorrect because the possessive pronoun is needed. Options (2) and (3) are wrong because appearance and length are spelled correctly. Option (4) is incorrect because the possessive form is needed.

22. **(3) Because they dislike** (Sentence structure/Subordination) Option (3) correctly establishes the first idea as causing the second. Options (1) and (5) show the opposite cause-and-effect relationship. Option (2) incorrectly shows one idea as a concession to the other. Option (4) incorrectly contrasts two similar ideas.

23. **(4) caught; then, it rakes** (Sentence structure/Combining sentences) Option (4) correctly sets up a time sequence for these ideas. Option (1) is a run-on. Option (2) is a comma splice. Option (3) incorrectly contrasts the two ideas. Option (5) makes no sense; the second idea cannot be negated as an alternative to the first.

24. **(3) have stood up to** (Sentence structure/ Clarity) Option (3) retains enough of the verb to keep the proper tense—present perfect. Option (1) changes the meaning; because the subject of the sentence is now badgers, the verb must change form. There is no reason for

Answers and Explanations   **313**

the past tense, as in options (2) and (5).
Option (4) is an incorrect verb form.

25. **(3) move without claws after animals**
(Sentence structure/Misplaced modifiers)
Option (3) is correct because it moves the
misplaced phrase next to the word it modifies.
Option (1) is incorrect because a comma is
necessary after the introductory phrase.
Option (2) is incorrect because it leaves
without claws in an incorrect location. Option
(4) is incorrect because bad is the correct
modifier for feel.

26. **(4) change to catch prey to catching prey**
(Sentence structure/Shift of focus) Option (4)
is correct because it creates a parallel series of
participles. Option (1) is incorrect because the
singular verb needs disagrees with the plural
subject cats. Option (2) is incorrect because it
changes the participle to a present-tense verb,
which does not correct the parallel structure
error. Option (3) is incorrect because it
changes the participle to a plural noun, which
does not correct the parallel structure error.

27. **(5) great damage if** (Sentence structure/
Subordination) Option (5) is correct because if
correctly shows the conditional relationship of
the second idea. Option (1) is incorrect
because it reverses the condition. Option (2) is
incorrect because so indicates an effect
relationship not present in the two original
sentences. Option (3) is incorrect because
before indicates an incorrect time relationship.
Option (4) is incorrect because or incorrectly
indicates alternate possibilities.

28. **(1) Cat owners who are parents worry**
(Sentence structure/Sentence combining)
Option (1) is correct because it uses the
relative pronoun who to incorporate essential
information from the first sentence. Option (2)
is incorrect because the essential phrase who
are parents should not be set off by commas.
Options (3) and (4) are incorrect because they
leave out the main idea of the first sentence.
Option (5) is incorrect because making parents
the subject incorrectly changes the meaning of
the original sentences.

POSTTEST
(Pages 220–233)

1. **(4) change have to has** (Usage/Subject-verb
agreement) Option (4) is correct because the
subject of the sentence is number, which is

singular, so the singular verb has increased
must be used. There is no reason for the
changes in options (1), (2), and (3).

2. **(5) family and to the workplace** (Sentence
structure/Parallelism) This sentence does not
have parallel structure. Option (5) is correct
because the phrases to the family and to the
workplace are parallel. Options (2), (3), and (4)
do not result in parallel structure.

3. **(2) if it allows** (Usage/Pronoun reference—
agreement with antecedent and subject-verb
agreement) Option (2) is correct because it is
singular and requires the singular verb
allows. The pronoun it correctly refers to job,
which is singular. Therefore, options (3) and
(4) are incorrect. Allowance is not a verb, so
option (5) is wrong.

4. **(3) replace they with it** (Usage/Pronoun
reference—agreement with antecedent)
Option (3) is correct because the antecedent, a
job promotion, is singular and requires the
singular pronoun it. Option (4) does not
correct the pronoun to singular. There is no
reason for the changes in options (1), (2), and
(5).

5. **(1) change the spelling of Sucessful to
Successful** (Mechanics/Spelling) The correct
spelling is successful, so option (1) is correct.
There is no reason for the changes in options
(2), (3), and (4).

6. **(5) no correction is necessary** (Usage/Verb
tense, clarity, and pronoun reference—
pronoun shift) Option (1) is incorrect because
the present tense is used throughout the
paragraphs. The plural jobs, in option (2), is
needed because of the plural kinds, to which it
refers. Option (3) is incorrect because the
pronoun you should be used for consistency.
Option (4) changes the meaning and does not
make sense.

7. **(2) training, and experience are required**
(Sentence structure/Parallelism; Usage/
Subject-verb agreement and verb tense;
Mechanics/Punctuation) Option (2) is correct
because the three items in series should be of
parallel structure; the first two items, skills
and training, are nouns, so the last one should
be a noun, experience. Are required is the
correct verb because it agrees with the plural
subject, skills, training, and experience, and
maintains the present tense. Options (1), (3),
and (4) are incorrect because they do not

include the needed verb form. Items in series should be separated by commas, not semicolons, as in option (5).

8. **(2) who are** (Usage/Pronoun reference—wrong relative pronoun) In option (2), who is the correct relative pronoun because it is the subject of the verb are. The relative pronoun which refers to animals, places, or things, but not to people. Therefore, option (4) is incorrect. Who and whom refer to people or animals. Option (3) is incorrect because it uses the objective form whom. Option (5) is incorrect because the comma would separate the subject and the verb.

9. **(4) change we have to you have** (Usage/Pronoun reference—pronoun shift) The pronoun you is used throughout the passage. We should be changed to you for consistency, so option (4) is correct. There is no reason for the changes in options (1), (2), and (3).

10. **(5) restaurant; however, you** (Sentence structure/Run-on sentences and fragments; Mechanics/Punctuation) Independent clauses may be joined by a comma and a conjunction or by a semicolon. Option (5) is correct because however is a conjunctive adverb and requires a semicolon before and a comma after it. Options (1) and (2) would create run-on sentences. A comma is not required after the conjunction but, as in option (3). In option (4), because is not logical and creates a sentence fragment.

11. **(4) change needed to need** (Usage/Verb tense—sequence of tense in sentence and paragraph) Option (4) is correct because the verb tense throughout these paragraphs is present tense. Needed is past tense and should be changed to present-tense need for consistency. There is no reason for the changes in options (2) and (3).

12. **(3) learn about the business and the job** (Usage/Pronoun reference—vague reference) The pronoun it makes a vague reference; it is not clear what the pronoun refers to. Option (3) is correct because it uses the specific words instead of pronouns. Options (2), (4), and (5) change the pronoun but do not clarify the reference.

13. **(5) your interest in the job** (Sentence structure/Parallelism) Option (5) is correct because the list of things to stress should have

a parallel structure. Option (2) is not clear in its meaning. Option (3) does not result in parallel structure. In option (4), you're, meaning "you are," is incorrect.

14. **(4) change ben franklin to Ben Franklin** (Mechanics/Capitalization) Option (4) is correct because the name Ben Franklin is a proper noun and each word should be capitalized. Therefore, option (3) is incorrect. Postal Service should be capitalized because it is a proper noun. Therefore, options (1) and (2) are incorrect.

15. **(4) change midwest to california to Midwest to California** (Mechanics/Capitalization) Option (4) is correct because both a section of the country, Midwest, and the name of a state, California, should be capitalized. There is no reason for the change in option (1). Options (2) and (3) each make only one of the two necessary capitalization corrections.

16. **(4) finally, the airplanes** (Sentence structure/Parallelism and clarity) Option (4) is correct because items in series should have parallel structure. The verb came should not be repeated, so option (2) is incorrect. Also, a comma is needed after finally to set it off because it interrupts the sentence. The extra words super and speedy in options (1), (3), and (5) are unnecessary; the sentence is clearer and more concise without them.

17. **(4) days; airmail** (Mechanics/Punctuation—semicolons) Option (4) is correct because these two sentences should be joined with a semicolon. Option (1) is incorrect because the original sentence is a run-on sentence; it contains two sentences with no punctuation between them. If the two sentences are joined with a comma and without a conjunction, as in option (2), a comma splice results. A semicolon should not be used with and or but, making options (3) and (5) incorrect.

18. **(3) change rose to risen** (Usage/Verb tense; Mechanics/Capitalization) Option (3) is correct because the past tense rose does not need the helping verb has; has risen is the correct present perfect tense. Option (2) is incorrect because mail is singular and requires the singular verb has. There is no reason for the changes in options (1), (4), and (5).

19. **(3) cents, and it appears** (Mechanics/Punctuation—commas between independent

clauses) Option (3) is correct because the two sentences should be joined with a comma and conjunction. The original version has a comma splice (two independent clauses joined by a comma with no conjunction). Removing the comma in option (2) creates a run-on sentence. Option (4) incorrectly uses a semicolon with the conjunction and. Option (5) shows a cause-and-effect relationship, which is incorrect; both ideas are of equal rank.

20. **(3) Service, despite its faults, does** (Usage/Subject-verb agreement; Mechanics/Punctuation) Option (3) is correct because the interrupting phrase despite its faults should be set off with commas. The subject of the sentence is Service, which is singular, so the singular verb does is correct. Options (1) and (2) are incorrect because they use the plural verb do. Options (4) and (5) incorrectly use a semicolon to set off the interrupting phrase.

21. **(3) change are to is** (Usage/Subject-verb agreement) The subject of the sentence, cost, is singular and requires the singular verb is. In terms of dollars is a prepositional phrase, so dollars cannot be the subject of the sentence. There is no reason for the changes in options (1), (2), and (4).

22. **(3) change intensive to intensely** (Usage/Adjectives and adverbs) Option (3) is correct because an adverb is used to describe an adjective; in this case, intensely describes the adjective controversial. There is no reason for the changes in options (1), (2), and (4).

23. **(2) change constitution to Constitution** (Mechanics/Capitalization) Option (2) is correct because Constitution must be capitalized; it is the title of a specific document. There is no reason for the changes in options (1), (3), and (4).

24. **(5) or to prohibit** (Sentence structure/Parallelism) This sentence does not have parallel structure because has prohibited does not follow the same verb form as to regulate. Option (5) is correct because to prohibit is parallel with to regulate. Options (1), (2), (3), and (4) do not create parallel structure in the sentence.

25. **(2) change who to that** (Usage/Pronoun reference—wrong relative pronoun) Option (2) is correct because the relative pronoun that refers to animals, places, or things; who and whom refer to people. The antecedent bill is a

thing, so that is the correct pronoun to use. There is no reason for the changes in options (1), (3), (4), and (5).

26. **(3) as a "cooling off" period** (Mechanics/Punctuation and capitalization) When quotation marks are used to set off an unusual term or an exact phrase in a sentence, the first word does not need to be capitalized. Therefore, option (3) is correct and options (2) and (4) are wrong. It is not necessary to use a comma to separate the phrase from the rest of the sentence, as in option (5).

27. **(1) change They to It** (Usage/Pronoun reference—agreement with antecedent) Option (1) is correct because the pronoun they is referring to the waiting period in sentence 5. Waiting period is singular, so the neuter singular pronoun it is needed. The pronoun He, in option (2), is incorrect. There is no reason for the changes in options (3), (4), and (5).

28. **(3) sales prevented by background investigations** (Mechanics/Punctuation—overuse of commas) Because the phrase prevented by background investigations is essential information to the meaning of the sentence, no commas or semicolons should be used; therefore, option (3) is correct and options (2) and (5) are incorrect. Prevented is the correct verb tense, so option (4) is incorrect.

29. **(5) their** (Usage/Pronoun reference—agreement with antecedent) A plural possessive pronoun is needed to refer to the plural antecedent criminals. Therefore, their in option (5) is correct. He and she in option (2) is neither plural nor possessive. Them, in option (3), is plural but not possessive. Option (4) is incorrect because our would refer to a group of which the author is not a part.

30. **(1) when** (Sentence structure/Improper coordination and subordination) Option (1) is correct because the word when shows the relationship between the two sentences. Options (2), (3), (4), and (5) do not properly use a subordinate conjunction to connect the dependent clause and the independent clause.

31. **(4) Hundreds** (Sentence structure/Clarity) The sentence is wordy. Eliminating the words virtually and countless makes the sentence concise; therefore, option (4) is correct.

Answers and Explanations

Options (1), (2), (3), and (5) do not eliminate the wordiness.

32. **(3) lost** (Usage/Verb tense) Because the paragraphs and the rest of this sentence are written in past tense, the past-tense lost, in option (3), is correct. Loose, in option (2), means "not tight." Options (4) and (5) are incorrect because they are the wrong tense; also, option (4) is a singular form and does not agree with the plural subject.

33. **(3) change they to the people** (Usage/Pronoun reference—ambiguous reference) It is not clear whether they refers to countries or to people. Option (3) is correct because using the people eliminates the ambiguous reference. Options (1) and (2) do not clarify the pronoun reference. Option (4) is incorrect because succeed is spelled correctly.

34. **(3) change your shoulder to our shoulders** (Usage/Pronoun reference—pronoun shift) Because the first pronoun in the sentence is we, for consistency the second pronoun should be our, rather than your; therefore, option (3) is correct. There is no reason for the change in option (1). Options (2) and (4) shift to other incorrect pronouns.

35. **(5) change had gave to gave** (Usage/Verb tense—verb form) Option (5) is correct because the past-tense gave does not need a helping verb. There is no reason for the changes in options (1), (2), (3), and (4).

36. **(3) cooperation and understanding** (Mechanics/Punctuation—overuse of commas) Option (3) is correct because the conjunction and joins two nouns that are objects of the preposition of. There is no reason to use a comma or a semicolon as in the other options.

37. **(2) the free world** (Sentence structure/ Improper coordination and subordination) Option (2) is correct because this is a complex sentence and no conjunction is needed. The clauses are improperly coordinated in options (1) and (5), the ideas being joined are not of equal rank, so no coordinating conjunction is needed. Options (3) and (4) are incorrect because they result in two dependent clauses.

38. **(4) reached 300; however, since then** (Sentence structure/Clarity) Option (4) is correct because it combines the two related sentences using however. Options (1), (2), (3), and (5) are incorrect because they do not show

the contrast in the relationship between the two ideas. Option (3) also creates a comma splice.

39. **(5) no correction is necessary** (Usage/Verb forms; Mechanics/ Punctuation—overuse of commas and spelling—homonyms) Showing in option (1) is an incorrect verb form because it needs a helping verb. Option (2) is incorrect because a comma would separate subject and verb in the dependent clause. Option (3) is incorrect because their is the correct plural possessive pronoun referring to people; They're is the contraction for "they are." Option (4) is incorrect because a comma is not used where two items are joined with and.

40. **(3) LaRosa, chairman of the American Heart Association's task force on cholesterol issues, keeping** (Mechanics/ Punctuation—appositives) Commas are used to separate a descriptive phrase (appositive) from the noun being described when the description is not essential to the meaning of the sentence. Notice that the commas are used on both sides of the phrase. Therefore, option (3) is correct and options (1), (2), and (5) are incorrect. In option (4), the second comma is placed incorrectly.

41. **(2) change are to is** (Usage/Subject-verb agreement) Public is a group word and is considered singular, so the singular verb is, as in option (2), is correct. There is no reason for the changes in options (1), (3), and (4).

42. **(4) Today, doctors recommend** (Usage/ Subject-verb agreement; Mechanics/ Capitalization) Option (4) is correct because doctors is a plural noun and must have a plural verb, recommend. Possession is not shown, so options (2) and (3) are incorrect. In option (5), there is no reason to capitalize doctors because it is not used as a proper noun.

43. **(2) fiber, oat bran, and beans** (Mechanics/ Punctuation—commas between items in series) Option (2) is correct because commas are needed between each of the items in a simple list. Option (3) incorrectly uses a semicolon instead of a comma. Options (4) and (5) have commas placed incorrectly.

44. **(5) no correction is necessary** (Mechanics/ Spelling and punctuation; Sentence structure/Fragments; and Usage/Pronoun reference) In option (1), Exercising is spelled

correctly. Since exercising creates a sentence fragment, making option (2) incorrect. The sentence does not show possession, so the pronoun you should not be changed to your, as in option (3). Option (4) is incorrect because no comma is needed after the word fit.

45. **(5) no correction is necessary** (Mechanics/Spelling; Usage/Subject-verb agreement, verb tense, and adjectives and adverbs) In option (1), resistance is spelled correctly. Option (2) is incorrect because the singular verb has agrees in number with the singular noun resistance. Option (3) is incorrect because it changes the verb tense of the passage. Option (4) is incorrect because the comparative adjective form stronger is needed.

46. **(3) This, we now know, has** (Usage/Subject-verb agreement with interrupting phrase; Mechanics/Punctuation—commas with parenthetical expressions) Option 3 is correct because the subject This is singular and requires the singular verb has. Options (2) and (5) are incorrect because they use the plural verb have. We now know is an interrupting phrase and should be set off with commas, so option (4) is incorrect.

47. **(2) change children, they to children, and they** (Sentence structure/Comma splice) The original sentence has a comma splice (two sentences improperly joined together with a comma). Option (2) is correct because the two sentences must be joined by a comma and a coordinating conjunction. Option (3) is incorrect because a semicolon is not used with the coordinating conjunction and. There is no reason for the changes in options (1) and (4).

48. **(3) that are sterile so they** (Usage/Pronoun reference—agreement with antecedent and wrong relative pronoun) Option (3) is correct because the pronoun must agree with its antecedent insects. Insects is plural, so the pronoun should be they, which is plural. Options (2), (4), and (5) are incorrect because the relative pronouns who and whom refer to people, not insects.

49. **(1) change Its to It's** (Mechanics/Apostrophes) It's is a contraction for "it is." Its is a possessive pronoun. Option (1) is correct because It is the subject of the sentence and is is the verb; no possession is being shown in the sentence. There is no reason for the changes in options (2), (3), and (4).

50. **(5) no correction is necessary** (Mechanics/Punctuation—commas after introductory elements and between items in series; Usage/Subject-verb agreement and clarity) Unfortunately is an introductory element that should be set off with a comma, so option (1) is incorrect. Option (2) is incorrect because the comma is necessary to separate adjectives in series. Option (3) is incorrect because the subject pesticide is singular and requires the singular verb is. The word than is used in comparisons and should not be changed to then, meaning "at that time," as in option (4).

51. **(2) controversial, contradictory, and** (Sentence structure/Fragments; Mechanics/Punctuation—commas between items in series) Both sentences are fragments; combined they contain a series of three adjectives—controversial, contradictory, and emotional—that describe the subject. Items in series should be separated by commas, so option (2) is correct. Option (3) is incorrect because and should be used only between the last two items in the series. Options (1), (4), and (5) do not correct the sentence fragments.

52. **(5) parlors is legal, but private** (Usage/Subject-verb agreement with the interrupting phrase; Mechanics/Punctuation—commas between independent clauses) The subject of the first independent clause is betting. Betting is singular, so the singular verb is is correct. Therefore, option (5) is correct and option (2) is incorrect. When a coordinate conjunction joins two sentences (independent clauses), a comma, not a semicolon, is needed before the conjunction; therefore, options (3) and (4) are incorrect.

53. **(2) change There is to There are** (Usage/Subject-verb agreement—expletive and verb tense) Option (2) is correct because the subject of the sentence is organizations, which is plural; the plural verb are is required. The paragraphs are written in present tense. Option (1) is incorrect because the past-tense were would not be consistent with the verb tense in the other sentences. Use of the pronoun they, as in option (3), is incorrect. There is no reason for the change in option (4).

54. **(3) change nevada, to Nevada** (Mechanics/Capitalization; Mechanics/Punctuation—overuse of commas) Option (3) is correct because the name of a state, Nevada, should

be capitalized. Because the dependent clause is restrictive, a comma after Nevada is not needed, so option (4) is incorrect. There is no reason for the changes in options (1) and (2).

55. **(3) insert a comma after card game** (Mechanics/Punctuation—appositives) A card game, an appositive that further explains Poker, should be set off by commas; therefore, option (3) is correct and option (1) is incorrect. There is no reason for the changes in options (2) and (4).

SIMULATED GED TEST

(Pages 236–249)

1. **(3) insert a comma after past** (Mechanics/Punctuation—commas after introductory elements) Option (3) is correct because a comma, not a semicolon as in option (2), should be placed after the introductory phrase in the past. Past is a noun meaning "a time gone by"; passed, in option (1), which means "to transfer something to another person," is incorrect. There is no reason for the change in option (4).

2. **(5) no correction is necessary** (Mechanics/Spelling—homonyms and punctuation) In option (1), hear means to gain information through the ear; here refers to a location. In option (2), eye refers to the organ of the body that one sees with; I is a pronoun that refers to oneself. Option (3) is incorrect because a nonessential (unnecessary) clause should be set off with a comma. Option (4) is incorrect because addition means more; edition refers to a version of printed material.

3. **(3) people who are** (Usage/Pronoun reference—wrong relative pronoun and verb tense) Option (3) is correct because the pronoun who is used when referring to people, and since people is plural, the plural verb are is needed. Option (2) uses which, the relative pronoun that is used to refer to things, not people. Options (2) and (4) are incorrect because they use the singular verb is. Option (5) is incorrect because the sentence is written in present tense and the verb were is past tense.

4. **(3) is that the body receiving the transplant** (Usage/Pronoun reference—vague reference and subject-verb agreement; Sentence structure/ improper coordination and subordination) Option (3) is correct because

the pronoun it has no clear antecedent. The vague pronoun it should be replaced by the body receiving the transplant. Option (2) still has the vague pronoun reference. Options (2) and (4) are incorrect because the subject problem is singular and requires the singular verb is. Option (5) is incorrect because the word because creates an incorrect subordinate structure in this sentence.

5. **(1) is sometimes required** (Usage/Subject-verb agreement with interrupting phrase) Option (1) is correct because the subject use is singular, so the singular verb is is needed. Options (2) and (5) are incorrect because they use the plural verb are. Option (3) is incorrect because the verb were does not agree with the singular subject and is past tense; the rest of the sentence (and paragraph) is written in present tense. Options (4) and (5) are incorrect because the phrase in any case is wordy; eliminating it will make the sentence clearer.

6. **(4) concerns are heard that** (Mechanics/Punctuation—overuse of commas) Option (4) is correct because commas are not needed before or after the verb are heard. Options (2), (3), and (5) are incorrect because commas should not separate the subject and verb or set off an essential clause.

7. **(5) no correction is necessary** (Usage/Verb tense; Mechanics/ Possessives) Option (1) is incorrect because selling is present tense and the paragraph is written in present tense. Option (2) is incorrect because their should not be changed to they're, the contraction for "they are." Options (3) and (4) are incorrect because his and its are both singular, and the plural possessive their is required to agree with people.

8. **(2) change its to their** (Usage/Pronoun reference—agreement with antecedent; Mechanics/Spelling—homonyms) Option (2) is correct because the pronoun its must agree with its antecedent people; people is plural, so the plural pronoun their is correct. Option (1) is incorrect because they're is the contraction for "they are." There is no reason for the changes in options (3) and (4).

9. **(4) change todays to today's** (Mechanics/Possessives) Option (4) is correct because the singular possessive today's is required in this sentence. Option (3) is incorrect because it shows the plural

possessive todays'. There is no reason for the changes in options (1) and (2).

10. **(1) arrives, we** (Sentence structure/Sentence fragments; Mechanics/Punctuation—commas after introductory elements) Option (1) is correct because the rewritten sentence starts with a dependent clause; a comma, not a semicolon, as in option (2), should follow a dependent clause at the beginning of the sentence. Options (3) and (4) are incorrect because the semicolons create sentence fragments and because these options contain the unnecessary words because and as a result. The conjunction but in option (5) is also unnecessary.

11. **(2) change There is to There are** (Usage/Subject-verb agreement—expletive) Option (2) is correct because the subject of the sentence, computers, is plural, so the plural verb are is correct. There is no reason for the changes in options (1), (3), and (4).

12. **(4) at the supermarkets and discount stores,** (Sentence structure/Parallelism) Option (4) is correct because all three items in this series should start with prepositions: in, at, and on. Options (1), (2), and (3) do not maintain parallel structure. Option (5) uses the preposition on incorrectly.

13. **(1) satellites. They** (Sentence structure/Run-on sentence and comma splice) Option (1) is correct because the two independent clauses can stand alone as two sentences. Option (2) is incorrect because a semicolon is not used with a coordinating conjunction. Option (3) is incorrect because a comma is needed to join two independent clauses with the conjunction and. Option (4) is incorrect because it creates a comma splice. Option (5) is incorrect because it creates a run-on sentence.

14. **(1) is that, at least so far, they** (Usage/Subject-verb agreement; Mechanics/Punctuation—commas with parenthetical expressions) Option (1) is correct because the subject of the sentence is problem. Problem is singular and requires the singular verb is. Options (2), (3), and (5) are incorrect because the plural verb are does not agree with the singular subject problem. Option (4) is incorrect because the parenthetical phrase at least so far should be set off with commas.

15. **(1) change the spelling of benifit to benefit** (Mechanics/Spelling) Option (1) is

correct because the correct spelling is benefit. There is no reason for the changes in options (2), (3), and (4).

16. **(1) change is to are** (Usage/Subject-verb agreement and verb tense) Option (1) is correct because this sentence has a compound subject, keyboarding and data entry, which requires a plural verb are. Option (2) is incorrect because the paragraph is written in present tense and is is present tense. There is no reason for the changes in options (3) and (4).

17. **(3) change united states to United States** (Mechanics/Capitalization) Option (3) is correct because United States, the name of a country, should be capitalized. There is no reason for the changes in options (1), (2), and (4).

18. **(4) change with is to with are** (Usage/Subject-verb agreement) Option (4) is correct because the subject forms is plural, requiring the plural verb are. There is no reason for the changes in options (1) and (2). Option (3) is incorrect because our is a possessive pronoun showing ownership; the verb are is needed in the sentence.

19. **(1) movies, videotapes, and magazines** (Mechanics/Capitalization) Option (1) is correct because none of these words should be capitalized. Options (2), (3), (4), and (5) are incorrect because none of the words in this series is used as a proper noun.

20. **(1) when** (Sentence structure/Subordination) Option (1) is correct because when expresses the cause-and-effect relationship between the two ideas. Options (2), (3), (4), and (5) do not show this relationship.

21. **(3) change is to was** (Usage/Verb tense in paragraph) Option (3) is correct because the word clue long ago earlier in the paragraph (sentence 5) indicates that a past-tense verb, was arrested, is correct. There is no reason for the changes in options (1) and (4). Option (2) is incorrect because will be arrested is future tense.

22. **(4) change see hear and say to see, hear, and say** (Mechanics/Punctuation—commas between items in series) Option (4) is correct because the three items in series, see, hear, and say, should be separated with commas.

Answers and Explanations

There is no reason for the changes in options (1), (2), and (3).

23. **(1) change You tend to We tend** (Usage/Pronoun reference—pronoun shift) Option (1) is correct because the rest of the sentences are written in first-person plural we. This sentence shifts to second-person you; for consistency this sentence must also use first-person plural we. There is no reason for the changes in options (2), (3), and (4).

24. **(5) forms, and we** (Sentence structure/Run-on sentence; Mechanics/Punctuation—commas between independent clauses) Option (5) is correct because a comma and a coordinating conjunction are required to join these sentences correctly. In option (1), the two sentences joined by the conjunction and with no comma create a run-on sentence. Options (2) and (3) are incorrect because a semicolon is not used with a coordinating conjunction. Options (3) and (4) are incorrect because a comma is not needed after the conjunction and.

25. **(3) remove the phrase back in the beginning** (Sentence structure/Clarity) Option (3) is correct because the phrase back in the beginning is unnecessary. The sentence is clearer and more concise without it, since originally means the same. Options (1), (2), and (4) do not make the sentence clearer.

26. **(2) change social security act to Social Security Act** (Mechanics/Capitalization) Option (2) is correct because Social Security Act is the name of a particular law and should be capitalized. Option (1) is incorrect because the word act also needs to be capitalized. There is no reason for the changes in options (3) and (4).

27. **(2) those who have disabilities** (Usage/Pronoun reference—wrong relative pronoun) Option (2) is correct because who is the subject of the verb have and is correct; whom, as in options (1) and (4), is objective case and cannot be the subject. Option (3) is incorrect because the relative pronoun which does not refer to people. Option (5) is incorrect because the last item in the series must name a category of people.

28. **(3) years, and the** (Mechanics/Punctuation—commas between independent clauses) Option (3) is correct because sentences joined by a coordinating conjunction need a comma before

the conjunction, not a semicolon as in options (1), (2), and (4). Option (4) is incorrect because the coordinating conjunction and should not be followed by a comma. Option (5) is incorrect because no possession is shown.

29. **(2) health care, the number** (Sentence structure/Fragment; Mechanics/Punctuation—commas after introductory elements and capitalization) Option (2) is correct because a parenthetical dependent clause should be set off with a comma. Sentence 5 is a fragment. Option (3) is incorrect because a dependent clause should not be separated from an independent clause by a semicolon. Option (4) is incorrect because using while creates two fragments (two dependent clauses) with no independent clause to make a complete sentence. Option (5) is incorrect because there is no reason to capitalize health care.

30. **(3) change which to who** (Usage/Pronoun reference—wrong relative pronoun) Option (3) is correct because the relative pronoun which does not refer to people; who or whom refers to people. Who is the subject of the verb were working. Option (4) is incorrect because whom is objective case and cannot be used as the subject of a verb. There is no reason for the changes in options (1) and (2).

31. **(5) move temporarily between the words using and to** (Sentence structure/Modification) Option (5) is correct because the adverb temporarily should be moved as close as possible to the verb it modifies, to fund. There is no reason for the changes in options (1), (2), (3), and (4).

32. **(2) youth if we want** (Mechanics/Punctuation—overuse of commas) Option (2) is correct because the dependent clause is essential to the meaning of the sentence; it should not be set off by a comma. Options (1), (3), (4), and (5) are incorrect because the commas and semicolons are used incorrectly.

33. **(1) change academy to Academy** (Mechanics/Capitalization) Option (1) is correct because Academy is part of the name of an organization and should be capitalized. There is no reason for the changes in options (2), (3), and (4).

34. **(3) An Oscar is a gold-plated** (Sentence structure/Clarity) The combination in option (3) is the most concise and clear version. Options (1), (2), and (5) are wordy and

incorrectly use the comparison word like. Option (4) is incorrect because the pronoun it has no antecedent.

35. **(4) change Spring to spring** (Mechanics/Capitalization) Option (4) is correct because the names of seasons should not be capitalized. There is no reason for the changes in options (1), (2), and (3).

36. **(3) actress, and the Oscars are** (Usage/Pronoun reference—ambiguous reference and subject-verb agreement; Mechanics/Punctuation—comma between independent clauses) Option (3) is correct because it eliminates the ambiguous reference of the pronoun they. In the original sentence it is not clear whether they refers to the Oscars or to every actor and actress. Options (2) and (5) are incorrect because a semicolon is not used with the conjunction and. Option (4) is incorrect because the plural subject they requires the plural verb are.

37. **(5) no correction is necessary** (Mechanics/Punctuation—appositives) Option (5) is correct because the phrase a device that reads the prices on groceries at the checkout and records them is an appositive that further explains what a scanner is; an appositive should be set off with commas, as in the original sentence. Options (1) and (3) are incorrect because they remove these commas. There is no reason for the change in option (2). Option (4) is incorrect because an appositive is not set off with a semicolon.

38. **(4) these devices is** (Usage/Subject-verb agreement with interrupting phrase and verb tense) Because the subject of the sentence, name, is singular, the singular verb is is correct; therefore, option (4) is correct and options (1) and (2) are incorrect. The rest of the paragraph is written in present tense, so the present-tense verb is is correct. Changing the verb tense, as in options (3) and (5), is incorrect.

39. **(4) replace who with that** (Usage/Pronoun reference—wrong relative pronoun) Option (4) is correct because the relative pronoun in the sentence refers to a computer voice. The relative pronoun who refers to people; that refers to things. There is no reason for the changes in options (1), (2), and (3).

40. **(4) move on the package after spacing** (Sentence structure/Misplaced modifier)

Option (4) is correct because it clarifies the meaning of the sentence. The original sentence does not make clear whether the package or the lines have different widths and spacing. There is no reason for the changes in options (1), (2), and (3).

41. **(4) Nobel, a Swedish chemist, invented** (Mechanics/Punctuation—appositives and capitalization) Option (4) is correct because the phrase a Swedish chemist further explains who Alfred Nobel was. It is an appositive and should be set off with commas. Options (1), (2), and (3) do not correctly show the appositive set off with commas. Option (5) is incorrect; Swedish should be capitalized because it is an adjective derived from a proper noun.

42. **(3) world peace, chemistry, physics, literature, and** (Mechanics/Punctuation—commas between items in series) Option (3) is correct because three or more items in series should be separated with commas. Options (1), (2), (4), and (5) are incorrect because they do not separate each item with a comma.

43. **(2) change dynamite, he to dynamite; he** (Mechanics/Punctuation—semicolons; Sentence structure/ Comma splice and run-on sentence) Option (2) is correct because two sentences joined without a coordinating conjunction require a semicolon. Option (1) is incorrect because removing the comma after dynamite creates a run-on sentence. The original sentence is incorrectly joined by a comma, which options (3) and (4) do not correct.

44. **(5) no correction is necessary** (Mechanics/Punctuation—commas and capitalization; Usage/ Verb forms) Options (1) and (3) are incorrect because the phrase which began in 1901 is a nonessential phrase and should be set off by commas. Option (2) is incorrect because the verb begun needs a helping verb; began is the correct tense. Option (4) is incorrect because the proper noun Sweden should be capitalized.

45. **(4) change norwegian to Norwegian** (Mechanics/Capitalization) Option (4) is correct because Norwegian is an adjective formed from a proper noun and should be capitalized. There is no reason for the changes in options (1), (2), and (3).

46. **(1) established** (Usage/Verb tense and subject-verb agreement) Option (1) is correct

because the phrase In 1969 indicates past tense; the verb established is past tense. Because the revision also changes the sentence from passive voice to active voice, the subject of the sentence is now the Swedish Central Bank, not prize. Therefore, was established, as in option (2), is incorrect. Options (3), (4), and (5) are incorrect because the verbs are not past tense.

47. **(3) year on December 10, the** (Mechanics/Capitalization) The name of a month, December, is a proper noun and is always capitalized; therefore, option (3) is correct and options (1) and (2) are incorrect. Options (4) and (5) are incorrect because there is no reason for a comma before or after the preposition on.

48. **(3) change are to is** (Usage/Subject-verb agreement) Option (3) is correct because the subject cash is singular and requires the singular verb is. There is no reason for the changes in options (1), (2), (4), and (5).

49. **(4) change the spelling of alot to a lot** (Mechanics/Spelling) Option (4) is correct because a lot is two words. There is no reason for the changes in options (1), (2), and (3).

50. **(4) power plants that burn** (Mechanics/Capitalization and punctuation—overuse of commas) Option (4) is correct because the phrase that burn high-sulfur coal is essential to the meaning of the sentence and should not be set off by a comma as in options (1) and (5). Power plants is a common noun and should not be capitalized, as in option (2). Changing that burn to burning, as in option (3), would be an acceptable change, but setting off the phrase with a semicolon is incorrect.

51. **(1) change midwest to Midwest** (Mechanics/Capitalization) Option (1) is correct because the name of a specific section or region of a country, such as Midwest, should be capitalized. There is no reason for the changes in options (2) and (4). Option (3) is incorrect because Northeast is capitalized correctly.

52. **(1) trees. It** (Mechanics/Punctuation—commas between independent clauses; Sentence structure/ Run-on sentence) Option (1) is correct because both sentences are complete and can stand alone. Options (2) and (5) are incorrect because a semicolon is not used with a coordinating conjunction

separating two independent clauses. Option (3) is incorrect because two independent clauses joined with a coordinating conjunction and without a comma create a run-on sentence. Option (4) is incorrect because if a coordinating conjunction is used, a comma should not be placed after the conjunction.

53. **(3) cleaner coal, oil, gas, or** (Mechanics/Punctuation—commas between items in series) Option (3) is correct because three or more items in series should be separated by commas. Options (1), (2), (4), and (5) do not show commas correctly placed between each item in the series.

54. **(3) replace it with the coal** (Usage/Pronoun reference—vague reference) Option (3) is correct because the pronoun it has no antecedent in this sentence; the pronoun should be replaced with a noun to make clear what it refers to. Options (1) and (2) are incorrect because the commas separate the subject and verb. Option (4) is incorrect because its is a possessive pronoun; no possession is shown in the sentence.

55. **(3) soon; however, it will not** (Mechanics/Punctuation—Semicolon) Option (3) is correct because the two independent clauses should be joined with a semicolon and the conjunctive adverb however. The conjunctive adverb must be followed by a comma, so options (2) and (5) are incorrect; also, no comparison is made, so sooner in option (2) is wrong. In option (4), because shows a cause-and-effect relationship that does not make sense.

Glossary

abbreviation a shortened form of a word, such as A.M. and P.M., Dr., and Mr.

adjective a word that describes or modifies a noun or a pronoun by telling what kind, how many, or which one or ones. Example: The house is on a steep hill.

adjective clause a subordinating clause that begins with a relative pronoun. Example: A dog that is well trained will not jump on the furniture.

adverb a word that describes or modifies an action verb, an adjective, or another adverb by telling when, where, how, or to what extent. Example: He walked slowly.

adverb clause a group of words that begins with a subordinating conjunction and gives information about the main idea in a sentence. Example: Rather than leave after dark, we will wait until morning.

antecedent the particular noun or phrase to which a pronoun refers. Example: The people and their pets marched in the parade. (People is the antecedent for their.)

apostrophe a punctuation mark (') used to form possessives and, in contractions, to take the place of a missing letter or letters. Examples: We're (we are) certain the book is Randy's.

appositive a word or phrase that explains or gives further information about a noun or pronoun. Example: Sara, the right fielder, has the highest batting average.

article the words *a, an,* and *the.* They are used with nouns to limit their meaning. Example: I am looking for the book.

capitalization beginning a word with a capital letter to signal a new sentence, or to show that it is the name of a specific person, place, or thing. Example: We are going to Memphis. I is always capitalized.

clause a group of words that has a subject and a word saying something about the subject but that forms only part of a complex or compound sentence. *See* dependent clause *and* independent clause.

comma a punctuation mark (,) that marks the separation of words or groups of words in a sentence. Example: She bought a dress, shoes, and a hat.

comma splice an incorrect use of a comma to join two independent clauses. Example: Pack your bags, leave town.

comparative a degree of comparison of the characteristics of two people, qualities, or things that show a change in the quantity, quality, or relationship described by an adverb or adjective. Example: Paul is a good mechanic, but Alex is a better one.

complex sentence a sentence that has at least one dependent and one independent clause. Example: If the restaurant is closed, we will have to eat at home.

compound antecedent two or more nouns to which a pronoun refers. Example: Jeff and Carol are riding their bikes. (Jeff and Carol is the compound antecedent to their.)

compound object two or more nouns, pronouns, or phrases that together are affected by the action of a verb or that follow a preposition. Example: Cheryl bought tickets for Jesse and me.

compound sentence a sentence with two independent clauses which are related. Example: We traveled by boat, and we had a wonderful time.

compound subject two or more nouns, pronouns, or phrases that together are the doers of the action of the main verb in a sentence. Example: Sally and John enjoy riding bikes.

conjunction a word that connects words or groups of words. Example: Kevin scored a goal, but Tim did not.

conjunctive adverb a word that connects two main ideas in a sentence and shows a connection between them. A conjunctive adverb requires a semicolon and is followed by a comma. Example: He had to leave; however, his report is on the desk.

consonant any letter of the English alphabet except *a, e, i, o, u,* and sometimes *y*

contraction a word formed from two words that are combined and shortened by leaving out a letter or letters. An apostrophe takes the place of the missing letter or letters. Example: he's (he is) Exception: won't (will not)

coordinating conjunction a word that joins two independent clauses and shows a relationship of equal rank between the ideas. Example: She works hard, but her performance could improve.

dangling modifier a modifying phrase that is misplaced in a sentence. Example: Reaching under the bed for the ball, the cat scratched his hand.

dependent clause a clause that has a subject and a verb but does not express a complete thought. Example: If the money is not available, we will not buy the new computers.

direct address words that name the person who is being spoken to. In direct address, a comma is used after the person's name. Example: Carol, I need help with the landscaping.

direct quotation the exact words someone has used; a direct quotation is set off with quotation marks. Example: Montaigne said, "Cowardice is the mother of cruelty."

double negative two negative words used in a sentence when only one is needed. Example: She isn't never going to find her keys.

end punctuation a period, question mark, or exclamation mark. They are used at the end of a sentence to signal a pause and to make the meaning of the sentence clear.

exact quotation *See* direct quotation.

exclamation mark a punctuation mark (!) used at the end of a phrase or sentence to express a strong feeling, such as surprise, shock, or enthusiasm. Example: I love it!

first person the form of verbs or pronouns that refers to the speaker or writer of the speech. Example: I am here.

fragment *See* sentence fragment.

future perfect tense a verb tense that expresses a future action that will begin and end before another future action takes place. Example: He will have completed three courses by the end of this year.

future tense a verb tense that shows that an action will take place or a condition will be true in the future. Example: You will see your brother next week.

gender the masculine, feminine, or neuter form of a word that determines agreement with other words. Example: Susan bought her father a present. (The feminine pronoun her agrees with Susan.)

grammar the rules of the English language, including mechanics, usage, and sentence structure

homonyms words that sound alike but have different spellings and/or different meanings. Example: Before we swim in their pool, let's put our towels over there.

indefinite pronoun a word that makes a general reference to a person, place, or thing. Example: Anyone can answer the phone.

independent clause a group of words that has a subject and verb and expresses a complete thought. Example: To their surprise, they all passed the test.

infinitive the form of a verb that normally consists of the word *to* plus the first-person singular present tense. Example: to go

intensive pronoun a pronoun that adds emphasis to another noun or pronoun. Example: I did it myself.

interjections words that display extreme emotion or excitement. Example: Wow! I'm very excited about the party tomorrow.

interrupter a word or expression that interrupts the main thought in a sentence. Example: The company said, of course, that the check was in the mail.

introductory element a word or phrase at the beginning of a sentence that is not an essential part of the main idea. Example: However, your term paper is still due on Monday.

irregular verb a verb that changes its spelling to form its past and past participle. Example: begin (present), began (past), begun (past participle)

items in series in a sentence, a list of words or phrases that appear one after the other. When there are more than two items in a list, they are separated by commas. Example: He brought the soft drinks, hot dogs, and chips to the picnic.

linking verb a verb that expresses a state or condition by linking the subject of a sentence to words that describe the subject. Common linking verbs are forms of *be*. Example: I am the first high school graduate in my family.

linking words words that join clauses that could stand alone. Example: I'm angry; furthermore, you're out of line.

mechanically correct writing that uses correct capitalization, punctuation, and spelling

mechanics the aspect of grammar that includes capitalization, punctuation, and spelling

misplaced modifier a descriptive word or phrase placed in such a way as to confuse or change the meaning of the sentence. Example: Joey bought the car from the neighbor with the broken headlight.

modifier a word or phrase that describes another word or phrase. Example: Joan decided to buy the red dress. (Red modifies dress.)

nonrestrictive clause a clause that is not essential to the meaning of a sentence

noun a word that names a person, place, thing, or quality. Example: We visited the museum.

number the form of a noun or pronoun that shows it is singular or plural

object a word or phrase that is affected by the action of a verb or that follows a preposition. Example: He hit the ball over the fence.

object pronoun a pronoun used as the object of a verb or preposition or when restating a noun object. Example: Give it back to him.

parallel structure a series of words, phrases, or clauses in a sentence that are written in the same form. Example: We spent the money because we earned it, wanted something new, and needed the car.

parenthetical expression a phrase that adds nothing essential to the meaning of a sentence

and that interrupts the main thought. Example: That's the last time, if you want to know the truth, that I'm going to get the old car fixed.

participle a form of a verb that is always with a helping verb to indicate certain tenses. Participles can also act as adjectives. Examples: I have been, you have seen, the frightened child, the barking dog

parts of speech the different kinds of words that make up a sentence

past participle the principal part of a verb that uses a helping verb to form the present perfect, future perfect, and past perfect tenses. Example: They have loaded the truck.

past perfect tense a verb tense that expresses an action that began and ended before another past action began; it is formed by using the helping verb had with the past participle. Example: We had chosen to stay home before we realized the party was for us.

past tense a verb tense that expresses an action that took place or a condition that was true in the past. Example: We talked for hours yesterday.

period a punctuation mark (.) that is used to indicate the end of a sentence. Periods are also used in abbreviations, such as A.M. and P.M. Example: That's all, folks. We'll be back tomorrow at 8 A.M.

phrase a group of related words that acts as a single part of speech. Example: We hid the present under the bed.

plural more than one. Plural nouns usually end in s. Examples: dogs, houses

possessive a word that shows ownership. Examples: Harriet's project, my father's keys

possessive pronoun a pronoun form that shows ownership. Example: She said it was her umbrella, but I recognized it as mine.

predicate the part of a sentence that usually consists of the main verb and that tells about the subject

prefix a word part added at the beginning of a word that changes the meaning of the word. Example: He is certain, but I am uncertain.

preposition a word that shows direction, location, or time. Example: <u>After</u> dinner we put most <u>of</u> the dishes <u>on</u> the counter.

prepositional phrase a phrase that begins with a preposition, and includes its object, and any words that modify the object. Example: We found the wallet <u>in the red car</u>.

present participle the verb form ending in <u>-ing</u>. The present participle can be used as an adjective or combined with the verb *be* to make the progressive forms of verbs. Example: I <u>am walking</u> three miles every day.

present perfect tense a verb tense that expresses an action that was completed or a condition that was true at some indefinite time in the past. It also refers to an action that began in the past and has continued into the present. It is formed using either <u>have</u> or <u>has</u> with the verb's past participle. Example: <u>She has worked</u> long and hard on that report.

present tense a verb tense that expresses an action that takes place now or a condition that is true now. Example: He <u>runs</u> every morning.

pronoun a word that takes the place of a noun. Example: Lisa is sixteen, so <u>she</u> is old enough to drive.

proper adjective an adjective that is formed from a specific place name. It is capitalized. Examples: <u>American</u>, <u>Russian</u>

proper noun a noun that names a specific person, place, or thing. A proper noun is always capitalized. Examples: <u>Henry</u>, the <u>Alamo</u>, the <u>Declaration of Independence</u>.

punctuation the use of special marks to show how the parts of a sentence are related to each other and where and how the sentence ends. Examples: Did you hear the news? The drawing was held; we won the money, the car, and the trip!

question mark a punctuation mark (**?**) used at the end of a question. Example: Where are you taking that letter?

quotation marks punctuation marks used in pairs (**" "**) to set off a special term or a person's exact words. Examples: Some people do not like to be called "yuppies." "I know I don't," said Luke.

reflexive pronoun a pronoun used when the subject is both the doer and the receiver of the action. Example: Let's treat <u>ourselves</u> to some ice cream.

regular verb a verb whose past and past participle forms are made by adding <u>-d</u> or <u>-ed</u> to its present form. Example: dance (present), <u>danced</u> (past), have <u>danced</u> (past participle)

relative pronoun a pronoun used to introduce a subordinate clause. Example: I fully trust the doctor, <u>whom</u> I've consulted many times. (<u>Whom</u> refers to the doctor.)

restrictive clause a clause that is essential to the meaning of a sentence

run-on sentence two or more sentences incorrectly strung together as one sentence. Example: In time I hope to get my GED I will look for a better job.

second person the form of verbs or pronouns that refers to the person being written or spoken to. Example: <u>You are</u> ready to graduate.

semicolon a punctuation mark (**;**) used to join the independent clauses of a compound sentence when a coordinating conjunction is not used or when a linking word such as <u>however</u> is used. Examples: I got rid of that old car<u>;</u> it didn't run well anyway. He went to the doctor this morning; <u>however</u>, he still doesn't have the test result.

sentence a group of words with a subject and a verb that expresses a complete thought. Example: I attended high school in Chicago.

sentence fragment an incomplete sentence. A fragment may lack a subject or a verb, begin with a word that makes it dependent on another sentence for meaning, or begin with a relative pronoun. Examples: Whoever challenged the present system. Running on empty.

sentence structure the part of the writing process that deals with correctly expressing related ideas in a sentence and with combining clauses

singular one person, place, or thing

spelling the correct or accepted formation of words from letters

split infinitive when the two parts of the infinitive form of a verb are separated. Split infinitives are not grammatically acceptable. Example: We decided to finally go.

subject the noun or pronoun a sentence is about; the doer of the action of the main verb in a sentence. Example: Jim found a great job.

subject pronoun a pronoun used as the subject of a sentence or dependent clause. Example: He starts his new job next week.

subject-verb agreement when the form of the main verb of a sentence matches the subject. Example: The team practices daily. (singular subject, singular verb) Example: We know. (plural subject, plural verb)

subordinate clause a group of words that adds details about an independent clause but is dependent on the main sentence and cannot stand alone. Example: We finished cleaning up after nine o'clock.

subordinating conjunction a word that sets up a relationship of unequal rank between the main ideas in two clauses. Example: I'll go to the party even though I may have to leave early.

subordination secondary ideas related to a sentence's main idea by such subordinating words as *because, although, since,* and *while.*

suffix a word part added to the end of a word that changes the meaning of the word. Example: My dog likes to be comfortable.

superlative a degree of comparison among more than two people or things that indicates an extreme or unsurpassed level. Example: Joe's is the best coffee shop in the city.

tense refers to when the action of a verb takes place or when a condition is true. *See* verb tense.

third person the form of verbs or pronouns that refers to the person or thing being spoken or written about. Example: She is president of the company.

title an identifying name for a rank, office, or honor. When attached to a specific person's name, a title is capitalized. Example: Because he decreed the freeing of the slaves, President Lincoln was known as the Great Emancipator.

usage the standard ways of constructing ideas and using language, including the formation of verbs and use of pronouns, adjectives, and adverbs

verb the state of being or action of the subject in a sentence or dependent clause. Example: He baked only three cakes for the sale because he was out of flour.

verb tense the form of a verb (present, past, future) which communicates how the action of a sentence relates to the passage of time

vowel the letters *a, e, i, o,* and *u* (and sometimes *y*) of the English alphabet

Index

Answer Sheet

GED Writing Skills, Part I

Name: _____ Class: _____ Date: _____

○ Pretest   ○ Posttest   ○ Simulated Test

1 ① ② ③ ④ ⑤	11 ① ② ③ ④ ⑤	21 ① ② ③ ④ ⑤	31 ① ② ③ ④ ⑤	41 ① ② ③ ④ ⑤	51 ① ② ③ ④ ⑤
2 ① ② ③ ④ ⑤	12 ① ② ③ ④ ⑤	22 ① ② ③ ④ ⑤	32 ① ② ③ ④ ⑤	42 ① ② ③ ④ ⑤	52 ① ② ③ ④ ⑤
3 ① ② ③ ④ ⑤	13 ① ② ③ ④ ⑤	23 ① ② ③ ④ ⑤	33 ① ② ③ ④ ⑤	43 ① ② ③ ④ ⑤	53 ① ② ③ ④ ⑤
4 ① ② ③ ④ ⑤	14 ① ② ③ ④ ⑤	24 ① ② ③ ④ ⑤	34 ① ② ③ ④ ⑤	44 ① ② ③ ④ ⑤	54 ① ② ③ ④ ⑤
5 ① ② ③ ④ ⑤	15 ① ② ③ ④ ⑤	25 ① ② ③ ④ ⑤	35 ① ② ③ ④ ⑤	45 ① ② ③ ④ ⑤	55 ① ② ③ ④ ⑤
6 ① ② ③ ④ ⑤	16 ① ② ③ ④ ⑤	26 ① ② ③ ④ ⑤	36 ① ② ③ ④ ⑤	46 ① ② ③ ④ ⑤	
7 ① ② ③ ④ ⑤	17 ① ② ③ ④ ⑤	27 ① ② ③ ④ ⑤	37 ① ② ③ ④ ⑤	47 ① ② ③ ④ ⑤	
8 ① ② ③ ④ ⑤	18 ① ② ③ ④ ⑤	28 ① ② ③ ④ ⑤	38 ① ② ③ ④ ⑤	48 ① ② ③ ④ ⑤	
9 ① ② ③ ④ ⑤	19 ① ② ③ ④ ⑤	29 ① ② ③ ④ ⑤	39 ① ② ③ ④ ⑤	49 ① ② ③ ④ ⑤	
10 ① ② ③ ④ ⑤	20 ① ② ③ ④ ⑤	30 ① ② ③ ④ ⑤	40 ① ② ③ ④ ⑤	50 ① ② ③ ④ ⑤	